Indianapolis 500
YEARBOOK

Superfamily

AUTO STICK 2 . . . Shifter now provides positive performance control of your car's automatic transmission, born on the track for excellence on the street. Auto Stick 2.

HURST SUPER AIR SHOCKS . . . Add super air power to your family car, street rod or station wagon. Super Air Shocks provide needed load supporting power for safety, control, and performance.

HURST/AIRHEART SCR ELECTRONIC IGNITION . . . The SCR Ignition by Hurst/Airheart performs at an affordable price. Compact size, simple installation, and a 5-year guarantee makes it THE wise choice in ignition efficiency.

SCHIEFER'S . . . Line of flywheels, discs, and pressure plates are long lasting and trouble free. Give your car "the choice of champions."® Schiefer!

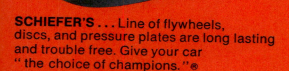

HURST/AIRHEART DISC BRAKE KITS . . . Engineering performance that stops the pros. Hurst/Airheart disc brake kits are dependable braking systems professional race cars use for life saving results.

HURST PERFORMANCE INC. Warminster, Pa. 18974

Above products are available from your local authorized Hurst outlet.

A Continuing Tradition

Buz McKim

INTRODUCTION

This, our second annual Indianapolis 500 Yearbook affirms our belief that race fans of the world will indeed support a book dedicated to "The Greatest Spectacle in Racing." As many of you know, the tradition of the Indianapolis 500 Yearbooks was begun in 1946 by the late Floyd Clymer and continued through 1968. Clymer died in 1970 without having published the 1969 book and except for a brief attempt made in 1970, the book was dormant until 1973 when we revived the tradition. Our first printing sold out in less than 120 days and we have only a few copies left from a third printing we found necessary.

For our second edition we have been fortunate enough to compile some of the most famous writers and photographers known to the sport. Long-time enthusiasts will immediately recognize names of award-winning journalists and photographers who have been covering the sport since the Thirties.

In reference to the Thirties and the current preference for nostalgia in general that prevails throughout the country, this year's 500 Yearbook has been designed in an attempt to bring you the best of the current era compiled with our memorable past.

We again solicit your comments about the publication and appreciate the hundreds of complimentary notes received about last year's book.

--Carl Hungness, Editor and Publisher

CARL HUNGNESS PRESENTS:

The Indianapolis 500 Yearbook

Volume II   Number II

Unequaled in Coverage of the World's Most Famous Automobile Race

EDITOR & PUBLISHER .... Carl Hungness
ART & PHOTOGRAPHIC DIRECTOR .... Jim Chini
HISTORICAL EDITOR .... Jack C. Fox
FEATURE EDITOR .... Jerry Miller
DISTRIBUTION MANAGER .... Dr. Harlen Hunter

BOOK DESIGN CONCEPT BY
Jim Chini and Carl Hungness

A special thanks to Al Bloemker, director of publicity, Indianapolis Motor Speedway and his staff for their assistance in compiling this book.

COLOR AND COVER CREDITS
Our cover, as well as all color photos and layouts in this book were photographed and designed by Jim Chini.

Library of Congress Catalog Card Number 74-84562
Library Binding $8.95 ISBN 0-915088-03-7
Paperbound $4.50 ISBN 0-915088-02-9

This publication subscribes to standards set by the American Auto Racing Writers and Broadcasters Association.

American Auto Racing Writers and Broadcasters Association

Contributing Writers
Dusty Brandel
Dustin W. Frazer
John Fugate
Steve Kelly
Bob Laycock
Tom Lucas
Johnny MacDonald
Robin Miller
Bob Russo
Ted West

Staff Artists
Jack Fox
Joe Henning
Don Kihara
Buz McKim
Joe Stevens

Editorial Assistants
Terri Gunn
Ray Briskey

Contributing Photographers
Vincente Alvarez
R. J. Brizzolara
Bruce Craig
Tom Dick
Jack C. Fox
Frank H. Fisse
Ray Golub
Dr. Harlen Hunter
Steve Kelly
David G. Knox
Don Larson
Sam Linde
Steve Lingenfelter
Dick Miller
Jerry Miller
Ron McQueeney
Jerry Nolan
Robert P. Tronolone
Ted West
Eric Williams
Phil Whitlow

The editors wish to thank Charlene Ellis and her Indianapolis Motor Speedway photographic staff for their contributions:

Fred Abel
Harold Bergquist
Dick Bundy
Charles Duffy
Harry Goode
Jim Haines
Jack Householder
Bob Scott
Dave Stringer
Marion Thomas
Bill Watson
Walt Wheeler
Dale Wines

USAC Triple Crown to Valvoline. Again.

Unser once.

The California 500. First leg of USAC's Triple Crown. Won by Bobby Unser. In Dan Gurney's Olsonite Eagle-Offy. On Valvoline® Racing Oil.

Rutherford twice.

The Indianapolis 500. The Schaefer 500. Both won by Johnny Rutherford. Who becomes the first driver ever to win two USAC Triple Crown races in the same season. And he won them both on Valvoline Racing Oil.

Valvoline all three times.

USAC's Triple Crown. Each race 500 miles long. Each race dominated and won by Valvoline drivers, for the second year in a row. As a matter of fact, more professional race drivers at Ontario, Indy and Pocono*, on major drag strips, and on road race courses run on Valvoline Racing Oil than any other brand.

Valvoline. We have the right kind of motor oil for every kind of car, every kind of driving.

Valvoline
The motor oil the pros run on.

Valvoline Oil Company, Ashland, Ky. *Ashland*® Division of Ashland Oil, Inc.

*Ontario: 29 of 33 starters ran on Valvoline; Indy: 28 of 33 starters ran on Valvoline; Pocono: 28 of 33 starters ran on Valvoline.

PRESENTING

THE CONTENT

Improvements	8	Pancho Carter	131
The Prelude	11	Jan Opperman	134
The Race	34	Tom Sneva	136
Driver Earnings	59	Fire Crew	138
Starting Field	61	Ex-Drivers	140
Great Hot Air Controversy	62	Young Mechanics	143
Davey Crockett	64	Inspector Is A Lady	146
The Past	66	Ladies Are Welcome	147
The Sampson	70	All Engines Banned	148
20 Years Ago	75	Bill Simpson	149
The Riley	79	Triple Crown	154
1954 Field	84	Performance Records	167
The Iron Duke	91	The Drivers	170
Oldtimers	96	Technical Scene	192
The Rookies	98	The Chiefs	197
A. J. Foyt	103	The Facts	207
Johnny Rutherford	107	Cartoons	222
The Field	111		

Because we didn't experience the Indianapolis 500 during the Great Depression years of the Thirties, we cannot draw a direct parallel to the state of the economy then and the definite economic slump of 1974. Months before this year's race the feared gas shortage was upon us and millions of motorists waited in line, many for the first time in their lives, to purchase fuel.

Fuel. Shortage. Next to Watergate, those two words dominated the automobile racing scene in 1974. In compliance with governmental requests for self-regulation, officials at the Indianapolis Motor Speedway voluntarily reduced the number of days the track would be open. And in response to public outcry following the 1973 event, USAC officials cut the fuel supply allocated to "500" cars. While the former act made this year's practice period a thing of, "let's get down to business and up to speed in a hurry," the fuel regulation served to help make the actual racing more competitive.

More competitive racing . . . that's what it is all about. Fortunately, after this year's "500" there were no special board meetings to adjust, regulate and change car specifications for safety's sake. There were, however, rumblings going on keyed to the old tune of "let's bring down the costs" by making some changes. Throughout the summer of 1974 the talk about Indianapolis 500 cars centered around the "stock-block" engine controversy. It is claimed that the modern-day Indianapolis car is far too expensive and the best way to cut back its cost is in the engine department. The popular Offenhauser (and Foyt) engines cost in excess of $20,000 per copy and stock-block (an engine utilizing many of the same components you run in your everyday passenger car) supporters naturally claim that a competitive engine can be built for far less.

While the bench racers as well as the rules makers, argue which type engine is best and consider what specifications should apply to each, the fan in the stands is currently enjoying some of the most competitive Championship style racing ever staged. The current state of the economy naturally has more than one car owner spooked and it's no surprise that entries in other Indianapolis car races in 1974 were down a bit. But blaming a lack of interest on powerplant cost is plugging the light in the wrong socket.

We could write several pages on the pros and cons of both the special racing engine and the stock-block and come back to you with the same result: You'll eventually wind up with a ready-to-race vehicle. That they might cost $20,000 as compared to $100,000 doesn't mean a thing unless: 1) they'll run 500 miles and 2) they put on a good show.

The show at Indianapolis 1974 was a memorable one indeed. It contained all the ingredients of a successful automobile race. The winner didn't have an unfair advantage over the field; there was wheel-to-wheel competition throughout the day; the new fuel regulations added a bit of mystery as to whether or not there was enough fuel to finish, etc., etc.

The fact Johnny Rutherford's McLaren was powered by an Offenhauser engine probably didn't cause too much comment among Indianapolis' fan population. The fact that he drove his heart and existing rules made for 33 nearly equal race cars that the fan in the stands could identify with probably made more of an impact with the rank and file. The balance that exists today at Indianapolis might just have happened by accident, literally. Current car specs are a direct result of a meeting held after last year's race that was held in an attempt to slow all the vehicles down. The resultant wing-width rule, fuel load rule, car weight, etc. all seem to fit the proper equation for close, safe racing. Drivers we know report that today's racing conditions are at least liveable and they can race one another on the track rather than wait for each other's car to break or a lay back and wait for a mistake because they didn't used to feel confident enough to run alongside each other.

We're hoping the rules makers continue in their search for more inexpensive ways to go racing but hope they don't upset the balance that now exists. And rather than obsolete existing investments we hope they'll consider that the sports dollar can be divided up just so many ways and in times of economic strain, even Singer Sewing machine engines in race cars might not help the situation.

Rutherford's score with the venerable old Offenhauser is another notch for the traditionalists. In years to come they'll say, "Indy 1974 was one of the best." Maybe this quarter is aging, but if they don't change a thing for the running and outcome of next year's race, it'll be just fine with us.

performance plus...

faster starts, reduced plug fouling, longer tune-up life!

Top racers know the performance benefits of the ACCEL Super Coil: extra spark energy for improved acceleration and maximum engine performance; heavy-duty construction for severest racing applications; special tower design to prevent carbon tracking and voltage flashover.

The race-winning features of the ACCEL Super Coil also make it an outstanding performer on the street. Increased spark energy

helps eliminate misfire for faster acceleration and improved engine performance under load. Heavy-duty construction and special windings produce maximum firing voltage for faster starts. Greater available spark energy improves combustion, thus extending tune-up life by reducing deposit build-up and minimizing plug fouling.

The ACCEL Super Coil . . . for extraordinary performance on street and track.

AN ECHLIN COMPANY
Box 142, Branford, Conn. 06405
In Canada: 500 Carlingview Drive
Rexdale, Ontario M9W 5H1

For 1974 Catalog, brochure, decals and jacket emblem send $2.00 to: P.O. Box 11946, Santa Ana, Calif. 92711

IMPROVEMENTS

by Carl Hungness

Although construction of the Indianapolis Motor Speedway began in 1909 and the first 500-mile International Sweepstakes was run back in 1911, modifications to the 539-acre facility have never fully ceased.

Maintaining "The Capitol of Auto Racing", as the words read on the Speedway's main office and current museum, is Clarence Cagle, a self-taught grounds supervisor who has received nation-wide recognition as the foremost authority on the many and varied aspects of running a large race track.

A tall, lanky man in his fifties, Cagle has spent all of his adult years working for the family that owns the facility, the Hulmans of Terre Haute, Ind. Since Tony Hulman purchased the plant in November 1945, Cagle has supervised the continual upgrading of the facility and today not much more than the original soil remains from the way the place looked in 1911.

Cagle didn't start out to be a grounds superviser. Moreover, he was a capable Hulman employee who had a variety of duties and was asked to help out on Tony's new project on a temporary basis. To hear Clarence tell the story, he was simply "on loan" to the Speedway "until we got the place straightened out."

To Clarence Cagle, the Speedway has been a permanent home. Just as a new mortage holder trims his grass and

The Speedway as it appeared in 1945.

sweeps the sidewalk on his own little piece of the world, Cagle cannot walk past a Dixie cup without picking it up.

While Tony Hulman has been described as one of Indiana's most benevolent businessmen, an outsider might believe otherwise if he caught a glimpse of Cagle riding his tractor on New Year's Day or picking up wayward napkins after a late-hour press party in May. Moreover, Cagle doesn't know how to relax and isn't very interested in learning, thank you.

Between Tony Hulman's foresight and Cagle's unrelenting work schedule, they have transformed the Indianapolis Motor Speedway into an American Institution without equal in the auto racing world.

They began their continual upgrading soon after World War II with a tight schedule to meet before the running of the 1946 race. Several of the Speedway's famous garages in

The first turn, 1974.

its publicized Gasoline Alley had been destroyed by fire in 1941. New garages were constructed utilizing the pleasing and traditional styling that was a holdover from the pre-war days. A new grandstand and paddock were also put up for the 1946 event.

The following year the press was treated to new seating and the always present automotive accessory companies also found new headquarters. From 1948 through 1953, 10 new garages were constructed and four

The start of the 1974 Classic. Hulman and company have transposed IMS into the world's finest racing facility.

more grandstands were erected to seat the ever-growing crowd.

By 1956, the current museum and business office was built and the following year the control tower, tower terrace and pit area were finished. A new tunnel under the backstretch was completed in the same year also and new asphalt was applied in the turns.

Clarence Cagle

Tony Hulman

The old Pagoda which was once destroyed by fire in 1928 and then reconstructed finally gave way to the ultra-modern structure that now stands. Construction of the new tower was completed in 1957 and a fourth tunnel (under the backstretch) was finished. By the following year, the tower terrace seating area had been extended.

Cagle and crew were indeed busy during the Sixties as several new grandstands were built. The existing golf course was expanded to 27 holes; a 96-unit motel was erected at the east end of the track; an electric scoreboard reacing some 68' 8" high and containing 6000 light bulbs was built near the starting line; more new tunnels were dug under the two and one-half mile track, etc., etc.

Among the most publicized improvements made to the Speedway took place between the 1973 and 1974 event. Six hundred feet of the existing inside retaining wall was removed near the fourth turn. The move aided drivers entering

approximately 856 feet and widened another five feet. The latter move extended each individual pit from 30 feet to 40 feet. The wall was also raised to a uniform height of 32 inches all around the track. Two of Clarence Cagle's men, Charlie Thompson and Luther Ray report that the retaining wall job and pit modifications took 26 men nearly 10,000 man hours to complete the job.

Last year, construction of a new 96,000 square foot complex at the

All new flag stand flanks the world famous row of bricks across the finish line.

Coming out of the fourth turn, drivers are now greeted by a higher retaining wall.

(continued on page 145)

south end of the track, between the first and second turn, was begun. The new building will serve as executive offices and will also be used as a new museum containing some 50 vintage race and passenger cars. Curator Karl Kizer reports he will more than welcome the additional space as the current facility has been overflowing. The new executive offices will complement the three-level hospitality suites (located on the outside of the second turn) which were completed in time for the 1973 race.

While most of the Speedway's con-

Under two inches of Indiana snow, the Speedway in January doesn't look like a very inviting facility. In photo at left worker prepares the huge scoreboard with a new coat of paint.

We fly with the Eagles.

Dan Gurney's Eagles are the most popular cars on the USAC Championship trail, regularly dominating the top ten finishers in each race.

At Jorgensen Steel, we're proud to supply the steel and aluminum used in every Eagle chassis. Including Gurney's new Jorgensen-sponsored SCCA Formula 5000 contenders.

What's more, our steel and forgings also go into the turbocharged Drake-Offy engines that power most of the USAC Indy entries.

But you don't have to build racing cars to enjoy Jorgensen's service.

Whether your orders are large or small, call us for anything in steel, aluminum or forgings. You'll receive the fastest on-schedule delivery in the business.

The same that Dan Gurney gets.

JORGENSEN STEEL
The Full Service Center

EARLE M. JORGENSEN CO. LOS ANGELES • SAN DIEGO • PHOENIX • OAKLAND • SAN FRANCISCO • HONOLULU
SEATTLE • HOUSTON • DALLAS • TULSA • DENVER • KANSAS CITY • CHICAGO • PHILADELPHIA • BALTIMORE

ALLOY STEELS, INC. DIVISION OF EARLE M. JORGENSEN CO. DETROIT • FLINT • LANSING • DAYTON • CINCINNATI • CHICAGO

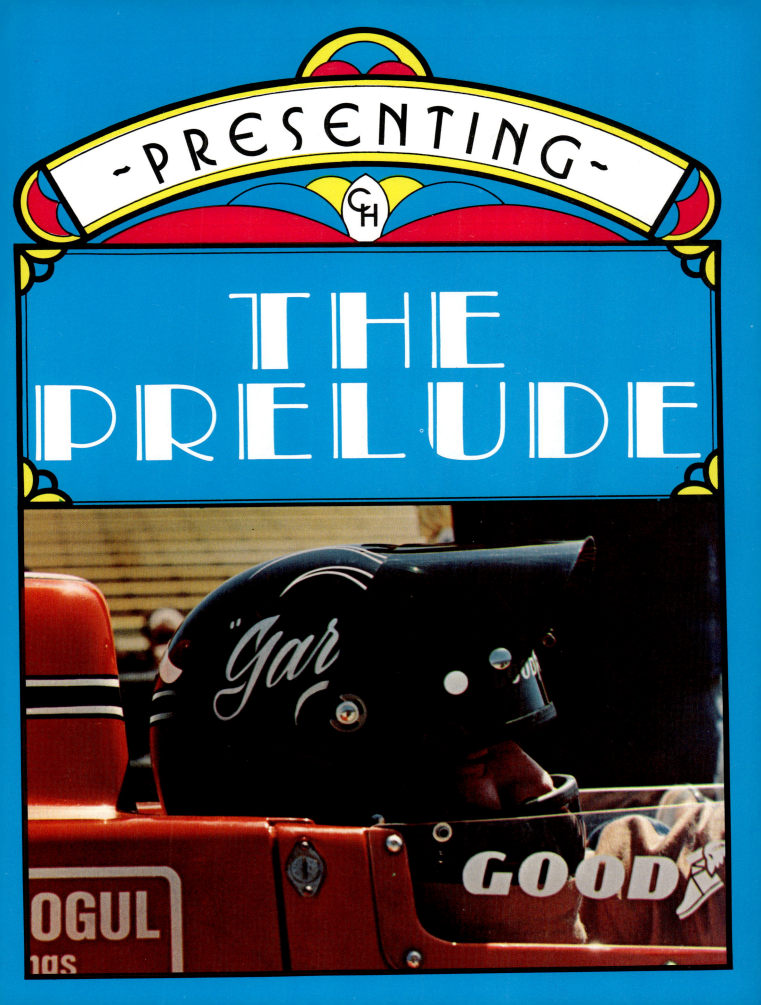

The Prelude To The 1974 Indianapolis 500 Was Shortened to 14 Days (From the Usual 20 Plus) By The Energy Crisis. An All Business Atmosphere Prevailed For One of The Safest and Most Competitive Practice Periods In History

by Jack Fox

Link

PUBLISHER'S NOTE: Once again, we extend our thanks to the USAC News Bureau and the Gilmore Racing Team for their assistance in compiling the following information. Gilmore sponsored the Daily Track Summaries this year, a tremendous asset to journalists.

May 6

With the thought in everyone's mind that this year must be better than the tragic 1973, the opening day of practice for the 1974 Indianapolis 500 brought the year's first injury even before the track was officially opened. In a senseless effort to be the first car on the track, the Roger Penske and Rolla Vollstedt crews jumped new Chief Steward Tom Binford's green light and sent Mike Hiss in No. 68 and Tom Bigelow in No. 27 in a dash down the track before given the go-ahead. In trying to get out of the way of the two cars, Waly Myers, the track's 71-year-old steward tripped and fell breaking his hip and wrist. The popular Myers who has been associated with the 500 since 1934 when he was a riding mechanic for Mauri Rose was rushed to Methodist Hospital where it was estimated he would have to spend four to six weeks after undergoing an operation. Walt later reported to friends that when he was wheeled into the operating room he saw a collection of drills and saws and inquired if he had been taken into the hospital's carpenter shop by mistake. He was informed that he was in the correct room to repair his injured hip.

Both Penske and Vollstedt were fined the maximum USAC penalty

Charlene Ellis again headed the IMS photo crew.

Magnesium wheel manufacturer Ted Hallibrand was on hand as usual.

Tom Binford replaced Harlan Fengler as chief steward in 1974.

of $100 by Binford for their over-anxiousness.

When the actual green light was flashed, Bigelow was first out to win the dubious honor and in a few minutes Binford almost assessed the third fine when Salt Walther exceeded the 160 mph speed limit by five miles. The young chauffeur who was so badly injured last year was let off with a stern warning.

Binford lifted the speed limit which was imposed to blow the sand and dirt off the track's surface at 1:24 p.m. which was a record for the speed in which the cars have been allowed to attempt qualifying speed. Fastest of the group of 27 cars which eventually took to the track before the 6 p.m. closing was Bobby Unser who toured the oval in his Olsonite Eagle at 188.245. Mike Mosley was next in the Lodestar Eagle/Offy at 184.312. Pole position favorite, A.J. Foyt, was doing some last minute adjustments in his garage and announced that he would be on the track the following day.

May 7

The first accident of the month was a spectacular one and the first practice incident in a number of years involving two cars. At 4:27 Tom Bigelow and Lee Brayton were racing each other down the front stretch. Bigelow hit the first turn first but lost control and spun directly in front of Brayton who was driving the No. 28 Eisenhour Eagle. Lee's white car climbed the left rear wheel of Bigelow's mount and took off on the fly for the wall which he hit with teriffic impact. The car skidded down the short chute, smoking badly. Bigelow also caught the wall and some large pieces flew off his No. 27 car. Neither driver was injured and both were released from the infield hospital. The cars were not so fortun-

Longtime entrant Andy Granatelli was a spectator at the Speedway this year.

ate and both were withdrawn when it was found that they could not be repaired in time to qualify. Bigelow sent an SOS for his backup car which was still enroute to the track. The identical backup, although entered as No. 17 will carry No. 27.

A.J. got his orange Coyote on the track for the first time and apparently had the hotter setup as he toured the premises in 192.349 for the fastest

Larry Bisceglia was the first spectator in line for the 26th consecutive year.

Car owner Ralph Wilke again entered a car for Mike Mosley.

time of the day (and year). Johnny Rutherford and Bobby Unser, considered A.J.'s foremost foes for the pole spot, also got over the 190 mark.

Duane "Pancho" Carter Jr., who took the first three phases of his driver's test on opening day became the first rookie to complete the four-phase test, and he passed it in excellent form. Jigger Sirois finished his refresher test in the blue and white

Steve Krisiloff left, STP team mechanic Howard Gafford and Wally Dallenbach talk about the state of Wally's shoes before his qualifying run.

A.J. Foyt and his deep concentration furrow his brow before the veteran charger makes his qualifying attempt.

Specator on the right gives A.J. the universal "OK" sign as Foyt pulls out of pits to qualify. Four quick laps later and A.J. was set to start the 58th annual "500" from the number one position.

NORTON

SPIRIT

Sophomore driver Mike Hiss proved his prowess at Indianapolis this year by putting his Roger Penske-prepared McLaren in the front row. One of the most gleaming machines ever to appear at the Speedway, the No. 68 car carries one of the only industrial sponsors at Indianapolis. The Norton Company is the world's largest manufacturer of abrasive products.

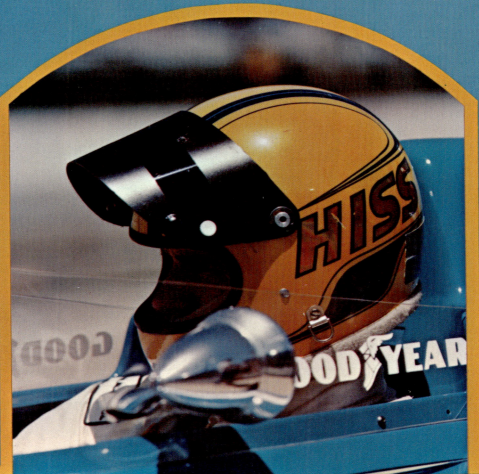

Cicada No. 25.

A new record for practice runs on a second day was broken when 36 cars left the pits. The day started under cloudless skies but in the late afternoon it began clouding up and there was a threat of rain in the air.

May 8

A heavy rain the previous night soaked the track and it was 3:46 before Tom Binford turned on the green light. Only 11 cars were able to brave the damp, cool air and strong winds before things were shut down 25 minutes later. Al Unser had the fastest time of the abbreviated period in Parnelli Jones' No. 15 at 185.337 mph.

The real action happened far from the Speedway with Tom Bigelow as the chief participant. It seemed that the car towing his backup car thru Iowa broke down and Tom had to call a friend in Davenport to tow it to his shop while Tom set out from Indianapolis to the rescue. The return trip was another mishap-laden adventure.

"The spring on the trailer broke near Galesburg, Ill." quoth Tom. "That dropped the axle down and the tire rubbed against it until it blew out. We used a two-by-four to wedge it up and when we stopped 20 minutes later, the tire was red-hot again. This time we used a rope to pull the axle forward but two hours later the rope broke. We finally pulled the axle up and put a wedge underneath it and it held until we got back to the Speedway."

May 10

The final day of practice before the start of qualifying was just as busy as usual and the pressure of the moment produced several minor accidents. Hard-luck Lloyd Ruby looped

Steward Walt Meyers tripped getting out of the way of Mike Hiss, left, and Tom Bigelow as the two raced each other for "First on the Track" honors.

Dr. Vicente Alvarez, noted Argentine photographer, tried out the 1973 Viceroy Parnelli for size. Helping him "suit-up" are Al Unser, left, and Parnelli Jones.

Sprint car stylist Larry Cannon made the starting field in his second year at the Speedway. He started in 33rd position.

Jim Hurtubise was at the Speedway for the 14th consecutive year, but this year without his beloved front-engined Roadster.

Johnny Rutherford, driving a Champion-equipped McLaren Offenhauser, took the checkers at an average 158.589 mph.

For the 35th time, a driver using Champion spark plugs wins the Indianapolis 500. Motor racing's biggest and richest event. Champion. World's No.1 selling spark plug brand.

CHAMPION ®

Toledo, OH 43661

We've got your plug.

THE ENGLISH LEATHER CHAMPIONS

Roger McCluskey:
current U.S.A.C. Champion.

Craig Breedlove:
first man to break 600 mph on land.

Tom "Mongoose" McEwen:
Funny Car champion at NHRA Supernationals

Ed "The Ace" McCulloch:
holder of the 1973 "Driver of the Year" Award.

Ed, Roger, Craig & Tom know that part of being a champion is smelling good. And they like the clean, honest scent of English Leather®. You can find out why for just $1. That's all it costs to get the English Leather Travel Set. Mail $1.00 (check or money order) to Mem Co., Inc., P.O. Box 359, Dept. IY-1, Passaic, N.J. 07055.

All our champions wear English Leather. Or they wear nothing at all.

MEM COMPANY, INC., Northvale, N.J. 07647 © 1974
Available in Canada

This young fan may not realize it, but that's Johnny Rutherford signing her flag.

Two hot shoes from the USAC Midget racing ranks, Bill Engelhart, left, and Larry Rice, 1973 USAC Midget Champion, discuss Larry's chances of making the '74 "500."

coming out of the southeast turn and after sliding approximately 400 feet, his Unlimited Racing Eagle caught the wall and then slid another 280 feet. The car was moderately damaged although Lloyd was uninjured.

Denny Zimmerman spun coming into the front stretch. His MVS was also moderately damaged after contact with the wall. A little later, Larry McCoy broke a half-shaft on the Eastern Racing Atlanta/Offy, his father's car, and spun coming out of turn No. 3. There was no contact nor damage to the car. McCoy had recently completed his refresher test.

Jan Opperman, the racing hippie, was granted his Championship license and stepped into his first Championship car in time to get in three phases of his driver's test. The colorful chauffeur who got his start in BCRA Midgets in northern California but who really developed his talents in the Supermodifieds in Pennsylvania was signed to the Parnelli Jones "Super Team" to replace Joe Leonard, another BCRA graduate who started his career in the small cars in 1955 - not 1958 as his official Speedway biography states. Joe is recovering from serious leg injuries incurred in a crash during the California 500 at Ontario. Previous to his test, Opperman had only driven on two paved tracks which we would assume to be San Jose and Stockton. His current residence is a farm near Beaver Crossing, Neb., which rates when it comes to odd names right along with David Hobbs' Upper Boddington, England.

It was another busy day which saw Bobby Unser set fast time at 192.513 closely followed by Johnny Rutherford and Foyt over the 190 mark.

USAC Sprint car regular Joe Saldana helped out on Jerry Karl's crew this year.

Driver-fabricator Eldon Rasmussen made it to the Speedway in 1974 and looked smooth, but he was caught waiting in the qualifying line.

Mario Andretti, who had been practicing all week in the Viceroy/Parnelli, switched to their spare Eagle when the former car would go no faster than 186 mph.

After the track was shut down for the afternoon, the drivers and owners gathered for the annual drawing for opening day qualifying positions and who should draw the first spot...A.J. Foyt. Bill Simpson got the second slot for the No. 18 American Kids Eagle and third went to...yes, A.J. Foyt for his No. 82 piloted by George Snider. All told, 46 cars drew for qualifying positions.

RAIN was predicted for the morrow.

May 11

With the prediction of precipitation for later in the afternoon, the pre-qualifying practice period opened at 9 a.m. under a sunny sky. By 10:30 when the track was shut down, there had been a lot of activity and several tow-ins but no spins nor accidents. There was, however, a pit member on Al Loquasto's car, Jim Vorgin, fell off and was run over by the car in the pits.

At 11:05 the track was declared open for qualifying and the first car

Car Care by Castrol

Castrol. Lube oil specialists. Since 1899. Trusted on the track. Respected on the road. Famous worldwide. Dedicated to the finest engine care and protection of motorcars. For as long as men put on goggles, helmets or homburgs. Try Castrol GTX, the World's Finest Motor Oil. Castrol Oils Inc. New York, N.Y. Member Burmah Group **Burmah**

Celebrating 75 Years of Lubrication Excellence

away from the line was A.J. in his Gilmore Racing Coyote/Foyt. His first lap was 46.74 (192.555) and from here on, the entire qualifying procedure was an anti-climax. This was to be the fastest lap of the entire day and Foyt's average speed of 191.632 gave the others a mark to shoot at.

Bill Simpson posted a 181.041 and there immediately was some conjecture as to whether it would be fast enough to make the starting field. Bill, while not too impressed with his efforts seem to think it would be safe. Snider in the second Coyote ran 183.993 and it began to appear that times, indeed, would be much slower than last year and that no valid minimum speed estimate existed. One reason for the reduced speeds seemed to be the addition of the 80 lb. manifold pressure popoff valve which USAC rules demanded on the turbochargers.

At 11:30 Pancho Carter went out in the turquoise and copper Cobre No. 11 and turned in a speed of 180.605 for his four-lap run. Bentley Warren followed in Tassi Vatis' yellow and black Finley/Offy. He ran his three warmup laps but did not take the green flag from Pat Vidan.

Bobby Unser disappointed those who thought he would give Foyt a close run for the pole when his announced speed was only 185.175. Steve Krisiloff became the first member of the Patrick-Bignotti-STP team to qualify with 182.519 and teammate, Wally Dallenbach, was right behind with the best challenge to A.J. 189.683 mph was good enough to give Wally a spot in the middle of the front row.

About this time the black clouds began rolling in from the southwest and the predicted 70% chance of rain began to look like 100%. Jerry Grant made his run in the turquoise No. 55 Cobre, 181.781, and David Hobbs secured his starting spot with a 184.833 in the black and red McLaren sponsored by Carling Black Label Beer, a sponsorship which would have been unheard of during some of the more stuffy years of AAA sanctioning, although not entirely unheard of in 500 history -- remembering Lou Schneider's Edelweiss and Louie Tomei's Falstaff. As David came in, a slight sprinkle of rain was reported but it did not keep Mike Mosley from going out in the Agajanian-Lodestar Eagle and qualifying at 185.318 which was beginning to look like a reasonably good time.

Lloyd Ruby lost control of his racer as he negotiated the second turn late in the afternoon of May 10. Despite considerable damage to the car, Chief Mechanic Mike Devin and crew performed a yeoman repair job and had Lloyd's car ready to qualify the next morning.

Deep concentration flashes from the eyes of these veteran drivers. Top, left to right: Jerry Karl, Wally Dallenbach, Bob Harkey. Bottom, left to right: Bill Vukovich, Gary Bettenhausen, Rick Muther.

The sprinkles soon got heavier and the yellow light came on as qualifying was temporarily suspended at 12:25. Fans scurried for cover and soon the track was quite wet. The shower was short-lived, however, and the tremendous task of drying off the racing surface began as the day's first streaker was reported in the "Snake Pit" at 1:06. He was a lad being tossed high in the air from a blanket held by his buddies. One young man's girl friend was also tossed--and when he took exception, a fight started which was quelled by helmeted state police. An arrest triggered the crowd to shower the men in blue with beer bottles and soon a full-fledged riot was going in the infield. Reinforcements were called in and order restored. With the police diverted or otherwise occupied, the streakers had a field day. At one

time there must have been 10 or 15 in the first turn playing frisbee or running thru the creek to get on the track surface. One portly, unclothed gentleman got onto the front stretch and climbed Pat Vidan's new starter's and officials' stand. He fell and injured himself quite badly. For the most part, the lads in the first turn were well-behaved although some non-streakers broke down a fence to get a better look at the doings. When the pace car came by and it looked like qualifying would be resumed, they began heading back over the fence. As one of the daily papers said, "Never have so many removed so much to expose so little."

With the track back in condition the trials were resumed at 3:31 and Lloyd Ruby immediately made his run with an average of 181.699. Not too fast for the perennial hard-luck driver

but apparently quite safe. Jimmy Caruthers followed with 184.049 in the third Cobre/Eagle to qualify and Gary Bettenhausen next got a 184.492 in the Roger Penske McLaren. Billy Vukovich qualified Jerry O'Connell's Sugaripe Prune Eagle at 182.500 and again the rain drops started as Tom Sneva started on his run in Grant King's Kingfish. The young former junior high school principal from Sprague, Wash., pulled in when the yellow came on but in a few minutes was back out. His run was a good one, 185.847. Before Gordon Johncock, last year's winner could get the flag, it began raining again, harder this time, and the track was shut down for the afternoon. The qualifying line for the following Saturday was set with Johncock first followed by Mike Hiss, John Mahler, Salt Walther, Vukie's backup

Betty Rutherford watches as husband Johnny dons his helmet in preparation for qualifying his car.

car, Al Loquasto, Dick Simon, Tom Bigelow, Jerry Karl and Mario Andretti. Since Johnny Rutherford and Al Unser had been taken out of the original line, due to engine trouble, it was announced that they would start a new qualifying line and would therefore be ineligible for the pole position although those remaining in their original places would have a shot at Foyt's spot.

May 12

It was a slow day both on the track and in the infield as only 11 cars got on the track and no cars were allowed in the infield other than those with official parking stickers. Clarence Cagle's crew was doing their best to let the grounds dry off after an all night rain. Jan Opperman passed his drivers' test in the Parnelli car and was seen to sport a new haircut -- much shorter than the one he first unveiled. George Bignotti filed a protest with USAC when it was learned that he will be required to use the special large turbocharger in the race which was on Dallenbach's car when it qualified. The protest hearing was set for Tuesday.

Mike Hiss was fast for the day and National Midget Champ Larry Rice was out in the blue and orange La-

Warre stock block Chevy in an ancient Eagle chassis. Larry's chances of getting enough speed to pass his test looked rather doubtful as the car just didn't have much speed.

May 13

Johnny Rutherford drove the hottest laps of the day at over 190 mph although he was not eligible for the pole. Roger McCluskey took some laps in his new Riley/Offy which will be sponsored by English Leather. An extremely low car, it was first seen with a low slung tail, later replaced by a more conventional wing. Lindsey Hopkins is the owner of the attractive blue and white creation.

Word was received of the death in Beverly Hills, Cal. of Wes Mahaney, long-time friend of the racing fraternity. Wes, an insurance company executive passed away on his 74th birthday and his last words to his old friend attorney Don Bringgold were to give the boys at the Speedway his regards.

May 14

Tom Binford ruled that the big turbo on the Wally Dallenbach car would have to remain in place for the 500, despite the protest of George Bignotti. Binford and officials Art Meyers and Don Cummins issued the

statement that there was "a significant difference in performance characteristics between the two types of blowers."

Eldon Rasmussen took three phases of his driver's test in his attractive Ras-Car No. 58. It is bright yellow with blue numbers and appears to be a re-worked Atlanta chassis. Rasmussen was entered in 1973 but not allowed on the track as he lacked the necessary racing experience.

Due to gusty winds and afternoon rain, track activity was held to a minimum with only 10 cars on the track. Foyt in a shakedown run was fast with 189.913.

May 15

The weather was better and 32 cars got out to find the extra few miles an hour that will be needed on Saturday.

Jan Opperman also found that the concrete wall can be hard when you run a race car into it. He got into the grass in the southeast turn, tried to drive it back on the track, did a half-spin and slid 250 feet to the wall which he hit and then bounced off into another half-spin and hit it again. Fortunately the car wasn't badly damaged and Jan received only a sprained

Al Unser, right, discusses his car's handling with Chief Mechanic Phil Casey.

Lee Kunzman, left, talks with Ron Falk during a lull in practice. Lee was still recuperating from a tire-testing crash at Ontario last December.

Goodyear tire engineer Paul Lauritzen, right, listens intently to Wally Dallenbach's comments on the type of rubber compound used in Wally's tires.

Mike Mosley and his Chief Mechanic A.J. Watson, right, had one of the fastest combinations at the Speedway with their Lodestar Eagle/Offy.

wrist. He had been running almost 180 a few laps before the accident but was running at a much slower speed as he had just stopped at the pits. Rasmussen was the last driver to complete his test as time for the rookies to show their ability expired at 6 p.m. Rutherford ran almost 192 in his orange McLaren for fast time honors.

May 16

It was another day of bad weather and not much action although a streaker did his thing in the first turn on a motorcycle. High winds held down much of the practice with Al Unser being high with 187.617.

In the Oldtimers Club trailer, Charles Lytle, the Speedway's perennial bon vivant, raconteur, wit and historian was reliving some of the amusing incidents in his 55 years around the world's speedways. An Indy fixture since the 1930's, Charles

(don't call him Chuck) carries the official title of assistant curator of the Speedway Museum. He started his rounds upon arrival from Sharon, Pa. with a cane but as the days passed, the cane became conspicuous by its absence. Harry Hartz, another of the better known Oldtimers, hospitalized for a few days after an automobile accident on May 6th, reported to the trailer for the first appearance.

May 17

For those who make their homes in the midwest and are acquainted with tornado weather, Friday was one of apprehension, but to those of us who like a good storm it was "neat"! About 1 p.m. black, low-hanging clouds began scudding over the grandstands and tower and soon it looked like midnight. Lights came on and the clouds turned to greenish-brown. High winds and the following rain soon

Johnny Rutherford listens to what Herb Porter and Tyler Alexander, on Porter's left sitting on the wall, have to say about aerodynamics.

turned the Speedway area practically into a short-lived disaster area. Just before the storm hit three cars got on the track amid thunder and lightning but came in just in time to beat the

PERFECT CIRCLE® AT INDY

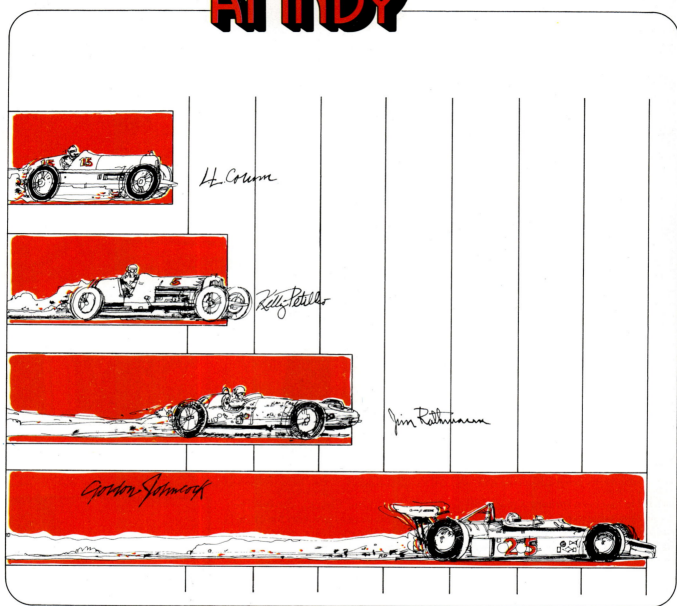

L.L. Corum

Kelly Petillo

Jim Rathmann

Gordon Johncock

THE FASTER THE PACE, THE BETTER THE RINGS.

Perfect Circle Piston Rings have been in 33 Indy 500 winners since we first made the racing scene in 1924. That year, the winning speed was 98 mph.

Last year, Gordon Johncock won at 170 mph, using far better, more sophisticated Perfect Circle rings. Down through the years, Perfect Circle has kept pace with the technology which has brought about ever-greater speed and performance at Indianapolis.

Perfect Circle rings are in almost every USAC type racer. We make a ring that's right for every engine, whether it's a race car, passenger car, tractor or truck engine.

Perfect Circle

DANA

A Doctor of Motors Product

The men of the press at the Speedway include: Shav Glick of the L.A. Times, left, and Johnny MacDonald of the San Diego Union. . . .

Ray Marquette of the Indianapolis Star. . . .

John Totten of WRTV, right, with Vel Miletich. . . .

Don Hein of WLWI interviewing A. J. Watson. . . .

and Jim Wilson of WISH.

downpour which reportedly showered an inch and a half of rain in a half-hour. The area behind the tower terrace stands was soon a river and the men and womens conveniences were flooded with a foot of water. Hurredly erected dykes kept some of the torrent out of the Champion and Perfect Circle rooms but there were a lot of wet pedestrians in the environs. One big tree was blown down near the Speedway hospital and many limbs broken off of those in the "Snake Pit." A large wheeled trash container got loose in front of the press room and just missed a parked Cadillac. It did, however, score a direct hit on radio announcer Paul Page's WIBC press car.

The storm passed without the expected pointy clouds showing themselves although a story reached California that one had taken the roof off Parnelli Jones' garage. In a few minutes, the rain stopped and a few intrepid "Snake Pit" spectators climbed the fence and began swimming in the swollen creek inside the first turn. A covy of guards went down to watch the bathers but were disappointed when their appearance caused the lads to scurry back behind the fence to content themselves with belly-flopping in the huge mud puddles left by the storm. A subsequent short sprinkle shut down the track for the day.

May 18

In order to prevent the previous Saturday's rash of streakers and rioters, the state police force was beefed up with many more men, dogs and long, healthy-looking clubs. This made the younger spectators quite orderly and the streaking was confined to the race track where some desperate ef-

forts were made to make the starting field. First away when the track was finally opened for qualifying after being delayed by a damp surface and a mandatory 30-minute practice period was Gordon Johncock. He made a fine run with a speed average of 186.287 and then Mike Hiss in the blue and yellow Norton Spirit Eagle, a Roger Penske entry, toured at 187.490 to place him on the outside of the front row. John Mahler, next out in the Deutch-Roy Woods Eagle took two laps on the flag at 179.4 and 180.6 and then came in after, apparently, experiencing some sort of mechanical problem.

Salt Walther took a very slow warmup lap around the oval to wave to his many fans who followed his well-publicized fight against the critical burns he sustained last year. While it was a fine piece of showmanship, it did cut into the qualifying time of those cars still in line. Once on the

llector's Dream

**A SENSATIONAL
CONVERSATION STARTER!**
For Your Office or Den

SIZE: DIAM. 27"

Parnelli Jones, left, reminisces with J.C. Agajanian.

Mel Kenyon's car was the only one equipped with a roll cage.

Sammy Sessions, shown with Chief Mechanic Smokey Yunick, was next to qualify when time ran out.

flag, he did a creditable job with 183.927 in his blue, white and orange McLaren. Al Loquasto in his yellow and white McLaren, mechanicked by veteran Clint Brawner, got out on the track but failed to take the flag, only the second driver to do so—Bentley Warren was the other on the previous Saturday.

In rapid succession, five cars qualified who still theoretically had a shot at Foyt's pole position. None came close, but all made the race: Dick Simon, 184.502; Tom Bigelow in the Vollstedt backup now carrying the No. 27, 180.144; Jerry Karl in the blue Hopkins/Eagle, 181.452; Mario Andretti in Parnelli's Viceroy/Eagle, 186.027 and John Martin in his dark red McLaren recently renamed the Sea Snack Shrimp Cocktail Special -- a tongue twister for the track's announcers -- 180.406. This ended the "first day qualifiers" under the new qualifying rules which few spectators really seemed to understand.

Next up was Rick Muther in the yellow and red Eisenhour Coyote/Foyt. He was the first driver to accept a run of under 180 mph when he clocked 179.991. In the meantime, it had clouded up and rain began falling while Bob Harkey was warming up Lindsey Hopkins' red No. 79. This was at 12:43 and the track didn't get dried off until 4:20. Time was getting critical and those at the end of the qualifying line were in a state of panic hoping that there would be enough time for at least one shot at the green flag. Far back in line sat the Vatis No. 94 which had been in line since it clocked thru the pit gate at 8:03 in the morning. Johnny Parsons had replaced Bentley Warren in the cockpit and as the car was up for its second time, it appeared by the fine print in the entry

blank that when it got its second chance, the chain of events which would guarantee those cars behind it their one chance to qualify would be broken. Just what was said by who and to whom would be a matter for the courts to decide.

Harkey was not very impressive with 176.687 as the first car on the track after a rain had a lot of dirt and sand to contend with as well as a cold groove. Jim McElreath followed in the Thermo King No. 46 and was only a little better with 177.244. Johnny Rutherford finally had made his way to the front of the line and went out to try to break Foyt's mark. He came close with 190.446 but even if it had been 200 mph, he could have started no further up than right behind the slowest qualifier of the first group which had ended with John Martin. The ever-popular Jim Hurtubise did a good job in his McLaren--180.288--and the friendly Herk was in the field. "We have to get in every year or so just so they'll know we're still here," he later quipped.

Al Unser got Parnelli's third car in with 183.889, not particularly impressive for a two-time winner but in nevertheless and IN safely. Rookie Larry "Boom Boom" Cannon could only get 173.963 out of the orange Hoffman Eagle but at this point no car could afford to turn down a time, no matter how slow.

As the second Thermo King car reached the front of the line, a decision was made to withdraw the No. 46 and let Jim McElreath try to get a better time with No. 45. It was better --but not much--177.279. Jigger Sirois could get no better than 173.360 in the Cicada and began sweating. Larry McCoy warmed up the Surefine Foods Atlanta (Ras-Car) but didn't take the

flag. National Champion Roger McCluskey made the field with 181.005 in the Riley No. 1. Denny Zimmerman bested Sirois with a 173.569 in the MVS, which he had wrecked several days before, and the field was full.

Now Johnny Parsons' mount, the Tassi Vatis owned No. 94 was next in line. Young John, who had been dreaming of landing an Indianapolis 500 ride since 1968 was granted his chance. He performed well and turned 180.252 to bump Sirois from the field. Jan Opperman was last out and bumped Zimmerman with a 176.186. Likeable Sammy Sessions was left waiting when the 6 o'clock gun went off.

Steward Binford was immediately deluged with owners, drivers and pitmen of the cars still in line who demanded a chance to qualify. He was deaf to their protestations due to his interpretation of the rules for qualifying as stated in the entry blank. The gang next cornered Speedway Vice-President Joe Cloutier, but were referred back to Binford. Most vocal of the group was a Connecticut lawyer, Wright Hugus, a member of the Roy Woods pit crew. The hassle went from the track to the USAC office where the official protest by six "left at the gate" car owners was denied by Binford.

May 19

While the track was quiet and closed to outsiders, the qualifying controversey continued and meetings were held at various places. It was ruled that a reopening of the trials could only occur if all owners of qualified cars and the two alternates would sign a waiver allowing the qualifying runs to resume. Since this would have quite

Nothing but the finest from our family to yours.

The Stokely-Van Camp family of quality fruits, vegetables, and other fine products for your table.

Stokely-Van Camp, Inc. Indianapolis, Indiana 46206

Chief Mechanic Clint Brawner, back to camera with straw hat, talks qualifying strategy with his driver Al Loquasto.

Referee Don Cummins was always present to consider any situation requiring his years of experience.

possibly meant that one or more of the already qualified cars would be bumped from the race, the prospect of such an action seemed quite remote.

May 20

The Speedway's legal problems began to mount and the qualifying procedures were debated by contestants, officials and those in the press room, while the annual Oldtimers Barbeque was being held behind the tower. All day long, the grand old men of auto racing had been assembling in their trailer parked behind the Press Building. Red caps were very much in evidence and there were some great former drivers among the attending members. The evening's festivities were conducted by Tom Carnegie and sponsored by the Hook Drug Stores, great friends to auto racing.

May 21

It appeared that the legal forces of the "Unqualified Six" were going to court to force a reopening of qualifying or at least to get an injunction to prevent the holding of the race on Sunday. Wright Hugus, or as he was becoming known by press room wags "Lawyer Fungus", has been granted a hearing on his proposed injunction by Marion County Superior Court Judge Frank A. Symmes Jr. Trial date was set for Wednesday morning at 9:30 and subpoenas began flying faster than some of Saturday's qualifiers. The Grant King team and Lindsey Hopkins disassociated themselves from the suit.

Doris King had Don Bringgold dictate a telegram to attorney Don Tabbert who would handle the actual trial work for Hugus and crew, dropping from the suit. While she felt that the qualifying was handled poorly, she also felt that any court action to interfere with the running of the race was even more wrong.

May 22

"Gentlemen, start your injunctions." Many of the track regulars were in the court room of elderly Judge Symmes as lawyer Don Tabbert began calling witnesses. First on the stand was Tony Hulman who had been subpoened to bring a number of track financial statements, entry blanks and

his income tax returns for the past several years. The presentation of these records, other than the signed entry blanks, was objected to by James Donadio, representing the Speedway and sustained by Judge Symmes. Henry Ryder, representing USAC, and Donadio asked for a change of venue out of Marion County. When asked how much a reopening of qualifying would cost the Speedway, Tony, after a long delay finally answered "somewhere in between someplace," which convulsed the courtroom. Cloutier testified as to his discussions with the contestants and then Tom Binford tried to explain the fine print in the entry blank and his

Former chief steward and now consultant to Tom Binford, Harlan Fengler shares an old racing memory with USAC President Reynold MacDonald.

and the Speedway's interpretation of it. Tony had earlier testified that should he reopen time trials and should anyone from the original field be bumped, the Speedway would be open to legal action by those contestants. Judge Symmes refused an evening session when the case dragged to 5:30.

May 23

The traditional carburetion tests were held as usual despite the court action, which was still going on downtown. Most of the cars were on the track and then pit practice took over. As the rookie drivers were having a group picture taken on the starting line, · Johnny Parsons yelled "Look out! Here comes Eldon Palmer!" (driver of the pace car which t-boned the photographers' stand several years ago).

At 3 p.m. a bicycle race for a prize of $3000 was held. It was a two-lap affair with drivers running one lap and friends, relatives, press, etc. riding the other lap. Dick Simon and his son Tim were the winners of the event which unfortunately produced the month's most serious competitive injury. Dick Wallen, one of the country's best racing movie makers, took a nasty spill in the north chute and received four broken ribs and a punctured lung. He was removed to Methodist Hospital. Just before the race he had told your writer that he was too old for this but it would be his only chance to race against A.J. Foyt.

As the bikes were lining up for the race, word was received that Judge Symmes had rejected the plea for an injunction and that the 500 would proceed as planned.

May 24

The weather was perhaps the best of the entire month but there was no activity other than some feverish work in the garage area getting cars ready for the big grind two days hence. In the evening, Foyt entered and won both 50-mile Sprint car features at the Indiana State Fairgrounds. "Boom Boom" Cannon got upside-down but was not injured, which once again calls attention to the risk of a qualified 500 driver competing in another event.

May 25

The traditional Drivers' Meeting brought out the usual number of politicians, pseudo-celebrities and trophy givers. It is a show for the laymen but not particularly interesting when you remember that the real meeting was held under the tower the previous Thursday. Perhaps the most applauded celebrity was Charlie O. Finley--controversial owner of the Oakland A's ballclub--a Hoosier who makes his home in LaPorte.

All in all, it was an interesting three weeks in May and, fortunately, a safe one. We really needed that!

Jim McElreath received a set of training wheels at the Driver's Meeting.

Mario Andretti acknowledged applause at the '74 Driver's Meeting.

The "Snake Pit" was as lively as ever, maybe more so considering the abundance of 'streakers' this year.

One of the very few wall bangers this year was car No. 27 driven by Tom Bigelow.

Former driver Freddie Agabashian, right, and racing P.R. man Dave Blackmer watch the start of the bicycle race.

Former builder Frank Kurtis and Champion's Bobby Strahlman visit the track each May.

Gary Bettenhausen chomps on a chicken leg during a break in practice.

Two of the most devoted golfers among the ranks of the drivers are Lloyd Ruby, left, and Bill Vukovich. Both can shoot the tough Speedway course in the low 80's with ease.

Wally Dallenbach, left, and Bob Harkey attended the picnic staged in the late Art Pollard's honor.

Pit practice is allowed several days before the race to perfect that all-important technique. This is Mike Hiss and crew.

Chief Mechanic Mike Devin, installs a new set of spark plugs just prior to start of the race.

Aviator, race driver and ambassador of the sport, Bob Harkey, left, and Bell Helmet's Jimmy Coughlin survey the starting field.

From one winner to another: Parnelli Jones, left, listens to last minute comments from Mario Andretti. Chief Johnny Capels is on the right.

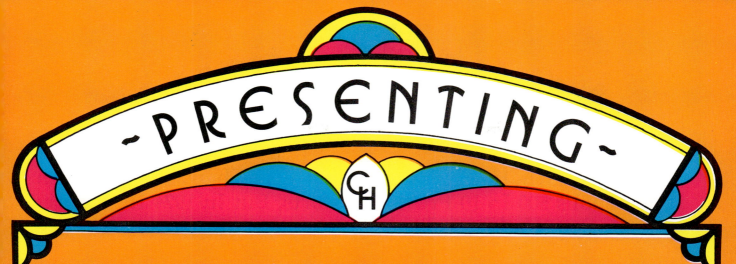

PRESENTING

THE RACE

JOHNNY WINS
And So Does Racing

He Started 25th, Had Not Completed More Than 337 Miles In An Indianapolis 500 In 10 Previous Efforts, But In 1974 He Figured Enough Dues Had Been Paid.

By Carl Hungness
Editor and Publisher

Historians will remember 1974 as the year the President of the United States resigned his office; energy crisis and inflation were headlined words and economy was something you strived for in everyday life. One Henry (Hank to millions) Aaron achieved baseball immortality and more than one endorsement by breaking the mighty Babe Ruth's all-time home run record in '74. While Hank had been plodding along for nearly two decades in the security of a guaranteed pay check for each season of ball played, one John Rutherford, III had been dreaming, scheming and working his way toward achieving the status of professional race car driver. Walk up to the man on the street and ask him to give you his definition of a pro race driver and if only remotely interested he might reply, "I don't know, maybe those guys who run in the Indianapolis 500."

Through a display of driving ability that has been described as "downright frightening" John Rutherford the third convinced the powers that be (and there are many of them in auto racing) that he should have an opportunity to compete in the 1963 Indianapolis 500-Mile Sweepstakes, the oldest and richest car race of them all. Rutherford appeared on the scene during a year of change: The traditional Indianapolis 500 Roadsters had heard the death summons from the cigar-shaped Lotus-Ford cars that migrated to Indianapolis from England. A pair of the rear-engine little cars were entered for two driving greats who had taken a different road to Indianapolis than the one John Rutherford had followed. The quiet Jimmy Clark was in the fastest "Lotus-powered by Ford" and had not come to America from the Grand Prix circuit to show the "yanks" how it was done, Jimmy just came to race and he always considered it his good fortune that he was one of the greatest race car drivers of all time in Formula One racing. The

Knox

There's no quiet before the storming 33 cars of the Indianapolis 500 start their trek around the world's most famous race track. Bands, balloons, box lunches and fast heartbeats are the order of the day.

other Lotus was entered for the man with the magnetic smile, Mr. All-American Boy himself, Dan Gurney. No traditionalist he, Gurney could convince you that you should stop drinking coffee in the morning because the coffee bean plants in South America needed a rest. Gurney had convinced FoMoCo and a race car designer named Colin Chapman that Indianapolis should be rid of the Roadsters. Moreover, Daniel probably would have convinced Chapman that Indianapolis didn't need rear-engine cars if Daniel had in fact been a Roadster driver himself.

No matter. John Rutherford wasn't about the politics of the vehicles involved, or baseball, he had himself a Watson-Offy Roadster for the show and after being bumped around the nation's dirt tracks for the past four years he knew he was in store for the largest payday of his career by running the '63 "500." His chances of winning the race were remote to say the least. After all, he was starting way back there in the ninth row, in 26th spot. He had heard that the race's first winner ever, Ray Harroun had started in 28th spot in 1911 and Lou Meyer did the same thing in 1936 from the 28th position and maybe somebody else came from way back in '32, Fred Fame or Frame or something like that. But there was hope. After all, Parnelli Jones was sitting on the pole in a Watson-Offy, even if Clark was next to him in a Lotus.

J.R.'s hopes ended after some 43 laps of the 200-mile grind had been completed. Transmission failure was listed as the cause of his leaving the race. And so it came to pass that Johnny Rutherford was introduced to the Indianapolis Motor Speedway and the aura surrounding the place that makes competing there something special in itself. In the beginning it was, "I have to get a ride at THE Speedway," then it slowly changes to "I have to get a good ride at the Speedway," to "I can win the darn thing." At Indianapolis, you don't win the race, you win the Speedway as in "Foyt has won the Speedway three times now."

Throughout the next 10 years Rutherford wasn't anywhere near the front of the pack at race's end. He was usually back in the garage area somewhere contemplating the floor and wondering just what it was that made all those race cars break under him. While the Lotus-Fords and a couple of other rear-engine machines with Chevrolet engines built by a southern Californian named Mickey Thompson were leaving their effects on Indianapolis, Rutherford had gone back to the most dangerous and competitive form of automobile racing ever designed, Sprint car racing, and proven himself a champion. He had proven that he could race with the front runners at Indianapolis because most of them joined John in the midwest throughout the summer to run the half-mile dirt and paved tracks that had always been considered the apprentice grounds for Indy greats. And Lord knows you have to drive a Sprint car hard: It sure seemed strange that he couldn't get a Speedway car to last 500 miles around the two and a half mile smooth pavement. Why, one of these things wouldn't last two laps around a place like Terre Haute or Eldora, a pair of dirt half-miles with holes knee deep to a tall Indian.

Nevertheless, John was eeking out a living from automobile racing, a sport where the guaranteed salary is the exception rather than the rule. John was fully aware of the 40 percent paycheck: the car owner usually takes 60% and you get 40. . . .unless you win and then a benevolent owner might split with you. John Rutherford had spent more than one night sleeping on someone's floor in search of monetary security and the fame that goes along

Believe it or not, there are 33 race cars amidst this crowd. Scene is taking place 10 minutes before Tony Hulman gives the "Gentlemen Start Your Engines" command.

Official Starter Pat Vidan annually gives a flag (signed by all drivers) to the winner.

The Hurstettes, good-will ambassadors from the Hurst Co. add to the glamour of the "500."

Dick Beith, a for
shop teacher who made
million in the custom wheel
dustry bought an Indy car and dedi
ed it to the kids of America. Beith
rookie Bill Simpson, a successful businessma
his own right, were among the most popular par
pants in this year's "500."

AMERICAN KIDS
RACER

VUKY

JERRY

JUD

Sugaripe

Second-generation star Billy Vukovich, veteran Chief Mechanic Jud Phillips and Sugaripe Prune Special car owner Jerry O'Connell make up one of the most formidable trios at Indianapolis. Their consistency has proven that a "500" win is in store for them.

with it. He also spent his share of "sheet time" when a vicious Sprint car spit him over the wall at Eldora and got burned a couple of times, too, at places you don't even want to remember. Or the ones you want to go back and conquer.

Handsome John was always there in the Sixties. His reputation was that of being a hard-charger but he was always the guy that was involved, or sitting in the pits with a broken something or other. In 1964 his car was forced into a flaming wreckage taking place on the main stretch: John was burned slightly and out for the day. He lasted 15 laps in '65, missed the 1966 show because he had broken both arms in a Sprint race; he hit the wall in the 1967 event; Billy Vukovich spun in front of him in '68 and he lasted a whole 24 laps in

Actor Jim Nabors among the celebrities on hand.

A pillar of the Speedway staff, Safety Director Jo Quinn is easily recognized by his checkered attire.

'69 and surprised everyone but himself by qualifying in the front row in 1970 but lasted only 135 laps. A bad battery blew his chances in '71 and he went 55 laps in '72 and 124 laps in 1973. He got their attention again in '73 when he set a new track record for qualifying that was just an eyelash under 200 mph.

With his not-very-enviable finishing record, it was a rare sportswriter indeed who chose Rutherford to come home first in the 1974 classic. A veteran from the *Indianapolis Star* newspaper named Bob Collins picked J.R., but Collins pens a daily column titled "The Lighter Side" and most of us figured he'd poke a little good natured fun at Rutherford. After all, it was almost 1963 again. Rutherford was back there in the ninth row again, this time he was on the inside rather that in the middle so his official starting position was listed as 25th. He wondered if anyone had ever won it from 25th. Oh hell, it doesn't make any difference if they start me 34th, he was probably thinking, the car's good, I'm good, and if I finish this thing, I'm certainly going to be up front knockin' on the door.

Speculation had it that Rutherford would 1) hang it on the fence in a banzai charge to the front; 2) turn up the boost and run out of fuel; 3) something will break.

No matter what happened to him, fans knew that he would be spectacular. He had set second-fastest qualifying time but not on the right day so for whatever the rules and reasons, J.R. was back there among 'em. It was, just a little blow to his ego, too. A couple rows up he could see Duane "Pancho" Carter starting his first "500." Carter's dad had started a couple of rows ahead of John back in '63, and John could have been thinking that time had passed him by. After looking around a bit he noticed that only five other guys in the race were with him back in the '63 "500." Man, you don't start thinking of where everybody went because it will scare you.

Now everybody is in rear-engine cars and there isn't a Lotus in the show. Matter of fact, most of the cars in the program are a product of Dan Gurney's All-American Eagle shops in Santa, Ana, Cal. After a couple of second-place finishes, 'ol Daniel said enough of trying to beat this place and hung up his goggles to concentrate on building some very fine

Set for his 27th consecutive broadcast, Voice of the Indianapolis 500, Sid Collins is a study in concentration.

Rookies (and half-brothers) Pancho Carter and Johnny Parsons before race: Right, Speedway historian Charles Lytle.

Johnny Rutherford is looking at eight rows of race cars ahead of him: He passed them all.

Bud Poorman, Gurney mechanic Butch Wilson share a light moment.

The Greatest Spectacle in Racing is about to begin but this little guy isn't interested yet.

racing machines. Colin Chapman hasn't been around for a long time it seems. Now Foyt owns all the Fords and they don't call them Fords any more. Nowadays everyone has a turbocharger on his engine and they're considering a move back to the stock-block engines. Mickey Thompson's cars used Chevies back in '63 and the Lutis-Ford was basically a stock-block, too. Forty-three laps in 1963. You sure can't win a "500" that way.

Well, let's see now. Other than starting back in 25th spot, what other unsurmountable problems could you have in trying to win this thing? There's the wings, they cut the width down this year, but we qualified second-quick. Tires? No, Goodyear and Firestone both have everything dialed in. Wonder whatever happened to Allstate? They were here in the Sixty. . . .something. Engine life? Since they made us cut back on the fuel allotment, engines have been living longer. The fuel allotment. That's it! They're saying we're all going to run out of fuel and this will be the "500" that nobody finished. It would be kind of nice if somebody else didn't finish once in a while.

The McLaren people say we've got the fuel thing handled. We have to get at least 1.8 mph 'cause we're only allowed 285 gallons for this race. McLaren. They weren't around in 1963. But car for car, the McLaren record is second to none at this track. They don't build many of them, like the Eagles, but the ones they do build are sure good.

Going into the 58th annual Indianapolis 500, John Rutherford could have found a lot on his mind. Nevertheless, he told wife Betty before the start, "I love you and I'll see you in Victory Lane."

Rutherford lived up to his promise. In one of the most memorable and competitive "500's" of all time, Johnny Rutherford drove a flawless race and came home first much to the delight of everyone in attendance. Even A.J. Foyt, who for much of the race appeared to be well on his way to an unprecedented fourth victory commented that he was very pleased J.R. won the race: Foyt conceded the fact he himself was just "too busy" to devote as much time to being a "good champion" as Rutherford could. On one hand, Foyt appears as though he would give his proverbial eye teeth for a fourth Indianapolis victory and his complimentary comments directed to Rutherford were the mark of a true sportsman, a title that has not often been pinned on Foyt. Throughout the years, many journalists have failed to understand Foyt's competitive spirit and have often translated his attitude of "second place is losing" to mean that he isn't interested in anyone else but A.J. Foyt. Not so. Foyt wants a win to be the result of hard competition: Backing into a victory is a bit hollow.

Two nights before this year's "500," for example, Foyt brought his Sprint car to the Indiana State Fairgrounds to compete in one of the most publicized and anticipated Sprint car races of the season. The

(continued on page 45)

Far left: Mel Leighton has been in racing since the Thirties. Champion's Rocky Phillips and Art Lamey before race.

STP TEAM

Brightly painted and as competitive as ever, the STP team with Gordon Johncock (20), Wally Dallenbach (40) and Steve Krisiloff (60) was back for the '74 race. Wally occupied the middle of the front row after qualifying while defending winner Johncock was only two positions behind, once again pointing out the fact that cars prepared by George Bignotti are a threat to win any event.

jimmy caruthers

Beginning in Quarter-Midgets when he was less than a decade old, Jimmy Caruthers has been dedicated to a life of automobile racing ever since. Along with Fletcher Racing teammate Pancho Carter, Jim is also a former USAC National Midget Champ. Although a serious racer, he's first on the scene where there's fun to be had.

jimmy mcgee

Jimmy McGee worked his way up the mechanic's ladder of pro auto racing by serving an apprenticeship under crafty veteran mechanic Clint Brawner. McGee learned the trade well and is one of the most respected mechanics in Championship racing today.

The most awesome sight in all of sports is the way the start of the Indianapolis 500 has been described. Wally Dallenbach leads A.J. Foyt into the first turn to begin one of the safest and most competitive ''500's'' ever run.

Speedway owner Tony Hulman starts the million dollar race with his annual ''Gentlemen, Start Your Engines!'' Right, Gordon Johncock raised some eyebrows when he came in on the pace lap for a consultation.

The front row: Foyt in a Coyote, Dallenbach in an Eagle and Hiss in a McLaren.

Sprint race was a virtual reunion for the people of professional auto racing, including personalities of yesterday and today. A.J. was under a great deal of pressure by virtue of his pole position qualifying for the "500" and he considered the Sprint race to be a place he "could have some fun."

A couple dozen Sprint racers looked forward to the race on the mile Fairgrounds track as a place to impress the many Indianapolis 500 car owners, mechanics and officials that would be in attendance and Foyt was just out for a good time. A couple of days prior, in the annual golf tournament

A.J. was needling Pancho Carter, the current Sprint points leader about the upcoming Sprint race. Gary Bettenhausen was needling Foyt that Jan Opperman would "blow his doors off at the Fairgrounds" and in general, the race was to be a showdown between the Sprint car regulars for the legendary Foyt, whose Sprint appearances are quite rare nowadays.

Young Pancho might have been a Rookie in the 500, but he was performing like a veteran at the Fairgrounds. Midway through the race he was leading Foyt lap after lap much to the delight of the youngsters in attend-

ance. Pancho sports an Afro hairdo that's a bit more in style than A.J.'s somewhat balding pate. There was a red flag that stopped the race, however, and the seasoned Foyt jumped out of his Sprint car, poured 10 gallons of fuel in it, made a minor adjustment to the right rear torsion bar, went back out and passed Carter with no trouble. Carter's car owner, builder Steve Stapp commented, "Well, that's what happens when you build cars for guys." Foyt too, was in a Stapp creation and knew just what to do to make it handle better. After

(continued on page 53)

A grandstand photo of Gordon Johncock at over 200 mph.

Rutherford making his charge through the pack early in the race. He's passing Jim McElreath on the inside of the front straight.

This happy group is occupying the infield near the first turn, known affectionately as the "snake pit." Weather was beautiful.

In early stages of the race we doubt the drivers can take time to read their pit boards when running close together.

Dick Simon was credited with completing only a single lap in the event. He waits above, for diagnosis: A valve was cracked and his day was over.

Frustration shows on Chief Mechanic Johnny Capels' face as his machine, driven by Mario Andretti, burned a piston only two laps into the race.

Hunter

IMS

Fox

IMS

Hungness

Chini

AL UNSER

Al Unser and Mario Andretti, two of the nation's superstars are always favorites to win at Indianapolis. Al is one of the few two-time winners of the classic event while popular Mario has one win. The Viceroy-sponsored cars are among the cleanest in racing.

MARIO!

RUBE

Lloyd Ruby's name was in the national racing newspapers in the late Forties. Like a good wine, this timeless veteran has become more popular with age. Quiet and unassuming, 'ol Rube has cut a swath as wide as his native Texas through Championship racing. But like Sam Snead and his unreachable Open victory, Lloyd Ruby is still searching for the win at Indianapolis that should have been his on several occasions.

Young Chief Mechanic Mike Devin, left, passed up a teaching career to follow the sport of speed and is gaining honors during his tenure. Car owner Mike Slater, right, has become one of the sport's unwavering supporters.

Larson

Whitlow

There is but one fast "line" through Indy's turns: Above you may see how turn two is entered. . . .and exited.

IMS

Link

The veteran and the rookie: Lloyd Ruby about to put some distance between himself and Pancho Carter.

Haines

Dick

Jim Hurtubise (No. 56) isn't racing here, he's merely re-entering the track after a pit stop.

Bundy

Alvarez

Two-time winner Al Unser leads '73 champ Gordon Johncock through the first turn. Close racing was the order of the day.

Watson

Nolan

A classic duel unfolded between Foyt and Rutherford. From top, they come through the fourth turn, down the main straightaway and lap Salt Walther and head into number one. Then, Foyt broke and the throngs were curious.

George Snider (No. 82) is taking a run at rookie Bill Simpson. Veterans credited Simpson's first race as "smooth."

McQueeney

McQueeney

Nolan

From the top, Jan Opperman has already lost it in this shot. . . .goes completely sideways as Billy Vukovich comes on the scene. . . . Vuky dives inside while Jerry Grant goes around. No contact was made.

Pancho Carter was forced (unintentionally) out of his groove and spun, causing Jim McElreath an anxious moment. Pancho was restarted and finished the race. Winner Rutherford apologized for the incident.

Brizzolara

Brizzolara

Larson

Larson

Brizzolara

Amiable Jerry Karl knows that his every movement in the above sequence is on film. His wall tapping incident looks worse that it was. He nearly saved the vehicle from making wall contact....but.

Although Johnny Parsons has just had the biggest payday of his career, he doesn't appear happy in this photo.

Hungness

American Kids Racer owner Dick Beith, left, and Bill Simpson show their disappointment at dropping out before race's end.

Stringer

Rutherford's crew kept a constant check on fuel supply. They finished with an ample supply.

Champion's Art Lamey checks a spark plug from a car that has falled out of the race.

Jimmy Gerhardt in the middle of a tire change: The pin in his mouth is a safety device used so wheel nut cannot back off.

Popular Jim Hurtubise pleased his many fans by making the race this year but lasted only 31 laps.

Left, Lloyd Ruby takes on tires and fuel while Bob Harkey, right, does the same. Note tremendous heat waves above the Harkey car.

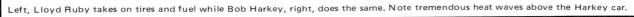

Jerry Karl relaxes with a swig of water during one of the many pit stops required this year. Two veteran names in racing, Louis Meyer left, and Wally Meskowski service Gordon Johncock's STP entry in right photo.

the race Foyt noted over the P.A. system that he would not have beaten the young Carter if the race had not been stopped. Again, he was conceding victory and taking the win lightly by saying, "I was just clowning around." The fickle teeney-boppers flocked to Foyt's pit after the race in search of his autograph, Afro hair or not. It was truly a memorable night of racing for Foyt as he also won the second 50-lap feature run the same night.

Foyt wasn't quite so lucky in this year's "500." Fortunately, there was no red flag to stop the race, and even if there had been, A.J. and crew couldn't have done much to make his car go faster. His bright orange Coyote was performing flawlessly for a full two-thirds of the event.

Right from the clean start it was evident to the near 300,000 in attendance that A.J. would most likely win the event....if he finished. A late blooming Wally Dallenbach took about a 10-car length lead at the start but retired after only three laps had been run. He wasn't first into the pits, though. Dick Simon was credited with one lap in his Foyt-engined Eagle when a valve let go. Gary Bettenhausen faired a little better in his continuing search for an Indianapolis victory, his Offy made two laps before losing a valve also and former winner Mario Andretti was out on the second lap with a broken piston.

While the usual mechanical ills were slimming the field somewhat, Foyt was leading the race from the third through the 24th lap. Rutherford was threading his way up through the pack and says of his performance, "I had to be very careful. It was a matter of being smart, doing a good job and paying attention to what I was doing."

J.R. was in third place at the end of 13 laps and second on the 21st circuit but Foyt appeared to be long gone by this time. Rutherford made the first of his eight pit stops on the 23rd lap and stayed only 17 seconds to pick up a load of fuel. Foyt managed a right rear tire change and fuel in 19 seconds on the very next lap and gave up the lead to Bobby Unser for two laps in the process.

Fans along the front chute were treated to the highest number of pit stops recorded in memory by all participants. Each car had to visit his pit every 20-25 laps or so to take on fuel and many times make a tire change. All in all, some 195 pit stops were recorded throughout the race.

For those who term "excitement" spins, crashes and the like, the 1974 Indianapolis race didn't live up to their

IMS

Tronolone

Knox

IMS

Opposite page: From the top, Rutherford, Foyt, Bobby Unser, Billy Vukovich and Gordon Johncock. Cars are travelling at over 200 mph in these photos.

From top: During their duel, Rutherford, left, and Foyt pulled in pits at the same time. Rutherford's crew has no tire changing problems (as Foyt's did, momentarily) and J.R. leaves pits first.

Tronolone

Roger McCluskey probably felt as though there was a black cloud over his head after being put out of his 13th Indianapolis 500 race with mechanical ills.

expectations. For those who enjoy out-and-out automobile racing, nose-to-tail style, Indy '74 was just what the doctor ordered.

"The eyes of the world are on you," said newly-installed Chief Steward Tom Binford at the annual driver's meeting. He was referring of course to the criticism levied at the running of last year's event that was plagued by rain, crashes and fire.

No one really made a spectacle of himself during the race that saw the yellow flag displayed seven different times for a total of 34 minutes and a couple of seconds. Jerry Karl became the only wall smacker of the day when he spun in the northwest turn. He had to be pried from his mount but suffered no more than a minor leg injury and was walking around later in the afternoon.

Rutherford himself was nearly a party to two separate altercations which to the observer both appeared to be his own doing. First, after a pit stop he re-entered the track in front of Billy Vukovich who had to back off for the Texas charger. Vuky gathered his Sugaripe Prune Spl. back up, shook his fist at Rutherford and continued his fine drive to third place. Then, while lapping fellow Texan Jim McElreath and Pancho Carter, Rutherford dove periously close to Carter and the rookie spun in the process. There was conjecture that the two had actually touched wheels but Rutherford said he felt nothing. McElreath had to perform some quick maneuvering to miss Carter's spin but all turned out roses as Pancho was restarted and went on to cop "Rookie of the Year" honors. As noted, Rutherford made more or less of a public apology to Carter for "getting close" after the race on the track's P.A. system.

Jan Opperman also "lost it" in the fourth turn but avoided wall contact

(continued on page 58)

Dick

Whitlow

Left, Jimmy Caruthers seems to be wondering "What happened?" after stepping from his Cobre Firestone entry. George Snider, right, only made seven circuits in his Gilmore Racing Team car before being sidelined with engine difficulty.

As announcer Tom Carnegie was saying, "And HERE he comes," Pat Vidan was waving the checkered flag for Johnny Rutherford as the spectators stood and cheered. Our gracious Texan returned the salute two-fold as he drove down pit road and acknowledged all in attendance with both hands.

"That's my Johnny!" A totally smitten Betty Rutherford listens to her John tell the crowd what a wonderful day it has been.

Chris Economaki gives Rutherford a chance to tell the ABC audience what it was really like out there. Economaki is always first on the scene and known to all racers.

For John Martin, Indianapolis 1974 was not as successful as he would liked it to have been. He'll be back.

A proud "Pappy" Carter listens to son, Pancho, describe his first "500" to mechanic Gary Bond just after the race.

Track announcer Tom Carnegie knows a future star when he sees one. "How did it feel, Panch?"

DEADLINE! Less than two minutes after Rutherford crossed the finish line, every seat in the press room was filled with an anxious writer rushing a story in. Words come slow, though, as many appear to be thinking.

POST RACE

After the race Jimmy Caruthers changed back into his Levi's and played with his motorcycle.

The "Bike Guys" and "Car Guys" are a close-knit bunch.   After the "500" Jimmy Caruthers, right, Tom Sneva (with glasses), Sprint car owner Don Shepherd, left and mechanic Mike Tzouanakis went to watch Gene (Burrito) Romero compete. Romero and Caruthers are room-mates. Popular bike racers Chuck Palmgren, Charlie Seale, Mert Lawill, Don Castro, Frank Gillespie, David Aldana, John Hateley, etc. are usually found with the Indy car crowd.

The racers go bike ridin' and the writers go racin'. Sort of. 500 Yearbook Publisher Carl Hungness, right, and Photo Director Jim Chini duscuss Hungness' performance in a Midget race after the "500." Chini says, Retirement is imminent if you want to get the Yearbook finished!"

Alvarez

"My Daddy is a winner!" Rutherford's children, Johnny Rutherford IV (called Ivy by fellow competitors) sits atop his father's winning McLaren after the race while his daughter stands guard.

Link

Local Indianapolis newscaster John Totten interviews second place Bobby Unser after his second place drive, while Chuck Palmgren, right, carries Dan Gurney's AAR and Eagle emblems to another AMA win. Gurney owns and built the bike Palmgren campaigns.

although he was parked for the day after running in the top 10. Opperman's performance was indeed creditable considering the lack of pavement experience he has compiled throughout his career as a Sprint car driver.

Opperman and Carter were leading the large (seven) rookie contingent in this year's event but every first-year driver in competition had no trouble in adapting to the rear-engine "funny-cars" as they have been termed by traditionalists. One of the more noteworthy performances was turned in by Tom Sneva, who was running in the top five before being sidelined by mechanical troubles. Safety equipment manufacturer Bill Simpson was also impressive and running in the top 10 when he too was put out with a balky engine.

While the rookies were gaining valuable experience, veterans Foyt, Rutherford, Bobby Unser, Johncock and Vukovich were playing a cat and mouse game for the first half of the race. Bobby inherited the lead after Foyt's first pit stop on the 24th lap and the Albuquerque star led laps 25-26 but relinquished up through the 49th lap again when Foyt pitted. Bobby then led laps 50-52 and relinquished again when Foyt re-entered the fray. Rutherford was faster than Unser throughout and was pecking on Foyt's tail for the best display of a rear-engine car race seen to date at the historic oval.

Both Foyt and Rutherford pitted on the 64th lap and up until this point J.R. had never led a lap in Indianapolis competition. Foyt's crew slowed with a tire change and was clocked at 54 seconds while Rutherford's team put him back in competition in 14 seconds with a fuel load only. The spectators

went absolutely wild over the suspense of "who will get out first" as Foyt and Rutherford's pits were close to each other, one on each side of the scoring tower.

Rutherford hung on to the lead through two more pit stops that both he and Foyt made. Foyt went by John on the 125th lap (when Rutherford again pitted for 20 seconds) and led until the 135th lap when Foyt pitted. Johnny took over for laps 136-137 but A.J. again commanded the lead for laps 138-140.

Foyt's costly pit stop only served to make the race more exciting. He was clearly faster than Rutherford down the chutes, but J.R. made up lost time in the turns. When Foyt pulled alongside John on the front stretch and dove under him going into the first turn (lap 136) the price of admission had been taken care of: Anything from here on out was frosting. A moan loud enough to drown out the loudest Offy when the black flag was displayed for Foyt on the 139th lap. It was waved again, lap 140 and once more on lap 141 when A.J. finally heeded the "come in for consultation" directive. He stayed only 15 seconds (for fuel) to the astonishment of a USAC official who had come over to talk about the oiling problem Foyt appeared to be having. Not feeling that A.J. had really taken time for a summit meeting, officials again commanded the black flag on the next lap (142) and A.J.'s day was over. He didn't take time to stop at his pit but turned left for the last time of the day and headed directly toward Gasoline Alley.

A huge crowd of newsmen gathered around his locked garage and after about 15 minutes Foyt emerged, said a

couple of words to the national TV audience, "Scavenger pump broke" and he jumped on his motorcycle and exited the premises without further comment. What did they want him to say?

Rutherford commanded all but one lap of the remaining 60 circuits (Bobby U. led lap 176 while John was in the pits) and sailed home with a 22 second lead over Unser. Bobby allowed as to how he was simply outrun. He said, "I could have boosted up and maybe caught Johnny at the end, but I would have run out of fuel doing it." And he was right. Unser finished with just enough fuel to cross the line and coasted most of the way around back to the pits.

Several other teams encountered fuel mileage problems, most notably Johncock and Steve Krisiloff who both ran out of fuel on the same lap but were able to restart. Tom Bigelow's crew also told him that he would have to drive with a very light foot in order to finish, a most frustrating thing for a race car driver to hear.

Since his victory, Rutherford has appeared on most of the popular TV talk shows and has been following a relentless personal appearance schedule. His attitude about his victory was expressed shortly after the race: "I hope this will ease people's minds, that we're not a bunch of idiots here trying to see how many people we can wipe out."

Automobile racing needed you, Johnny Rutherford. And next time we see a rookie start back there in the eighth or ninth row, we'll remember that the road to an Indianapolis 500-Mile Race victory consists of more than passing a couple of dozen race cars.

TOTAL WINNINGS AT THE SPEEDWAY BY ACTIVE DRIVERS

By Bob Laycock

	DRIVER	YEARS	RACES	TOTAL WINNINGS	MILES	POINTS
1	Al Unser**	1965-74	8	$749,806.94	3,502	3,850
2	A.J. Foyt***	1958-74	17	743,698.94	5,967	4,950
3	Bobby Unser*	1963-74	12	481,019.62	3,807	3,100
4	Gordon Johncock*	1965-74	10	405,480.09	3,155	2,750
5	Mario Andretti*	1965-74	10	401,828.43	2,267	2,350
6	Johnny Rutherford*	1963-74	11	375,223.61	2,385	1,200
7	Lloyd Ruby	1960-74	15	264,255.53	5,745	2,900
8	Bill Vukovich	1968-74	7	251,851.54	2,157	2,300
9	Joe Leonard	1965-73	9	215,244.12	3,162	2,050
10	Roger McCluskey	1961-74	13	210,437.52	3,920	900
11	Jim McElreath	1962-74	11	206,633.40	3,982	2,900
12	Mel Kenyon	1966-73	8	193.171.13	2,875	2,400
13	Gary Bettenhausen	1968-74	7	153,727.52	1,562	650
14	George Snider	1965-74	10	142,434.60	1,572	114
15	Jerry Grant	1965-74	8	133,966.86	2,617	650
16	Mike Mosley	1968-74	7	123,492.01	1,990	400
17	Sammy Sessions	1968-73	6	117,991.13	2,025	900
18	Wally Dallenbach	1967-74	8	115,444.51	1,865	0
19	Jim Hurtubise	1960-74	10	100,194.93	2,235	0
20	Dick Simon	1970-74	5	91,069.82	1,515	0
21	Steve Krisiloff	1971-74	4	76,102.32	1,202	400
22	Mike Hiss	1972-74	3	70,723.11	1,112	300
23	David Hobbs	1971-74	3	69,018.47	1,025	600
24	John Martin	1972-74	3	64,854.10	1,135	350
25	Bob Harkey	1964-74	4	56,361.45	1,182	500
26	Rick Muther	1970-74	3	56,241.14	732	250
27	Jimmy Caruthers	1972-74	3	55,166.10	827	200
28	Salt Walther	1972-74	3	46,697.23	352	0
29	Denny Zimmerman	1971-72	2	44,978.11	762	250
30	Lee Kunzman	1972-73	2	44,250.68	645	300
31	Sam Posey	1972	1	37,410.89	495	500
32	Jerry Karl	1973-74	2	35,022.22	342	0
33	Duane Carter, Jr.	1974	1	26,758.42	477	300
34	Tom Bigelow	1974	1	20,769.42	415	50
35	Bill Simpson	1974	1	19,922.42	407	0
36	Tom Sneva	1974	1	19,136.42	235	0
37	Graham McRae	1973	1	19,038.80	227	0
38	John Mahler	1972	1	16,062.87	247	0
39	Jan Opperman	1974	1	15,617.40	212	0
40	Larry Cannon	1974	1	15,429.40	122	0
41	Johnny Parsons	1974	1	14,497.40	45	0
42	Bentley Warren	1971	1	14,486.24	190	0

*Former Winner

TOTAL PRIZE MONEY EACH YEAR OF THE TONY HULMAN REGIME

1946	$ 115,450
1947	$ 137,425
1948	$ 171,075
1949	$ 179,050
1950	$ 201,135
1951	$ 207.650
1952	$ 230,100
1953	$ 246,300
1954	$ 269,375
1955	$ 270,400
1956	$ 282,052
1957	$ 300,252
1958	$ 305,217
1959	$ 338,100
1960	$ 369,150
1961	$ 400,000
1962	$ 426,162
1963	$ 494,030
1964	$ 506,575
1965	$ 628,399
1966	$ 691,808
1967	$ 734,634
1968	$ 712,269
1969	$ 805,127
1970	$1,000,002
1971	$1,001,604
1972	$1,011,845
1973	$1,006,105
1974	$1,015,686

USAC CHAMPIONSHIP BOX SCORE -- INDIANAPOLIS, INDIANA -- MAY 26, 1974

Track: Indianapolis Motor Speedway   Avg. Speed: 158.589 mph   Basic Purse: $ 817,500
Type Track: 2½-Mile Paved   Time: 3:09:10.06   Lap Prize: $ 40,000
Organizer: Anton Hulman   Distance: 500 Miles   Accessory: $ 158,156
Weather: Sunny   Event No. 4   TOTAL: $1,015,686

FIN. POS.	ST. POS.	DRIVER	CAR NAME/ NUMBER	PTS. WON	MONEY WON	LAPS COMP.	RUNNING/ REASON OUT
1	25	Johnny Rutherford	McLaren (3)	1000	$245,032	200	Running
2	7	Bobby Unser	Olsonite (48)	800	$ 99,504	200	Running
3	16	Billy Vukovich	Sugaripe Prune (4)	700	$ 63,411	199	Running
4	4	Gordon Johncock	STP Dbl. Oil Filter (20)	600	$ 36,329	198	Running
5	9	David Hobbs	Carling Black Label (73)	---	$ 32,074	196	Running
6	30	Jim McElreath	Thermo King (45)	400	$ 27,220	194	Running
7	21	Duane Carter, Jr.	Cobre Firestone (11)	300	$ 26,258	191	Running
8	31	Bob Harkey	Peru Circus (79)	250	$ 23,735	189	Running
9	18	Lloyd Ruby	Unlimited Racing (9)	200	$ 22,732	187	Out of fuel
10	17	Jerry Grant	Cobre Firestone (55)	150	$ 21,266	175	Running
11	22	John Martin	Sea Snack (89)	100	$ 20,643	169	Running
12	23	Tom Bigelow	Bryant Heating (27)	50	$ 20,019	166	Running
13	20	Bill Simpson	American Kids Racer (18)		$ 19,422	163	Piston
14	3	Mike Hiss	Norton Spirit (68)		$ 21,697	158	Running
15	1	A. J. Foyt	Gilmore Racing (14)		$ 35,674	142	Oil line fitting
16	27	Roger McCluskey	English Leather (1)		$ 18,347	141	Rear end
17	14	Salt Walther	Dayton-Walther (77)		$ 17,447	141	Piston
18	26	Al Unser	Viceroy (15)		$ 17,492	131	Valve
19	19	Jerry Karl	Ayr-Way Lloyd's (42)		$ 16,583	115	Accident
20	8	Tom Sneva	Raymond Companies (24)		$ 18,386	94	Ring & pinion gear
21	32	Jan Opperman	Viceroy Parnelli (51)		$ 15,617	85	Spun out
22	15	Steve Krisiloff	STP Gas Treatment (60)		$ 15,276	72	Clutch
23	12	Jimmy Caruthers	Cobre Firestone (21)		$ 15,563	64	Gear box
24	33	Larry Cannon	American Financial (59)		$ 14,679	49	Differential
25	28	Jim Hurtubise	Miller High Life (56)		$ 14,824	31	Blown engine
26	29	Johnny Parsons	Vatis (94)		$ 14,497	18	Turbocharger
27	24	Rick Muther	Eisenhour (61)		$ 13,998	11	Piston
28	13	George Snider	Gilmore Racing (82)		$ 14,027	7	Valve
29	6	Mike Mosley	Lodestar (98)		$ 15,685	6	Blown engine
30	2	Wally Dallenbach	STP Oil Treatment (40)		$ 15,472	3	Piston
31	5	Mario Andretti	Viceroy (5)		$ 15,587	2	Valve
32	11	Gary Bettenhausen	Score (8)		$ 14,230	2	Valve
33	10	Dick Simon	TraveLodge (44)		$ 13,774	1	Valve

FAST QUALIFIER: A. J. Foyt, No. 14 -- 3:07.86 (191.632 mph)
LAP LEADERS: Laps 1—2, Dallenbach (No. 40); Laps 3—24, Foyt (No. 14); Laps 25—26, B. Unser (No. 48); Laps 27—49, Foyt; Laps 50—52, B. Unser; Laps 53—64, Foyt; Laps 65—125, Rutherford (No. 3); Laps 126—135, Foyt; Laps 136—137, Rutherford; Laps 138—140, Foyt; Laps 141—175, Rutherford; Lap 176, B. Unser; Laps 177—200, Rutherford.
YELLOW LIGHTS: Seven for a total of 14 laps and total time of 34 minutes, 2 seconds.

THE OFFICIAL STARTING FIELD, 1974 INDIANAPOLIS 500-MILE RACE

Courtesy Dick Sauer, Director of Timing and Scoring Indianapolis Motor Speedway

A. J. Foyt Jr., No. 14	3:07.86	**191.632**	
Gilmore Racing Team	46.74	192.555	
	46.82	192.226	
Qual: 5/11 @ 11:06	47.00	191.489	
	47.30	190.275	

Wally Dallenbach, No. 40	3:09.79	**189.683**	
STP Oil Treatment	47.19	190.718	
	47.35	190.074	
Qual: 5/11 @ 11:57	47.66	188.838	
	47.59	189.115	

Mike Hiss, No. 68	3:12.01	**187.490**	
Norton Spirit	48.02	187.422	
	47.90	187.891	
Qual: 5/18 @ 11:25	48.07	187.227	
	48.02	187.422	

Gordon Johncock, No. 20	3:13.25	**186.287**	
STP Double Oil Filter	48.24	186.567	
	48.26	186.490	
Qual: 5/18 @ 11:15	48.30	186.335	
	48.45	185.759	

Mario Andretti, No. 5	3:13.52	**186.027**	
Viceroy Special	48.22	186.645	
	48.29	186.374	
Qual: 5/18 @ 12:16	48.48	185.644	
	48.53	185.452	

Mike Mosley, No. 98	3:14.26	**185.319**	
Lodestar Special	48.46	185.720	
	48.60	185.185	
Qual: 5/11 @ 12:20	48.56	185.338	
	48.64	185.033	

Bobby Unser, No. 48	3:14.41	**185.176**	
Olsonite Eagle	48.33	186.220	
	48.45	185.759	
Qual: 5/11 @ 11:40	48.63	185.071	
	49.00	183.673	

Tom Sneva, No. 24	3:14.44	**185.147**	
Raymond Companies Spec.	48.33	186.220	
	48.41	185.912	
Qual: 5/11 @ 4:13	48.70	184.805	
	49.00	183.673	

David Hobbs, No. 73	3:14.77	**184.833**	
Carling Black Label	48.79	184.464	
McLaren	48.57	185.071	
Qual: 5/11 @ 12:12	48.63	185.071	
	48.72	184.729	

Dick Simon, No. 44	3:15.12	**184.502**	
TraveLodge Eagle	49.24	182.778	
	48.84	184.275	
Qual: 5/18 @ 11:52	48.42	185.874	
	48.62	185.109	

Gary Bettenhausen, No. 8	3:15.13	**184.492**	
Score Special	48.62	185.109	
	48.61	185.147	
Qual: 5/11 @ 3:47	48.86	184.200	
	49.04	183.524	

Jimmy Caruthers, No. 21	3:15.60	**184.049**	
Cobre Firestone	48.74	184.653	
	48.57	185.300	
Qual: 5/11 @ 3:38	48.97	183.786	
	49.32	182.482	

George Snider, No. 82	3:15.66	**183.993**	
Gilmore Racing Team	48.30	186.335	
	48.94	183.899	
Qual: 5/11 @ 11:21	49.11	183.262	
	49.31	182.519	

Salt Walther, No. 77	3:15.73	**183.927**	
Dayton-Walther Special	48.99	183.711	
	48.88	184.124	
Qual: 5/18 @ 11:38	38.87	184.162	
	48.99	183.711	

Steve Krisiloff, No. 60	3:17.24	**182.519**	
STP Gas Treatment	49.26	182.704	
	49.27	182.667	
Qual: 5/11 @ 11:46	49.39	182.223	
	49.32	182.482	

Billy Vukovich, No. 4	3:17.26	**182.500**	
Sugaripe Prune Special	49.58	181.525	
	49.16	183.076	
Qual: 5/11 @ 3:56	49.11	183.262	
	49.41	182.149	

Jerry Grant, No. 55	3:18.04	**181.781**	
Cobre Firestone	49.26	182.704	
	49.74	180.941	
Qual: 5/11 @ 12:04	49.53	181.703	
	49.51	181.781	

Lloyd Ruby, No. 9	3:18.13	**181.699**	
Unlimited Racing	49.42	182.113	
	49.38	182.260	
Qual: 5/11 @ 3:30	49.71	181.050	
	49.62	181.378	

Jerry Karl, No. 42	3:18.40	**181.452**	
Ayr-Way/Lloyd's Special	49.29	182.593	
	49.42	182.113	
Qual: 5/18 @ 12:10	49.65	181.269	
	50.04	179.856	

Bill Simpson, No. 18	3:18.85	**181.041**	
American Kids Racer	49.31	182.519	
	49.60	181.452	
Qual: 5/11 @ 11:14	49.98	180.072	
	49.96	180.144	

Duane Carter Jr., No. 11	3:19.33	**180.605**	
Cobre Firestone	49.71	181.050	
	49.67	181.196	
Qual: 5/11 @ 11:28	50.04	179.856	
	49.91	180.325	

John Martin, No. 89	3:19.55	**180.406**	
Sea Snack Shrimp	49.49	181.855	
Cocktail	49.90	180.361	
Qual: 5/18 @ 12:22	50.00	180.000	
	50.16	179.426	

Tom Bigelow, No. 27	3:19.84	**180.144**	
Bryant Heating and	49.60	181.452	
Cooling	50.04	179.856	
Qual: 5/18 @ 12:01	50.06	179.784	
	50.14	179.497	

Rick Muther, No. 61	3:20.01	**179.991**	
Eisenhour Special	50.23	179.176	
	49.76	180.868	
Qual: 5/18 @ 12:30	49.89	180.397	
	50.13	179.533	

Johnny Rutherford, No. 3	3:09.03	**190.446**	
McLaren	47.09	191.123	
	47.11	191.042	
Qual: 5/18 @ 4:36	47.24	190.517	
	47.59	189.115	

Al Unser, No. 15	3:15.77	**183.889**	
Viceroy Special	48.84	184.275	
	48.77	184.540	
Qual: 5/18 @ 4:53	48.96	183.824	
	49.20	182.927	

Roger McCluskey, No. 1	3:18.89	**181.005**	
English Leather Special	49.85	180.542	
	49.62	181.378	
Qual: 5/18 @ 5:30	49.73	180.977	
	49.69	181.123	

Jim Hurtubise, No. 56	3:19.68	**180.288**	
Miller High Life Special	49.27	182.667	
	49.51	181.781	
Qual: 5/18 @ 4:45	50.42	178.501	
	50.48	178.288	

Johnny Parsons, No. 94	3:19.72	**180.252**	
Vatis Special	49.82	180.650	
	49.79	180.759	
Qual: 5/18 @ 5:46	50.19	179.319	
	49.92	180.288	

Jim McElreath, No. 45	3:23.07	**177.279**	
Thermo King Special	50.67	177.620	
	50.64	177.725	
Qual: 5/18 @ 5:08	50.89	176.852	
	50.87	176.922	

Bob Harkey, No. 79	3:23.75	**176.687**	
Peru Circus Special	50.93	176.713	
	50.98	176.540	
Qual: 5/18 @ 4:19	50.77	177.270	
	51.07	176.229	

Jan Opperman, No. 51	3:24.33	**176.186**	
Viceroy Parnelli Special	50.95	176.644	
	51.10	176.125	
Qual: 5/18 @ 5:53	51.17	175.884	
	51.11	176.091	

Larry Cannon, No. 59	3:26.94	**173.963**	
Hoffman Auto Racing	51.74	173.947	
	51.74	173.947	
Qual: 5/18 @ 5:00	51.70	174.081	
	51.76	173.879	

The average speed of the 33 cars that started the race in 1973 was 192.329 miles per hour.
The average speed of the 33 cars that started the race in 1974 was 182.787 miles per hour.

Official Indianapolis Motor Speedway Records as of June 1, 1974
By Bob Laycock

Laps	Miles	Time	Miles Per Hour	Driver	Car	Year
				QUALIFYING RECORDS		
1	2½	45.21	199.071	Johnny Rutherford	Gulf McLaren	1973
4	10	3:01.44	198.413	Johnny Rutherford	Gulf McLaren	1973
				RACE RECORDS		
1	2½	48.91	184.011	Wally Dallenbach	STP Oil Treatment	1974
2	5	1:35.93	187.637	Wally Dallenbach	STP Oil Treatment	1974
4	10	3:14.21	185.366	A. J. Foyt Jr.	Gilmore Racing Team	1974
10	25	8:06.28	185.079	A. J. Foyt Jr.	Gilmore Racing Team	1974
20	50	16:22.35	183.234	A. J. Foyt Jr.	Gilmore Racing Team	1974
30	75	25:05.67	179.322	Bobby Unser	Olsonite Eagle	1972
40	100	33:44.08	177.859	A. J. Foyt Jr.	Gilmore Racing Team	1974
50	125	42:16.91	177.381	Bobby Unser	Olsonite Eagle	1974
60	150	50:57.29	176.627	A. J. Foyt Jr.	Gilmore Racing Team	1974
70	175	1:04:28.79	162.842	Johnny Rutherford	McLaren	1974
80	200	1:14:27.29	161.172	Gary Bettenhausen	Sunoco McLaren	1972
90	225	1:23:36.58	161.465	Al Unser	Johnny Lightning 500 Special	1970
100	250	1:32:31.68	162.113	Gary Bettenhausen	Sunoco McLaren	1972
110	275	1:40:45.43	163.760	Gary Bettenhausen	Sunoco McLaren	1972
120	300	1:49:03.76	165.043	Gary Bettenhausen	Sunoco McLaren	1972
130	325	1:58:21.78	164.747	Gary Bettenhausen	Sunoco McLaren	1972
140	350	2:06:46.87	165.640	Gary Bettenhausen	Sunoco McLaren	1972
150	375	2:18:20.45	162.642	Gary Bettenhausen	Sunoco McLaren	1972
160	400	2:26:34.94	163.739	Gary Bettenhausen	Sunoco McLaren	1972
170	425	2:35:57.25	163.510	Gary Bettenhausen	Sunoco McLaren	1972
180	450	2:46:23.97	162.260	Jerry Grant	Mystery Eagle	1972
190	475	2:55:01.16	162.839	Mark Donohue	Sunoco McLaren	1972
200	500	3:04:05.54	162.962	Mark Donohue	Sunoco McLaren	1972

Paris wouldn't be Paris without the Eiffel Tower, San Francisco wouldn't be San Francisco without the Golden Gate and Indianapolis wouldn't be Indianapolis without a seering, furious, knuckle-busting rules controversy at the Speedway during the month of May. While in most parts of the world spring is known as bringing out fruit blossoms, at Indy spring is best known for bringing out angry press statements, tight-lipped glares between competitors and organizers, complaints and threats of team withdrawals and a vast assortment of other official and unofficial nose-thumbings. In 1974, Indy was in full-bloom as usual.

This year's great controversy centered on the STP team which, if you remember the turbine years and certain other annual rumblings in the press, is no stranger to the white-hot printed word. Even with Andy Granatelli no longer in evidence the STP team managed yet again to gain the spotlight during qualifying, thanks to a huge snail-shaped piece of metal whose

Chini

The exhaust header on this unassuming Offenhauser leads into an equally inconspicious turbocharger, used for years on over-the-road diesel trucks. Now they're using them at Indianapolis and sure enough, they caused a controversy.

qualifying line with it firmly in place. USAC was caught off guard. They had no idea anyone would bring out a T18, so there was no pressure gauge available. Furthermore, no warning had been given to Bignotti that he had to have a gauge and there was nothing in the rules that said the T18 was illegal. Dallenbach qualified the car on the front row next to A.J. Foyt's pole-winner and everyone else screamed "Foul!"

The controversy got hotter when Bignotti applied for permission to return to a TEO-691 for the race. He argued that it is common for teams to switch turbos from 691's to smaller 690's between qualifying and a race, but USAC said removing the T18 would violate the spirit of the rule which stated that a car must use the same configuration for a race that it had used for qualifying. An earlier STP-USAC squabble over the same point had happened in 1969 when Andretti's chief mechanic, Clint Brawner, wanted to add an oil cooler for the race that hadn't been there during qualifying. The oil cooler was disal-

THE GREAT HOT-AIR CONTROVERSY of 1974

By Ted West

chief claim to notoriety was that it could ram huge quantities of air into the team's Drake-Offenhauser engine at a speed of 600 mph. This snail-shaped object bore the innocent-sounding name of "Airesearch T18-17A" and was of course a turbocharger.

The story began long before anyone arrived at the Speedway. In mid-winter, Mark Donohue of Roger Penske Racing had been considering using such a T18-17A. The reason for using the T18 is that it is much larger than the TEO-691 used on most cars at Indy. Since cars would be required to use a "pop-off" valve which was meant to limit the engines to a maximum of 80 inches of manifold pressure, Donohue reckoned that even if

the T18 stayed at 80 inches like the TEO-691, the sheer volume of air being forced into the engine would be greater, and thus in effect more horsepower would be available. But when Donohue took the idea to USAC they said a pressure gauge would have to be attached to the unit during qualifying to prove it had stayed at 80 inches pressure. Unsure they could prove this, the Penske people abandoned the T18.

Months later, on the day before qualifying, a man named Skip Cooley walked into George Bignotti's STP garage and said he could give him a hundred horsepower overnight. He explained to George the magical powers of the T18-71A, the team spent the night installing it on Wally Dallenbach's car and Wally appeared on the

lowed and Mario went on to win the 500 anyway.

With Bignotti forced to leave the T18 on Dallenbach's car for the race just about everyone thought the car would be unable to finish on the allotted 280 gallons of fuel. Surely, they said, greater air volume requires more fuel to maintain the proper mixture and avoid burned pistons.

But then Bignotti shocked everyone. On the second weekend of qualifying he had a T18 mounted on Johncock's STP Eagle too, though the third car driven by Steve Krisiloff ran a 691 blower. This time USAC had a pressure gauge ready and sure enough, it said that the engine had grossly exceeded 80 inches during Johncock's run to fourth spot on the grid. The engine was put on a dynamometer though, and Bignotti's claim that the high-pressure reading came about only when the engine was shut off, such as for going into a turn, was upheld. Otherwise the T18 produced a legal 80 inches under normal running. Thus the car was allowed to race.

On the question of fuel mileage, everyone else still thought the T18 had no chance. Bignotti's men claimed in private though that when the engine's boost was turned down, as it would be in the race, the blower's greater air volume cooled the fuel and let the engine run as efficiently as with a smaller blower. Furthermore, much greater power was available whenever needed by simply turning up the T18's boost. Bignotti's people said things were fine and everyone else said they didn't have a chance. Only the race would tell.

At the green flag, Dallenbach showed what kind of power he had by putting a hundred yards on A.J. Foyt before Turn 2, but Wally only lasted three laps before he burned a piston. Johncock, however, was running like a train. After being so high as third on lap 10, he dropped back to the middle of the field and then began moving up again to seventh by lap 130, then sixth, fifth and fourth where he finished. So the T18 could finish 500 miles on 280 gallons after all.

Well yes, sort of. During the race there had been seven incidents taking 34 minutes and 21 seconds of yellow flag time, every minute of which helped Johncock conserve fuel. When USAC's Frankie DelRoy checked fuel in the finishing cars though, he found both Johncock's on-board tanks and his pit tank dry. If there'd been one minute less yellow time, Johncock would probably have coasted to a stop on the track out of fuel. But Bignotti won his point--by a drop!

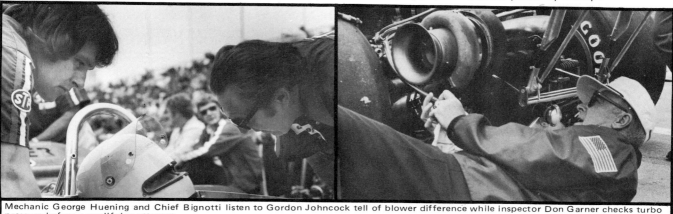

Chini

West

Mechanic George Huening and Chief Bignotti listen to Gordon Johncock tell of blower difference while inspector Don Garner checks turbo pressure before a qualifying attempt.

DAVEY CROCKETT

By Robin Miller

How did Walter Oliver Howell Jr. find success and fame as Davey Crockett? With 20 years of hard work, a bunch of knowledge and no coonskin cap.

Crockett, or Howell if you prefer, is the lone independent engine man still in operation on the United States Auto Club's Championship Trail. He started out to be a driver and has developed into a master constructor of the powerful Offenhauser engine.

Today, tucked inside his growing shop in tiny Lizton, Ind., Crockett tears down and assembles the powerplants for many of the top teams in USAC. But way back in 1955, he was just Walter Howell, a laborer on the CRA Roadsters of the late and great Johnny Poulsen.

It was in the wee hours of the morning during a thrash at Poulsen's Gardena, Cal. shop that Walter was renamed. "Poulsen needed a part and somebody pointed to me and said, 'Let Davy Crockett get it,' and that was it. I've been Davey Crockett ever since," laughs Howell.

"Then I began my career as the world's worst race driver," says D.C. shaking his head, "and looking back I'd say I was very lucky to get through that period of my life."

While Davey was attempting to drive, he continued to work for Poulsen and another legendary character named Lee Roy Neumeyer. He drove Sprinters and Midgets up to 1963 and that's when he red flagged his career. "A very good friend of mine named Bud Sterett was killed in a race at El Centro. It really affected me and calmed me down because that kid had

a hell of a future," reflects the 40-year-old father of one.

So Crockett hung up his shoes for a wrench and came back to the midwest and began stooging on a Sprint car for a kid named A.J. Foyt. He decided he wasn't going anywhere in

the fall of 1964 so he hoofed it back to the coast and got hooked up with Carroll Shelby. Crockett became the chief on Shelby's Mark 4 GT-40 prototype machine and accompanied the car to LeMans. Following that assignment, Davey went to work for a California

insurance salesman named George Follmer who drove a Lotus 23 with a Porsche engine to the ARRC championship.

The next stop was employment at the Traco Engine Plant. A fellow named Mike Goth persuaded D.C. to go Can-Am racing for the 1967 season and then it was back to Traco. It was that point in his life that Howell became acquainted with Herb Porter in a Goodyear deal.

Porter, the long-time Indy mechanic was the tire company's new engine saviour. "That's when I got out of mechanics and began specializing in engines. It was also the biggest break I ever got -- working with Herb. He has helped me more than anyone and I've had a bunch of help," exclaims Crockett.

He was with Porter for three years and in 1971 he was hired by Roger Penske, where he did all the engine work for the Mark Donohue team. Davey went with McLaren in 1972 and as he put it, "snapped defeat from the jaws of victory" as Donohue captured the Indy 500 that year for Penske. He parted company with McLaren midway through the year and finished it out with the Vel Miletich-Parnelli Jones team.

Then, in January 1973, Davey Crockett went into the woods of competition by himself. "It was something I always wanted to do," he replies. "I've never been motivated by money and I guess that's one of my problems. But I'm happy being my own boss and things are going pretty good."

As of May, 1974, Davey's three steadiest customers were the Thremo King team, Lindsey Hopkins' cars and the American Kids Racer team headed by Dick Beith. Since Davey's roots filter back to the nation's dirt tracks, he still finds time to build an occasional Sprint car engine and is now doing more and more Road Race engines, too.

When a team brings Davey an Indy engine to overhaul, it takes him a minimum of 50 hours and costs in the neighborhood of $750. As a man entrenched deeply into auto racing, Davey is not only price conscious of his own work but has some poignant views about the overall cost of the sport in general. He is growing increasingly tired of hearing self-proclaimed experts talk about the future of engines in USAC racing.

"The guys that think they're gonna' get stock block engines to run with any life are just kidding themselves," opines D.C. "They never have lived and they never will. Those little dudes just don't know about those big, long tracks. The engine life of an Offy today is better than it's ever been. The motors run farther and they're more economical than ever before.

"When a guy goes to Drake to purchase a new engine, he pays $24,000 and the next one costs $20,000. A guy buys a Chevy stock block for, well say $11,000. But when he junks it, he pays no less than $5,000 to repair it. And it doesn't take long to hit $40,000 the way stock blocks blow."

Davey Crockett speaks his piece. With a grin as wide as an axe handle, 'Ol Davey also has that enviable knack of turning those tight situations that always crop up in auto racing into humorous memories. He can sit for hours and tell you of the practical jokes he has pulled on his friends throughout the sport.

When Crockett went to work for the regimented Roger Penske team, Davey's friends told him that he would have to "clean up his act." Crockett has always been considered clean-cut mind you, but he has never believed that a shirt should be tucked inside one's pants. Members of the Penske crew not only tuck their shirts in, but it has been reported that Penske would prefer it if crews' buttons were shined.

Two weeks after joining the Penske stable, Davey's clean blue shirt tails were flying in the breeze. After all, who ever heard of a man named Davey Crockett dressing up to go to work?

PAST

Chet Miller, Dr. - Eddie Tyren ...
Indianapolis M... ...1929

1924

By Jack C. Fox

Drivers and their cars arrived by train and the cars were unloaded at the Prest-O-Lite siding across from the track. . .Harlan Fengler was confined to Methodist Hospital after flipping his Wade Special in the northeast turn in practice. . ."Racing Luck" staring Monty Banks was playing at the Circle "The Temple of the Silent Art". . .French driver Antoine Mourre (pronounced More) was being tutored by Ernie Olson. . ."Mutt and Jeff," "Uncle Wiggley," "Mr. and Mrs." and "You Know Me, Al" by Ring Lardner, were in the funny papers. . .Ora Haibe took the track in his Schmidt Special, a 1923 Mercedes. . .boys' wool knickers were .95 cents and men's union suits sold for .88 cents. . .Coast drivers used Richfield gas brought back in tank trucks from Los Angeles. . .Buster Keeton was showing at the Colonial in "Sherlock, Jr.". . .Jimmy Murphy's car was called the "Golden Tornado" . . .You could go to San Francisco on the Pacific Limited for $95.70 round trip. . .Eddie Hearne tore himself away from the radio loud speaker in his garage long enough to pose for a picture with Murphy and Earl Cooper . . .Womens' coats sold for $9.50 and summer dresses were $30. . .Alfred Moss, who had been working for over a month on the Schmidt Special signed to drive one of the Barber-Warnocks, Model T Fords converted for racing by the Chevrolet Brothers. . .two-toned baby carriages listed at $38.50 and Lillian Gish starred in "The White Sister" at the Ohio. . .It was estimated that you could buy a Miller and campaign it for one year for $30,000 (car, $10,000; upkeep $10,000; shipping $2,000; driver's personal expenses $5,000; mechanic's wages $2,000; mechanic's railway fare $1,000. . .The White Star Line advertised their "magnificent trio of oil burners, Majestic, Olympic (sister ship to the Titanic), and Homeric. . .The phonograph in Harry Hartz' garage played "It Aint Gonna Rain No Mo". . .McDonough's car was announced as Milton's 1923 winner with a new chassis and running gear. . .L.S. Ayres and Company sold "Speedway clothes for those who appreciate the fashion possibilities of a great sport event". . .Dutch Baumann was the favorite in the dirt track races at Hoosier Motor Speedway. . .spare ribs sold for 8 cents a pound and potatoes were 6 lbs. for 25 cents. . . Frithlof Ramsen hit the wall practicing in one of the Barber-Warnocks. . .Jerry Wonderlich's car was painted Mojave brown. . .Player pianos sold for $395 and you could buy a Victor record of Gigli singing "Martha" for $2. . . Young Louis Schneider sneaked on the Speedway in a dirt track car and drove a lap with the Army chasing him in a motorcycle and side car. . .He pulled into the pits, was taken to the Speedway Office and then sent home. . . Grover Cleveland Alexander and Dazzy Vance led the National League in pitching. . .Al Waddell, P.R. man for wealthy Cliff Durant, went to a fortune teller who told him a red car would win the 500. . .Durant's car, said to be the most expensive ever built, was polished aluminum with a nickel plated frame. . .Eddie DeBiase was serving spaghetti for the fourth year at his Venice Gardens. . .Earl Cooper was deluged with good luck charms after he said he needed one. . . Henry Ford arrived on the eve of the race and walked the track. . .He also bought a $10,000 insurance policy on each driver. . .Loeb and Leopold confessed to murdering Bobby Franks in Chicago and the Indiana Republican Convention endorsed Calvin Coolidge for President. . .Qualifying deadline was 6:00 a.m. the morning of the race. . .Henry Ford toured the track in the Cole pacemaker and then drove a lap in a Barber-Warnock. . .When Joe Boyer pulled into Victory Lane in his dark RED Duesey, owner Fred Duesenberg kissed him on BOTH cheeks (Andy Granatelli please note). . .Fred later announced that he was going to retire from racing. . .Results of the race were carried over radio station WGN in Chicago sponsored by Carl G. Fisher's Prest-O-Lite Company.

Joe Boyer in car, drove 92 laps in this Duesenberg while L.L. Corum (inset) drove the other 102 laps to record the 1924 win.

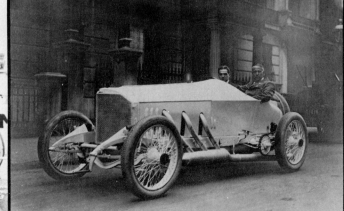

Ten years prior to the '24 event the much heralded Ralph DePalma failed to qualify this Mercedes due to excessive vibration. Note chain drive.

Three-time winner Mauri Rose (1941-47-48) was a capable craftsman as well as driver. In photo at left he is shown filing the cowl of his Blue Crown Spark Plug Spl. which appears as the finished product at right.

First meeting of the Champion Spark Plug 100-Mile Per Hour club included, from left, front row; Howdy Wilcox, Wilbur Shaw, Lou Moore, Lou Meyer, Bill Cummings, Dave Evans. Back row, from left; Cliff Bergere, Fred Frame, Russ Snowberger, Chet Gardner, Mauri Rose.

Legendary Ralph DePalma poses when the "Golden Age of Auto Racing" was coming to a close (1929) in his beautiful Miller Spl.

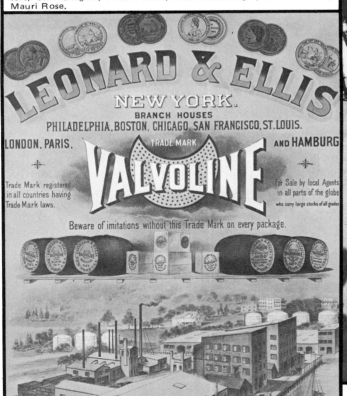

Valvoline Oil, as evidenced by this poster, has been around quite a few years.

The "Clown Prince of Auto Racing" the late Eddie Sachs, peers upward for the photographer taking this shot that depicts the bulky but smooth lines that were common to the Roadsters of the Speedway. Sachs was fatally injured during the running of the 1964 classic.

A. J. Foyt hikes the left front wheel of his Roadster in a memorable duel in 1961 with Eddie Sachs. The pair finished just this way.

Duane Carter (No. 1) and another all-time favorite, Tony Bettenhausen pose in the two Murrell Belanger cars. Both drivers' sons are current stars, Gary B. and Pancho Carter.

The era of the two-man racer has long since passed. This photo is of Louis Tomei and his mechanic John Peck in 1937.

Duane Carter's first Speedway appearance in 1948 wasn't as successful as his son Pancho's was this year. He's losing a wheel here in 1948.

The last Kurtis-Roadster to be built for the Speedway sported a full roll-cage assembly.

Face familiar? The little guy in the cockpit is Mickey Rooney telling from right, Thomas Mitchell, Mary Hatcher and Allen Jenkins what's wrong with his Offy. Scene is from the 1950 movie "The Big Wheel."

Just a trace of grease around his brow, but a young Johnny White couldn't be happier. He had just won "Rookie of the Year" honors in 1964.

Herb Ardinger and the memorable Novi on the bricks in 1947.

SAMPSON / SCHROEDER

THE SAMPSON

By Jack C. Fox

A tall, blond young man made his way through the pit area of the Indianapolis Motor Speedway. It was just a few days before the race and already-qualified cars were making last minute tune-ups before the final inevitable tear-downs and mechanics of un-qualified cars were feverishly working to squeeze those few extra miles out of their shiny little Millers or less shiny although equally potent Duesenbergs. It was late May of 1928.

Seeing a group of men sitting on the pit wall, he walked up to the youngest, a chunky, round faced youth, tanned from a California sun. Seated next to him was an older man, who, despite his bushy eyebrows bore a strong resemblance to the younger.

"Hi, Louis," said the blond, "just got in from Ohio. What are you driving?" "Not a darn thing, Sam. Looks like it's going to be just like last year. All of the good cars have drivers. Maybe I can get in a few laps driving relief like I did for Shaw last year."

This is an approximation of the meeting between Alden Sampson and Louis Meyer prior to the 1928 "500." Supposedly their meeting had taken place at a race in the Midwest the previous year. Meyer was a youngster from Huntington Park, Cal., and Sampson was the grandson of the founder of a successful steam tractor business in Ohio.

For Meyer it had been a short though rather successful career in West Coast dirt track racing and in 1927 his mechanical ability had earned him a trip to Indy as mechanic for Frank Elliott. When Elliott got a chance to drive one of the new 91-cubic-inch Millers, he gave the 22-year-old Meyer permission to drive the older rebuilt 122 which Jimmy Murphy had driven to his death in 1924.

Dubbed the "Murphy Death Car" by railbirds and officially named the Jynx Special for a self-sealing tire compound, it still gave the rookie a fine chance to make the big race and Meyer jumped at the opportunity to qualify the gold-colored car. Elliott, however, (once he had a better ride) offered the old car for sale and shortly before the race, Wilbur Shaw and Fred "Skinny" Clemons with the financial backing of Fred Holliday of the Holliday Steel Co., decided to purchase the car for Wilbur, ace of the "outlaw" dirt tracks, to make his "500" debut. Although bitterly disappointed, Meyer asked to remain as mechanic with the agreement to serve as relief driver for the dapper Shaw.

In the 1927 "500" the driving team of Shaw and Meyer finished a surprising fourth in a car which was at least 10 miles an hour slower than the new Millers and updated Dueseys. Later that season, Meyer had met Sampson and

The first time Alden Sampson and Louis Meyer teamed for the 500-mile race, they won it! In the above photo, Louis Meyer's father, left, joins Sampson, center, and Louis Meyer, in the car, in a victory pose. The top photo shows Meyer, left, and Sampson, right, at the Speedway in 1930.

Having won the ''500'' and the National Driving Championship in 1938, Meyer and Sampson returned to finish second in the 1929 Indy 500.

The all-new Sampson car, built by Myron Stevens with the Leo Goosen-designed 16 cylinder engine. Sampson and Meyer came in fourth.

Dale Drake, who later teamed with Meyer to build the famous Offy racing engine, rode with Meyer for Sampson in 1932.

Chet Gardner stepped into the cockpit of the radio-equipped Sampson car in 1933 and brought it home in fourth position.

Although five-years-old, the car continued to perform well in 1935 finishing seventh for Sampson with Chet Gardner again driving.

Sampson's new driver, Harry McQuinn drove well all day but ran out of gas before he could finish the 500-miles of 1936 with a standard Miller engine.

The new Sampson car for 1939. This Myron Stevens design featured the 16 cylinder Lockhart engine. A broken rear axle forced driver Bob Swanson out early.

Alden Sampson's last ''500'' entry. Walt Ader drove this super-charged Offy-powered car to 22nd place before rain halted the 1950 event.

a friendship was formed which would be most successful for both men.

When Sam learned that Meyer had no ride for the 1928 race and having an independent income so that he would never have to work very hard for a living he determined to help his friend in a most tangible way while also entering auto racing himself as a car owner. Meyer told Sampson that there was, indeed, a fine Miller for sale and that it could be purchased reasonably.

The car they chose was a gold 91-cubic-inch Miller which Tony Gulotta had driven to third in 1927. Entered by Phil "Red" Shafer, it was actually owned by Albert Champion and his A-C Spark Plug Company. Shaw had originally been signed to drive it but when a new fuel pump that the A-C people were testing proved to be unsatisfactory for Speedway use--they decided to offer the car for sale. It was a chain of events surprisingly similar to that of the previous year with Meyer and Shaw reversing their roles.

Sampson approached Shafer who named a price. Sampson whipped out his checkbook but "Red" wanted cash. Sampson had to repair to the nearest Western Union office, telegraph the family attorney and have the desired amount wired to him in Indianapolis. The transaction finally

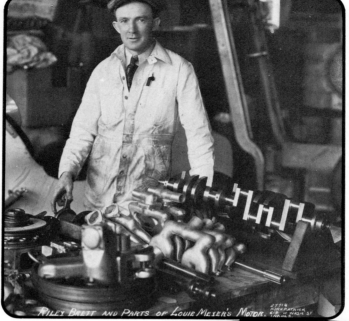

Riley Brett.

completed, Meyer and his father began to prepare the car for the race and after starting 13th, won the event after Jimmy Gleason's Duesey--which held a good lead--was forced into a long pit stop when a mechanic spilled water on the magneto and the next leader, Gulotta, dropped back with a clogged fuel line.

Meyer and Sampson were in the racing business although their immediate success was never repeated while they were teamed. In 1929, it looked like the Meyer-Sampson team would make it two in a row, but when Louis made his last pit stop, he killed

Alden Sampson is shown here examining the disassembled engine from Frank Lockhart's ill-fated Land Speed Record car which went in Sampson's 1939-41 Speedway car.

(continued on page 150)

his engine and it was seven minutes before he could get restarted. By that time, Ray Keech was far in front. Meyer was still able to salvage second place in front of Jimmy Gleason. A second Miller had joined the team but it did not gain the starting field. Ralph DePalma, far past his prime, didn't have much luck getting it up to speed. Phil Pardee, who replaced the popular Italian-American, qualified the car for the starting field but wrecked it in practice just before the race and there was no time for repairs.

The coming of the new "junk formula" in 1930 and the return to two-man cars found a new Sampson

The Leo Goosen-designed engine which powered Sampson's 1930-36 Speedway entry.

BILL VUKOVICH SR.   53-54   INDY WINNER

Buz mc Kim

20 YEARS AGO
at the indianapolis motor speedway

By Bob Russo
Photos courtesy Indianapolis Motor Speedway

Twenty years ago, crew cuts were in; it **only** cost about $23,000 to field a first-class Championship race car; Fess Parker created a $100 million market for Davey Crockett hats; "Sh-Boom," "Hey There," "Wanted" and "Little Things Mean a Lot" were among the top tunes; Sam Hanks was the defending AAA National Driving Champion and Marilyn Monroe was the sex symbol of the decade.

Rocky Marciano twice beat Ezzard Charles to defend his heavyweight title; a 23-year-old Willie Mays was the National League's batting champion and MVP; the rear-engine Championship car was something to be scoffed at; Navy beat Army 7-0; "I Love Lucy" topped the television ratings; and the first atomic submarine was commissioned at Groton, Conn.

The 270 cubic-inch Offy engine was going for about $6,600; superchargers definitely were NOT the way to go, unless you happened to own a Novi; "Dark Star" was a 25-to-1 long shot winner in the Kentucky Derby; Hi-Fi was a new household word; long hair was frowned upon; From Here to Eternity won an Oscar as best picture; Indianapolis Motor Speedway boss Wilbur Shaw accepted 65 entries, all but three of them powered by the four-cylinder Offy; and USC beat Wisconsin 7-0 in the Rose Bowl.

The nation's younger set was switching from Pop to Rock; the Hula Hoop was still four years away; comedian Sid Ceasar's popular "Show of Shows" died from over-exposure after 160 TV performances. . . .and at 2:52 p.m. on Monday, May 31, 1954, Bill Vukovich won the 38th annual Indianapolis 500-Mile Race.

Of all the nostalgia, none can be recalled so vividly, perhaps, as Vukovich's historic ride to Victory Lane. Although a clear-cut favorite when May 1 rolled around and activity began in preparation for the rich 500 classic, ensuing mechanical problems with his Fuel Injection Special, and a starting berth far back in the 33-car field appeared to dim Vukie's chances of becoming a two-time winner. The skeptics, evidently, didn't know Bill Vukovich.

There was no shortage of pre-race predictions in 1954. Some were lost and forgotten long before race time, but one—a prominent forecast for record speeds—grew stronger each day there was activity on the two and one-half mile course, and soon became a rather startling reality.

There were valid reasons for the speed predictions. Firestone, then the one and only tire company represented at Indianapolis, had developed a new tire for the 1954 race, featuring an extra wide tread and cross sections for increased traction.

Additionally, the new roadster-type chassis design of the cars themselves had reached perfection, following two years of development after Frank Kurtis first introduced the innovation in 1952. True, there still were more than a dozen of the conventional Dirt Track machines in the field of entries, but the low-slung Roadsters, with the driveline offset and running beside the driver had already proven to be far superior and more costly.

Vukovich, after dominating the 1952 race until an inexpensive steering part cheated him out of a certain victory with less than 10 laps to go, and then coming back to win the 1953 classic, was among the early favorites to crack the existing track record of 139 mph set by the late Chet Miller.

But instead of making records, the poker-faced veteran paced the garage area or stood quietly in the turns watching others turn it on while his own machine lay denuded in its garage where mechanics Frank Coon and Jim Travers searched for solutions to the mysterious engine problems that were keeping Vukie's speeds down.

The assault on the record books started early but then hit a snag. Sam Hanks and Art Cross, teammates in a pair of Bardahl Specials were among the early speed setters in their conventional Dirt Track machines as track action began to pick up. Frank Armi and Johnnie Tolan were spin victims without serious consequence, and then the weather turned cold and rainy.

Adding to the woes, the piston ring problem that had hit Vukovich's car earlier began spreading throughout Gasoline Alley, and one week before the first day of qualifications, only a few cars were termed ready.

But the problems somehow seemed to vanish almost as suddenly as they appeared. Two days before the first qualifying weekend, the big numbers began to show with increased regularity.

Troy Ruttman, back in action for the first time since suffering a compound arm fracture after winning the 1952 race, cut a sizzling 136 mph lap in the Auto Shippers Special, a combination Dirt Track and Roadster, before Duane Carter, Ruttman's teammate, upped the practice record to 137 mph. A day later, Carter tapped the mark still further, zipping over the course at 139.1.

So the stage was set for qualifying and records were

anticipated, but few persons if any were quite prepared for such a mass assault when official trials unfolded. The only disappointment of the day was the fact that Vukovich still wasn't ready, and there were those pessimists who concluded that Vukie's luck had run out. Again, they didn't know their subject very well.

Jim Rathmann, in Andy Granatelli's Grancor Special was the first qualifier but was waved in after three laps. Carter went out but forgot to fasten his safety belt and nearly lost control in the first turn before coming back in. Eddie Johnson tried but his 136 mph effort was termed too slow and he was waved in.

Muscular, tattooed arms, rolled-up sleeves and an open-faced helmet described a 1954 race driver. Andy Linden makes a pit stop. Note the wire wheels.

Finally, chunky Jimmy Reece became the day's first official qualifier, driving the Malloy Special, a Dirt Track machine, to a respectable 138.312 mph average. The cheers for Reece had barely subsided when Johnny Thomson took the green flag.

Slowest qualifier in 1953 and as yet to hit the peak of his great career, Thomson was not considered a serious contender for the pole position. His Chapman Special, once known as Basement Bessie when it belonged to Paul Russo and Ray Nichels, also was an underdog. But Thomson surprised and delighted the fans with four quick laps, each faster than the previous one, included the last which broke Miller's official mark by a tick of the watch. Thomson wound up with an average of 138.487 mph.

But Johnny's fame, too, was short lived, for Jack McGrath was next out in the sleek yellow Hinkle Special, one of the latest of the Kurtis Roadsters, and the fans didn't need an official announcement to let them know new records were in the making.

140 mph Barrier Broken

McGrath circled the course in 1:03.79 and became the first man to lap the historic track at 140 mph. His official speed was 141.088 mph. Jack turned two more at better than 140 mph, then cut his quickest of the four with a thundering 141.287 mph effort, winding up with a record 10-mile average of 141.033 mph.

Before the day ended, 11 other drivers bettered the Miller record but

McGrath had the pole with Jimmy Daywalt alongside in the Sumar Roadster. On the outside of the front row was a husky, cigar-smoking Arizonian who was to figure prominently in the 1954 race and in ensuing years. His name: Jimmy Bryan.

Thirteen positions were filled the first day. On Sunday, it rained again and Vukovich still wasn't ready, but three more drivers made it into the field which was now half-full. Heading the trio was likeable rookie Pat O'Connor with a 138.084 mph effort while Bob Scott was the slowest at 137.504 mph.

During the week that followed, 1951 winner Lee Wallard announced his retirement and was followed by 1950 AAA National Champion Henry Banks and veteran George Connor. Vukovich's problems continued with a cracked block and rain was predicted for the final weekend of qualifying.

But things began getting brighter as the weekend approached. Vuky finally found what he had been looking for and was clocked at 140 mph in practice. The rain clouds never materialized and 18 more cars qualified as the bumping process began, and among the first to go was Duke Nalon in the popular Novi, a victim of Andy Linden's 137.820 mph effort.

Vukovich made it but his 138.478 mph average was disappointing to those who were looking for another new record. It gave Vukie the 19th starting slot, and dimmed his prospects for a repeat victory since no winner in recent years had ever started that far back in the field. Johnnie Parsons also made the field in his immaculate Be-

lond Special, joining Vukovich and Ruttman as the only former winners in the race.

Before qualifying ended on Sunday, one of the most heart-breaking stories in 500 history unfolded in full view of the excited audience. Bob Scott, the quiet, likeable Californian who had qualified the Travelon Trailer Roadster the first weekend had been bumped despite a seemingly safe 137.504 mph mark. With only a short time remaining, Scotty jumped into one of the Brady Specials, and without previous experience in the machine, began doing a sensational qualifying job.

Three times Scott circled the course at better than 138 mph, safe enough to get him in the race. Then, as he came around for what normally would have been the checkered flag lap, Bob pulled into the pits. He had mistaken the white flag for the checkered. With tears streaming down his cheeks, Scotty bolted from the cockpit and took the long walk down pit row. Two months later he died in a crash at Darlington, S.C.

In all, 10 cars were bumped from the 1954 field, with credit for the slowest average going to Frank Armi in the Martin Brothers Special at 137.637 mph. Armi's speed was faster than the entire field in 1951. Equally startling was the fact that only two qualifiers from the 1953 race could have made the 1954 lineup.

McGrath was installed as the top choice to win. He was clearly the class of the field, with nearly a two mile per

Race day 1954 was muggy and here Vuky shows his method of beating the heat during a pit stop. . . .a cup of water down the back.

hour advantage over the next fastest qualifier. Among the former winners in the pack, Ruttman--in the fourth row--appeared to have the best shot at a repeat victory, based on his practice performance during the month.

Rain Threatens

The weather on Race Day was worrisome. Sometime around 7 a.m. there were unmistakable sounds of thunder and soon the skies opened up and drenched the entire Speedway and its occupants. But by 9 o'clock the sun was shinning as the weatherman gave his okay for the start.

Celebrities on hand included Roy Rogers (without Trigger) and Marie Wilson who was to greet the winner in Victory Lane. Dean Martin and Jerry Lewis, then still together as a comedy team, had paid the Speedway a visit earlier in the month.

Seth Klein, noted for his knickers and checkered sox during the many years he served as chief starter for the 500-mile race had retired and handed his flags over to Bill Vanderwater. The rain threat had disappeared but the humidity hung low and it was apparent that the race would be run under hot, uncomfortable conditions, although not nearly as bad as the previous year.

McGrath and Vukovich both appeared in the pits as their machines were pushed toward the starting line. The pole winner appeared happy, re-

sted ("I had 10 hours of sleep") while Vukie was his usual quiet self.

O'Connor topped the six rookies in the field, starting his Hopkins Special from the fourth row with Bill Homeier, Larry Crockett, Len Duncan, Ed Elisian and Armi lined up throughout the field behind the popular Irishman.

James Melton sang the traditional "Back Home In Indiana," and then it was time for Speedway President Wilbur Shaw to give the historic command that brought the 33 cars to life. Moments later, the Dodge pace car was underway with the field trailing.

The start was a perfect one. McGrath grabbed the lead with Daywalt and Bryan tucking in behind as they hit the first turn. By the time they reached the back chute, however, Ruttman had charged all the way from 11th place and was running fourth.

Records began to fall early. McGrath erased Vukie's 1953 mark for 10 laps with a blistering 136.945 mph average. Bryan was second, and Ruttman had taken third. Back in the pack, Vukovich had picked up ground and at the end of 50 miles was running sixth and locked in a tight duel with Hanks. McGrath enjoyed a 25-second lead over Bryan.

At the 100-mile mark, veterans were astounded to note that all 33 cars were still running and no one could remember such lack of attrition so far

into the race. McGrath held his biggest lead thus far and Vukie had succeeded in taking fourth place.

When McGrath pitted for fuel and rubber on his 44th lap, Daywalt sailed into the lead. Cross was second, followed by Vukie, Art Cross and Hanks. Earlier pit stops had dropped Ruttman and Bryan in the standings but both were still charging.

Ruttman's bid soon ended when a tire shredded and sent his car into a sideway skid. Somehow, Troy kept control, drove to the pits and rejoined the race but had lost too much ground.

The Ruttman incident brought out the yellow flag and Daywalt pitted, followed by Vukovich. Cross inherited the lead. More pit stops followed but no car had yet left the race. In the mass of pit stops, Bryan came out the leader with McGrath second and Vukovich third.

Shortly past the 200-mile mark, the first car left the race. It was the Jones & Maley Special driven by Homeier. While in the pits for servicing, the car lurched into the pit wall when Bill's foot slipped off the clutch. Front-end damage kept the machine from continuing. McGrath regained the lead just past the half-way mark when Bryan pitted for fuel and tires but a few laps later, he too came into the pits and the lead was taken by Vukovich. The average speed was 133.726, two miles an hour faster than Vukie's 1953 pace.

Relief Needed

Once in front, there was no stopping Vukovich. He gradually pulled away but Bryan, giving a surprising performance in his Dean Van Lines Dirt Car kept the leader in sight. McGrath, too, remained a challenger until his next trip to the pits when his Hinkle Special stalled and cost the pole winner valuable time.

As expected, the hot humid weather took its toll. Many drivers were calling for relief as the race continued. Walt Faulkner and Chuck Stevenson traded seats several times in the Agajanian Special, Eddie Johnson took over the Sabourin Special from Rodger Ward, Marshall Teague relieved Carter in the Auto Shippers car, 1949 winner Bill Holland later relieved Teague, Tony Bettenhausen relieved

(continued on page 82)

National Champions

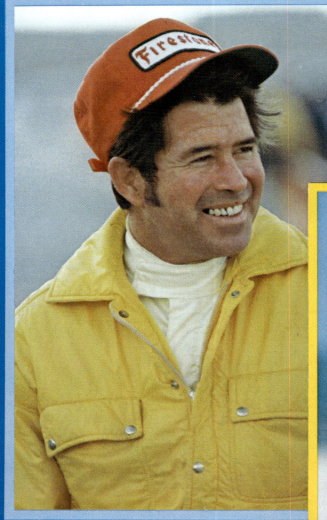

Defending National Driving Champion Roger McCluskey and his mechanic Don Koda came to the Speedway in 1974 with their brand new English Leather Special and within just a few days had the car operating well enough to qualify.

The Riley

By Ted West

Of all the cars that appeared at the Speedway this year the 1974 English Leather Special was without doubt the most radically new. It was certainly new in point of time, so new that Roger McCluskey's crew didn't have nearly enough time to get it fully sorted out for qualifying and the race. But its potential can be judged by the fact Roger qualified the car at an average speed of 181.005 mph after having run it only three days. Of course that didn't satisfy the defending National Champion who kidded after his qualifying run, "The speed stinks, but then maybe English Leather can do something about that." English Leather and maybe another day or two of testing and the car should be a front-runner.

If the car is similar to any other car this year it is of course A.J. Foyt's Coyote. The similarity isn't accidental. The English Leather Special was designed by Bob Riley, the same pleasant, easy-going automotive engineer who did the drawings for Foyt's car. Riley is a southerner who has had experience designing Road-racing cars, notably the very successful Zink Formula Vee cars, but Bob only started working on the peculiar design problems of the Speedway cars three years ago. His first conspicious design was the 1973 Coyote which, with modifications in radiator location and engine compartment aerodynamics, has blitzed the USAC competition this year by winning the pole at both Ontario and Indy.

Moonlighting from his full-time job as an engineer for one of the Big Three in Detroit, Riley decided to take the Coyote design approach one step further. Since his working relationship with Foyt ended after Indy in 1973, he began drawing the new car. McCluskey approved the drawings in mid-winter and the new Riley materialized in the pits at Indy only days before the race.

While the similarities between the English Leather Special and the Coyote are evident at first glance, they

Chini

Chini

Alvarez

Bearing a striking resemblance to a duckbill platypus, the nose of the Riley negates the use of additional wings such as used on conventional Speedway cars.

Foyt's Coyote utilizes virtually the same front-end treatment as the Riley. Foyt's car is basically the same one he ran in '73 with some modifications.

are superficial. Technically, the cars are very different. In fact, it seems fair today that if Foyt had built a new car for 1974 it would have been this Riley. Of course the most obvious difference (and Foyt wouldn't have gone along on this) is the change from the Coyote's Foyt (Ford) engine to an Offy. McCluskey's car had a super short-stroke (2.600 x 4.375) engine and a "standard short-stroke" (2.750 x 4.281) engine at his disposal, both breathed on by Dick Jones of Champion Spark Plugs.

The basic physical and aerodynamic theory behind the Riley and the Coyote is the same. The car's tub has been made wide and extremely low to get the car's center of gravity as close to the ground as possible. In fact, the Riley's tub is only 8¾ inches high (a ¼-inch smaller than the Coyote) and stands a total of 11 inches off the track. Take out a ruler and measure 11 inches from the floor and you'll see how radically low the Riley really is.

Of course neither driver nor engine can fit into a nine inch space, so the cockpit and engine compartment are contained in an ultra-clean central housing interrupted only by mirrors and the Offy's intake log -- which could have been tucked in also but was left as is because Dick Jones said efficient fuel intake flow required the present log configuration. Aerody-

namically the car is very efficient and as Riley put it, "With everything so low we don't think we'll need as much downforce to get through the turns quickly." And of course the less aerodynamic downforce you need to generate, the less drag is produced, which in turn gives a car great straightaway speed. As in any really sophisticated design, the Riley is a well-balanced package of low center of gravity, low drag and proportionately high downforce.

But how can the car be so much lower than the others? Starting with the 1973 Coyote, Bob Riley began experimenting with new suspension ideas which allow the attachment or

When the Riley appeared at the track it sported this ultra-low wing and semi-fender assembly. Initial teething problems were found in the new configuration and a conventional wing was installed.

The ridgid fully triangulated suspension arms used on the Riley are designed so as to allow precise tuning of spring and shock absorber rates. All tubing is of aircraft quality.

The rear suspension of the English Leather Special is a real first. Virtually all component parts are mounted below the centerline of the driving axle thus allowing most of the structure to be covered by bodywork.

"pick-up" points on the tub to be sufficiently low to make an ultra-low profile practical. In the 1973 Coyote he devised a conventional "rocker-arm" front suspension which for the first time was mounted no higher than the center line of the front hub. In the Riley he has improved on even this. Still mounted at the hub centerline, the rocker arms have been replaced by multi-tubular, fully triangulated suspension arms which are much more rigid than rocker arms and allow the spring and shock absorber rates to be tuned more precisely. Normally such a multi-tubular affair would give up in increased drag what advantage it had in structural stiffness, but since the front suspension is in the aerodynamic "shadow" of the Riley's "sports car" nose anyway, there is no increased drag.

Where the Riley has made big improvements on the Coyote, however, are in the rear suspension. While the Coyote's front suspension had been lowered to the hub centerline, its rear suspension was strictly conventional with a high mounted sway-bar, full height rear uprights and an upper link mounted on the rear wing mount sub-frame. This was all out in the airstream and Riley believed he could design a rear suspension which was not only aerodynamically cleaner but also lower and with better geometry. The English Leather Special's rear suspension is a first. The sway-bar was mounted below the half-shafts (as was the winning McLaren's, by the way) and instead of having a "top-link" mounted above the half-shafts, the Riley had a "forward-link" mounted at the same height as the half-shafts but just ahead of it. Thus the rear suspension presented a much lower

and narrower shape to the air and also maintained the idea of keeping all suspension parts at, or below the hub centerline (and the tub topline).

Furthermore, instead of conventional rear radius rods angling out from the rear bulkhead to the hubs, as the Coyote had, the Riley's radius rods were brought straight back from the side-mounted radiator housings. This meant that yet another area of aerodynamic turbulence was avoided at the rear. This feature is extremely important because the cleaner the air is as it passes over the engine to the wing, the more efficient the wing will be. Speaking of wings, the Riley also has a very unusual "body wing" integral to the rear of the tub, but the crew was so far behind trying to qualify for Indy that they used a conventional wing. With some development time the other wing will probably find its way into regular use.

There is one final difference between the English Leather Special and most cars that came to the Speedway in 1974. Only this car and the single 1974 Parnelli (which Andretti chose not to qualify) were designed to the new smaller fuel tank rules for 1974. This allowed the English Leather Special to incorporate its main radiators within the sides of the tub instead of building a high housing on top of the tub like the Coyote had in 1973. In 1974, the unwiedly Coyote radiators were moved to the nose, which had to hurt the effectiveness of the Riley designed nose and which also might account for the Coyote being slower than the McLarens in the turns. The English Leather Special, on the other hand, should be excellent in the turns without paying the penalty of those high Coyote side radiators. In fact, the

housings on the rear sides of the English Leather Special's tub are only exhaust ducts to keep hot air off the tires. Otherwise the weight of the radiators themselves is down low at the center of gravity where it is least harmful to the car's handling.

All in all, this car was the newest and most inventive machine at the Speedway in 1974. English Leather, which has been so active in other sports areas, looks like it has picked a thoroughly viable combination in chief mechanic Don Koda, fabricator Chuck Looper, defending USAC National Champion Roger McCluskey and the man behind the scenes, the brilliant Bob Riley.

Every available inch is utilized in the Riley's compact design. On the left is the Accel transistorized ignition flanked by a Simpson fire extinguisher bottle.

Bill Holland, 1949 500 champion, poses in the car he was scheduled to drive in 1954, the last time he was entered as a driver. Jim Rathmann eventually qualified the car for the race and was relieved by Pat Flaherty.

Holland, Carter replaced Ruttman, Pat Flaherty relieved Rathmann, George Fonder replaced Armi and Bob Scott finally got into the race as replacement for Andy Linden.

But it was a safe race. As Vukovich continued on toward his second straight victory, not a single incident marred the running, and the average speed continued to climb.

Bryan continued to drive a brilliant race as Vukovich's only threat. He stayed close to the leader and actually closed the gap several times but never could pull even. No one knew it at the time, but Bryan was taking a terrible physical beating.

Somewhere around the 130th lap, the front spring broke, making handling difficult and later the shock absorbers added to the pounding Bryan was taking. Still later, the throttle return spring broke and the big Arizonian had to pull the pedal back with his toe each time he decelerated.

The most serious accident of the day came three-quarters of the way through the race. Daywalt and Flaherty, the latter driving Rathmann's car, collided coming out of turn four. Both cars came to a safe stop but were out of the race, Daywalt with tears in his

Mr. "First in Line," Larry Bisceglia and his pet dog Wiggles were on hand as usual when May 1, 1954 rolled around.

eyes, his chances for victory ended after a fine drive.

Bryan took the lead for the final time when Vukovich made his last pit stop, but the Dean Van Lines car also was in need of servicing and Jimmy gave up the front position which went back to Vukovich.

Rain again became a threat around the 400-mile mark, and more drama was added when Vukovich's crew hung out a sign reading "E-Z TIRES." On his last stop, Vukie was forced to swerve in the pits to miss another car and he wound up with the inside wheels too close to the pit wall to be serviced. His crew changed only the outside tires and replenished the fuel, and now there was concern about the left side tires.

At this point, Vukie held nearly a full lap lead on Bryan, gaining the distance in the exchange of pit stops, and in response to his crew's warning, reduced his speed. Had Bryan's car not been crippled, the finish might have been more dramatic.

Meanwhile, the skies darkened and a few drops of rain began to fall. Unfortunately, the freakish shower dropped rain only on one part of the track and that happened to be where O'Connor was running. The sudden wetness caused Pat to spin and brought out the yellow flag, giving Vukovich a break.

Shortly after the green was displayed again, the Bardahl Special originally started by Hanks and now driven by Rathmann began careening down the main stretch after the engine seized. Rathmann bumped the wall and was able to make a safe stop.

Laps Second Place

The final bit of drama came on the final lap, as Vukovich came out of turn four for the checkered flag. Spotting Bryan three cars ahead of him, Vukie pulled to the inside and in a burst of speed, passed the two stragglers and then went past Bryan, putting a lap on the Arizona driver just a few feet from the finish line.

Vukovich's average speed for the 500 miles was 130.840 mph, bettering his 1953 mark. Bryan was second, followed by McGrath, Ruttman (relieved by Carter), Mike Nazaruk, Freddy Agabashian, Don Freeland, Paul Russo, Crockett and Niday. All of the first five finishers broke the old re-

The Queen of the 1954 "500," the late Marie Wilson, arrives in town via the Borg-Warner Company plane. In '54 Miss Wilson was best known as television's "My Friend Irma."

While being relieved because of excessive heat, Troy Ruttman and Marshall Teague tried to cool off under a tarp. Ruttman was the 1952 "500" winner and Teague was famous as the driver of Hudson Stock cars.

cord.

Vukie's victory put him in the exclusive company of Wilbur Shaw and Mauri Rose as the only drivers to win the race twice in succession. Bryan, who had to be helped from the cockpit afterwards, was black and blue from the beating his car gave. In addition to the broken spring, broken shocks and broken throttle spring, Chief Mechanic Clint Brawner discovered another serious problem when he tore the Dean Van Lines Special apart after the race.

The right front wheel bearing was ground to powder, but by some miracle had held the wheel in place and allowed Bryan to finish the race.

Ruttman in his Automobile Shippers Spl. Note how high he sat in the car with no roll bar to protect him!

1954 FIELD

By Jack C. Fox

All Photos IMS

Car No. 14
BILL VUKOVICH
Fuel Injection Special

Bill Vukovich, a veteran of the California Midget bull rings started driving in 1938 and was at once recognized as a talented, agressive driver. He reached the Speedway in 1950 and qualified for his first race in '51 at the wheel of the Central Excavating Special, finishing 29th. He almost won in '52 but hit the wall when his steering failed with nine laps to go. He won both the 1953 and '54 500s and was fatally injured while on the way to his third straight win in 1955.

The gray and red Fuel Injection Special was owned by oil executive, Howard Keck, Jr., and mechanicked by the "Whiz Kids" Jim Travers and Frank Coon. It was a Kurtis-Kraft 500a Roadster, first run in '52 by Vukie. It carried him to his '53 and '54 victories but was retired by Keck after the second win. After Vukovich's death, it was donated to the Speedway Museum by Keck where it remains as a memorial to one of the greatest Speedway drivers of all time.

Car No. 9
JIMMY BRYAN
Dean Van Lines Special

Like Vukie, big, blond, cigar-chewing Jimmy Bryan was a graduate of the Midget wars and had never driven a big car in competition until he came to the Speedway in 1951 to drive the Viking Trailer Special for Doug Caruthers. While he passed his test he failed to qualify fast enough to make the starting field. He was 6th in '52 and 14th in '53. Following the 1954 race, the native of Phoenix, Ariz. remained a Dean Van Lines driver with finishes of 24th, 19th and 3rd. In 1958 he switched to the Belond laydown Roadster and survived the big first-lap crash to win the 500. In 1959 he lost his clutch on his first lap, was 19th in 1960, and the following month crashed to his death in Langhorn's infamous "Puke Hollow".

The white and blue Dean Van Lines car was built in 1953 by Eddie Kuzma and was a Dirt Track chassis. Bob Sweikert retired it after 151 laps with a broken radius rod. In '55 it had a Dodge under the hood but did not qualify and Marshall Teague failed to qualify it in 1956. Last heard, it was running as a Sprint car in the Arizona area. Clint Brawner was its mechanic.

Car No. 2
JACK McGRATH
Hinkle Special

Jack McGrath, a lanky, soft-spoken leadfoot with white eyebrows was one of a number of Speedway drivers who got their start in the old California Roadster Assn. He moved to Midgets and Sprint cars and then into Championship racing. He was a very highly thought of Speedway driver from the time of his first race in 1948. In 1950 he started his long association with owner Jack Hinkle, finishing 14th in the rain-shortened 500. Jack was 3rd in '51, 11th in '52, 5th in '53, 3rd in '54 and had just retired with magneto trouble in the '55 race when his old adversary, Vukovich crashed to his death. On November 6, 1955, McGrath was fatally injured on the dirt track at Phoenix, Ariz., driving the

Hinkle Dirt Track car.

Jack Hinkle had a new cream and black Kurtis-Kraft 500c for McGrath in 1954. McGrath drove it in 1955 and after McGrath's death, Hinkle sold his equipment to Cecil McDonald of Farmington, New Mexico and got out of racing. The car, as were all of those in the 1954 starting field, was Offy-powered.

Car No. 34
TROY RUTTMAN
Automobile Shippers Special

The phenominal Rutt was winning races when most youngsters his age were shooting marbles and he was the Speedway's youngest driver at 19, thanks to a faked birth certificate, being flagged in 12th place in '49 driving the ancient Carter Special. His early career had been in Roadsters,

Sprints, Midgets and Stocks and he remained active in these various cars until he was badly hurt in a Sprint car accident in 1952 shortly after winning the 500. He made a comeback in '54 and his career lasted until he flipped at Trenton 10 years later. He rarely failed to lead the race at least for a few laps. Last heard, he was in the Go-Kart business in Michigan.

Gene Casaroll's orange and black Auto Shippers Special was a Kurtis 500a Roadster, mechanicked by Miles Spickler. It was new in 1952 but Walt Faulkner failed to qualify it. He did better the next year and was flagged in 17th place. 1954 was the car's last 500 appearance in the Auto Shippers stable although it came back in 1958 when Rex Easton failed to qualify it as the Wyandotte Tool Special.

Car No. 73
MIKE NAZARUK
McNamara Special

"Nasty Mike" was a colorful driver from the Midget and Sprint car ranks in the Pennsylvania area with lusty tastes and a picturesque vocabulary. He finished 2nd in his first 500 (1951) but failed to qualify M.A. Walker's Zink Special the following year. In '53 he started driving for Lee Elkins' McNamara team and was fatally injured in a Sprint race at Langhorne on May 1, 1955.

The red and gold Lee Elkins McNamara Special was a Kurtis-Kraft 500c which was new in 1953. It was originally owned by Ed Walsh and was wrecked in practice by Cliff Griffith who was badly burned. The remains of the car were rebuilt by the Elkins crew and Nazaruk finished 5th in '54. Len Duncan wrecked the car in practice the following year. Floyd Trevis was the car's chief mechanic.

Car No. 77
FREDDY AGABASHIAN
Merz Engineering Special

Fred was one of the finest drivers to come from northern California and got his start in the San Francisco Bay area driving Sprint cars in the mid-1930's. He soon became a winner in Midgets and after the War he teamed up with owner, George Bignotti, to win the 1946, '47 and '48 BCRA Midget crowns. His first Speedway

race was in 1947 when he finished 9th in the Ross Page car. His best finish in a 500 was 4th in '53 at the wheel of Andy Granatelli's Kurtis-Kraft. He retired after failing to qualify two cars in 1958 and is now a veteran member of the Champion Spark Plug Highway Safety Team.

The Merz car which was a Kurtis-Kraft 500c, entered by Miklos Sperling and mechanicked by Benny Benefield and Frank DelRoy. The maroon and cream beauty was driven to 5th in '55 by Walt Faulkner. Ed Elisian was in the seat for '56 and stalled after 160 laps. It was then owned by Fred Sommer and ran as the Hoyt Machine Special. Jimmy Reece drove it in '57, Gene Hartley failed to qualify it in '58 and it was wrecked on the northeast turn in '59 by Red Amick when it belonged to LeRoy E. Foutch. This was its last appearance.

Car No. 5
PAUL RUSSO
Ansted Rotary Engineering Special

Russo was a top driver in the 1930s and did most of his racing in Midgets. His older brother, Joe, was a 500 competitor before losing his life in an accident at Langhorn. Paul drove his first 500 in 1940 and started 14 races. He went the distance six times and his best finish was 4th in 1957 at the wheel of the Novi. After his retirement in 1965 he became associated with Perfect Circle Piston Rings

Car No. 7
DON FREELAND
Bob Estes Special

Don Freeland was another of the rapid gang of CRA hotrodders who descended upon the Speedway after

the War. Don, starting in 1953, drove five of his first six 500s in cars owned by Bob Estes finishing 7th twice and 3rd once. His last race was in 1960 although he failed to qualify in '61, '62 and '63. After his retirement he was rarely seen around the tracks.

Jud Phillips and his friend A.J. Watson built the Estes car which was somewhat similar to a Kurtis-Kraft. Jud was its chief mechanic and it ran in the '54, '55 and '56 races with Freeland at the wheel. It was painted in the usual Bob Estes colors of red and light yellow.

and is now their trackside representative.

The dark blue Kurtis-Kraft 500a was owned by the Hoosier race team of Roger Wolcott and Bill Ansted and mechanicked by Herb Porter. It made its debut in '53 when it was Chrysler-powered and driven by George Connor, who failed to qualify and announced his retirement. An Offy was installed in '54 and in '55 LeRoy Warriner failed to qualify it. Duke Dinsmore was flagged after 191 laps in '56 after it was sold to the Shannon Bros. of Dayton, Ohio. The car's last appearance was in '57 when Gene Force failed to make the starting field.

Car No. 28
LARRY "CRASH" CROCKETT
Federal Engineering Detroit Special

Larry had a short, spectacular career as a Sprint and Championship driver. He hailed from Columbus, Ind. and was named "Rookie of the Year" for his '54 performance. He also became a victim of the notorious Langhorn track on March 20, 1955 when he crashed to his death in a Sprint car.

Veteran 500 contestant, Russ Snowberger, turned the wrenches and ran the Speedway team of owner Dan LaVine's yellow and blue Federal cars. Crockett's ride was a Kurtis-Kraft 3000 which was new and driven by Walt Brown in 1951. George Connor finished 8th in it in '52 after a qualifying spin from the starting line to the middle of the first turn. Paul Russo was in the seat in '53 and it was retired after the '54 race.

Car No. 24
CAL NIDAY
Jim Robbins Special

Cal was a veteran driver of the Midget wars whose first races were in the Rocky Mountain area. Cal, who lost a leg in a motorcycle accident in his youth, drove in the '53 thru '55 500s, retiring after a serious accident in the fourth turn. He spent a number

of years in Hawaii and now makes his home in Oxnard, Cal.

Car No. 98
CHUCK STEVENSON
Agajanian Special

Chuck was National Champ in 1952 and a two-time winner of the Mexican Road Race who got his start racing Midgets with both URA and BCRA while making his home in Fresno, Cal. His first 500 was in 1951 and

Car No. 45
ART CROSS
Bardahl Special

Art was a Midget driver from the East when he finished fifth in his first 500 in 1952. He won "Rookie of the Year" honors to add to his 1951 National Midget Championship. Art finished second in '53 and later bought a farm near LaPorte, Ind., which gradually took up most of his time and he phased out his racing activities. His last race was in 1955 although he occasionally returns for the annual Oldtimers Club barbeque.

Ed Walsh's black and white Bardahl was a Kurtis-Kraft 4000 Dirt Track car which had been entered for Roy Hamilton by Clyde Dillon in '53. Barney Christensen was chief mechanic and after '54 the car did not compete in the 500.

The maroon and cream Offy which Cal drove was originally built by Roscoe Ford and Myron Stevens for the late Bobby Ball in 1952. Andy Linden wrecked it on the third lap in '53 and its most notable performance was in 1955 when Jerry Hoyt snookered the hot shots to capture the pole on a windy qualifying afternoon. Its last 500 was in the hands of Cliff Griffith and Cliff finished 10th in the '56 500. Roscoe Ford was the mechanic from '52 thru '54.

---

following the '54 race, Chuck was out of racing until 1960 when he made a comeback and competed in the '60 thru '65 events. When he failed to qualify in 1966 Chuck once again hung up his goggles.

The Agajanian Special, mechanicked by the late Clay Smith first made its appearance as a Studebaker-powered, Eddie Kuzma-built Dirt Track car. Allen Heath couldn't qualify it but Stevenson drove it the following year. Duane Carter drove it in '55 for the colorful J.C. Agajanian and the car was then used exclusively on the mile tracks. As usual with the Aggie cars of that era, it was painted red and cream.

Car No. 88
MANUAL AYULO
Schmidt Special

Manny was a Peruvian born in Los Angeles who came up thru the Roadster and Midget ranks in southern California. He first made the 500 in 1949 driving for Bill Sheffler. He next qualified in 1952 although he drove relief for Jack McGrath in '51. Manny drove the same Schmidt car in '53 and was fatally injured in it practicing for the '55 race.

Rotund Pete Schmidt, a St. Louis butcher, owned the attractive Eddie Kuzma-built Roadster. The red and silver creation was officially mechanicked by J.M. Seely although Ayulo did much of the mechanical work himself. After Ayulo's death, the car was sold to Pete Salemi and was driven in the '56 500 by Eddie Johnson.

Car No. 17
BOB SWEIKERT
Lutes Special

Bob was a big, handsome Midget,

Car No. 16
DUANE CARTER
Automobile Shippers Special

Duane came to the Speedway in 1947 after over a decade in the Midgets which he started driving in his native Fresno, Cal. in 1934. Duane first qualified for the 500 in '48 and

Car No. 32
ERNIE McCOY
Crawford Special

Ernie came to the 500 from the ARDC Midget ranks. He drove in both the '53 and '54 events (8th his first year), but did not qualify in 1955 and went back to the Eastern racing circuits.

Ray Crawford's Kurtis-Kraft 500b was new and driven by Bill Holland in '53. Crawford drove it in both '55 and '56 when he crashed in the northeast turn. That was the car's last time on the track. It's '54 mechanic was Ricky Iglesias and, as always, it was painted red and cream.

Sprint and Roadster driver from Hayward, Cal. who made his first race in 1952 after failing to qualify the two previous years. In '55 he survived a tragic race to win the grind and also cop the National Championship. Bob was 6th in 1956 and on June 17 of that year was fatally injured in a Sprint car accident at Salem, Ind.

Frances Bardazon's red Lutes Special was a Kurtis-Kraft 4000 Dirt Track car, new in '53 when Eddie Johnson failed to qualify it. The car was equally unsuccessful in '55, its last appearance.

---

his best finish was a 4th in 1952. After the ill-fated '55 race he was asked to head the newly-formed USAC which he did until he returned to competition in 1959. He drove in the '60 and '63 events and retired after an unsuccessful attempt to qualify in '64. Now with the Champion Highway Safety program, Duane recently saw his son, Pancho, gain "Rookie of the Year" honors in the '74 500.

Gene Casaroll's orange and black Dirt car was a Kurtis-Kraft 4000 new in '53 when it was owned by Blakely and Hinkle and unsuccessfully qualified by Johnny Tolan. In 1954 it was mechanicked by J.L. Zimmerman and did not again appear in the 500.

Car No. 25
JIMMY REECE
Malloy Special

Jimmy was a 22-year-old serviceman when he drove in his first 500, the 1952 event, finishing 7th. Jimmy's career started when he drove Midgets as a teenager in Oklahoma City and his best 500 finish was a 6th in '58. Jimmy was fatally injured at Trenton on September 29 of the same year.

Rocky Phillip turned the wrenches on Emmett Malloy's black Offy which had been built by former Midget driver, Bob Pankratz. It failed to qualify in '53 but Reece made the '54 and '55 events in the bulky Dirt Track car.

Car No. 27
ED ELISIAN
Chapman Special

Ed was a controversial driver who came from the Roadster ranks of northern California. His involvement in several fatal accidents and some legal troubles occasionally made the papers but he could drive a race car. 1954 was his first race and he continued to make the starting field thru 1958 when he triggered the multi-car accident which killed Pat O'Connor. Ed was fatally injured on August 30, 1959 at Milwaukee.

Myron Stevens, who built many cars for Harry Miller, constructed the red and turquoise car for wealthy Indian, H. Allen Chapman. Art Sims was the mechanic and it was originally driven in 1952 by the late Bill Schindler, and in '53 by Ernie McCoy.

Car No. 1
SAM HANKS
Bardahl Special

Sam was yet another driver to get his start in California Midgets -- his first race was in 1936. He won the Coast Championship in 1937, drove his first 500 in 1940 and qualified for the '41 race but crashed in practice the day before and did not compete. Sam drove all but the '47 race and capped a very successful career by winning the '57 500, immediately announcing his retirement in Victory Lane. Sam is now director of racing for the Speedway.

Harry Stephens was chief mechanic on Ed Walsh's Kurtis-Kraft 4000 black Bardahl. It was new in 1953 and driven by Joe James. Sam Hanks had it in '53 and besides finishing 3rd in the 500 he won the National Championship.

Car No. 71
FRANK ARMI
Martin Brothers Special

Hard-driving Frank Armi came out of the URA Midgets and after an occasional Sprint car ride in southern California he came to Indy in 1951 but failed to qualify until '54. He went to work for a movie studio after he gave up racing.

The salmon-colored car was built by New York's Frank Curtis and was new in '54. Al Herman drove it in its only other appearance the following year and finished 7th. Bill DeJournett was the mechanic.

Car No. 12
RODGER WARD
Dr. Sabourin Special

Rodger first made a name for himself by beating the red-hot Offy Midgets with a Ford V8-60 at Gilmore Stadium and again the following night at San Bernardino. He came to the Speedway in '51 to drive the Bromme Offy and his career extended until 1966 when he retired "because it wasn't fun any more." He won the grind in both '59 and '62 and also scored two 2nds, one 3rd and a 4th. He has had a number of occupations since leaving racing and is one of the very few winners in recent years who has not become wealthy.

The white and blue car owned by Dr. R.N. Sabourin, New York chiropractor, was built by Johnny Pawl and it was mechanicked by Ernie Casale, Eddie Russo drove it the following year in its only other appearance.

Car No. 35
PAT O'CONNOR
Hopkins Special

O'Connor was a product of Indiana Roadster, Sprint and Midget car ranks and tried to make the 500 in '53 but didn't qualify until '54. He finished 8th in both '55 and '57 and was fatally injured in the big first-lap crash in 1958. Pat was one of the most popular drivers of the era and lived in North Vernon, Ind.

Lindsey Hopkins was just getting started in his car-owning career, relatively speaking, since his string of 500 entries which continues to this day started in 1952. Bill Cheesman was the mechanic on the beautiful blue and orange Kurtis-Kraft 500c which Bill

Car No. 43
JOHNNY THOMSON
Chapman Special

The Massachusetts speedster got his early training in Midgets, moved to Sprints and came to the Speedway in

Car No. 31
GENE HARTLEY
John Zink Special

Gene was born to auto racing as his father, Ted, has driven Midgets from their inception in the early '30s until the present day. Gene's first 500 was in 1950 and drove in all but three races until he retired to become a promoter in 1962. His best finish was 11th and he accomplished this four times.

Jack Zink's Kurtis-Kraft 4000 which first ran in '52 with Jimmy Reece at the wheel, was red and white. Dave Burket was the chief mechanic.

Vukovich drove to his death in 1955. Jim Rathmann drove it in '56. It came back in '57 and Don Edmunds took his drivers' test in the car, then owned by Doug Caruthers. It was last seen in '59 when it was owned by Frank Arciero and Maserati-powered, but Shorty Templeman couldn't make the race.

'53 to drive the Sabourin Offy. The little Scot surprised a lot of railbirds by even making the starting field. He was soon recognized as a great driving talent and finished in the money in five of the six races in which he drove before his death in a Sprint car accident on September 24, 1960.

The Chapman Offy was a rebuilt, up-dated version of the famous "Basement Bessie" which was originally constructed by Paul Russo and Ray Nichels in 1950. It failed to qualify in 1951 and was not at the track in '52 or '53. Chief mechanic of the turquoise and red car was Howard Moore.

Car No. 74
ANDY LINDEN
Brown Motor Special

Andy started in CRA Roadsters and then moved to URA and AAA Midgets. His first 500 race was in 1951 when he took 4th in the long-tailed Leitenberger Special. He had failed to qualify in '50 and was the first car to drop out of the race in both '52 and '53. His career at Indy lasted thru the 1957 race when he took 5th. Andy was critically injured in a Midget accident at Clovis, Cal. late that year and has never fully recovered from his injuries.

Verlin Brown's attractive metallic brown and gold Offy was built by Gordon Schroeder in 1951 with Duke Dinsmore driving it until it overheated. Gene Force was bumped the following year and Sport car driver, John Fitch, also failed to qualify in '53. The car was sold to George Walther in '55 but neither Elmer George nor Jim McWithey could make the starting field that year. Henry Meyer was the '54 mechanic.

The famous Belanger 99 was originally built in 1949 by Frank Kurtis and utilized a number of Midget parts. It was small and light but mighty on the Speedways. Lee Wallard drove it to victory in '51 and Tony Bettenhausen won the National Championship with it. Tony failed to qualify it in '52 and Cal Niday went only 30 laps in '53. It was retired in 1954 and eventually was presented to the Speedway Museum.

his racing from the rough and ready "Chicago Gang" of the 1930s. His 500 record was long although Tony preferred a dirt surface. He won the AAA National Championship in 1952 and his best 500 finish was 2nd in 1955. He competed in 12 events and was fatally injured in 1961 while testing a car for old friend Paul Russo.

Mel Wiggers' Kurtis-Kraft 500c was new in '54 and the white and gold car was operated by Wiggers and mechanic Johnny Rae. It was sold to Allen Chapman for the '55 race where Bettenhausen and Paul Russo combined to finish 2nd. Its last race was '56 when it was driven by Andy Linden.

Car No. 38
JIM RATHMANN
Bardahl Special

During his career, Rathmann compiled some very impressive statistics, winning the '60 event and finishing 2nd three times. His first race was in '49 and his last in '63 when he retired to be a car dealer in Florida. Jim often returns to Indianapolis to drive the pace car.

Ed Walsh's third entry, mechanicked by W.D. Sparks under the guiding hand of Harry Stephens, was a new Kurtis-Kraft 500b painted the usual black and white of the Bardahl cars. This was the car's only appearance.

Car No. 99
JERRY HOYT
Belanger Special

Jerry was the son of racing mechanic Art Hoyt who secured a 500 ride for him just as soon as he was old enough for an AAA license. Jerry drove the Morris Special in the '50 race but missed the show in Pat Clancy's car in '51. After a stint in the service, he returned in '53 to drive for Jack Zink. Jerry won the coveted pole in '55 and was killed in a Sprint car wreck at Oklahoma City on July 10 of that year.

Car No. 19
JIMMY DAYWALT
Sumar Special

Daywalt started trying to make a starting field in 1949 but didn't get a starting spot until '53 when he took 6th in the Sumar Spl. This was the best finish in his Speedway career which lasted until his retirement after he failed to qualify in '63. Jimmy competed in a total of eight 500s and passed away of cancer on April 4, 1966.

John Blouch was head mechanic for Chapman S. Root's Sumar Racing Team which included both Speedway, Dirt and Sprint cars. The blue and white Kurtis-Kraft 500d was new in '54. It was wrecked by Johnny Boyd in the Vukovich accident in '55 and the rebuilt car was around thru 1958 being driven by Daywalt, Marshall Teague and Jerry Unser in that order.

Car No. 10
TONY BETTENHAUSEN
Wiggers Special

The leadfoot from Tinley Park, Ill. came up from the Midgets learning

Car No. 51
BILL HOMEIER
Jones and Maley Special

Bill was a friendly, popular Texan out of the southern California Midget ranks who failed to qualify a Cadillac-powered car in '53. He was unsuccessful qualifying in '55, '58 and '59 but made his second and last race in 1960. He returned to Texas and is an auto shop teacher. One of his young students was Tony Bettenhausen, Jr. and undoubtedly Bill has been able to give him some excellent racing advice.

The red and white Kurtis-Kraft 500c was new in '54. Sam Hanks drove it in '55 and '56 (2nd place), and Bob Christie made the race in 1957. It was then sold to Eddie Shreve and from then on it was known as the Safety Auto Glass Special. In succeeding years LeRoy Warriner, Johnny Kay and Duke Dinsmore failed to qualify it and finally in 1961, Bill Randall wrecked it beyond repair in practice. It suffered a most interesting fate and for the past 13 years it has been perched high on the roof of the Safety Auto Glass Co. serving as a sign.

Car No. 65
SPIDER WEBB
Advance Muffler Special

Spider was a top Sprint car driver in the midwest during the '30s and '40s and did some Midget racing in California before the War. His first race was in 1928 and he drove his first 500 20 years later. 1954 was his sixth race and he retired after failing to qualify in '55.

Bruce Bromme owned this most successful rail chassis and while obsolete by Speedway standards, the car didn't know it and continued to qualify. It was in every race except for 1950 between '48 and '54. The chassis was used on dirt for many more years, finally with a Chevy under the hood. J.N. Meyer was the mechanic on the red and orange car which had been built by Bromme and his father, Lou.

Car No. 15
JOHNNIE PARSONS
Belond Special

Johnnie came up from URA and AAA Midgets and won the rain-shortened 1950 500 on his second attempt. He had been 2nd in his first race but after the win he was never able to come close to Victory Lane again. He retired after the 1958 race, his 10th. Son Johnny qualified for his first 500 in '74. Johnnie lives in Van Nuys, Cal. and works with Red Caruthers constructing Volkswagen-powered Midgets.

Sandy Belond's dark yellow and red Kurtis-Kraft 500c was new in '53 and also driven by "J.P." This was the car's second and last 500 race and its mechanic was talented Ray Nichels.

Car No. 33
LEN DUNCAN
Ray Brady Special

A 43-year-old rookie in the 1954 race, Len got his start in Midgets when they first came east in 1934 and served as European chauffeur to President Truman during the latter days of the War. This was his only 500 as he failed to qualify in '53, '55 and '56. He still

Ray Brady's "Tank" was built for George Fonder to drive in 1950 by Gordon Schroeder and Emil Deidt and originally housed a six-cylinder Sparks engine. An Offy was installed in '51 but the car didn't crash the starting field until the '54 race. It finally retired in 1957 after making only one race in eight attempts which may qualify it for "least-successful" honors. Brady did his own mechanical work on the cream and black rail job.

THE IRON DUKE

Duke Nalon Drove Race Cars When Words Like NOVI and Midgets Were Popular. The Name Nalon Was Popular Then Too, Because, He Drove Better Than Most Guys.

Compiled by
Ed Hitze and Tom Lucas

Duke Nalon. To racing buffs who are over 30-years-old, those two words immediately bring to mind a tall, well-built good-looking race driver whose nerves of steel could tame any race car no matter how tempermental it might be, even if that car was the famous Novi. Over the years the words Nalon and Novi have become almost synonymous, to the point that many people think that the Duke never drove anything but the Novi. Before the Novis ever existed, Duke made a name for himself in the Midgets and the "big cars," the forerunners of today's Sprint cars.

Dennis Nalon began his racing career in his home town of Chicago, Ill. in 1933 driving the Christie Miller Dirt Track car. In no time at all, Nalon became one of the midwest's top "hot shoes" to the extent that in 1935 he was entered in the Indianapolis 500 in the Jeeter-Morris Spl. which was powered by a Ford V-8. For some reason the car was withdrawn and Duke didn't return to the Speedway until 1937. In the meantime, Nalon was expanding his racing activities to include the "big car" circuit along the East Coast in addition to running the competitive midwestern tracks.

Duke returned to the Speedway in 1937 at the wheel of the Elgin Piston Pin Spl., but failed to qualify for

Hitze

IMS

The above highly-publicized photo shows Nalon's spectacular crash which occurred while he was running away with the 1949 500-mile race. 1947-48 winner Mauri Rose scoots by, avoiding the blazing car. Top photo: The Duke in his prime, 1947.

Nalon set a new track record at Winchester, Ind. in 1940 with this car. Note the stock early-Ford front suspension.

Nalon again at Winchester (1941) battling for the lead in the pole No. 2. Elbert Booker is driving the dark No. 2, Tony Bettenhausen No. 5 and Tony Willman No. 7.

The Duke had pole-position for this race at Ft. Wayne, Ind. in 1940. Notice the lack of a guard rail at the top of the high-banking.

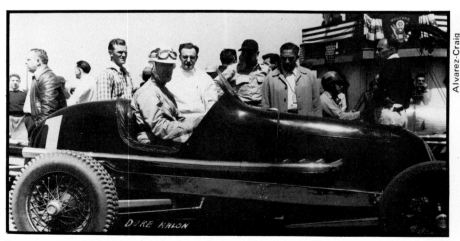

Some race cars had nicknames in the early days. Nalon sits in "Poison Lil" owned by Paul Weirick in this scene from Williams Grove, Pa., 1946.

the race. In September of the same year, Nalon was seriously injured in an accident at Nashville, Tenn. Nalon was leading the feature on an extremely dusty track when Howdy Cox spun in front of him and Nalon was unable to avoid a crash. Vern Orenduff, Chet Gardner and Ted Horn also couldn't avoid piling into the spinning Cox. Orenduff, Gardner and Horn were injured enough to require hospitalization. Cox died in the accident.

Nalon, of course, recovered and returned to the Speedway in 1938. By this time he had acquired the nickname "Duke," supposedly because of his habit of wearing white and always appearing super clean when he raced--a sharp contrast to the greasy overalls which were the standard racing apparel of the day. In 1938 Nalon was at the wheel of Henry Kohlert's Miller, the chassis of which was built by none other than Harlan Fengler, one time "Boy Wonder" of the board tracks and former Indianapolis 500 chief steward. Nalon started 33rd, drove a consistent race and was flagged off in 11th-place after completing 178 laps. 1939 was a dry year at the Speedway as Nalon failed to qualify Murrell Belanger's car.

The next year, 1940, was much better for Duke. Although he only lasted until the 120th lap when a connecting rod let go in his Marks Spl., Nalon won the 100-mile Championship race at Langhorne, Pa. As a matter of fact, Duke won the same race in 1941 also. In '41, Nalon drove the Elgin Piston Pin Maserati to 15th-place in the 500 having run 173 laps.

Racing returned to the scene in 1946 and so did Duke Nalon. He landed one of the few foreign-entered cars in the race when he drove a Maserati for Corvorado Filippini as a teammate to Gigi Villoresi. Duke's car fell victim to universal joint problems

on the 45th lap. This was nothing to be especially ashamed of in 1946 because before the race was even half over, there were only 15 cars still running, and only nine were running when George Robson won the event. Duke didn't give up when his car

dropped out, however. When Russ Snowberger brought his Maserati in and requested relief, Nalon was there, ready to take over. Nalon's new mount lasted until lap 134, differential trouble being the cause of dropping from competition. Nalon also returned

The large photo shows the "Tuffy's Offy" Midget team in 1947. Duke Nalon drove the No. 21 car and Johnny Roberts was his teammate in car No. 22. The small photo on the left shows Nalon adjusting his car's carburetors after making an engine change. The photo on the right shows Duke at speed after having made the engine swap. The above scenes took place at Hinchcliff Stadium, Paterson, N.J., in June, 1947.

to the Midget wars with occasional forays into the big car races.

For the 1947 race, Duke qualified second-fastest in one of the more exotic cars to run at the Speedway. The car was a W-163 Mercedes which was owned by Don Lee. The car reputedly was a getaway car especially built for Adolph Hitler which spent the war years hidden in a Swiss barn. Duke moved the car from its 18th starting position to fifth on lap two, and ran strongly until a piston let go shortly after the half-way point of the race.

By now you could be thinking Nalon certainly wasn't setting the world on fire at the Speedway. That kind of observation can be made very easily when merely examining statistics, not having seen Nalon actually running in those years. It's not uncommon for a driver to go quite a few years without success before he gets it all together and his star really shines. A good contemporary example of this is Johnny Rutherford.

In 1948, Duke gave the Speedway another go, this time in the cockpit of

the car with which he was to become most famous—the Novi. Duke qualified the car on the second day of qualifications with the fastest four-lap average in the field. It was on this day that Nalon proved he had ice water running through his veins.

Cliff Bergere had been Duke's teammate until a spin in practice caused Bergere to declare the beastial V-8 "too dangerous to drive." Bergere was replaced on the team by Ralph Hepburn, a veteran of 15 500's who drove the original Novi in 1946. Hepburn left the pits to begin his qualifying attempt in the car with which he set the track record in 1946. Maybe Bergere was right. While warming the car up to start his run, Hepburn lost control going into the third turn and hit the wall head on, dying instantly.

The 1948 500 is best remembered for the classic drive of Nalon who had the race all but won when he had to stop for fuel late in the race. During an earlier stop, the sloshing fuel in the Novi's tank had caused air bubbles to form, making the tank appear full when it actually was, at most, three-quarters full. Duke and the Novi had to settle for a third-place finish, the

Floyd Dreyer's super-fast car was Nalon's ride in a race at Hohokus, N.J. in 1938.

Nalon races fellow driver Rex Mays' Midget, steering with one hand, braking with the other.

best either would do in the race, ever.

If Nalon could still finish third with a late pit stop in 1948, then with a little preventive maintenance, he ought to be a shoe-in in 1949. This

Duke Nalon drove for Fred Peters at Langhorne, Pa. in 1947. The car is the former Noc-Out Hose Clamp Spl. which Floyd Davis and Mauri Rose shared when they won the 1941 Indianapolis 500.

Nalon led much of the 1950 Langhorne 100 before running out of fuel. Vince Conze, left, and Frankie DelRoy, right, push the car as Duke jogs along behind them.

The first car Nalon drove in the "500" was Henry Kohlert's Miller Spl. in 1938. Kohlert himself drove in the "500" twice in the late 1920's.

Two famous Sprint car drivers of the late 1940's, Duke Nalon and Cletus "Cowboy" O'Rourke, occupied the seat of the 1937 Elgin Piston Pin Spl. Unfortunately, their qualifying speed was too slow to make the field.

Two Grand Prix aces of the '30's flank Nalon in this shot. Luigi Villoresi, left, and Achille Varzi, right, together with Nalon comprised the Corvorado Fillippini Maserati team in 1946.

Duke drove the maroon and silver Marks Spl. in the 1940 Indianapolis 500. Tiny Worley, who later gained fame as the chief mechanic for the Belanger Spl. team stands second from the right.

Seven of the best dirt track drivers before World War II gathered for this picture at Winchester, Ind. in the early '40's. In the back row from left are, Tony Willman, Everett Saylor, Tony Bettenhausen and Elbert "Grandpappy" Booker. The front row contains Duke Nalon, George Connor and Emil Andres.

A smiling promoter Ted Doescher congratulates Duke after Nalon set a new one-lap qualifying record on the treacherous Winchester (Ind.) high-banks. Note lack of a roll-bar.

should have been The Year for Duke and the Novi, and certainly started out that way. Nalon qualified for the pole position with a 132.9 mph average and found teammate Rex Mays alongside him in the front row for good measure. Nalon supposedly said before the race, "There is about one inch of the throttle on that Novi that I don't want anything to do with." Sequential photographs of the start show Nalon noticeably pulling away from the rest of the field, Mays included.

In one lap, Nalon had a lead of several hundred feet over Mays and continued to pull away until a broken rear axle sent him flashing into the north turn wall on lap 24. The car erupted in flames as it hit, but somehow Duke scrambled out and over the wall, rolling over as he did to extinguish the flames on his driving suit.

Recovery was slow and painful, but it didn't keep him from coming back in 1950. However, a late arrival due to an "appearance money" dispute between Lou Welch, owner of the Novis, and the Speedway management cut into preparation time so severely that Nalon and teammate Chet Miller were unable to work their cars up to qualifying speed.

In a comeback comparable to those of Jim Hurtubise and Salt Walther in recent years, Duke Nalon came blasting back in 1951 to win the pole position at a record average of 136.498 mph to retrieve the record for the Novi team which it lost to Walt Faulkner in 1950. Ironically, Faulkner came back a week later and regained the record. In the race, Duke was content to run in the vanguard of the field but not quite at the blistering pace being set by Cecil Green, Jimmy Davies, Jack McGrath and Lee Wallard. One by one, the "hot dogs" dropped out and Duke moved into contention. But, not to be denied, the famous Novi Jinx struck again and the car stalled on the backstretch on lap 152. Wallard won the race and Duke finished 10th.

Bill Vukovich was the big story in 1952 with his Roadster which was to point the way into the next decade at the Speedway. Vuky set new qualifying records with the car the second day of qualifying. Nalon started fourth by virtue of a strong qualifying effort the first day. Teammate Chet Miller didn't qualify until the last weekend, but when he did he provided the glory

Duke Nalon and the memorable Novi are truly classics of the sport.

for the Novi camp. The 49-year-old elder statesman of racing obliterated Vukovich's record with an average of over 139 mph, almost breaking through the 140 mph barrier which at that time was as spectacular as 200 mph is today, maybe more so. The race was all Vukovich and Ruttman. Nalon's car lasted 84 laps and Miller's 41 with broken supercharger shafts being the common cause of elimination.

They say history repeats itself, and in 1953 it seemed to for the Novi team. The two Novi Governor Specials arrived at the track early in May and again were among the fastest. Late in the afternoon of May 15, Chet Miller was out "hot lapping" looking for the 140 mph lap which eluded him in 1952 and which he hoped to run the next day in his run for the pole position. As he entered the first turn, Miller made the same mistake Ralph Hepburn had made May 16, 1948 on the other end of the track in the same car. The car dipped down into the grass of the infield and then shot head-on into the wall. Chet died instantly and Duke had to again qualify with a heavy weight on his shoulders.

Nobody knew it at the time, but the 191st lap of the 1953 500 was the last Duke would turn in competition at the Speedway. Gene Hartley, relieving Tony Bettenhausen, spun entering the third turn and Nalon was forced to spin to avoid a collision. He was awarded 11th place.

Duke Nalon was in the twilight of a great career in 1954 and so was the front-drive version of the Novi. The

magic of Nalon and the Novi was still there but the speed wasn't. And when a error in signaling caused Duke to qualify at an average of 136.395 mph, the magic was over. The speed was too slow to qualify for the race, and two grand careers at the Speedway ended.

Although Duke had missed the program at Indianapolis in 1954 after having competed in 10 previous races there, he was far from being considered a has-been. Some five months after the running of the 1954 classic, Nalon entered the longest Midget car race ever run on the legendary Terre Haute (Ind.) half-mile dirt track. After 200 laps, that's 100 miles of continual broadsliding, bouncing and eating dust, Duke Nalon had won one of his last automobile races.

The front-drive Novi returned in 1955 with Troy Ruttman in the cockpit, and Duke Nalon was entered in a conventional Offy-powered car owned by John McDaniel. Neither the Novi nor Nalon qualified for the event. The Novi came back, as a rear-drive model in 1956. So did Duke Nalon, as a spectator, as he has ever since.

Today, Nalon holds an administrator's job with the Arizona State Highway department. He's an interested and welcome spectator at the USAC races held annually in Phoenix, Ariz., and is usually accompanied by his son, Pat. The younger Nalon, currently a college student, has expressed a desire to follow in his father's footsteps. We hope Pat enjoys as successful and safe a career as his dad did. Unfortunately, no matter how hard young Patrick tries, we doubt that the magic of Nalon and the Novi will ever again be witnessed at the Indianapolis Motor Speedway.

OLDTIMERS

By Jack C. Fox

All Photos by Alvarez

The running of the annual Indianapolis 500 draws fans and participants from all over the world. Another annual event held on the Speedway grounds on the Monday before the race draws a group of participants just as devoted to their event as the former are to the 500-mile race. These are the Speedway Oldtimers. Each year they congregate, starting on the day the track is open for practice, in a large house trailer furnished by Huddleston Bros.

Personable Mrs. Mary Owen, official "den mother" of the club, handles registration and last-minute book work for club Secretary, Bob Laycock, as well as overseeing the serving of snacks and lunches. Often on hand to assist Mrs. Owen and greet the steady

flow of former "knights of the roaring road" is Oldtimers' President Bill Klein and Vice-president, Herman Winkler.

Activity in the trailer picks up as the annual barbeque nears and the stories of past Speedway glories fly thick and fast. It is a thrilling sight to see these lenendary men of steel relive the days of the cloth helmets, physically-punishing, stiff-sprung race cars, wire wheels and primitive tires.

Perhaps these veterans of the smoke paths lack the polish of today's millionaire drivers, weighed down with their safety equipment but they are a breed apart. That any still live is miracle enough, for they used to ply their profession in rock-strewn, dust-laden dirt tracks, often in lumbering two-man cars designed primarily for the "brickyard."

Their driving uniforms might be slacks, or knickers with dress shirts and neckties or in later years a light pair of pants and a T-shirt which would work up under the arm pits after the start leaving the driver practically bare-chested for the remainder of the four or five hour grind. They made giants in those days.

The barbeque itself was attended by over 250 club members and only a few guests (the club is an exclusive one and intends to remain so). Tom Carnegie traditionally presides at the meeting and introduces the donors of the various awards. The AP Parts Award was won by Roy House. Fred Young presented his Young Radiator plaque to Freddy Agabashian, the Officials plaque was given to Chief Timer Ray House and Bob Laycock presented

Mr. William H. Davidson of the Harley-Davidson Co., presented Joe Petrali's record-setting Harley-Davidson motorcycle to Speedway President Tony Hulman at this year's Oldtimers's Bar-B-Q. Mr. Davidson, left, and Mr. Hulman, right, flank the venerable two-wheeler in this photo.

Kurt Freudenthal with the Press Award. When Lindsey Hopkins received the Car Owner Award he told of being invited to a race in the mid-thirties by Eddie Rickenbacker and later watching a race from the box of Bill Klein where he was plied with champagne, fried chicken and caviar. He thought that was what racing was all about but learned quite differently when he became a car owner several years later.

Paul Russo received an award for his contribution to auto racing and Tony Hulman accepted the late Joe Petrali's Harley-Davidson, on which he set many records in the thirties from William H. Davidson. Tony told some humorous incidents about his career as a motorcycle rider, one how he went thru the fence on the half-mile at Terre Haute at the tender age of 12 and another about how he was unseated by his Harley at Yale which proceeded to cross a quadrangle (riderless) and flatten itself against a very well-built stone building. It was one of Tony's best speaking efforts.

The Oldtimers Plaque, the club's highest honor, went to three-time winner and club Vice-president, Louis Meyer.

Some of the great driving names of yesteryear who attended the party or visited the trailer were Freddy Agabashian, Emil Andres, Henry Banks, Frank Brisko, Duane Carter Sr., Floyd Davis, Pete DePaolo, Billy DeVore, Harlan Fengler, Dick Frazier, Cliff Griffith, Ira Hall, Sam Hanks, Gene Hartley, Harry Hartz, Jack Holmes, Norm Houser, Luther Johnson, Cy Marshall, Johnny Mauro, Harry McQuinn, Louis Meyer, Duke Nalon, Cowboy O'Rourke, Johnnie Parsons, Hal Robson (who confirmed that the family name was, and has always been, ROB-SON not ROBE-SON as is often mispronounced), Paul Russo, Babe Stapp, Myron Stevens (who built many cars for Harry Miller as well as finished fourth in 1931), Steve Truchan, Doc Williams and Cliff Woodbury.

For the first time, the barbeque was hosted by Hook Drug Stores and a fine one it was with plenty of food and an interesting story from Bud Hook about how he ushered and announced over a public address megaphone (in the days before the electric PA system) when he was a teenager.

Once again it was a very happy time for so many men who have done so much to make the 500 what it is today.

Jimmy Jackson, Clay Ballinger, Henry Banks. . . .

Myron Stevens, Fred Post, Duke Nalon. . . .

Babe Stapp and Emil Andres were some of the notables in attendance.

Lindsey Hopkins received the Car Owner Award from Al Bloemker.

[97]

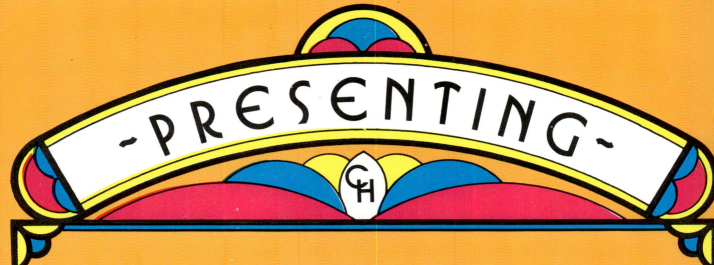

~PRESENTING~

THE ROOKIES

Pancho

Duane "Pancho" Carter, Jr. was accorded an opportunity to qualify for his first Indianapolis 500-Mile Race by car owner Bob Fletcher of Phoenix, Ariz. Fletcher also hired rookie Chief Mechanic Gary Bond for Pancho's car and the pair responded like veterans by winning "Rookie of the Year" honors.

Rookie Class

By Jerry Miller

1974

The Rookie Class of 1974: Tom Sneva, Duane Carter Jr., Bill Simpson, Jan Opperman, Tom Bigelow, Larry Cannon and Johnny Parsons.

When you're an Indy 500 rookie, the check they hand you at the Victory Dinner isn't just a check. It's your diploma.

Once you've walked up to that podium and have that piece of paper in your hot little hand, you have graduated. No one will ever dare call you "rookie" again.

So it was for the graduating class of '74, a fraternity of seven "greenies" who made the grade as Indy 500 drivers. Not the biggest freshman class in 500 history, but not the smallest either. And certainly one of the most interesting.

Answering the roll call were:

--A former schoolteacher who had given the Sprint car boys a few lessons in the science of rear-engine race driving.

--A long-haired, free-spirited vagabond racer from Beaver Crossing, Nebraska.

--Two sons of former Indy 500 greats.

--A racing uniform manufacturer with a new outlook on life.

--A couple of top Sprint car drivers looking toward bigger and better things.

Clay Ballinger served as "Guidance Counselor" in Walt Meyer's absence.

Not every rookie comes to the Speedway with a set driving assignment. Some comb the garages for the opportunity to prove their prowess, others study their more-fortunate counterparts from the pit wall. Falling into the latter category in the above photo are Butch Wilkerson, Rollie Beale, Sheldon Kinser and Sammy Sessions--a veteran who had a ride but failed to qualify. In the right photo, Jigger Sirois poses with the man who provided Jigger with his ride, car owner Tom Adams.

for high speed marks.

While Carter was the big news out on pit row, the talk back in the garage area was mostly about Jan Opperman, the controversial free-wheeler whose sudden appearance at the 500 Speedway was as unexpected as a gypsy at the policeman's ball. Even though he had been running with the USAC Sprinters the past few weeks, Opperman, racing's resident counter-culturist and Jesus freak, just didn't seem the type to be even a little interested in the Establishment stronghold of big-time racing.

Jan was known to be partial to those backwoods tracks, most of them dirt and less than a mile around--Indianapolis meeting neither of those prerequisites. And, wandering around Gasoline Alley in his rag-tag jeans, denim jacket and floppy bush hat, he hardly looked like a walking invitation for some Captain America car owner to lay a $100,000 race car at his feet.

But, by the middle of the first week, the rumors had it that Jan had landed a ride in the Minnesota Serendipity car--not too much of a shocker, since the Serendipity operation was something of a maverick, too. But when, the very next day, Opperman was wearing a new Firestone jacket and chumming around with Parnelli Jones--whose hair always used to be shorter than a Marine recruiter's--the gossip grapevine really started smoking.

Before the week was out, one of the year-old Parnellis was rolled out (continued on page 128)

(continued on page 128)

It was an intriguing collection of new blood, its color and potential at least approaching that of the most spectacular rookie crop in modern times, the famous class of '65. That was the group that, on reflection, read like an honor roll of "most likely to succeed" candidates -- Mario Andretti, Al Unser, Gordon Johncock, Joe Leonard, Jerry Grant, George Snider, Billy Foster, Arnie Knepper, Maston Gregory, Mickey Rupp and Bobby Johns.

It was also a marked improvement over the preceding semester's graduates. The class of '73 was lacking in both size and genuine "rookie-ness."

Two of the three '73 newcomers who picked up their checks at the Victory Dinner, Bobby Allison and Graham McRae, had already earned advanced degrees in the hallowed halls of Grand National and International Road Racing, respectively. The third, Jerry Karl, was a little closer to the traditional rookie image, but even he could boast of previous 500-mile experience at Pocono and Ontario.

The new bunch had them beat on both counts. There were seven of them, of course, and some of them were admittedly wet behind the ears when it came to Indianapolis-style racing.

Two of them had never even sat down in a Speedway car before. Another had no previous 500-mile experience.

Three of them were under 30 years of age and all but one of the year's magnificent seven had come up through the old-fashioned Sprint car farm system.

Little wonder, then, that the new kids in school were the talk of the campus, right from the time they opened the gates May 6.

The first of the frosh to gain attention was Duane Carter Jr., the curly-haired, 23-year-old son of former Indy driver Duane Carter Sr. (but of course). The fact that Pancho's name did not appear on the 500 entry list and he had a total of zero Champ car starts under his belt heightened the barnyard buzzing when the former USAC Midget Champion rolled out to the pit line in the No. 11 Cobre Firestone Eagle of Arizona businessman Bob Fletcher.

"I just feel very fortunate he picked me to drive the car," Pancho latter offered, on his new boss. "There were a lot of other capable drivers around."

Carter, who already owned a real sheepskin from Long Beach State College in his native California, went through his Indy orientation course like a graduate student. The business administration major got right down to business, cramming his 40-lap rookie test into two days and quickly joining the old hands in the search

Bill Simpson finally qualified for the "500" after several years of trying and a complete change in his outlook on life. Here he shares a pleasant moment with his chief mechanic Ted Swiontek, left, and his car owner Dick Beith.

JAN

Jan Opperm[an]
proved that [a]
good racer c[an]
drive anythi[ng.]
With virtua[lly]
no prior pa[ve]
ment ex[pe]
rience, J[an]
won the r[es]
pect of fa[ns]
and fellow d[ri]
vers alike [by]
qualifying [for]
his first [In]
dianapol[is]
"500."

Other Times & Other Places
A.J. Foyt

Above: A.J. and his newly-rebuilt Sprint car ready for the mile race at DuQuoin, Ill. in 1963. Below: Doin' it in the dirt at Terre Haute in his new Stapp-built Sprinter, 1974.

Upper left: Just before he notched his first Indianapolis 500 victory, A.J. still found time to run a Midget race. Scene is from San Bernardino. Middle: Two nights before this year's "500" A.J. won both ends of twin 50-lap races at the Indy Fairgrounds mile. Right: Exploding Mother Earth in a 1973 Dirt race at the Fairgrounds.

Numero Uno has been a Foyt trademark. Left and middle photos show him at Sacramento in 1965 and '68. He's on the DuQuoin mile in '64 in right photo.

The beginning of the most phenomenal record ever recorded in Championship auto racing began here in Phoenix, Arizona in 1964. Foyt won 10 out of 13 races.

He tried Stock cars and won the championship. Scene is Riverside, Cal.

Before the start of the 1964 "500." He won that one, too.

Superstardom was bestowed upon A.J. by the time 1967 rolled around. Above is another Dirt Track victory: Sacramento, 1967.

A.J. Foyt Was Competitive In The Fifties; He Dominated The Sixties and The Seventies Haven't Slowed Him Down.

On the left you can still see remains of a burn on his cheek. Middle: Would you buy a used car from this man? Right, Phoenix, 1971 and frustration. His car broke.

Left and middle, concentration before a night Sprint race at California's Ascot Park. Right, at DuQuoin with former driver, now builder Steve Stapp.

Even the King trips once in a while. While battling for the lead at DuQuoin in 1970, A.J. tipped over. Most photographers missed this shot because they couldn't believe it was happening.

AJ

GILMORE Racing Team 14

CHINI '74

The Rough Road to Indianapolis

Johnny Rutherford

Through Crashes, Fires and More Than A Normal Amount of Frustration, Johnny Rutherford's Performance In a Race Car Can Be Described In One Word . . . . . Spectacular.

All Photos by Jim Chini

El Centro, Cal. 1962 Johnny Rutherford on the inside of Tiger Gene Brown. After this weekend of racing, Johnny's car owner told him politely, "Kid, I don't think you're gonna' make it."

He did make it: To the pro ranks at Springfield in 1963 and had pole position sewn up til A.J. Foyt bumped him.

Moments after photo above right was taken, J.R. and Foyt led the field for the pace lap.

Before the start of Indy 1964. He was burned in a first lap accident in this race.

1963 again, and John again had to settle for second starting spot next to Roger Ward at Sacramento. He led the race until steering broke. Moviemaker Dick Wallen checks him over.

The Texas Lone Star getting another heart-stopping ride with John at the Hoosier 100 in Tim DelRose's Dirt machine.

Left: Before deciding Sprint title race, 1965 Ascot. He was champion some 15 minutes later. Right: Waiting for crew to replace broken battery at Indy in 1970.

A young John Rutherford at DuQuoin, Ill. in 1963 sported a crew cut.

Rossburg, Ohio 1966 nearly made J.R. an obituary. Both arms were mangled in this spectacular Sprint car crash. (Eric Williams photo)

Always spectacular on the dirt. Sacramento, 1965 and he's over the "cushion" and standing on the gas.

Hanford, 1968 Rutherford inside, Art Pollard's STP turbine outside.

At Indianapolis (1970) in one of his favorite cars, "Geraldine," an updated Eagle.

A rare Midget car appearance, DuQuoin in 1964.

Above: Sprint car appearances for Rutherford are now rare. He is, however, as spectacular as ever when driving the competitive machines. Below: Johnny Rutherford, winner of the 1974 Indianapolis 500 Mile Sweepstakes. The road was a long one, but preparation finally met opportunity. Rutherford has become one of the 500's most popular winners.

PRESENTING

THE FIELD

No. 3 Johnny Rutherford, McLaren Spl. St. 25, Fin. 1. Denis Daviss was the chief mechanic on this updated 1973 McLaren. Mike Douneen was Daviss' chief assistant, and Don Bartos did the engine work. Team manager was Tyler Alexander. Colors: Orange, with blue and white trim.

No. 48 Bobby Unser, Olsonite Eagle, St. 7, Fin. 2. A 1974 Eagle/Offy entered by All American Racers and prepared by Wayne Leary. Colors: White, with blue, red, orange and yellow trim.

No. 4 Bill Vukovich, Sugaripe Prune Spl. St. 16, Fin. 3. Vukovich also drove this Jud Phillips-prepared car in the 1972 and 1973 "500's." Colors: Yellow, with burgandy, orange and white trim.

No. 20 Gordon Johncock, STP Double Oil Filter Spl. St. 4, Fin. 4. Defending champion Johncock drove this 1974 Eagle/Offy for George Bignotti and the STP-Patrick Racing Team. Colors: Dayglo red with black and white trim.

No. 73 David Hobbs, Carling Black Label McLaren. St. 9, Fin. 5. The only brand new McLaren in this year's race had Hywel Absalom as chief mechanic and Tyler Alexander as team manager. Colors: Black, with red and white trim.

No. 45 Jim McElreath, Thermo King Spl. St. 30, Fin. 6. Second-year Chief Mechanic Lynn Reid assembled this 1973 Eagle/Offy which was driven last year by Mike Hiss. Colors: White, with red and two-tone blue trim.

No. 11 Duane Carter, Jr. Cobre Firestone Spl. St. 21, Fin. 7. Rookie Chief Mechanic Gary Bond built "Pancho's" car to last. It was driven in 1973 by Jimmy Caruthers. Colors: Copper, with turquoise, white, black and gold leaf trim. and black trim.

No. 79 Bob Harkey, Peru Circus Spl. St. 31, Fin. 8. Oldest car in the race. First run in 1967 by Joe Leonard, McElreath in '68, Kenyon in '70 and '72. Rebuilt by Eldon Rasmussen for the '73 race when Harkey also drove it. Don Kenyon is chief on this reworked Coyote. Colors: Red with white, yellow and black trim.

No. 9 Lloyd Ruby, Unlimited Racing Spl. St. 18, Fin. 9. The driver-mechanic combination of Lloyd Ruby and Mike Devin also competed in the 1973 "500" with this car. Colors: White and brown, with orange and black trim.

No. 55 Jerry Grant, Cobre Firestone Spl. St. 17, Fin. 10. Driver Jerry Grant brought his 1974 Eagle/Offy home 10th for car owner Bob Fletcher and Chief Mechanic Ron Falk. Colors: Turquoise, with copper, white, black and gold leaf trim.

No. 89 John Martin, Sea Snack Shrimp Cocktail Spl. St. 22, Fin. 11. The late Peter Revson drove this 1972 McLaren in its first "500" and John Martin drove it last year. John's chief mechanic was Mike Mullins. Colors: Red, with white and black trim.

No. 27 Tom Bigelow, Bryant Heating and Cooling Spl. St. 23, Fin. 12. Rolla Vollstedt built this car for the 1973 "500," and this year Bigelow and Chief Mechanic Dick Oeffinger made the starting lineup. Colors: Yellow and blue, with white, red and black trim.

No. 18 Bill Simpson, American Kids Racer. St. 20, Fin. 13. Bill Simpson qualified for his first Indianapolis 500 in the 1973 Eagle/Offy Wally Dallenbach used to win the 1973 California 500. Chief Mechanic was Ted Swiontek. Colora: Silver, magenta and blue.

No. 68 Mike Hiss, Norton Spirit. St. 3, Fin. 14. Karl Kainhofer updated this 1973 McLaren/Offy for 1972 Rookie of the Year Mike Hiss. Colors: Light blue, with yellow and black trim.

No. 14 A. J. Foyt, Jr., Gilmore Racing Team Spl. St. 1, Fin. 15. Three-time "500" winner A.J. Foyt brought his modified 1973 Coyote/Foyt back in 1974 to record the fastest qualifying time for the race. A.J. Foyt, Sr. was chief mechanic. Colors: Foyt orange, trimmed in white, black and blue.

No. 1 Roger McCluskey, English Leather Spl. St. 27, Fin. 16. Defending National Champion Roger McCluskey qualified his Don Koda-prepared Riley/Offy for his 13th Indianapolis 500. Colors: White and blue, with yellow and black trim.

No. 77 Salt Walther, Dayton-Walther Spl. St. 14, Fin. 17. Salt Walther made his comeback to the Indianapolis 500 in the 1973 McLaren which Peter Revson drove last year. Tommy Smith again served Chief Mechanic. Colors: Blue and white, with orange trim.

No. 15 Al Unser, Viceroy Spl. St. 26, Fin. 18. Two-time 500 winner Al Unser drove a brand new Eagle/Offy assembled by master mechanic Phil Casey. Colors: White and red, with gold and blue trim.

No. 42 Jerry Karl, Ayr Way-Lloyd's Spl. St. 19, Fin. 19. Lee Kunzman drove this 1973 Eagle/Offy last year. Duane Glasgow was the chief mechanic then as now. Colors: Blue, with white, orange and black trim.

No. 24 Tom Sneva, Raymond Companies Spl. St. 8, Fin. 20. Sneva was the fastest rookie qualifier in his 1973 Kingfish/Offy which Steve Krisiloff drove last year. Grant King and Ted Hall were co-chief mechanics. Colors: Red, with white, black and yellow trim.

No. 51 Jan Opperman, Viceroy Parnelli Spl. St. 32, Fin. 21 Dirt track wizard Jan Opperman drove Al Unser's 1973 car in his first Championship race for Chief Mechanic Jimmy Dilamarter. Colors: White and red, with gold and blue trim.

No. 60 Steve Krisiloff, STP Gas Treatment Spl. St. 15, Fin. 22. Another George Bignotti-prepared Eagle/Offy of 1973 vintage. Colors: Dayglo red, with white and black trim.

No. 21 Jimmy Caruthers, Cobre Firestone Spl. St. 12, Fin. 23. Jimmy McGee handles the wrenches on this 1974 Eagle/Offy. Colors: Copper, with turquoise, white, black and gold leaf trim.

No. 59 Larry Cannon, American Financial Spl. St. 33, Fin. 24. A 1970 Eagle/Offy which Bobby Unser did not qualify for the 1970 Race. Entered as a spare car in 1971 and 1972. Failed to qualify in 1973 with Cannon driving. Chief mechanic this year was Glen Hall. Colors: Orange, with white, black and yellow trim.

No. 56. Jim Hurtubise, Miller High Life Spl. St. 28, Fin. 25. This is the 1972 McLaren with which Mark Donohue won the Indianapolis 500. It was a reserve car in 1973. Chief Mechanic in 1974 was Hank Higuchi. Colors: White, with red trim.

No. 94 Johnny Parsons, Vatis Spl. St. 29, Fin. 26. A 1973 Fleagle designed and built by Chief Mechanic Bill Finley. J.P. failed to qualify last year but made the starting field handily this year. Colors: Black and yellow, with red trim.

No. 61 Rick Muther, Eisenhour Spl. St. 27, Fin. 27. A.J. Foyt's 1972 Coyote was entered by Lee Brayton in 1973. For 1974, Chief Mechanic Jimmie Wright modified the car to accept Eagle suspension parts. Colors: Yellow, with red and black trim.

No. 82 George Snider, Gilmore Racing Team Spl. St. 13, Fin. 28. After two years of failing to make the starting field, this 1972 Atlanta/Foyt was qualified by George Snider, A.J. Foyt, Sr. served as chief mechanic. Colors: Foyt orange, with white, black and pink trim.

No. 98 Mike Mosley, Lodestar Spl. St. 6, Fin. 29. A new 1974 Eagle/Offy prepared by Chief Mechanic A.J. Watson. Colors: White, with red and blue trim.

No. 40 Wally Dallenbach, STP Oil Treatment Spl. St. 2, Fin. 30. The fastest car fielded by the STP-Patrick Racing Team. Wally Dallenbach's best qualifying effort in eight Indianapolis 500's. Colors: Dayglo red, with black and white.

No. 5 Mario Andretti, Viceroy Spl. St. 5, Fin. 31. Mario chose this 1974 Eagle/Offy over a 1974 Parnelli/Offy for his 10th Indianapolis race. Chief mechanic was Johnny Capels. Colors: White and red, with gold and blue trim.

No, 8 Gary Bettenhausen, Score Spl. St. 11, Fin. 32. Earle MacMullin, Jr. updated this 1973 McLaren for this year's effort and served as Gary's chief mechanic. Colors: Red, with black and white trim.

No. 44 Dick Simon, TraveLodge Eagle. St. 10, Fin. 33. The original Foyt-powered Eagle first raced at the Speedway by Simon in 1973. Keith Randol was chief mechanic for this year's race. Colors: White, with orange, red and black trim.

Jan Opperman:
"This is really a far-out place."

and Jan Opperman, his hair considerably shorter and his driving uniform shiny and new, went to work on his rookie test.

The cynics in the crowd began whispering that maybe their hippie-style hero had "sold out." "Everything costs something," answered Jan, "but in this case I think the price was right."

"This is really a far-out place," he added, slipping back into his customary dialect. "It kind of scared me at first, but this is what I want to do."

Meanwhile, the rookie everyone knew would be around and figured would be this year's valedictorian was living up to his advance billing. Tom Sneva, the 25-year-old ex-schoolmaster from Spokane, Wash., was having little trouble keeping up with the upper-classmen in Grant King's latest Kingfish creation, reaching the mid-180s during practice prior to the first Saturday of "500" time trials.

If no one talked much about it, it was because they had it figured long before May rolled around. Sneva, who made a rear-engine Sprint car the hottest item on the USAC Sprint car trail and in the USAC Board room in 1973, had already served notice by leading at Phoenix and qualifying second quickest at Trenton earlier in the spring of '74.

Tom Bigelow and Bill Simpson were progressing well, too. Bigelow,

Tom Bigelow:
"It takes a couple of days at least. . . ."

the popular Sprint car and Midget winner from Wisconsin, pushed Rolla Vollstedt's latest masterpeice into the 180 mph range by mid-week.

Simpson, the good-humored Sports car grad whose California company always prided itself on its top-grade driving suits, had finally found an Indy 500 car to match that standard. With California businessman Richard Beith's sparkling Eagle at his disposal, Bill soon was into the 180 bracket as well.

Bill Simpson:
"It's a lot slower than we've been going. . . ."

Bigelow, however, fell victim to Indy's school of hard knocks. He and another rookie, Lee Brayton, collided in the first turn before the week was out and put severe crimps in their cars

Larry Cannon:
"It's very disappointing."

and their hopes for making it to graduation day.

Bigelow had a second car on the way, which kept him from being an

Johnny Parsons, Jr. had the advantage of his father's savvy when it came time to discuss strategy. Here John, Sr. suggests what John, Jr. might do to go faster.

instant dropout. Brayton was fresh out of cars and his classmates would go on without him.

Larry Cannon, the barber-politician-racer from Danville, Ill., wasn't really in the commencement picture yet, struggling along in the low 170s with his four-year-old Eagle. But Larry, a terror on the dirt tracks, always took his time getting used to having asphalt under him, everyone knew.

The seventh man, Johnny Parsons, whose father won Indy 24 years be-

Johnnie Parsons:
"That's my boy!"

fore, didn't even look like he'd be allowed to enroll. The dark-haired Californian hadn't landed a ride when the first weekend of speed exams rolled around.

While the rain and the streakers got most of the headlines on the opening Saturday, the class of '74 at least got three of its candidates in line for their caps and gowns.

Simpson was first to be fitted, qualifying the Beith car at 181.041 mph. The moment could have been happier, though, since the speed was about three miles an hour slower than what Bill had been turning in practice.

"What can I say? It's a lot slower than we've been going," said the first rookie qualifier. "We'll just have to live with it."

Pancho Carter was next, and his story had that same familiar ring of

Pancho Carter:
"I tried too hard."

disappointment. His run at 180.605 mph wasn't what he wanted, either.

"I tried too hard," said the curly-haired rookie. "I went 184 in practice. Everyone told me to relax and not try too hard, but I went out and did just the opposite."

After some of the veteran drivers made their runs, the rains came, and the streakers had their fling in turn one, Tom Sneva got the chance to strut his stuff. Outracing the raindrops that would close down qualifying for the day, the class of the first-year men clocked in at 185.147 mph, fifth-fastest for the day.

If Sneva was the quickest of the freshmen, he was also the most awe-

Tom Sneva:
"I'm really in the 500!"

struck. On Monday, two days after his qualification run, the personable young driver still couldn't believe he'd made the Indianapolis 500 field.

"You don't realize at the time what you're doing, I guess, but now I look back at Saturday and tell myself, 'God, Tom, you're really in the 500.' It still excites me, obviously," Sneva related.

While Sneva tried to convince himself that he really had made the 500, his classmates still had to look ahead to the next Saturday's final round of qualifications. For most it meant business as usual, but for Tom Bigelow it was a new lease on life.

The rains had come just in time Saturday to preserve Tom's place in the first-day qualifying line, a bit of good fortune since Bigelow's new car

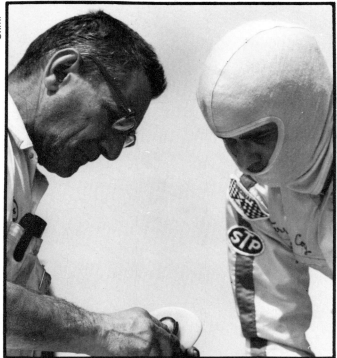

Veteran Chief Mechanic Jess Alu, left, and rookie Larry McCoy tried hard but were unable to crack the starting lineup.

Tom Sneva has shown great promise in his brief career with Indy cars. Mechanic Ted Hall, shown with Sneva, has been a major factor.

hadn't been sorted out enough to qualify that day. With another week to work out the bugs, without sacrificing his first-day qualifying status, Bigelow had found a silver lining in the black rainclouds that rained on the parade of qualifiers.

But, as Tom himself would admit, finding speed in an Indy car isn't as easy a proposition as breaking in an untested Sprint car. "You can jump in a new Sprint car and have it set up in a few minutes," explained Tom, "but, with these cars, it takes you a couple of days, at least."

It took Tom most of the week, but he found the handle again, getting the second Vollstedt car back into the 181 mph range he'd reached before his Indy crash course over in the first turn.

For the others, the second week demanded that they do some things they hadn't the week before. Opperman had to finish his rookie test, Cannon had to find more speed, and Parsons, naturally, had to find a car to drive.

And they did, each in his own time. Opperman

whipped through his test and moved quickly into the 180 mph category, but then he turned the Parnelli into what he called "a $100,000 lawnmower" with a spin through the infield that wound up against the retaining wall.

The car was back in shape by the end of the week, though, and so was Jan, it seemed, as the speed was still there.

Cannon put himself into the running, almost without warning, by cranking off some 180 mph laps near the end of the week. And Parsons not only found a ride, he found two of them-- starting off with Carl Gehlhausen's entry and then moving over to the Tassi Vatis car he'd driven through most of May in '73.

Then it was Saturday, and the four fledglings were about to earn their Indy wings.

Bigelow, who had been a last-minute bumping casualty the year before, was an early-hour success story this time. He qualified at 180.144 mph and spent most of the post-qualifying interview thanking everyone from Vollstedt to the fans in the stands for their part in the occasion.

Thanks to the ever-pesky Indiana rains, the other

"This sure beats cutting hair!" or so it seems barber-politician Larry Cannon is saying as he removes his "rookie stripes."

National Midget Driving Champion Larry Rice landed a Chevrolet-powered car this year but encountered mechanical troubles. Above he talks over the problem with his father, Bob, long-time auto racing supporter.

three student drivers had to squeeze their homework into the final hour of time trial test. At 5:05 p.m., Larry Cannon took his four laps, expecting to repeat those earlier 180 mph laps.

But the best he could do was a 173.963 average. Happy about it he wasn't. "It's very disappointing," said Larry, one eye on his time charts and the other on the clock. "We lost 300 rpm on the straightaways--heck, I ran 173 in my refresher test."

It was 45 minutes later when Parsons came to the line and he was about the only driver at the Speedway who wasn't at all disheartened by his qualifying speeds. "Oh baby, I can dig it," exclaimed the jubilant John, after his strong 180.252 mph run.

"I've wanted to be in this race for as long as I can remember," he went on. "It's really a thrill, I'll tell you."

Mr. Parsons Sr. was on hand for his son's big moment. "That's my boy," said the 1950 Indy winner.

Finally, with two minutes left on the clock, Opperman went out and proved that even an "outlaw" can have his place in the Indianapolis 500. Jan ran just as fast as he had to, 176.186 mph, and admitted he was "just tickled pink" to be in the big race.

He thanked the Lord, Parnelli Jones and Vel Miletich, in that order, and went off to run a Sprint car race.

The seven were in, and a lot of their buddies were on their way to sign up for next year's class. One, Jigger Sirois, had been bumped by Parsons. Bill Puterbaugh, Eldon Rasmussen, Al Loquasto, Larry McCoy, John Cannon, Larry Rice and Brayton had been left at the gate.

That left only the final exams, the race itself. It seemed likely that the new faces would play it close to the vest, since finishing at Indy is something you learn early in life.

But Tom Sneva, starting eighth, could afford to give a little thought to running faster than a strictly rookie pace. "The way I look at it, the main thing to consider is to be running at the end of 500 miles," observed Tom, looking to race day.

"Naturally, I expect to learn things as the race goes along, but I don't think we'll be laying back too far," he continued. "I think we can race with the other guys."

When it came time, Sneva did enough racing for the entire class. Looking more like teacher than student, Tom took the fight to the old pros, running fourth or fifth through the first 200 miles. But rear-end failure retired him 35 miles on down the pike.

Opperman, who rushed up from 32nd to 10th, had spun out shortly before. And Parsons and Cannon had parked with mechanical failures earlier.

So, the pride of the class of '74 came down to Carter, Simpson and Bigelow. Each had his own adversities to deal with, but they were still hanging in there when class was dismissed with the wave of a checkered flag.

Carter, who had brushed the wall once and spun in turn one when race winner Johnny Rutherford "spooked" him, kept on truckin' and was seventh at the end. Bigelow had been in the pits a lot, but he was still 12th when it was over.

He thanked the Lord, Parnelli Jones and Vel Miletich, in that order, and went off to run a Sprint car race.

Bob Fletcher, left, and Pat Patrick might be talking over the value of hiring a former Midget driver. Fletcher had Midget champs Pancho Carter and Jimmy Caruthers driving while Patrick has yet to gamble on any rookie.

Tom Bigelow, the fan-conscious chauffeur made the race despite a bout with the wall (and Lee Brayton) early in the month.

PANCHO CARTER

1974 Rookie of the Year

By Johnny McDonald

A slight tap of the fourth corner wall, a nerve-tingling bobble in the north chute, a "whoosing" spin and the grind of rubber in the first turn.

He could mark these down indelibly as reminders of his undergraduate course in obtaining a journeyman's credentials at the Brickyard.

But the end result for this California collegian was an eventual seventh position finish that placed him at the head of his 1974 graduating class at Indianapolis Motor Speedway.

Duane (Pancho) Carter Jr., was later to be honored with the Stark-Wetzel trophy for being "Rookie of the Year."

The 23-year-old son of Duane Sr., a man who had experienced the thrills of Indy 11 times himself, had studied well, accepted his "initiation" tests with aplomb and immediately set his sights for higher achievements.

"It felt real good. . .but I learned a lot out there," the curly-haired young man reviewed. "Running with those veterans out there. . .you learn a lot. . .like techniques of running through the corners. Yes sir, they really teach you a thing or two."

One such lesson came close to finishing him for the day. That was the time when eventual 500 winner Johnny Rutherford ducked underneath Carter and Jim McElreath as they approached the first turn.

"He dove in underneath me and I moved out into the gray," he said. "I

Chini

Pancho Carter leads brother Dana while both were serving their apprenticeships driving three-quarter Midgts on the West Coast. Pancho came from California directly to the professional ranks of USAC racing and in his first full year of competition won the USAC Midget Championship. As of this writing he has a comfortable point lead in the most competitive race car circuit in the world, the USAC Sprint car circuit. Brother Dana is currently running Midget and Sprint cars in the central Pennsylvania area, a hotbed of racing activity.

Pancho is shown here performing a simple but long awaited task: He's removing the traditional rookie stripes from the rear of his first Speedway ride. Now driving for car owner Bob Fletcher of Phoenix, Pancho and teammate Jimmy Caruthers have given hundreds of fellow Midget and Sprint car drivers renewed hope in "landing a Speedway ride." Owner Fletcher is to be commended for his far-sighted views in hiring a rookie and helping to develop him.

just started to spin and had to pull off."

In the turbulence created by Rutherford's McLaren as it swished into the groove, Carter's Cobre Firestone Special nosed downward and then as the rear tires grabbed, he was being pulled upward.

Englishman David Hobbs, Ruther-ford's McLaren teammate, went high and just missed contact.

Then he began motioning frantically to have someone pull or push him to the pits after he rolled to a stop in the grass.

"They started to push me but it was too slow to get me fired," the Midget and Sprint car star from Hun-tington Beach, Cal. added. "I was ready to go racing again but I knew I had to come into the pits to change all four tires."

The 5-10, 170-pound bachelor has been racing since 1967, receiving his early indoctrination at the little El Toro "bull ring" near Santa Ana, Cal., with three-quarter Midgets.

Dana Carter, left, Pancho and half-brother Johnny Parsons pose here along with patriarch of the family, Duane Carter Sr., one of yesterday's auto racing superstars.

Defending USAC Midget Division Champion Larry Rice hopes to land as good an opportunity as Pancho had for the 1974 race. Above he talks with Carter on a practice day.

Jimmy McGee, left, has made the transition from a young mechanic learning the trade to a veteran passing along his knowledge. Above he talks with Pancho and his mechanic Gary Bond.

The full-sized Midgets of the URA and ARDC associations were next, from 1969 through 1970, until he joined the USAC ranks.

Career highlights have been the winning of the Terre Haute Hundred, claiming the 1972 USAC Midget title and setting a world half-mile record of 16.27 seconds at Winchester, Ind.

The senior Carter, once director of competition of the United States Auto Club, was beaming as he praised his son's Indianapolis performance.

"I think he did a beautiful job," the 61-year-old parent judged. "He handled himself real well when Rutherford drove under him. That was a last-second maneuver by Rutherford, you know.

"Panch goes in pretty hot in the first half of the turn. He was aware that Rutherford was there and he saw McElreath, too."

Duane Sr. finished fourth in the 1952 Indy 500 but crashed on the 59th lap of his initial try back in 1948.

He recalls with a chuckle the days at Indianapolis when Pancho was only a few months old.

"I had him here when I was tire testing," he recalled. "When I was on the race track, some of the other guys. . .like (driver) Duke Nalon and Bill McCrary (now Firestone's racing director). . .had to change his diapers."

In discussing the race, the young Carter said his Eagle/Offy had some bad chassis problems at the start, that it wanted to spin out.

"It was really scarin' me," he admitted.

"We had some signals worked out and I motioned to my crew several times. We kept working on it and by about a third of the way through the race, it was working better."

Did he have any doubts about going the distance?

"Not really," he answered. "I kept tellin' everybody I had a great crew and all that.

"Joe Pittman built the engine and it ran just beautiful all day long. In fact, it was runnin' stronger at the end of the race."

Carter, who was graduated from Long Beach State (Cal.) University in 1973, had a great deal of competition in his chase for Indy freshman honors.

One of them was highly-regarded Tom Sneva, a junior high school principal from Lamont, Wash., who qualified in the middle of the third row.

There was businessman-driver Bill Simpson, another Californian, who finally made the grade after several tries. However, he had had excellent 500 experience at Ontario Motor Speedway.

Sprint car ace Tom Bigelow of Whitewater, Wis., had an 11th place finish in the California 500 as a strong recommendation, while auto racing's busiest driver Jan Opperman of Beaver Crossing, Neb., and Larry Cannon, a politician from Danville, Ill., had to battle up from the 11th row.

He even had competition from another member of the family, Johnny Parsons of Indianapolis, son of the 1950 winner, but Carter's half brother.

Duane Sr. viewed the race from several television monitors in ABC Network's track headquarters. Afterward, he said he thought the spin, plus the time lost in pulling Pancho into the pits cost his son a chance of finishing fifth.

JAN OPPERMAN

Jan Opperman, one of the nation's most talented and publicized Sprint car drivers came to the Indianapolis Motor Speedway in 1974 in search of a ride. He had been heralded for his accomplishments on the rough dirt tracks of the Midwest and central Pennsylvania area but no one thought of him as a pavement driver. Car owners Parnelli Jones and Vel Miletich were impressed enough with Jan's dirt track accomplishments to give him a ride in one of their Viceroy Specials. Thier judgement wasn't wrong, as Opperman proved his old quote of, "I came down off the mountain wantin' to stand on the gas." That he did.

Los Angeles' famed Ascot Park has spawned many a great racer. Above, Jimmy Caruthers goes outside of Jan Opperman in one of their early appearances in a race car. Photo taken in 1965. Opperman's car, the Ben Humke Ford was a popular machine in the Fifties. Caruthers' mount is reported to be the first Midget that popular builder Don Edmunds constructed.

Jan Opperman in his element: racing on the dirt. Opperman has won virtually every famous Sprint car race of note during his busy schedule in the past five years. He designed the chassis of this particular machine himself and it has proven to be perfectly matched to many half-mile dirt tracks.

When Jan appeared at the Speedway in May, he fit his publicized description of the "racing hippie." The hat, belonging to his younger brother (killed in a Sprint car accident) as well as the near-shoulder length hair were his usual race track trademarks. The jacket was borrowed from fellow Sprint racer Tom Bigelow.

"I really didn't know what to think of the guys driving Speedway Cars. I mean, sometimes, it looked like they were sort of strokin' it . . . because they always looked so smooth. Tell you somethin', . . . Nobody out there is a stroker. These things really get with it."

Like most rookies looking for a ride, Opperman had time on his hands at the Speedway. Above he and Sprint driver Chuck Booth listen as Billy Vukovich, right, tell 'em how it's done.

Success! Parnelli Jones, left, put Jan in his first Speedway car. Mechanics Johnny Capels, with screwdriver and Jimmy Dilamarter try to explain the complexity of an Indy car's guages.

The cooperative Opperman. After initial phases of his rookie test had been completed, Jan had time for the many reporters who were asking, ''What's it like out there?''

Oops! While warming up for his rookie test and following a very low groove on the race track, ''The blower came in and all of a sudden she broke loose.'' Damage was minor.

Graduation. Minus several inches of hair and a general sprucing up, Jan happily removes his rookie stripes denoting successful completion of his test.

Rookie, Tom Sneva

Chini

Whitlow

By Robin Miller

He was just a friendly, harmless rookie at the Indianapolis Motor Speedway in 1973, mind you. Getting through his test was definitely a chore because his car was far from competitive. But still, this kid smiled a lot and the racing fraternity smiled back-- they always do when they're not worried.

Today, Tom Sneva still possesses that infectous grin but he's got the competition frowning. In just one, short season, Sneva has broken into the upper echelon of USAC's Championship Trail.

To the average fan, he's a surprising darkhorse. But the people that know, saw this guy coming just like they did a decade ago with a fellow named Andretti. Sneva is fast-- very fast-- and smooth and a fireballer all the way. He knows chassis and he also knows he's still got plenty to pick up.

But you sure would have trouble telling this was his first full campaign in the world's quickest circuit. He was leading the Phoenix 150 in March; started next to Andretti in the front row of the Trenton 200 in April and was running fourth at Indianapolis this past May. In all three of those races, mechanical failure halted him, not his lack of experience.

And it wasn't very long ago that Sneva was attempting to control a building full of kids rather than a 1,000 horsepower Offy. "I was the

A racing driver's life is captured in the above photo. Tom Sneva is exiting Indy's fourth turn, all alone with nothing but his own judgement to rely upon. The former school principal has proven that he is equal to the task of competing with the nation's best race car drivers and is now pursuing his career on a full-time basis.

principal at Lamont Junior High School in Lamont, Wash. and I used to teach in the winter and race in the summer," explains the Sprague, Wash. native. "But that didn't work out so well and in 1969 I decided to go racing full time."

Tom' decision was to run rear-engined Super-modifieds. It was to be a wise one. After winning a couple of big Modified championships, Sneva came packing to Indy in 1973 with a hometown operation. As mentioned, the car just didn't have it so Sneva got hooked up with Carl Gehlhausen-- a low-buck independent on the Champ Trail and a regular on the Sprint circuit.

So the East Washington State College grad started to 'school' and ran in the back of the pack in the big car races at Michigan, Texas, Phoenix and Milwaukee. However, he "bolted" on the scene in the "Thunder and Lightning" division. Driving Gehlhausen's now-banned rear-engined Sprinter, Sneva won six pavement features (including three in a row) with most of them going away.

That began raising some eyebrows among car owners and Grant King signed him for the 1974 season. "There's no doubt that my rear-engine experience both here and back on the coast really made things happen a lot quicker," states the father of two charming little girls.

But, in fact, it was Sneva that made things happen. His initial go at Ontario for King wasn't spectacular but at Phoenix he started 10th, was leading and running second when a broken shock ended his sensational run.

Trenton was almost a duplicate as he nearly won the pole and was holding down fourth when his car broke down again.

But it was at Indianapolis that Sneva showed how he could handle himself. Late on the first Saturday of qualifying, with dark clouds encircling the 2½-mile oval, Tom went out to qualify. He was called in on his warm-up lap because an observer thought it was raining. He was sent right back out and ripped off his first three laps at 185-plus. But as he steamed into the second corner on his final go-around, he saw some big raindrops lite on his face shield.

Steve Long leans over Sneva's cockpit during a pit stop but probably cannot be heard over the roar of the engine.

Car builder Grant King gave Sneva his best ride to date in one of his "Kingfish" cars.

Rain on the Speedway surface with the slick tires is definitely dangerous but Sneva kept standing on the gas and completed his run-- with a cloudburst following him across the finish line.

"It got a little scary out there in two but it wasn't raining too bad," deadpanned Sneva later. "I slowed down a bunch in three 'cause I wanted to make sure there'd be a four."

His last lap of 183 mph cost him a second row spot but he was still quick enough for the middle of the third row. During the race he moved up to fourth before losing a bearing in his left-rear upright.

Sneva's destination to stardom has been helped along by his vastly underrated chief mechanic, Ted Hall, "Ted doesn't get much publicity but he's a multi-talented guy that's really helped me," praises Sneva.

Besides being an intelligent sort, Sneva is also a modest cat. He knows equipment helps make the racer and this is the first time he's had a competitive ride. But it shouldn't be too long now before the ex-teacher begins giving some of the boys a few lessons again.

INDY FIRE CREW

By Jerry Miller

Jim Brading, Bob McGruder and Don Traut didn't do much work during the month of May.

And no one, including their boss, was about to complain about it.

Brading, McGruder and Traut were the crew of Fire Truck No. 9 at the Indianapolis Motor Speedway in May. Stationed in the short chute between turns one and two from the opening day of practice through race day, the trio found itself with a lot of spare time on its hands.

"It's been a pretty easy month this year," said Traut, as he and McGruder relaxed in the shade of a tree during a late-month lull. "The only thing we had that amounted to anything was Brayton and Bigelow."

That was a reference to a first-week crash in the first turn, involving rookie drivers Lee Brayton and Tom Bigelow. The two had collided, sending Brayton into the outer wall and down the track in flames toward Truck No. 9.

"We saw it coming and were ready to go while he was still coming down the track on fire," recalled Traut, a lanky 39-year-old who has been working the fire beat at Indy for 10 years. "We had to wait for him to come to a stop—until they stop, we can't go out.

"But he stopped right in front of us, so it wasn't any problem. There were still flames coming up behind the driver, but they went out real quick.

"We helped Brayton get out, but he wasn't hurt. Just mad."

Except for occasional tow-ins, that was the bulk of Fire Truck No. 9's work for May, as the Speedway enjoyed one of its safest months in recent times. That didn't dampen the spirit of competition that has traditionally existed among the 10 fire crews spotted around the big 2½-mile oval.

Those crews take their work seriously and with the pride of any other racing participant. "You better believe there's competition between the trucks," said Traut.

"We'd hate to have something happen in front of us and Truck No. 1 beat us to it. That would be the day I'd quit," added McGruder, a husky 19-year veteran of the Terre Haute fire department in his first tour of duty at Indy.

It has been that kind of **esprit de corps** that has gained the Indy operation as the best fire and safety protection in the racing world. "That's what the drivers say, which makes us feel real good," noted Traut, who is also safety director at Indianapolis Raceway Park.

The duties of the three-man crew are clearly defined and methodically executed, according to the men on Truck No. 9. Brading, a 57-year-old mortician from nearby Plainfield (Ind.) with 13 years of experience on

Fortunately, the fire crews at Indianapolis in 1974 were not pressed into action. During one of the only wall-brushing incidents of the month (involving Lee Brayton and Tom Bigelow), firemen Jim Brading, Bob McGruder and Don Traut scurried from their infield position to aid the wrecked pair. Neither driver was injured.

the Indy fire brigade, is the captain of the unit and drives the rescue truck.

Traut and McGruder are the "jump men," riding in the bed of the red-and-white truck and rushing to the aid of any drivers caught up in a serious accident. "I'm the first one in, to help the driver and start fighting the fire, if there is one," reported McGruder, who wears the silver fireproof firefighting uniform for this crew. "Then the other two fellas come in to help out, if necessary."

While 1974 was a relatively calm year at the Speedway, the senior members of the fire crew have first-hand knowledge of the kinds of emergencies Indy is capable of having. Brading, who has been following racing for nearly 40 years, has seen racing crashes that would curl his gray-specked mustache. He grew up going to races at the old Jungle Park track near Rockville, Indiana--"That was a wild one"--and has been one of the first on the scene at the Indy crashes that claimed the lives of Eddie Sachs, Chuck Rodee and Art Pollard.

But none of it keeps Jim from doing his job. "I don't like to see accidents, of course; they actually upset me more than my work as a mortician," he related. "But, after nearly 40 years as a volunteer fireman or funeral director, nothing really bothers me too much."

Nonetheless, an almost accident-free May of '74 was a welcome "vacation" for everyone at the 500 track after the tragedies of 1973. Of course, the three crewmen on No. 9 look at their month-long vigil in the short chute as a vacation anyway, even if they're busy all month.

"I used to take my vacation to come out here and watch everything, so I figured I might as well get paid for it," admitted Traut, who works at the Eli Lilly chemicals plant in Indianapolis the rest of the year.

"Sure, it gets a little boring sometimes," he went on, "but you like it well enough to begin with or you wouldn't be here."

The month wasn't totally devoid of entertainment for Truck No. 9, however, as it had a ring-side seat for the "streaking" and related activities on the first Saturday of 500 qualifications.

"It's been pretty entertaining down here a couple of days," said McGruder, with a smile.

"Yeah, we've always got something going over there," Traut added, motioning toward the infield area traditionally known as the "Snake Pit."

But, as the three men knew, there wouldn't be any horseplay when race day came. With a fourth man added to the crew, they would have eyes for only one thing--trouble on the race track.

"We don't cover the whole track on race day, unless something major happens," explained Brading, a few days before the 500. "We cover what we can see, turn one, the chute, and turn two, plus part-way down the backstretch.

"Of course, when a red flag comes out, like it did for Swede Savage last year, we'll probably go."

For Brading and the rest of his crew, race day is the culmination of the drive that brings men to risk their own safety for that of others at the Indianapolis Speedway.

"It's a combination of liking auto racing and wanting to help somebody that might be in trouble," said Brading, from behind the wheel of Fire Truck No. 9.

EX DRIVERS

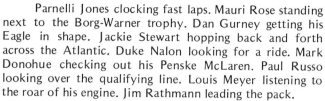

KIHARA

By Jerry Miller

Parnelli Jones clocking fast laps. Mauri Rose standing next to the Borg-Warner trophy. Dan Gurney getting his Eagle in shape. Jackie Stewart hopping back and forth across the Atlantic. Duke Nalon looking for a ride. Mark Donohue checking out his Penske McLaren. Paul Russo looking over the qualifying line. Louis Meyer listening to the roar of his engine. Jim Rathmann leading the pack.

A rundown of Indy 500 history? No, the year is 1974. And the names of yesterday are the names of today. They may not be in the cockpits of those loud and fast racing machines, but the big names of past Indy glory still stand out in the crowd around pit lane and Gasoline Alley. They are still part of the greatest spectacle in racing.

Parnelli Jones and Dan Gurney, of course, still race in the 500, albeit with stopwatches in their hands instead of steering wheels. Between them, they have collected more Indy car wins in the past five years than any two other car owners around.

Jones, the 1963 Indy winner and all-around tough-guy racer, has bridged the gap between success as a driver and success as a car owner. The cars he and business associate Vel Miletich have brought to Indianapolis have been big winners, with 500 victories by Al Unser in 1970 and 1971 included among their many trophies.

"I'm a hell of a lot luckier in business than I was in racing," says Jones, now a 40-year-old desk man. "I admit I still hate sitting in meetings all day," adds Parnelli, who used to sit in Indy cars and set track records with them, "but I do enjoy the decision-making part of it."

Gurney, the international driving star who never quite won Indy but finished second twice before retiring, heads up his own All-American Racers factory. The Eagles turned out in the Santa Ana (Cal.) shops have dominated Indy-style racing for the past three seasons, with Dan's factory entry for Bobby Unser setting speed records at every track along the Championship Trail.

So, Parnelli and Dan still battle each other at Indy, just like they did in the '60s, but from the other side of the

Chini

pit wall.

They also still have to contend with Mark Donohue, the soft-spoken master of all racing trades who won Indy in 1972. Donohue, who retired unexpectedly at the close of the '73 season, continues to ply his engineering skills as president of the Penske Racing organization for which he drove the most of his illustrious driving career.

The only advantage Jones and Gurney have over Mark is the fact that they have had time to overcome the natural urge to climb into their racing cars rather than watching someone else wheel them onto the track. "I'm experiencing some of the normal anxiety separation," admits Donohue, "but it's something I'm learning to live with."

Jackie Stewart, meanwhile, seems to have won that particular battle with himself. The mop-haired Scotsman who won three Grand Prix championships before calling it quits last year finds the answer in a whirlwind schedule of TV broadcasts and appearances for various automotive, tire and tobacco companies in America and Europe.

The routine was familiar at Indianapolis, where the squeaky-voiced Scot managed to squeeze in two 500 starts in his career. He bounced back and forth between Indy and Monte Carlo in May 1974, just like he did before he switched from driving to broadcasting.

"It's been quite a busy year," piped Jackie in May. "In fact, I'm busier now than I ever was in motor racing. I just hope, after this year, it slackens off a bit."

The less-recent retirees are there, too, along the pit row where they drove their famous cars to famous victories or near-victories.

Mauri Rose, the mustachioed little driver who won two of his three Indy 500s in the memorable Blue Crown Specials, is there, standing beside the big silver trophy with his name engraved on it in three places, stroking his mustache and watching the opening day of Indy time trials. It has become a traditional visit to the Speedway for the Detroit-based racing immortal.

Duke Nalon is in the crowd, too, looking fit and

prosperous in his business suit. He's looking for a ride back in Gasoline Alley--not another roaring Novi for himself, but a Stock car ride for his husky young son, Pat.

Paul Russo, another of the legendary string of Novi drivers, has his shingle out back of the pits, representing Perfect Circle piston rings at the big track where he raced 14 times.

Louis Meyer, the first three-time winner at Indy, is on the scene as usual, too. Though he turned his interest in Louis Meyer Inc. over to his son and son-in-law (George Bignotti), he still comes around to hear the sweet sound of the Offy engine he helped develop into racing's most venerable powerplants.

There is Sam Hanks, the good-natured, hawk-nosed winner of the 1957 500-miler. As the Speedway's director of racing, he still plays a big part in the spectacle that is May in Indianapolis.

Johnnie Parsons, the 1950 winner, and Duane Carter, one of his contemporaries, are on hand to watch their sons continue the family tradition.

They are almost everywhere, these racing legends from Indy's by-gone years. You see them working in official capacities--Clay Ballinger, Harlan Fengler, Elmer George, Harry Hartz, Henry Banks.

You find them, like Russo, representing the many racing accessory companies that are a part of Indy--Bob Veith, Freddie Agabashian, Johnny Boyd.

They may just be famous faces in the crowd--Cliff Bergere, Pete De-Paolo, George Souders, Gene Hartley, Rodger Ward.

And, when the latest field of 500 drivers comes around on the pace lap, one of them is leading the way. Jim Rathmann, the balding Florida car dealer who raced to victory here in 1960, is at the wheel of the pace car.

As it always was, Indianapolis remains the sights, the sounds, and the men of yesterday, today and tomorrow.

Top photo: Auto racing film maker Dick Wallen, left, chats with 1957 Indy 500 winner Sam Hanks while two-time Indy winner Rodger Ward tells George Bignotti of his most recent driving experience in a Stock car on the West Coast in middle photo. Former driver Elmer George, now director of the Speedway's radio network relates an incident to John Fugate, center, and D.A. Oil's Jack Martin.

Chini

Chini

Hunter

YOUNG MECHANICS

By Robin Miller

For the past few years, auto racing fans have been hearing about the young lions of the sport-- Mosley, Vukovich, Bettenhausen, Parsons, Carter, Caruthers, Sneva, Krisiloff-- and their rise to stardom in the sport of speed.

But what about the young lion tamers?

Yes, there just happens to be a large group of fellows in their early and mid-twenties that are currently helping make it possible for the hot shoes above to keep on smoking.

They're the guys that operate behind George Bignotti, A.J. Watson, Mike Devin, Don Koda, Jud Phillips and the other top mechanics on the United States Auto Club's Championship Trail. In almost every situation, they're the right-hand men of their respective teams.

In most cases, they started out tinkering with cars at a very early period in their lives and then began hanging around the various tracks-- serving apprenticeships as stooges.

And today, through quick adaptation, desire and experience, they've gained the ability and confidence it takes to massage a $100,000 race car.

In no particular order, the young men destined to be the future chiefs are John Barnes, Mark Bridges, Rick and Steve Long, Darrell Soppe, Gary Rovazzini, Steve Jordan, Randy Hunter, Mark Stainbrook, Larry Journey, Jim Gerhardt, Marv Webster, Pete Gross and Russ Newnes.

A couple of these fledglings-- Bridges and Webster-- have already assumed the responsibilities of that position. Bridges is a hulking Indianapolis native who became a boss at the tender age of 21.

It was just last summer that Bridges was named to replace Dick Cecil as chief for the MVS racing stable. Mark handled his job well but lost it when the team ran out of money. He's presently with Vel's-Parnelli Jones where he does much of the labor on Mario Andretti's mount.

Marvin Webster II was born with a creeper for a bed and a speed handle in his hand. Young Marv is the talented son of Marv, alias Pappy Webster-- the legendary car owner, mechanic, machinist, gear salesman from Mill Valley, Cal.

This season, Marv Jr. & Sr. are campaigning an Eagle by themselves. Since Pappy is getting up there in years, young Marv has become engine builder, chassis man and you-name-it. After missing the Indianapolis 500, Marv, Pappy and Jerry Karl finished Milwaukee and made the Pocono 500.

At 22, John Barnes has had about as much experience as a mechanic at 42.

Another Indy resident (Decatur Central High School), Barnes began his major league auto racing career with Paul Brooks. He also worked with Bill Finley and gained much valuable experience. Last June he worked with A.J. Watson and the Lodestar team and opened this year with Vel's Viceroy outfit.

Then Jimmy McGee snatched him up for the Cobre Firestone team. John currently handles the chassis for Jimmy Caruthers but can do engine work as well.

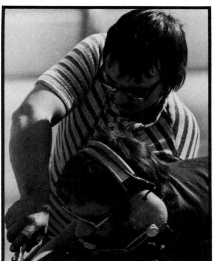

Chini

Two young men on their way to becoming chief mechanics include Gary Rovazzini (with headset) and Randy Hunter.

Mark Stainbrook is an easy-going 24-year-old who has stayed by A.J. Watson's side the past three years.

Mark, who started out working for the legendary Howard (Tilt) Millican, does whatever Watson asks on Mike Mosley's No. 98 Eagle.

Darrell Soppe is relatively new to the Championship scene-- as this is but his second year. But it didn't take the 23-year old Chula Vista, Cal. kid long to catch on.

Darrell landed a job as parts washer with Mike Devin early in 1973 and it wasn't long before he was assembling parts rather than scrubbing them. He takes apart and puts back together the chassis of Lloyd Ruby nowadays and it won't be long before Devin makes an engine constructor out of him.

Steve Jordan is a long, tall Texan that is employed by Anthony Joseph Foyt.

A kid who was financially set with some well-to-do parents, Jordan left the good life in 1967 to chase parts for Super Tex. Through his seven years, Steve has caught the brunt of some Foyt tornadoes but he's always been loyal to the cause. His forte is the fuel system but he also helps change engines, drive the trucks and set up the cars.

Russ Newnes is hardly "new" to the trade of big-time auto racing. He began some nine years ago with Dan Gurney and is currently hooked up with defending National Champion Roger McCluskey. Russ' primary function is that of chassis man but he is amply gifted in the field of fabrication.

Incidentally, it's Phillips and Vukovich who are graced with Hunter and Rovazzini.

While Jud does the engines, Randy and Gary take care of the chassis and gear boxes as well as the race day strategy.

Hunter, 29, started with Jud and has been associated with him for five years. Rovazzini, who just turned 27, drove Stock cars before breaking in with Bill Simpson's crew some six years back. Both are very competent and Vuky's longevity record of finishing can be directly attributed to this pair and Jud's preparation.

Another skilled duo is Pete Gross and Jim Gerhardt-- Lynn Reid's salvation on the Thermo King Eagle of Jimmy McElreath.

Gross, who is a mere 24 has eight years under his belt-- starting with Carl Gehlhausen's Sprint car in 1966.

Gerhardt, whose father is the car owner, has been around the Speedway ever since he could walk. Jim is just 20 but like Gross, has been involved actively since he was 16. Together, the two help overhaul the chassis and both are competent in many other areas.

And what group would be complete without a brother act? This one is the Long boys-- Steve and Rick-- and they make quite a team.

Steve, alias "Zoom" was not much more than a fence-hanging kid who begged builder Grant King for a job. With aspirations of becoming a race driver as well as a competent mechanic, Zoom has worked steadily for the past five years to accomplish his goals. He's currently driving his own Sprint car and working for the Lloyd Ruby team under Mike Devin's tutorship.

Brother Rick Long is currently employed by pioneer engine builder Herb Porter. Two of Porter's most recent protegees include Davey Crockett (see feature story in this book) and Carl Cindric, both considered by the racing fraternity to be among the top engine men in the country.

Devin's right-hand man, Danny Jones, an accomplished fabricator and chassis man is yet another who could well handle the title of chief mechanic.

Another young man on his way up the mechanic's ladder is likeable George Huening, currently serving under master mechanic George Bignotti.

Each of the above named young men, in addition to many more throughout the sport have followed the same pattern: Find a job working on a race car, any kind of race car, and slowly work your way toward the Speedway. Up until now it has been a long, tedious process. However, the chief mechanic's tutoring job might well be lessened considerably through the formation of a new school located just across the street from the Indianapolis Motor Speedway named Auto Racing Mechanics. Founded by George Eiler and Duke Pack, Indianapolis businessmen, young men will now have an opportunity to learn much more than the basics of the trade.

The Auto Racing Mechanics Institute includes not only mail-order courses but resident training on actual Indianapolis cars as part of the curriculum.

While you might surmise that the training necessary to become a chief mechanic comes slowly and carefully, it should be remembered that driver's lives are dependent upon the preparation of their machines. Rewards for the successful mechanic are high, however. Most receive a percentage of the car's winning's plus a better than average salary. Some are reported to make upwards of $60,000 annually. For that kind of money, the old term "Doctor of Motors" certainly applies.

struction is planned well in advance, Cagle's crew was pressed for time to erect a new official's tower at the start-finish line this past Spring. In just under 20 days, Starter Pat Vidan and Chief Steward Tom Binford had a new two-level structure from which to work. Binford now oversees operations from a height of 22 feet while Vidan works directly below him at 15 feet.

The press, drivers and crews alike have praised Speedway personnel for the safety improvements that appeared in 1974. With his usual smile, Tony Hulman simply commented, "We hope everyone is pleased with our efforts."

We're anxiously anticipating the completion of the new museum and wonder what other major improvements might be in store in the next few years. We know that one jovial journalist certainly commanded Clarence Cagle's attention last May at a press party when he asked the grounds supervisor, "When you gonna' put a dome over this place?"

Information Supplied By:
John Fugate, Indianapolis Motor Speedway Publicity Dept.

This view from high above the fourth turn depicts the line drivers follow for their entrance to pit row. The increased width has been heralded as a major safety improvement.

Clarence Cagle, left, leaves little to the imagination. Above, he explains precisely how he wants a barrier built around timing tower.

New energy absorbing barrier located at end of pit wall should help soften the blow should an errant race car get out of shape.

Several rows of seats have been removed along the front stretch to further insure spectator safety.

The Inspector Is *A Lady*

By Jerry Miller

From this day forward, they cannot call the officials who inspect the racing cars at the Indianapolis Motor Speedway "tech men." Thanks to Mitzi Graham, the term will have to be changed to "tech persons."

Mrs. Graham, a trim, publicity-shy housewife and grandmother, was a member of the United States Auto Club's technical committee for the 1974 Indianapolis 500. That automatically made her the first female official in the history of the Indy event.

Her duties with the tech committee in May included everything from assisting director Frank DelRoy to inspecting race cars to handing out the meal tickets to committee members at the beginning of the day. On race day, she helped tabulate official data on the pit stops made by cars in the 500-mile race.

It all came fairly natural to Mrs. Graham, whose father, the late Marshall Kerr, was a racing official at Indianapolis and other tracks around the country.

"I just grew up at race tracks," said the 45-year-old Indianapolis woman. "My father took me to my first race in a basket, when I was six weeks old."

That kind of upbringing made her approach to racing somewhat different than that of a typical race fan. "I always enjoyed watching the progress on the cars, the changes in the mechanical set-ups, and so forth," Mrs. Graham related.

With such an analytical interest in racing, it was almost inevitable that the Indianapolis woman would become the first of her sex to serve as an official at America's most famous and tradition-bound race track. But it wasn't really her idea.

"It was my husband's idea, frankly," she noted. "He told Frank DelRoy that, since I spend the month of May at the track every year, he might as well put me to work.

"I really wasn't that sure about it at first, but I figured I'd be willing to try anything once."

Mrs. Graham, whose husband is an Indianapolis businessman, was not, she pointed out, striking a blow for women's rights when she accepted the USAC invitation to become an Indy official. "I wasn't thinking about breaking any barriers," she said. "There was a job to be done and I felt I could do it.

"I'm not really a women's libber, although I've probably been one for 25 years without knowing it," she continued. "I've just gone ahead and done what I was capable of doing."

Among the things she had been capable of doing was serving as volunteer disaster coordinator for the American Red Cross unit in Indianapolis, supervising the maintenance of that organization's fleet of vehicles. She admitted to a fondness for "tinkering" with automotive things and occasionally doing minor mechanical work on the Red Cross vehicles.

In her job with the Indy tech committee, Mrs. Graham apparently did not encounter much resistance to her presence in the previously all-male domain. "It's really been wonderful," she reported. "The men I work with on the committee have been great.

"It was probably a bit of a shock to some of the crews and car owners but, after the first couple of days, they accepted me without any problem."

There was little about the operations of the tech committee that surprised Mrs. Graham, who had followed its workings as a child. "I knew quite a bit about the work, of course, but I was amazed at how thorough and detailed the inspections were," she said.

The one thing that actually threw her a curve, Mrs. Graham revealed, was the attention she drew from reporters at the Speedway. The mother of four grown children admitted she was reluctant to give interviews at first.

"I've always wanted to avoid any publicity," she said, "but I finally figured out there was no way I could avoid it."

By her own estimate, Mrs. Graham probably won't be a newsworthy item for long. "I would imagine there will be more women in racing before long," she related. "Some of the crews have women on them, working on the cars and so on.

"It really isn't the kind of work most women are very interested in. But there'll be more, I'm sure."

On the question of whether she would return as a "tech-person" at Indy in future years, Mrs. Graham said only, "It's too soon to say."

The Indianapolis woman reported her work at the Speedway had not caused any great problems in her home life. "I've had no complaints from my husband, because he knows what I'm involved in," said Mrs. Graham, with a smile, "but my dog misses me."

Mitzi Graham, the first female official in the history of the Indianapolis 500-Mile Race.

[146]

Ladies Are Welcome

By Dusty Brandel

They say that behind each successful man, there is a good woman. At Indianapolis in May, there's usually more than one woman behind each driver, official, mechanic and team sponsor.

Tony Hulman, President of the Indianapolis Motor Speedway, has two women. His lovely wife Mary and his secretary June Swango. Both work long, long hours during the month of May at the Speedway and many social functions that are part of the Indianapolis "500" Festival pagentry.

Mrs. Josephine Hauck, Executive Director of the "500" Festival Association, and her team work year 'round.

Mom Unser never misses the 'month of May' at Indianapolis. She has two sons racing and winning in the "500". Bobby won first in 1968 and brother Al captured the Memorial Day classic back to back in 1970-71!

Donna Snodgrass, Assistant Women's Editor of the Indianapolis Star, hits the track on opening day and continues, as she has for the past 12 years, writing stories on "what's happening" at Indy. Donna has brought the distaff side of racing to her readers, thus broadening the scope from — just the sports pages — to the women's page, plus special features in the Star.

It was Mari McClosky in 1971, when she was editor of a women's magazine, who really opened the doors for women reporters and photographers into Gasoline Alley and the pit area. Dorsey Patrick, Pat Singer, yours truly, and Ellen Griesedieck along with many other female media representatives are extremely grateful to Ms. McClosky. It has made it a lot easier to do our jobs covering racing.

The drivers' wives, who give moral support all year, through thick and thin with lot of love and understanding deserve a very special thanks too.

The nurses at the track hospital, Mrs. Lo Brinkley, Nashville, Tenn., Mrs. Connie Remke, Omaha, Neb., and Miss Arleen Hededus of Ann Harbor, Mich., who travel to Indianapolis each year and donate their time and experience deserve a note of thanks from the press, drivers and spectators.

Barbara Webb, director of nurses at the hospital said that this year's race was one of the best. Normally over 300 persons are treated for various ailments or overindulgence but, this year the number dropped to about 95 persons.

Linda Vaughn, Miss Hurst Golden Shifter, is one of racing's greatest supporters. Linda along with her Hurstette Team of June Cochran, Niki Phillips, Marsha Bennett, Kathy Kersh, Shelly Harmon and Tami Pittman, are all walking, talking encyclopedias of racing. They know the drivers and their families in championship, stock, sprint, and drag racing; Hurst products and customers; accessory company personnel, the rules and officials of all the race tracks plus the various sanctioning bodies.

Together, all these women — the wives of the drivers, the gal media representatives, secretaries, office personnel, nurses, the "500" festival ladies, sponsor representatives, the women spectators and the 'moms' — they all have helped in making the Indianapolis 500 the "Greatest Spectacle In Racing"!

Among the most interested lady spectators at the Speedway during the month of May are drivers' wives. Above, are two of the prettiest, Alice Mosley, left and Pat Muther.

ALL ENGINES Banned!

They held an extra race at Indianapolis this year and participants didn't have to invest anything except a few minutes time....The co-winners took home $3,000 out of a $15,000 purse while most of their competitors looked like they would have been satisfied with a healthy dose of oxygen....The Cool-Ray sunglass people and Indy public relations man Dave Blackmer put together the richest (per mile) bicycle race ever held and in doing so injected a bit of good old-time fun into the happenings at Indianapolis in '74....Each of the 33 drivers was invited to participate in the two-lap race, splitting the distance with a guest celebrity....There wasn't any particular order to the whole affair other than everyone began with a smile and most ended looking like they'd been whipped....Qualifying didn't exist so flagman Pat Vidan did his best to keep the first 33 riders behind the traditional yard of bricks before he waved the green....Equality prevailed as all participants rode the race on gleaming new Iverson 10-speeds....The bikes were distributed the week before the race and many crews were seen mixing special lubricants in an attempt to cut down all possible friction....Most should have spent their time practicing around the 2½-mile oval worrying less about their Iversons and more about their lungs....Jimmy Caruthers surprised everyone by handily winning the first leg of the affair....He turned his bike over to the "Winchester Man" Mike Haines, who ultimately finished third....The father and son team of Dick and Tim Simon made up lost ground (see photo) to win the event whereupon papa Dick told son to "go buy yourself a new car" when awarded the $3,000....Second place paid $1,000 (Tom Sneva and Chuck Dowd) and third was good for $500 with the remainder of the money being distributed among the participants in both the bike race and the actual "500".

Gary Bettenhausen isn't one to be caught wearing short pants. Thus, he figured his Nomex (flame-retardent) underwear would be ideal attire for running the race.

"Hope you're ok pop" might be what Tim Simon is thinking after his father, Dick, collapsed after having completed the first lap of the race.

Johnny Rutherford and A.J. Foyt displayed their sportsmanship and proved that they do better when the pedals they're pushing are connected to internal combustion engines.

Bobby Grim, Jr., son of the driving great of the same name was an early odds-on favorite but faded on the backstretch.

Speedway owner Tony Hulman, left, and Cool-Ray President Robert Reagan flank the victorious Simon team in victory lane while announcer Tom Carnegie (behind Reagan) humorously gives condolences to the rest of the field.

[148]

BILL SIMPSON

RESEARCHED BY STEVE KELLY
By Lin Black

"Everybody's aware of the fact that I'm a race driver and that's how I found out a lot of things. It's real hard to sit in an office chair and determine what a guy needs who's turning 200 miles an hour.

"At the Speedway this year, all 33 cars had something that came out of my factory, and I don't give my safety equipment away to anybody."

So said Bill Simpson, Race Driver, Businessman and Safety Expert.

Right now Simpson the businessman is busy working on a super-safe urethane fuel cell, not just for race cars, but hopefully for recreational vehicles and boats as well.

Bill claims that Laboratory tests show his cell is actually stronger than anything used up 'til now. Safer than a steel tank, the urethane cell absorbs shock. Its seam is almost stronger than the ballistic nylon that goes into it, due to thickness and construction.

"Fortunately we have had no track accidents to go by, but we do know that when filled to capacity with water, then dropped from 125-ft., our perfected cell has had no failures," Simpson said.

All USAC drivers use fuel cells for safety, but in accordance with USAC rules, the cell is made like a double bag with a belt between the outer and inner skin. Should a driver have a severe crash and puncture the fuel cell, only the outer layer should be affected. The belt and inner skin would remain unpunctured, with the outer skin acting as a shock absorber.

Although Goodyear and Firestone have supplied fuel cells in past years, they are not interested in the race car market, according to Simpson.

"They are so large that it is not a profit-making venture for them," Simpson continued, "so we seem to be a natural for the job."

Simpson's Torrance, Calif., company manufacturers all types of safety equipment — seat belts and harnesses, fire extinguisher equipment, clothing and now a heat shield that goes between the driver and the engine compartment. It acts as a heat shield rather than a fire protector. By making fuel cells, too, drivers can have one buying source for safety equipment.

Because Simpson banks on his own products for racing safety, other drivers have confidence in his products. And, he has 15 years of safety equipment manufacturing to prove it.

When Art Pollard, Swede Savage and Jim Malloy were tragically killed in severe crashes, Simpson found that their seat belts and harnesses, manufactured in his factory, were unharmed. "Swede's crash was so bad that it even surprised me that the harness was still in tact," Simpson commented. "But they didn't break and I would hope they never would . . . and I know they never will."

Simpson's newest venture into manufacturing fuel cells — from 1 gal. to 500 gal., he says (although the standard sizes are 11, 22, 28, 30, 35 and 40 gal. — has possibilities for the everyday driver and the boatsman. Fuel cells make it possible for drivers to carry additional fuel, hooked up to their fuel tanks in a safe, compact way.

The owner of a cruiser can carry up to 400 gallons of fuel in a cell on the deck safely. It folds up as he uses up the fuel and can be stored away when empty.

USAC, NASCAR and SSCA, have already O.K.ed use of the Simpson cell, and Simpson feels that the small ruling bodies will follow suit.

He's already talked with the small road car manufacturers who seem interested in the fuel cell idea for driver safety.

In the factory the fuel cell takes about four days to complete. A flat sheet of ballistic nylon is wrapped around an aluminum mold and rotated. The first coat of urethane goes over that to glue the seams together. Then the unfinished cell is "cured" for 24 hours and the procedure is repeated. After another 24 hours of "curing", it is taken off the aluminum mold and put on a foam mold where the open end is sealed off. The foam is pulled out through the inspection hole and the tank is washed, ready for accessories.

Simpson also will be making the spouts so that he can supply the entire fuel cell to the buyer.

Combining his two "businesses", the race-driver, inventor and businessman continually experiments with different types of suits, shoes, gloves, head socks and fire extinguisher systems — "a whole multitude of things," he says, "and we come up with a lot of really good ideas because of it."

Bill Simpson is just one man who helps to make racing a lot safer. Maybe it's because he's a part of this super sport.

Simpson, right, checks over progress of his new fuel cell manufacturing.

Special on the track. The bulky white No. 1 was built by Myron Stevens and Herman Rigling and it housed one of the most interesting engines in Speedway history. Under the direction of Riley Brett, Leo Goosen designed a wide crank case on which two parallel 91-inch Miller blocks were mounted, each with its own crankshaft. The total piston displacement was 201 inches for the 16 cylinders. The cranks were connected to a central driveshaft by spur gears. Downdraft manifolds through the top of the block much like today's Foyt engines were utilized. The engine was somewhat similar to the engine designed by Frank Lockart for his

engine. The Lockhart engine, incidentally, had been purchased by Brett although it was not used for a number of years.

The 1930 race under the new formula saw Meyer taking a fourth behind Billy Arnold, Shorty Cantlon and Louis Schneider. The neat black and white car had an equally neat pit crew dressed in white pants, black shirts and white neckties and trim. This would be standard for the Sampson through 1936. The bulky car weighed in at 2080 pounds but this was about average for the starting field which included a number of heavy semi-stock cars.

Meyer drove the

ill-fated beach car, although that engine had the case built so that the blocks were angled 15 degrees in either direction rather than straight up as was the Sampson

Brett-mechanicked Sampson 16 in both 1931 and '32, but with little luck. In '31, he finished 34th in a 40-car starting field, withdrawing on the

Building a race car 1930-style. Louis Meyer, left, Alden Sampson, center and Riley Brett, assemble their 1930 speedster.

Fox Collection

lap with an oil leak. The following year a skid resulted from both crankshafts breaking on the 50th laps and Meyer was awarded 33rd. The engine was reported as 220-cubic-inches (although the bore and stroke of 2.312 x 3.0 as reported on the entry blank were the same as the previous year). Meyer's riding mechanic was a man with whom he would be associated after World War II in the production of the famed Offy engine--Dale Drake.

Louis left the Sampson camp after the 1932 race and switched to Ralph Hepburn's Miller. It was a wise move as the new combination won the race -- making him the second two-time winner in Speedway history. Chet Gardner stepped into the Sampson and helped pioneer radio reception on Speedway cars. WOXAC were the call letters painted on the car and riding mechanic, Herschell McKee wore a specially-constructed helmet contain-

ing the car phones. Gardner finished in fourth place.

The likeable Gardner was back in the seat in both 1934 and '35. A connecting rod broke in the '34 race when Chet had completed 72 laps after working up as far as eighth place. The car performed better in '35 and Chet finished seventh.

Rough, tough Harry McQuinn, who had learned his auto racing with the rough "Chicago Gang" on the Midwest's dirt tracks was signed for the 1936 race when Gardner bought his own car--a Duesenberg chassis, powered with a 255 Offy engine. Harry worked his way through the pack and was running eighth on the 196th lap when the car ran out of gas. The fuel limit had been lowered to 37½ gallons of pump gasoline and McQuinn's plight was shared by six other drivers including Shorty Cantlon, Rex Mays, Doc Williams, Lou

Moore, Floyd Roberts and Frank Brisko. The aging 16 had been replaced for this race by a four-cylinder 247-cubic-inch Miller marine engine. Shortly after the race, Sampson sold the car to Billy Winn and young Billy DeVore drove it to seventh in the 1937 race. After several unsuccessful "500" entries, the car was retired in 1947 and has recently been restored by Pete Schneider of Thousand Oaks, Cal.

Sampson was out of racing for several years but he retained his connection with Riley Brett and when the car specifications were changed and two-man cars were replaced with narrower one-place jobs, Sam and Riley began making plans for a new car which would be the most powerful and most modern addition to American racing. Riley still had the Frank Lockhart engine, another 16-cylinder brute but with only 183-cubic-inchs. Superchargers were once again allowed

Two views of the 1939-41 Sampson car. The left photo shows the then-uncommon DeDion rear suspension. On the right notice the twin magnetos on the front of the engine and general massiveness of the engine compared to the rest of the car.

and two centrifugal units--one for each block of eight cylinders--were fitted just behind the fire wall.

Myron Stevens and Emil Deidt built the chassis and it contained both advanced European and American technoligical advances. The quarter-eliptic front springs were conventional but the axle was positioned above the frame. The rear-end utilized the torsion bar DeDion-type of independent suspension. The body was fully streamlined and with its cream and blue paint job it was one of the most attractive cars on the track.

Sampson and Brett chose their driver wisely. He was perhaps the hottest leadfoot in the history of Midget racing—Bob Swanson—who was also quite familiar with the "500." In his rookie year, he had dropped from the running early in the race at the wheel of the Sparks and Weirick car and then drove 50 laps of relief in the Hamilton-Harris Special for a tired and hot Ralph Hepburn. Many people still believe that had he remained in the car, he would have

won the race; although Hep stayed right on Shaw's tail to finish second by only 2.16 seconds. The soft-spoken Swede who claimed that he had the "luck of the Irish" riding with him, sat out the 1938 race due to a near-fatal Midget accident at Gilmore Stadium late in the '37 season and for the rest of his career walked with a noticeable limp.

Swanson qualified the new car at 129.431 mph which was only topped by Louis Meyer and the Chicago charger, Jimmy Snyder. The rear axle broke, however, after only 19 laps. Bob once again relieved Hepburn but, this time, with tragic results. He had just taken over when entering the backstretch on the 107th lap, he spun. Floyd Roberts was right behind and made contact, flipping Swanson's fuel-heavy car which immediately exploded in horrifying flames. Swanson was thrown to the middle of the track and the popular Roberts, winner of the previous year's "500" crashed over the outside wall to his death. In order to miss the prostrate Swanson, Chet Miller cranked his big Boyle

The builders pose proudly with their finished product in 1939. From left to right: Alden Sampson, unidentified mechanic, Gordon Schroeder, Leo Goosen and Riley Brett. Though it might look big and bulky by today's standards, in 1939 this car was every bit as streamlined as a 1974 Eagle is today.

After World War II, Gordon Schroeder bought the Sampson car and entered it in the first post-war "500" with Sam Hanks as the driver and band leader Spike Jones as the sponsor. Here Schroeder and Hanks pose for their official qualification photo.

two-man car to the left and flipped into the infield. Ironically, Bob suffered only minor injuries while Miller spent many weeks in the hospital.

While the big car was being made ready for the 1940 "500," Sampson and Brett got into the Midget business. They asked Leo Goosen to design an engine to rival the almost unbeatable 98-cubic-inch Offy. The engineering wizard who was responsible for almost every American racing engine over the past 55 years came up with a power plant which could still be quite competitive today. It was similar to the Offy so far as displacement was concerned although it contained five main bearings rather than the Offy's three and instead of the Offy's eight valves, the Sampson had 16. Ronney Householder scored many wins with his Sampson-powered Midget in 1940 and '41 but the engine was never put into mass production due to the War when Sampson's efforts were altered to military production.

Swanson was much more successful in the 1940 "500," taking a sixth after qualifying sixth-fast. The Sampson forces were delt a blow three weeks later when Swanson was fatally injured while qualifying for a Midget event in Toledo. In 1941, the last race before the Speedway was shut down by the War, Deacon Litz retired the car after 89 laps when oil trouble developed.

With Sampson and Brett out of the racing business for the duration of

the War, the car was stored until Gordon Schroeder purchased it in time for the 1946 race--first one under the Hulman-Shaw regime. Gordon had been a close associate with the Sampson operation since the car's first race and he had also acquired a Sampson-powered Midget just before the War shut down Midget racing. Popular entertainer, Spike Jones, was secured as a sponsor of the car which from that point on would be called "Old Spike." Sam Hanks, another top-flight Midget driver was fourth-fast and started the 1946 "500" on the outside of the front row although he lasted only 18 laps before he, like Litz, retired with a broken oil line.

With Sampson showing no apparent interest in re-entering the racing business, Brett bought the chassis from Schroeder and in 1948 leased it (minus engine) to Cotton Henning who was preparing a stable of cars for the Bennett Brothers. George Connor completed only 24 laps in the car. now powered with an in-line 268-cubic-inch eight cylindered Miller, when he retired with a broken drive shaft. That was the last trip around the brickyard for the car but not its last Indianapolis appearance, since Riley Brett later donated both the chassis, complete with the 16-cylinder Lockhart engine to the Speedway Museum.

In 1950, Sampson was back as a Speedway car owner. He had Johnny Rae build him a chassis for one of the little experimental 177-cubic-inch

supercharged Offys. Walt Ader drove the unattractive, box-like car and was running a poor 23rd when the clouds opened up and the race was red-flagged on Johnnie Parsons' 138th lap. Ader had only completed 123 laps when the downpour struck. This was to be the last Sampson car to make a "500."

The car was entered for the 1951 race but it was not to run. Sampson was driving through New Mexico in a pickup truck, heading for Indianapolis from his home in California's San Fernando Valley transporting an engine. Somehow he lost control and the pickup went off the road, turning over. Sampson was dead when help arrived.

Sam did much for auto racing with his substantial income. His cars were always immaculate and he used his resources to develop new engineering concepts and produce some of the best race cars of their time. While he never was able to repeat his success as a first-time entrant, Sam was always the owner--with the possible exception of his last car--of a potential "500" winner.

Personally, his friends remember him as a nice guy who loved good living but could really be a handful at times. Gordon Schroeder still owns several of his Midget engines and entertains hopes of running them in competition. Perhaps racing will once again hear of the name Sampson in the winner's circle.

USAC

POCONO   INDIANAPOLIS   ONTARIO

BOBBY UNSER, 1974 CHAMPION

Triple Crown

ONTARIO & POCONO

For Decades, The Indianapolis 500 Was The Longest Event In Championship Automobile Racing. Two New Tracks, One Built In The Beautiful Pocono Mountains and The Other In Swinging Southern California Now Stage Annual 500 Mile Championship Automobile Races. Their Success Adds Further Credence To The Adage "Automobile Racing is The Sport of The Seventies". Brief Coverage of Those Races Follows.

NTARIO

By Carl Hungness
Editor and Publisher

Back in 1937 the now legendary Wilbur Shaw edged Ralph Hepburn by 2.16 seconds to win that year's Indianapolis 500-Mile Race and in doing so set a record for the closest finish in 500-mile race competition.

Although the scene wasn't Indianapolis, the crowd of nearly 100,000 at this year's California 500 in Ontario, Cal. was treated to an even closer finish, only .58 of a second, as the eldest racing Unser, Bobby, led younger brother Al across the finish.

Bobby could not be termed the odds-on favorite going in to the fifth annual Cal 500 race as he had not scored a 500-mile race victory since his win at Indianapolis in 1968. In addition, he was starting the race from the front row and in previous runnings no one had won the California go from a top-three starting position.

The press and fellow competitors alike were reasonably certain that three-time Indianapolis 500 winner A.J. Foyt was going to be the class of the field and would be the man to beat barring mechanical failure. Foyt demonstrated his superiority in one of the two 100-mile qualifying races held at Ontario the weekend previous.

While everyone else was worrying about fuel mileage, (USAC rules for 1974 call for a 280 gallon limit to be issued to each entrant for a 500-mile race--down 60 gallons from a year ago) Foyt was concentrating on dialing in the chassis of his pancake-nosed Coyote. He far outclassed Bobby Unser in the qualifying race and led him to the checkered by some 17-plus seconds.

Nevertheless, Foyt did run into mechanical failure but it was of the unpredictable kind. He ran over a fiberglass body panel that had been shucked off of Salt Walther's car and

No, this isn't the 1974 Ontario 500 finish. Rather, it is an old race car demonstration which preceeded the running of the "500." The cars certainly looked out of place at what is one of the most beautiful and modern tracks in the world.

Chini

In the left photo, Bobby Unser is shown during a practice run in his Olsonite Eagle. Note how snugly he fits in the car's cockpit. The other photo shows the mascot painted on the cowling of George Snider's car. Could it have something to do with George having put on some weight over the winter?

Bobby Unser waves from Victory Circle as he accepts the plaque signifying his victory in the 1974 California 500. Brother Al Unser, right photo, finished only .58 seconds behind Bobby after over three hours and 500 miles of racing. This was the closest finish in any 500-mile Championship race in history.

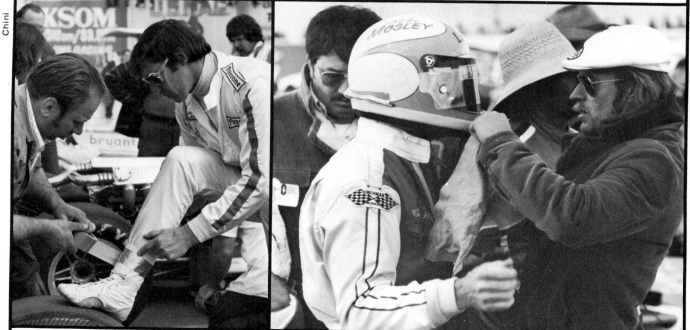

Getting suited-up for a 500-mile race isn't a one-man job. In the left photo, Bentley Warren gets some assistance in taping the cuffs of his uniform while Mike Mosley has brother Doyle give him a hand with his flame-retardant scarf which tucks inside the collar of the driving suit.

Chini

Chini

Winners of the two 100-mile qualifying races on March 3 were A.J. Foyt, top, and Johnny Rutherford, bottom.

the ensuing result was a broken oil tank for the Texas veteran.

At the start of the 500-mile race, it appeared as though Bobby had discovered some additional speed in his Olsonite Eagle as he led Foyt into the first turn and had a slight advantage when the pair came out of turn two. The other front row starter, Johnny Rutherford, who won the other 100-mile qualifying race, was third as the field completed the first lap.

On the backstretch, which is visible from every grandstand seat in the beautiful facility, Foyt demonstrated why he was nearly five miles an hour faster than anyone else during qualifying as he whisked around Bobby with no more effort than pushing the throttle down a little further. A.J. settled into a comfortable margin for the next 22 circuits until he ran over the Walther body panel that had been ripped off by the wind. Foyt knew his day was over and didn't bother to stop at his pit. He kept his orange No. 14 coasting all the way from the race track, through the pits and the tunnel that leads to the garage area. Anxious newsmen were a bit reluctant in approaching the sometimes short-tempered Foyt. Not only had he just lost some $70,000 in prize money, a win at Ontario would have given him a clean sweep of auto racing's Triple Crown, as he has already scored at Indianapolis and he won the Schaefer 500 at Pocono (Pa.) last year.

Once Foyt left the '74 season opener, the brothers Unser dominated the scene and swapped the lead back and forth some nine times before Bobby took final control on the 178th lap and held it to the end of the 200-lap grind.

In between times, Jimmy McElreath, winner of the initial Cal 500 in 1970, led a couple of laps while the Unsers were refueling. Steve Krisiloff also found himself occupying the No. 1 position under the same circumstances from laps 74—77 and again for laps 93—96, but was black flagged for a possible oil leak and tire check.

While in the pits, Steve's American Kids Racer Eagle/Offy burst into flames when the coupler on the refueling hose failed to shut off. Steve bailed out amidst a harrowing cloud of fire extinguishing smoke and found nothing but his feelings hurt after having put on another one of his impressive drives.

A lap prior to being called in, Krisiloff nearly spun in the first turn and officials feared that he may have worn a flat spot or two on his tires.

Although everyone was worried over the new fuel regulations (a few cars ran out during the prior weekend's qualifying races) the fact wasn't evident in the racing. The lead was swapped 21 times among the six drivers who led.

The anticipated action during pit stops occurred. Ontario's ultra-wide pit lane appeared as though it spawned high-speed entry and exit. Gary Bettenhausen and Joe Leonard nerfed one another around a bit during one of the pit stops. Gary B. suffered suspension damage in the fracas and spent several laps in his pit repairing the damage. He re-entered the race and quit worrying about fuel mileage as he had absolutely no chance of winning. As you might expect, the second-generation driving star became the fastest man on the race track and ran until the checkered flag flew. He had completed only 146 laps--but came to Ontario to race--and race he did.

Leonard's fate wasn't nearly so fortunate although the bumping incident with Bettenhausen had nothing to do with it. On the 152nd lap, Leonard apparently ran over some debris on the track thus causing a tire to lose air pressure. He whacked the inside pit wall, slid a couple of hundred feet down into the first turn where he again hit the retaining barrier.

All of USAC's fire prevention rules worked in the Leonard incident. Although the car was demolished, all systems held and flame did not erupt. After being pried from the car, Leonard was found to have suffered only a compound fracture of the left leg, foot lacerations and a gash over his left eye.

Earlier accidents were of the minor variety. Mike Hiss was up to sixth spot in 17 laps after starting 33rd. He lost control coming out of the second turn when he ran over some debris on the track and hit the outside wall. Amiable Jerry Karl bounced off the second turn wall after spinning and Gordon Johncock smacked the concrete wall in the first turn.

While the first seven spots in the race were taken by the tried-and-proven Dan Gurney Eagles, one of the more popular cars of the day came under a banner not seen in USAC Championship racing as frequently as it has been in the past. The Brabham driven by Bill Simpson chugged along all day and wound up a creditable 14th. Simpson obtained local sponsor-

Two-time USAC National Driving Champion Joe Leonard awaits his car in the Ontario pits. Leonard suffered serious leg injuries in a crash during the 500-mile race.

A. J. Foyt spooked his competition at Ontario by running fast WITHOUT a rear wing! He used a wing in the race, however.

The Ontario Queen and her Court posed for our photographer and appears to have met with Johnny Parsons' (background) approval.

Pit stops are a fine art. Two good examples are Al Unser's, left, and Jimmy Caruthers.

Bill Simpson stops for fuel during his fine Cal 500 drive.

Chief Mechanic Jimmie Wright, left, and driver Lee Brayton solving a problem.

Bobby Unser tried out a rear wing with super-large side plates. It proved unsatisfactory and was discarded.

Motorcycle racer Frank Gillespie hopes to switch his signboard for a race car someday.

Paul Russo, left, and Yearbook publisher Carl Hugness discuss race prospects.

The late Peter Revson and girlfirend Marji Wallace were spectators at Ontario.

Harold Gafford, left, and Roy Dickenson adjust Wally Dallenbach's shoulder harnesses.

ship for the Offy-powered car from a company called "Apple Annie's Speakeasy," a title that blends in with Simpson's easy-going personality.

While the Gurney-built machines scored impressively, the Offy engine again proved its reliability by taking the first 10 positions. A.J. Foyt's teammate, versatile George Snider brought home the first Foyt engine in 11th position.

Bobby and Al were the only drivers to complete the entire 200-lap distance. Third place went to Jerry Grant in one of the team Cobre Firestone Eagles, which was a terrific jump in finishing order for the veteran driver as he had placed last in his two previous attempts at Ontario. He was a lap behind at the finish and his teammate, the fun-loving Jimmy Caruthers was yet another lap back in fourth position.

The 1974 running of the California 500 firmly entrenched the race as a standard on USAC's Championship Trail. The grandstands were full and campers dotted the sanitary infield. ABC did their usual commendable job in broadcasting the event over live TV, which helped to relieve the once financially burdened facility to overcome some of its previously publicized troubles. General Manager Jim Cook could truthfully tell the press that the future looked bright for Ontario Motor Speedway and Speedway car racing in general.

After all, it's not everyday that one witnesses any race, much less a 500-miler that is separated by half a second between the winner and his pursuer.

USAC CHAMPIONSHIP BOX SCORE -- ONTARIO, CALIFORNIA -- MARCH 3, 1974

Track: Ontario Motor Speedway   Avg. Speed: 176.873 mph
Type Track: 2.5-Mile Paved   Time: 33:55.36
Organizer: OMS, Incorporated   Distance: 100 Miles
Weather: Sunny

FIRST QUALIFYING RACE

FIN. POS.	ST. POS.	DRIVER	CAR NAME/ NUMBER	PTS. WON	LAPS COMP.	RUNNING/ REASON OUT
1	1	A. J. Foyt	Gilmore Racing Team (14)	200	40	Running
2	2	Bobby Unser	Olsonite Eagle (48)	160	40	Running
3	7	Lloyd Ruby	Unlimited Racing (9)	140	40	Running
4	8	Jim McElreath	Thermo-King (45)	120	39	Running
5	9	Roger McCluskey	Lindsey Hopkins Buick Co. (1)	100	39	Running
6	10	Mike Mosley	Lodestar (98)	80	38	Running
7	4	Wally Dallenbach	Patrick Racing Team (2)	60	37	Running
8	5	Dick Simon	TraveLodge (44)	50	37	Running
9	11	Tom Bigelow	Bryant Gas Air Conditioning (27)	40	37	Out of fuel
10	6	Billy Vukovich	Sugaripe Prune (4)	30	37	Running
11	14	Lee Brayton	Eisenhour (28)	20	35	Out of fuel
12	13	Bentley Warren	Vatis (94)	10	34	Magneto
13	12	Tom Sneva	Grant King Racers (24)		33	Valve
14	3	Gordon Johncock	Patrick Racing (7)		23	Out of fuel
15	15	Skip Barber	Crower Cams (23)		17	Broken rod

SECOND QUALIFYING RACE

Avg. Speed: 172.673 mph   Time: 34:44.86

FIN. POS.	ST. POS.	DRIVER	CAR NAME/ NUMBER	PTS. WON	LAPS COMP.	RUNNING/ REASON OUT
1	1	Johnny Rutherford	McLaren (3)	200	40	Running
2	7	Jimmy Caruthers	Cobre-Firestone (21)	160	40	Running
3	6	Steve Krisiloff	American Kids Racers (18)	140	40	Running
4	11	Joe Leonard	Parnelli (16)	120	40	Running
5	4	Al Unser	Viceroy (15)	100	39	Out of fuel
6	12	John Martin	Unsponsored (89)	80	39	Running
7	8	Jerry Karl	Hopkins (42)	60	39	Running
8	9	Salt Walther	Dayton-Walther (77)	50	39	Running
9	3	Mario Andretti	Vieroy Parnelli (5)	40	37	Out of fuel
10	10	George Snider	Greer (82)	30	37	Out of fuel
11	2	Gary Bettenhausen	Penske Products (8)	20	28	Wing flap
12	14	John Cannon	Minnesota Serendipity (53)		18	Engine
13	5	Jerry Grant	Cobre-Firestone (55)		14	Magneto
14	13	Bill Simpson	Apple-Annie Speakeasy (92)		10	Handling
15	15	Bob Harkey	Cicada (93)		3	Oil leak

USAC CHAMPIONSHIP BOX SCORE -- ONTARIO, CALIFORNIA -- MARCH 10, 1974

Track: Ontario Motor Speedway   Avg. Speed: 157.017 mph   Basic Purse: $200,000
Type Track: 2½-Mile Paved   Time: 3:11:03.71   Accessory: $ 58,550
Organizer: OMS, Inc.   Distance: 500 Miles   P.F. Cont.: $ 500
Weather: Overcast, mild   Event No. 1   Appearance: $ 1,000
   Lap Prize: $ 55,000
   Entry Fee: $ 36,000
   TOTAL: $351,050

FIN. POS.	ST. POS.	DRIVER	CAR NAME/ NUMBER	PTS. WON	MONEY WON	LAPS COMP.	RUNNING/ REASON OUT
1	3	Bobby Unser	Olsonite Eagle (48)	1000	$88,758	200	Running
2	8	Al Unser	Viceroy (15)	800	$60,477	200	Running
3	17	Jerry Grant	Cobre-Firestone (55)	– –	$21,534	199	Running
4	4	Jimmy Caruthers	Cobre-Firestone (21)	600	$15,544	198	Running
5	6	Lloyd Ruby	Unlimited Racing (9)	500	$11,521	197	Running
6	10	Wally Dallenbach	Patrick Racing Team (2)	400	$ 7,312	196	Running
7	20	Mike Mosley	Lodestar (98)	300	$ 6,519	195	Running
8	9	Roger McCluskey	Hopkins Buick Co. (1)	250	$ 6,843	193	Running
9	21	John Martin	Unsponsored (89)	200	$ 5,861	193	Running
10	22	Tom Bigelow	Bryant Gas Air Cond. (27)	150	$ 5,203	192	Running
11	23	George Snider	Gilmore Racing Team (82)	100	$ 4,863	192	Running
12	25	Tom Sneva	Grant King Racers (24)	50	$ 4,498	192	Running
13	24	Bentley Warren	Vatis (94)		$ 4,369	187	Running
14	26	Bill Simpson	Apple-Annie Speakeasy (92)		$ 4,064	180	Running
15	7	Jim McElreath	Thermo-King (45)		$ 5,727	173	Water hose
16	28	John Cannon	Minnesota Serendipity (53)		$ 3,805	173	Running
17	30	Bob Harkey	Cicada (93)		$ 3,441	154	Gearbox
18	31	Al Loquasto	Martin Guitar (86)		$ 2,783	152	Timing gear
19	19	Joe Leonard	Parnelli (16)		$ 4,616	146	Accident
20	16	Gary Bettenhausen	Penske Products (8)		$ 3,769	146	Running
21	15	Bill Vukovich	Sugaripe Prune (4)		$ 3,406	141	Broken piston
22	13	Salt Walther	Dayton-Walther (77)		$ 3,535	128	Engine
23	27	Rick Muther	Webster Racing (76)		$ 2,548	121	Engine
24	5	Steve Krisiloff	American Kids Racers (18)		$ 6,551	93	Pit fire
25	14	Mario Andretti	Viceroy (5)		$ 5,152	91	Engine
26	18	Gordon Johncock	Patrick Racing Team (7)		$ 3,436	71	Accident
27	2	Johnny Rutherford	McLaren (3)		$ 9,738	49	Piston
28	12	Dick Simon	TraveLodge (44)		$ 3,503	38	Piston
29	11	Jerry Karl	Hopkins (42)		$ 3,323	32	Suspension
30	1	A. J. Foyt	Gilmore Racing Team (14)		$18,297	21	Oil tank
31	33*	Mike Hiss	Eisenhour (28)		$ 2,877	17	Accident
32	29	Skip Barber (23)	Crower Cams (23)		$ 2,595	8	Overheating
33	32	Johnny Parsons	Lodestar (97)		$ 2,078	0	Transmission

*Qualified by Lee Brayton

FAST QUALIFIER: A. J. Foyt, No. 14 – 190.617 mph.
LAP LEADERS: Lap 1, B. Unser (No. 48); Laps 2–21, Foyt (No. 14); Laps 23–34, A. Unser (No. 15); Laps 35–36, B. Unser; Lap 37, McElreath (No. 45); Laps 38–72, Simon (No. 44); Lap 73, Al Unser; Laps 74–77, Krisiloff (No. 18); Laps 78–87, B. Unser; Lap 88, A. Unser; Laps 89–92, Krisiloff; Laps 93–96, B. Unser; Laps 97–115, A. Unser; Laps 116–120, B. Unser; Laps 121–139, A. Unser; Laps 140–144, B. Unser; Laps 145–170, A. Unser; Laps 171–176, B. Unser; Lap 177, Al Unser; Laps 178–200, B. Unser.
YELLOW LIGHTS: Laps 18–23, Hiss (No. 28) hit wall; Laps 33–36, Karl (No. 42) hit wall; Laps 72–76, Johncock (No. 7) hit wall; Laps 87–91, Krisiloff (No. 18) spun; Laps 97–98, debris on backstretch; Laps 152–163, Leonard (No. 16) hit pit wall; Laps 176–180, debris on track.

Taking time off from a hectic schedule, Jim Leubbert of Lloyd Ruby's crew gets a quick haircut from Mrs. Doug Caruthers.

Jimmy Caruthers had a bicycle powered by a one-horsepower engine at Ontario. Here he demonstrates its features to Bobby Unser.

Steve Durst was assigned to the Thermo-King Spl., but was asked to gain more experience before tackling a 500-mile race by USAC officials.

USAC racing gets closer all the time! Al Loquasto leads a group of cars which includes Joe Leonard in No. 16, Jimmy Caruthers in No. 21, Jim McElreath and George Snider.

Bill Simpson's sponsor was a popular Southern California night spot. Bill's uniform patch was reminiscent of the old sandwich board type of advertising.

Johnny Rutherford flashes by in the late winter sun of Southern California on his way to victory in the second 100-mile qualifying race at Ontario on March 3. Rutherford started the 500-mile race in the front row but dropped out early due to mechanical trouble.

A. J. Foyt, left, does some last-minute fine tuning on his engine with a little help from Jack Starnes, center, and A.J.'s father, Tony.

Checking all-important fuel mileage figures are Tyler Alexander, left, team manager for Team McLaren and driver Johnny Rutherford.

Pocono

By Dustin W. Frazer
Associate Editor
National Speed Sport News

Texan Johnny Rutherford continued his hot streak on the USAC Championship Trail, coming from more than a lap behind to win the $400,000 Schaefer 500 at Pocono International Raceway.

Rutherford, driving the bright orange No. 3 Team McLaren Offenhauser, truly had Lady Luck in his pit. The Fort Worth veteran inherited the lead from Wally Dallenbach just 11 laps from the coveted checkered flag when Dallenbach, who looked like a sure winner, lost the engine in his red STP Eagle.

Johnny breezed home the winner by more than a lap over Jimmy Caruthers, completing the 200 laps around Pocono's 2.5-mile tri-oval in three hours, 11 minutes and 26.81 seconds. His winning average speed was 156.701 mph, erasing Joe Leonard's 1972 mark of 154.361.

The victory was the third straight for Rutherford. He won the Indianapolis 500 last May, and two weeks later came back to win the Rex Mays Classic at Milwaukee, Wis.

Rutherford had mixed emotions on Dallenbach's failure to finish. "I would have liked to see him stay in the race and hopefully catch him and beat him," he said, "but I'll still take the win. Wally was running very hard. He deserved to win if he had stayed in."

Trailing Caruthers' Cobre Firestone Eagle in third and fourth were Dallenbach's STP teammates, Gordon Johncock and Steve Krisiloff, finishing in that order. Rounding out the top five was pole starter Bobby Unser in the Olsonite Eagle.

A lengthy pit stop early in the race put Rutherford more than a lap down while crew chief Tyler Alexander and his crew made adjustments to correct a minor handling problem.

"I knew something was wrong with the car," said Rutherford, "so I went in for my second pit stop. The

Johnny Rutherford not only won the Indianapolis 500 but also the Pocono 500, the first man to win two 500-mile Championship races in a single season.

Wally Dallenbach drove a fine race at Pocono and appeared to have the race won when he suffered the heartbreak of a blown engine with only 12 laps to go.

crew changed one of the tires which appeared loose and also lowered the front wing. After that the car started to come around."

The race saw 18 lead changes among six drivers with Rutherford leading only 18 laps. The race's biggest leader was Bobby Unser, who led a total of 74 laps. Dallenbach led 40 laps. Other scored race leaders were Mario Andretti, Johncock and Krisiloff.

Andretti's race ended on the 133rd lap when Mario, running fifth, spun in oil from Bill Simpson's blown engine and hit the boiler plate retaining wall near the first turn.

"Bill Simpson blew an engine in front of me and dumped oil in my path," said Mario. "It all happened so quickly I didn't have time to react. I hit the wall pretty hard."

Mario was running well when a fuel leak in the turbocharger in his

Viceroy Eagle forced a 90-second pit stop and his car belched fire. Crew chief Johnny Capels suffered minor hand burns during the stop.

The only other accident of the day came on the 156th lap when rookie Tom Sneva, a former high school principal from Sprague, Wash., hit the wall in the first turn in his Grant King Offy. Sneva was badly shaken but otherwise unhurt.

Problems with fuel mileage in this year's Schaefer 500 was a big factor, as was the final outcome of last year's race when Roger McCluskey ran out of fuel on the final lap and A.J. Foyt went on to win.

Four of the six caution flags were to tow in cars that ran out of fuel and stalled on the track, including John Martin twice. Front running Al Unser ran dry in his Viceroy Eagle in the 25th lap, and Johncock ran out of fuel on lap 79 while leading.

Cars were only allowed 280 gallons of fuel for the race.

Bobby Unser's Olsonite Eagle would pick up only 27 of the 40 gallons it carried, making for additional pit stops. His rate of usage was also very high. On Unser's last stop, there was only eight gallons in the pit tank to add to the car, and team manager Dan Gurney slowed Unser to 150 mph so he could finish.

Unser had similar problems in this year's Indy 500 and was very discouraged. "It was sort of frustrating again," he said. "We were as fast as anybody else out there, but we had to turn the end of the race into an economy run to finish."

In contrast, Rutherford and Dallenbach had no fuel problems at all. "Nobody has a fuel formula like we have," Rutherford said. "Many of the car owners scream they need more fuel. If we can do it, why can't they?"

A.J. Foyt, last year's Schaefer 500 winner, was a strong pre-race favorite, but didn't last long enough to be a threat. Foyt was sixth fastest qualifier, but was forced to start 29th, having missed the first day of qualifying due to a mechanical problem and a spin.

Foyt passed 10 cars on the first lap and charged up to 12th place by lap 20 when the left front suspension upright cracked and sent his red Gilmore Coyote skittering up the track. It

Jimmy Caruthers finished second to Rutherford at Pocono, his best finish to date in a 500-mile Championship car race.

grazed the wall, but Foyt brought it back under control and drove it to the garage area.

Foyt said his week earlier spin "where I stood on the brakes so hard it nearly upended," probably fractured the part.

Two significant black flag incidents occurred during the race. Dallenbach was called in to the pits early when the emmission control valve on his Eagle came loose and was dangling. Eighth-place finisher Billy Vukovich was black flagged and lecutred for crossing the line exiting the pits too early, a costly penalty.

A crowd estimated at 62,000 saw 14 cars still running at the finish. Among the early drop-outs was Gary Bettenhausen, who lost a piston in his Sunoco McLaren. Defending USAC National Champion Roger McCluskey had overheating trouble in his English Leather Special. Mike Mosley lost a turbocharger on his Lodestar Eagle.

Jan Opperman, the popular rookie

who is probably the country's greatest dirt track Sprint car driver, was the first to drop out of the race when his Viceroy Parnelli overheated. "Something broke and blew through the radiator," Jan said.

Rutherford's victory gave him $92,625 and 1000 National Championship points. He still trailed Bobby Unser in the standings, however, 3100 to 2750. The Triple Crown title goes to Unser by virtue of his victory in the California 500 at Ontario last March, coupled with a second-place finish in the Indy 500 and a fifth at Pocono. Rutherford failed to finish at Ontario.

"This habit is getting to me, but it's one I'd like to keep for a while," Rutherford told the press after the race. "I tagged along somewhere back in the pack for several years as other drivers won races I should have won.

The racing at Pocono was close. Here A.J. Foyt leads Mike Mosley through a turn early in the race.

Then things begin going my way, and I'm winning. I hope it lasts for a while."

Dallenbach raced into the lead at the start from his outside front row starting position, beating Krisiloff and Bobby Unser into the first turn. Unser made a bid to pass Krisiloff on the second lap, but Steve held him back. Dallenbach's speed at the end of the first lap was 171.766 mph.

At the end of three laps, Krisiloff had faded and the top four were Dallenbach, B. Unser, Rutherford and Andretti. Unser moved into the lead on the fourth lap as Dallenbach dropped to fourth ahead of Krisiloff.

Andretti closed on Unser, not giving Bobby any breathing room at all. Andretti finally moved to the inside of Unser going down the front straightaway to start lap 10, and made the pass. Mario opened a six and a half second lead over Bobby at the end of 10 laps.

Mario led to the 23rd lap when he made a pit stop. Bobby Unser and Rutherford also pitted and Krisiloff went into the lead. Steve made his first pit stop two laps later, however, and Andretti was back out front once again.

Andretti opened a six second lead over Krisiloff at the end of 40 laps. The average speed was 160.946 mph.

Mario made his second stop on lap 47, getting in and out in 13.7 seconds, but Krisiloff was again the leader.

Krisiloff pitted on lap 51, giving the lead for the first time to Johncock. Two laps later, Johncock came into the pits and Andretti was once again out front. Bobby Unser closed to less than a second on Andretti by the 65th lap.

Unser came into the pits on lap 66, stopping for 13.3 seconds. Andretti's stop came on lap 73 and was in and out in 14.8 seconds, but Johncock was once again the leader. Five laps later, Johncock stalled on the second turn, out of fuel, and handed the lead to Bobby. Andretti was running second and Dallenbach third.

Team Manager Dan Gurney was faced with solving driver Bobby Unser's fuel consumption dilemma.

At the halfway or 100 laps, Jimmy Caruthers had moved into second behind Bobby Unser. Dallenbach was third followed by Lloyd Ruby, Krisiloff, Tom Sneva, Andretti, Rutherford, Billy Vukovich and Bill Simpson. The average speed was 159.753 mph.

Unser, enjoying a three second lead over Dallenbach, pitted on lap 118 and Wally was back in front. Unser was in and out of the pits in 17 seconds. Andretti and Rutherford had a drag race into the pits on lap 121 and Mario beat Johnny back out onto the track, making his stop in 17 seconds.

Unser passed Dallenbach for the lead on the 125th lap. The top five, Unser, Dallenbach, Caruthers, Andretti and Rutherford were all running within 17 seconds of each other.

On the 134th lap, Johncock overshot his pit and had to make an extra trip around the track before finally stopping. At 135 laps, it was Dallenbach, Caruthers, Bobby Unser now third, and Rutherford with just 8.6 seconds separating them.

Dallenbach pitted on lap 136 and Bobby moved to a .04 second lead over Rutherford. Bobby made a stop on lap 156 and Rutherford moved into the lead for the first time in the race. Rutherford pitted on lap 159, getting in and out in 21.9 seconds and Dallenbach moved back into the lead, passing Bobby Unser between the first and second turns. Rutherford was running third, right on Unser's rear bumper. Rutherford, the fastest on the track at this point, passed Bobby on lap 165 and began closing on Dallenbach.

Dallenbach and Rutherford darted for the pits on lap 181 in what was supposed to be their final stop. Dallenbach was in and out in 13.8 seconds while Rutherford stopped in 15 seconds.

Enjoying a six second lead over Rutherford, Dallenbach's STP racer suddenly slowed with a dozen laps remaining, its engine sputtering from a broken piston, and Rutherford cruised home the winner.

Bobby Unser won the pole position a week earlier with a four-lap average of 182.500 mph. Foyt missed out on a shot at the pole after being miles faster than anyone during practice.

A.J. came to Pocono with the fastest car and watched the first day of qualifying in utter frustration. "It means I'm going to have to start behind a bunch of idiots," Foyt said

Pancho Carter leads Steve Krisiloff, Mario Andretti and Gordon Johncock in this shot. Note the width of the main straightaway and pit area.

after blowing an engine in his first qualifying attempt early in the morning, and spinning his second time out later in the day.

Just moments before the gun went off at 6 p.m., ending the first day of qualifying, Foyt's car had been repaired and was ready to run. But two cars were in front of him on the line, the Rolla Vollstedt car driven by Tom Bigelow, and the Cobre Firestone Special of Duane (Pancho) Carter, Jr.

Bigelow took his car out on the track, and ever so slowly it built up speed, using the maximum of three practice laps over the 2.5-mile track. Then Bigelow began his four qualifying laps. After three at 168 mph, Vollstedt called Bigelow in, aborting the try. However, precious minutes had been used up in the futile try.

Rick Muther then crashed into the wall in the third turn, and also used up a couple of precious minutes.

Just as Carter started his run, the gun went off to end the session. Carter was allowed to complete his run, but no time was left for Foyt.

Bigelow pointed out that "Foyt has to play the game like everybody else. There was a time at Indianapolis when there were cars behind one of Foyt's, and he didn't move over."

For Foyt, there was little consolation. He had qualified for the pole for the California 500 and the Indianapolis 500. He could have made a sweep of the Triple Crown poles here.

It was a busy day with a record 28 drivers qualifying. Krisiloff, Dallenbach and Johncock of the STP team had been the fastest three drivers during the first day of practice. And in qualifications, the trio was again tightly bunched.

Krisiloff qualified second fastest with a four-lap average of 182.269

mph, Dallenbach third at 182.020 and Johncock fourth at 181.993.

The second day of qualifying on Sunday was washed out by rain and Foyt had to wait until the following Thursday to qualify. Foyt qualified at 181.415 mph, sixth-best overall among the 33 starters.

"I figured on qualifying at 183," Foyt said, "but the track wasn't in the best of condition. The track was dirty and I couldn't hustle the car. I should

be able to run the race at my qualifying speed." Three days of rain had washed most of the rubber off the track.

The only car bumped from the field was rookie Larry (Boom Boom) Cannon, who had to push his car across the finish line to end his run. The Offy engine in Cannon's ancient Eagle let go on the last lap. It coasted to a stop entering the third turn and he then pushed it the final mile.

USAC CHAMPIONSHIP BOX SCORE -- POCONO, PENNSYLVANIA -- JUNE 30, 1974

Track:	Pocono International Raceway	Avg. Speed:	156.701 mph	Basic Purse:	$300,000
Type Track:	2.5 Mile Paved	Time:	3:11:26.81	Accessory:	$ 67,030
Organizer:	Dr. Joseph Mattioli	Distance:	500 Miles	Lap Prize:	$ 3,000
Weather:	Sunny	Event No. 6 P.F. Cont.:		Appearance:	$ 1,000
				Entry Fee Dist:	$ 40,000
				P.F. Cont.:	$ 500
				TOTAL:	$411,530

FIN. POS.	ST. POS.	DRIVER	CAR NAME/ NUMBER	PTS. WON	MONEY WON	LAPS COMP.	RUNNING/ REASON OUT
1	5	Johnny Rutherford	McLaren (3)	1000	$92,200	200	Running
2	10	Jimmy Caruthers	Cobre Firestone (21)	800	$49,250	199	Running
3	4	Gordon Johncock	STP Dbl. Oil Filter (20)	700	$31,700	199	Running
4	2	Steve Krisiloff	STP Gas Treatment (60)	600	$17,020	198	Running
5	1	Bobby Unser	Olsonite (48)	500	$14,750	197	Running
6	12	Lloyd Ruby	Unlimited (9)	400	$ 9,905	197	Running
7	15	Bentley Warren	Lindsey Hopkins (42)	300	$ 9,050	196	Running
8	19	Billy Vukovich	Sugaripe Prune (4)	250	$ 8,480	194	Running
9	33	Eldon Rasmussen	Ras-Car (58)	200	$ 7,910	192	Running
10	3	Wally Dallenbach	STP Oil Treatment (40)	150	$ 7,540	188	Blown engine
11	17	Al Loquasto	Hess's (86)	100	$ 6,770	179	Running
12	27	Larry McCoy	Surefine Foods (63)	50	$ 6,215	174	Running
13	7	Tom Sneva	Grant King Racing (24)		$ 6,058	155	Accident
14	28	Lee Brayton	Sinmast (61)		$ 5,915	151	Running
15	22	Duane Carter Jr.	Cobre Firestone (11)		$ 5,772	146	Connecting rod
16	21	John Martin	Unsponsored (89)		$ 5,645	138	Running
17	8	Mario Andretti	Viceroy (5)		$ 5,288	132	Accident
18	16	Bill Simpson	American Kids Racers (18)		$ 5,345	131	Connecting rod
19	32	Tom Bigelow	Bryant Heating-Cooling (27)		$ 5,202	108	Engine
20	26	Salt Walther	Dayton-Walther (77)		$ 5,060	79	Transmission
21	9	Mike Mosley	Lodestar (98)		$ 4,918	70	Turbocharger
22	6	Al Unser	Viceroy (15)		$ 4,275	64	Connecting rod
23	23	Jim McElreath	Thermo King (45)		$ 4,632	46	Turbocharger
24	18	Jim Hurtubise	Miller High Life (56)		$ 4,490	31	Ignition
25	31	George Snider	Gilmore Racing (82)		$ 3,848	25	Radiator
26	25	Bob Harkey	Grant King Racing (26)		$ 4,205	21	Overheating
27	29	A. J. Foyt	Gilmore Racing (14)		$ 3,562	20	Broken upright
28	30	Roger McCluskey	English Leather (1)		$ 3,920	18	Overheating
29	13	Dick Simon	TraveLodge (44)		$ 3,778	18	Manifold
30	20	Sam Sessions	Oriente Express (30)		$ 3,135	15	Turbocharger
31	11	Gary Bettenhausen	Sunoco (8)		$ 2,992	9	Piston
32	24	Jerry Karl	Webster (76)		$ 2,850	4	Connecting rod
33	14	Jan Opperman	Viceroy (51)		$ 2,850	4	Overheating

FAST QUALIFIER: Bobby Unser, No. 48 - 3:17.26 (182.500 mph)

LAP LEADERS: Laps 1-3, Dallenbach (No. 40); Laps 4-9, B. Unser (No. 48); Laps 10-23, Andretti (No. 5); Lap 24, Krisiloff (No. 60); Laps 25-47, Andretti; Laps 48-50, Krisiloff; Laps 51-52, Johncock (No. 20); Laps 53-72, Andretti; Laps 73-77, Johncock; Laps 78-117, B. Unser; Laps 118-124, Dallenbach; Laps 125-130, B. Unser; Laps 131-136, Dallenbach; Laps 137-155, B. Unser; Laps 156-159, Rutherford (No. 3); Laps 160-162, B. Unser; Laps 163-180, Dallenbach; Laps 181-187, Dallenbach; Laps 188-200, Rutherford.

YELLOW LIGHTS: Six (6) for a total of 32 laps.

Performance Records

Year	Car	Qual.	S	F	Speed or Laps	Reason Out

MARIO ANDRETTI, Nazareth, Pennsylvania

Indianapolis 500 Record (Passed Driver's Test 1965)

Year	Car	Qual.	S	F	Speed or Laps	Reason Out
1965	Dean Van Lines	158.849	4	3	200	149.121
1966	Dean Van Lines	165.899	1	18	27	Engine
1967	Dean Van Lines	168.982	1	30	58	Lost wheel
1968	Overseas Natl. Airways	167.691	4	33	2	Piston
1968*	Overseas Natl. Airways			28	10	Piston
	*(Rel. L. Dickson)					
1969	STP Oil Treatment	169.851	2	1	200	156.867
1970	STP Oil Treatment	168.209	8	6	199	Flagged
1971	STP Oil Treatment	172.612	9	30	11	Accident
1972	Viceroy	187.167	5	8	194	Out of fuel
1973	Viceroy	195.059	6	30	4	Piston
1974	Viceroy	186.027	5	31	2	Piston

Pocono 500 Record

Year	Car	Qual.	S	F	Speed or Laps	Reason Out
1971	STP Oil Treatment	169.510	5	4	198	Flagged
1972	Viceroy	183.216	3	7	188	Flagged
1973	Viceroy	190.164	3	7	184	Valve
1974	Viceroy	179.964	8	17	132	Accident

Ontario 500 Record

Year	Car	Qual.	S	F	Speed or Laps	Reason Out
1970	STP Oil Treatment	174.199	8	10	182	Gear box
1971	STP Oil Treatment	177.191	8	33	0	Electrical
1972	Viceroy	191.499	5	27	52	Conn. rod bolt
1973	Viceroy	194.616	15	2	200	Running
1974	Viceroy	184.786	14	25	91	Engine

GARY BETTENHAUSEN, Monrovia, Indiana

Indianapolis 500 Record (Passed Driver's Test 1968)

Year	Car	Qual.	S	F	Speed or Laps	Reason Out
1968	Thermo-King	163.562	22	24	43	Oil cooler
1969	Thermo-King	167.777	9	26	35	Piston
1970	Thermo-King	166.451	20	26	55	Valve
1971	Thermo-King	171.233	13	10	178	Flagged
1972	Sunoco McLaren	188.877	4	14	181	Ignition
1973	Sunoco DX	195.599	5	5	130	Running
1974	Score	184.492	11	32	2	Valve

Pocono 500 Record

Year	Car	Qual.	S	F	Speed or Laps	Reason Out
1971	Thermo-King	165.563	13	6	198	Flagged
1972	Sunoco McLaren	182.766	5	19	77	Ignition
1973	Sunoco DX	186.056	11	27	37	Accident
1974	Sunoco	177.936	11	31	9	Piston

Ontario 500 Record

Year	Car	Qual.	S	F	Speed or Laps	Reason Out
1970	Thermo-King	175.046	5	19	93	Piston
1971	Thermo-King	177.444	27	3	198	Flagged
1973	Sunoco DX	(????)	6	19	79	Engine
1974	Penske McLaren	185.261	16	20	146	Running

JIMMY CARUTHERS, Anaheim, California

Indianapolis 500 Record (Passed Driver's Test 1971)

Year	Car	Qual.	S	F	Speed or Laps	Reason Out
1972	U.S. Forces—Steed	178.909	31	9	194	Flagged
1973	Cobre Firestone	194.217	9	21	73	Suspension
1974	Cobre Firestone	184.049	12	28	64	Gearbox

Pocono 500 Record

Year	Car	Qual.	S	F	Speed or Laps	Reason Out
1971	Gilmore Racing Team	164.394	20	13	183	Flagged
1972	U.S. Forces—Steed	175.584	18	10	160	Accident
1973	Cobre Firestone	186.625	9	16	124	Piston
1974	Cobre Firestone	178.050	10	2	199	Flagged

Ontario 500 Record

Year	Car	Qual.	S	F	Speed or Laps	Reason Out
1971	Thermo-King	173.904	16	19	122	Block
1972	Wynn's	190.336	7	12	171	Water line
1973	Cobre Firestone	192.823	20	15	119	Engine
1974	Cobre Firestone	181.397	4	4	198	Flagged

WALLY DALLENBACH, E. Brunswick, N.J.

Indianapolis 500 Record (Passed Driver's Test 1967)

Year	Car	Qual.	S	F	Speed or Laps	Reason Out
1967	Valvoline	163.540	15	29	73	Accident
1968	Valvoline	165.548	12	17	146	Engine
1969	Sprite	166.497	19	21	82	Clutch
1970	Sprite	165.601	24	17	143	Magneto
1971	Sprite	171.160	23	24	69	Valve
1972	STP Oil Treatment	181.626*	33	15	182	Flagged
1973	Olsonite Eagle	190.194	20	24	48	Conn. rod
1974	STP Oil Treatment	189.683	2	30	3	Piston
	*Qualified by Art Pollard					

Pocono 500 Record

Year	Car	Qual.	S	F	Speed or Laps	Reason Out
1971	Sprite	164.621	19	15	181	Flagged
1972	STP Oil Treatment	176.694	15	14	129	Rear end
1973	STP Gas Treatment	186.249	10	29	25	Valve
1974	STP Oil Treatment	182.020	3	10	188	Engine

Ontario 500 Record

Year	Car	Qual.	S	F	Speed or Laps	Reason Out
1970	Sprite	172.712	14	28	10	Piston
1971	Sprite	173.560	17	23	71	Gearbox
1972	STP Oil Treatment	182.264	32	21	108	Valve
1973	STP Oil Filter	193.632	5	1	200	Running
1974	Patrick Eagle	184.615	10	6	196	Flagged

A. J. FOYT, Houston, Texas

Indianapolis 500 Record (Passed Driver's Test 1958)

Year	Car	Qual.	S	F	Speed or Laps	Reason Out
1958	Dean Van Lines	143.130	12	16	148	Spun out
1959	Dean Van Lines	142.648	17	10	200	133.297
1960	Bowes Seal Fast	143.466	16	25	90	Clutch
1961	Bowes Seal Fast	145.907	7	1	200	139.130
1962	Bowes Seal Fast	149.074	5	23	69	Accident
1962*	Sarkes Tarzian		17	20		Starter failure
	*Rel. E. George 127-146					
1963	Sheraton-Thompson	150.615	8	3	200	142.210
1964	Sheraton-Thompson	154.672	5	1	200	147.350
1965	Sheraton-Thompson	161.233	1	15	115	Gearbox
1966	Sheraton-Thompson	161.355	18	26	0	Accident
1967	Sheraton-Thompson	166.289	4	1	200	151.207
1968	Sheraton-Thompson	166.821	8	20	86	Engine
1969	Sheraton-Thompson	170.568	1	8	181	Flagged
1970	Sheraton-Thomp ITT	170.004	3	10	195	Transmission
1971	ITT-Thompson	174.317	6	3	200	156.069
1972	ITT-Thompson	188.996	17	25	60	Engine
1973	Gilmore Racing	188.927	23	25	37	Conn. rod
1974	Gilmore Racing	191.632	1	15	142	Gearbox

Pocono 500 Record

Year	Car	Qual.	S	F	Speed or Laps	Reason Out
1971	ITT-Thompson	168.608	8	3	200	138.462
1973	Gilmore Racing	183.870	14	1	200	Running
1974	Gilmore Racing	181.415	29	27	20	Brkn. upright

Ontario 500 Record

Year	Car	Qual.	S	F	Speed or Laps	Reason Out
1970	Sheraton-Thomp ITT	174.343	7	15	131	Accident
1971	ITT-Thompson	175.618	9	16	157	Rear end
1972	ITT-Thompson	190.758	6	30	28	Gear box
1973	Gilmore Racing	191.327	26	10	191	Flagged
1974	Gilmore Racing	190.617	1	30	21	Oil leak

JERRY GRANT, Irvine, California

Indianapolis 500 Record (Passed Driver's Test 1964)

Year	Car	Qual.	S	F	Speed or Laps	Reason Out
1965	Bardahl MG Liq. Sus.	154.606	17	27	30	Magneto
1966	Bardahl Pacesetter	160.335	10	10	167	Flagged
1967	All-American Racers	163.808	30	20	162	Piston
1968	Bardahl Eagle	164.782	15	23	50	Trans. lubr. leak
1970	Nelson Iron Works	165.983	29	7	198	Flagged
1972	Mystery Eagle	189.294	15	12	188	Flagged
1973	Olsonite Eagle	190.235	18	19	77	Conn. rod bolt
1974	Cobre Firestone	181.781	17	10	175	Flagged

Ontario 500 Record

Year	Car	Qual.	S	F	Speed or Laps	Reason Out
1970	Nelson Iron Works	171.532	21	21	63	Ignition
1972	Olsonite Eagle	199.600	1	33	0	Conn. rod bolt
1973	Olsonite Eagle	194.259	2	33	1	Accident
1974	Cobre Firestone	185.150	17	3	199	Flagged

BOB HARKEY, Indianapolis, Indiana

Indianapolis 500 Record (Passed Driver's Test 1963)

Year	Car	Qual.	S	F	Speed or Laps	Reason Out
1964	Wally Weir's Mobilgas	151.573	27	8	197	Flagged
1971	Joe Hunt Magneto	169.197	32	22	77	Rear end
1973	Bryant Heating-Cooling	189.733	31	29	12	Engine
1974	Peru Circus	176.687	31	8	189	Flagged

Pocono 500 Record

Year	Car	Qual.	S	F	Speed or Laps	Reason Out
1971	MVS	160.751	31	29	39	Oil leak
1972	Niagara Falls Wine	173.001	23	29	13	Piston
1973	Norton	178.900	30	15	135	Flagged
1974	Grant King Racing	170.608	25	26	21	Clutch

Ontario 500 Record

Year	Car	Qual.	S	F	Speed or Laps	Reason Out
1970	Joe Hunt Magneto	172.307	17	17	100	Piston
1974	Cicada	No Speed	31	17	154	Gearbox

MIKE HISS, Tustin, California

Indianapolis 500 Record (Passed Driver's Test 1972)

Year	Car	Qual.	S	F	Speed or Laps	Reason Out
1972	STP-Pylon Windshield	179.015	25	7	196	Flagged
1973	Thermo-King	191.939	26	17	91	Valve
1974	Norton Spirit	187.490	2	14	158	Flagged

Pocono 500 Record

Year	Car	Qual.	S	F	Speed or Laps	Reason Out
1972	Page Racing	175.975	16	6	196	Flagged
1973	Thermo-King	184.521	12	6	191	Flagged

Ontario 500 Record

Year	Car	Qual.	S	F	Speed or Laps	Reason Out
1972	Sunoco McLaren	183.133	20	2	199	Flagged
1973	Thermo-King	190.416	19	27	28	Debris damage
1974	Eisenhour	165.001*	33	31	17	Accident
	*Qualified by Lee Brayton					

DAVID HOBBS, Upperboddington, England

Indianapolis 500 Record (Passed Driver's Test 1971)

Year	Car	Qual.	S	F	Speed or Laps	Reason Out
1971	Penske High Perf. Prod.	169.571	16	20	107	Accident
1973	Carling Black Label	189.454	22	11	107	Flagged
1974	Carling Black Label	184.833	9	5	196	Running

Pocono 500 Record

Year	Car	Qual.	S	F	Speed or Laps	Reason Out
1973	Carling Black Label	181.388	17	31	24	Engine

JIM HURTUBISE, Clermont, Indiana

Indianapolis 500 Record (Passed Driver's Test 1960)

Year	Car	Qual.	S	F	Laps	Speed or Reason Out
1960	Travelon Trailer	149.056	23	18	185	Conn. rod
1961	Demler	146.306	3	22	102	Piston
1962	Jim Robbins	146.963	29	13	200	135.655
1963	Hotel Tropicana	150.357	2	22	102	Oil leak
1964	Tombstone Life	152.542	11	14	141	Oil pressure
1965	STP Tombstone Life	156.863	20	33	1	Transmission
1966	Gerhardt	159.208	22	17	29	Overheating
1968	Pepsi Cola—Frito Lay	162.191	30	30	9	Piston
1972	Miller High Life	181.050	13	23	94	Penalty
1974	Miller High Life	180.288	28	25	31	Engine

Pocono 500 Record

Year	Car	Qual.	S	F	Laps	Speed or Reason Out
1971	Miller High Life	158.245	33	30	35	Engine
1973	Miller High Life	177.226	32	23	73	Piston
1974	Miller High Life	172.861	18	24	31	Ignition

Ontario 500 Record

Year	Car	Qual.	S	F	Laps	Speed or Reason Out
1970	Genesee	169.101	33	33	1	Accident

GORDON JOHNCOCK, Phoenix, Arizona

Indianapolis 500 Record (Passed Driver's Test 1965)

Year	Car	Qual.	S	F	Laps	Speed or Reason Out
1965	Weinberger Homes	155.012	14	5	200	146.417
1966	Weinberger Homes	161.059	6	4	200	143.084
1967	Gilmore Broadcasting	166.559	3	12	188	Spun out
1968	Gilmore Broadcasting	166.775	9	27	37	Gearbox
1969	Gilmore Broadcasting	168.626	5	19	137	Piston
1970	Gilmore Broadcasting	167.015	17	28	45	Engine
1971	Norris Industries	171.388	12	29	11	Accident
1972	Gulf McLaren	188.511	26	20	113	Valve
1973	STP Double Oil Filter	192.555	11	1	133	159.036
1974	STP Double Oil Filter	186.750	4	4	198	Flagged

Pocono 500 Record

Year	Car	Qual.	S	F	Laps	Speed or Reason Out
1971	Vollstedt	169.033	6	20	101	Fuel pump
1972	Gulf McLaren	183.457	2	22	64	Conn. rod
1973	STP Double Oil Filter	187.578	22	14	136	Accident
1974	STP Double Oil Filter	181.993	4	3	199	Flagged

Ontario 500 Record

Year	Car	Qual.	S	F	Laps	Speed or Reason Out
1970	Gilmore Broadcasting	173.385	11	4	200	155.481
1971	McLaren	178.491	7	27	51	Turbocharger
1972	Gulf McLaren	194.041	3	13	169	Accident
1973	STP Oil Treatment	197.542	3	32	3	Engine
1974	Patrick Racing Team	185.242	18	26	71	Accident

JERRY KARL, Manchester, Pennsylvania

Indianapolis 500 Record (Passed Driver's Test 1972)

Year	Car	Qual.	S	F	Laps	Speed or Reason Out
1973	Oriente Express	190.799	28	26	122	Flagged
1974	Ayr-Way/Lloyd's	181.452	19	19	115	Accident

Pocono 500 Record

Year	Car	Qual.	S	F	Laps	Speed or Reason Out
1972	Trailer Train	172.884	24	28	20	Split fuel tank
1974	Webster	171.095	24	32	4	Conn. rod

Ontario 500 Record

Year	Car	Qual.	S	F	Laps	Speed or Reason Out
1972	Oriente Express	187.454	25	29	45	Transmission
1973	Oriente Express	190.698	27	18	84	Valve spring
1974	Hopkins	180.073	11	29	32	Suspension

STEVE KRISILOFF, Parsippany, New Jersey

Indianapolis 500 Record (Passed Driver's Test 1970)

Year	Car	Qual.	S	F	Laps	Speed or Reason Out
1971	STP Gas Treatment	169.835	27	31	10	Accident
1972	Ayr-Way/Lloyd's	181.433	10	21	102	Turbocharger
1973	Elliott-Norton Spirit	194.932	7	6	129	Flagged
1974	STP Gas Treatment	182.519	15	22	72	Clutch

Pocono 500 Record

Year	Car	Qual.	S	F	Laps	Speed or Reason Out
1971	STP Gas Treatment	163.706	22	10	190	Flagged
1972	Grant King Racers	180.951	7	32	4	Block
1973	Tecumseh Comm.	188.353	6	22	67	Engine
1974	STP Gas Treatment	182.269	2	4	198	Flagged

Ontario 500 Record

Year	Car	Qual.	S	F	Laps	Speed or Reason Out
1970	Wagner Lockheed	171.895	19	29	8	Magneto
1971	STP Gas Treatment	174.089	15	5	196	Flagged
1972	R.A.C.	186.849	14	11	17	Flagged
1973	Pig Rig	191.939	11	12	184	Flagged
1974	American Kids Racer	182.223	5	24	93	Pit fire

JOHN MARTIN, Long Beach, California

Indianapolis 500 Record (Passed Driver's Test 1971)

Year	Car	Qual.	S	F	Laps	Speed or Reason Out
1972	Unsponsored	179.614	14	16	161	Fuel leak
1973	Unsponsored	194.384	24	8	124	Flagged
1974	Sea Snack Shrimp	180.406	22	11	169	Flagged

Pocono 500 Record

Year	Car	Qual.	S	F	Laps	Speed or Reason Out
1972	Unsponsored	175.529	19	17	89	Turbocharger
1973	Unsponsored	177.322	31	28	28	Ignition
1974	Unsponsored	172.323	21	16	138	Flagged

Ontario 500 Record

Year	Car	Qual.	S	F	Laps	Speed or Reason Out
1972	Lodestar Enterprises	183.878	28	32	18	Piston
1973	Unsponsored	189.934	23	5	196	Flagged
1974	Unsponsored	175.182	21	9	193	Flagged

ROGER McCLUSKEY, Tucson, Arizona

Indianapolis 500 Record (Passed Driver's Test 1961)

Year	Car	Qual.	S	F	Laps	Speed or Reason Out
1961	Racing Associates	145.068	29	27	51	Accident
1962	Bell Lines Trucking	147.759	9	16	168	Spun out
1963	Konstant Hot	148.680	14	15	198	Spun out
1965	All-American Racers	155.186	23	30	18	Clutch
1966	G. C. Murphy	159.271	21	13	129	Oil loss
1967	G. C. Murphy	165.563	22	19	165	Engine
1968	G. C. Murphy	166.976	7	29	16	Oil cooler
1969	G. C. Murphy	168.350	6	14	157	Exhaust header
1970	QuicKick	169.213	4	25	62	Crank case
1970*	Sprite *Rel. M. Kenyon			16	52	Accident
1971	Sprite	171.241	22	9	188	Flagged
1972	American Marine	182.685	20	24	92	Valve
1973	Lindsey Hopkins Buick	191.928	14	3	131	Flagged
1974	English Leather	181.005	27	16	141	Rear end

Pocono 500 Record

Year	Car	Qual.	S	F	Laps	Speed or Reason Out
1971	Sprite	164.852	18	25	79	Valve
1972	American Marine	178.434	9	11	135	Blower hose
1973	Lindsey Hopkins	182.547	16	2	199	Out of fuel
1974	English Leather	171.772	30	28	18	Overheating

Ontario 500 Record

Year	Car	Qual.	S	F	Laps	Speed or Reason Out
1970	QuicKick	171.151	24	25	26	Valve
1971	Sprite	172.686	21	28	40	Valve
1972	American Marine	189.723	8	1	200	151.540
1973	Lindsey Hopkins	194.238	7	4	199	Flagged
1974	Lindsey Hopkins Buick	179.856	9	8	193	Flagged

JIMMY McELREATH, Arlington, Texas

Indianapolis 500 Record (Passed Driver's Test 1962)

Year	Car	Qual.	S	F	Laps	Speed or Reason Out
1962	Schulz Fueling Equip.	149.025	7	6	200	138.653
1963	Bill Forbes Racing	149.744	6	6	200	140.862
1964	Studebaker STP	152.281	26	21	77	Magneto
1965	John Zink Urschel	155.878	13	20	66	Rear end
1966	Zink-Urschel-Slick	160.908	7	3	200	143.742
1967	John Zink Trackburner	164.241	11	5	197	Flagged
1968	Jim Greer	165.327	13	14	179	Stalled
1969	Jack Adams Airplanes	168.224	7	28	24	Engine
1970	Greer-Foyt	166.821	33	5	200	152.182.
1973	Norris Industries	188.640	33	23	54	Conn. rod bolt
1974	Thermo-King	177.279	30	6	194	Flagged

Pocono 500 Record

Year	Car	Qual.	S	F	Laps	Speed or Reason Out
1971	Dayton Steel Foundry	160.746	32	27	68	Valve
1973	Norris Industries	183.983	25	11	166	Ignition
1974	Thermo-King	172.175	23	23	46	Turbocharger

Ontario 500 Record

Year	Car	Qual.	S	F	Laps	Speed or Reason Out
1970	Sheraton-Thomp ITT	172.257	18	1	200	160.106
1971	Patrick Petroleum	174.969	12	8	183	Flagged
1973	Norris Industries	191.367	21	20	77	Conn. rod
1974	Thermo-King	180.777	7	15	173	Water hose

MIKE MOSLEY, Clermont, Indiana

Indianapolis 500 Record (Passed Driver's Test 1967)

Year	Car	Qual.	S	F	Laps	Speed or Reason Out
1968	Zecol-Lubaid	162.499	27	8	197	Flagged
1969	Zecol-Lubaid	166.113	22	13	162	Piston
1970	G. C. Murphy	166.651	12	21	96	Cracked block
1971	G. C. Murphy	169.579	19	13	159	Accident
1972	Vivitar	189.145	16	26	56	Accident
1973	Lodestar	198.753	21	10	120	Conn. rod bolt
1974	Lodestar	185.319	6	29	6	Engine

Pocono 500 Record

Year	Car	Qual.	S	F	Laps	Speed or Reason Out
1973	Lodestar	187.354	8	4	199	Flagged
1974	Lodestar	178.112	9	21	70	Turbocharger

Ontario 500 Record

Year	Car	Qual.	S	F	Laps	Speed or Reason Out
1970	G. C. Murphy	172.455	15	14	147	Turbocharger
1972	Vivitar	187.908	10	5	195	Transmission
1973	Lodestar	193.361	10	3	200	Running
1974	Lodestar	179.140	20	7	195	Flagged

RICK MUTHER, Laguna Beach, California

Indianapolis 500 Record (Passed Driver's Test 1968)

Year	Car	Qual.	S	F	Laps	Speed or Reason Out
1970	Tony Express	165.654	15	8	197	Flagged
1971	Arkansas Aviation	169.972	18	21	85	Accident
1974	Eisenhour	179.991	24	27	11	Piston

Pocono 500 Record

Year	Car	Qual.	S	F	Laps	Speed or Reason Out
1972	Vivitar	177.342	11	12	146	Overheating
1973	Lodestar	178.483	26	19	91	Magneto

Ontario 500 Record

Year	Car	Qual.	S	F	Laps	Speed or Reason Out
1970	Two Jacks	170.916	25	32	1	Valve
1972	Vivitar	182.990	30	16	162	Flagged
1974	Webster Racing	179.301	27	23	121	Engine

LLOYD RUBY, Wichita Falls, Texas

Indianapolis 500 Record (Passed Driver's Test 1960)

Year	Car	Qual.	S	F	Laps	Speed or Reason Out
1960	Agajanian	144.208	12	7	200	135.983
1961	Autolite	146.909	25	8	200	134.860
1962	Thompson Industries	146.520	24	8	200	138.182
1963	John Zink Trackburner	149.123	19	19	126	Accident
1964	Bill Forbes Racing	153.932	7	3	200	144.320
1965	DuPont Golden "7"	157.246	9	11	184	Engine
1966	Bardahl Eagle	162.455	5	11	166	Cam gear
1967	American Red Ball	165.229	7	33	3	Valve
1967*	Wagner Lockheed *Rel. G. Snider			26	82	Spun out
1968	Gene White Company	167.613	5	5	200	148.529
1969	Wynn's Spitfire	166.428	20	20	105	Fuel connector
1970	Daniels Cable Vision	168.895	25	27	54	Ring-pinion

Year	Car	Qual.	S	F	Laps	Speed or Reason Out
1971	Utah Stars	173.821	7	11	174	Gearbox
1972	Wynn's	181.415	11	6	196	Flagged
1973	Commander Homes	191.622	15	27	21	Piston
1974	Unlimited Racing	181.699	18	9	187	Out of fuel

Pocono 500 Record

Year	Car	Qual.	S	F	Laps	Speed or Reason Out
1971	Utah Stars	165.208	14	8	197	Flagged
1972	Wynn's	179.248	8	26	34	Accident
1973	Commander Homes	198.913	4	3	199	Flagged
1974	Unlimited Racing	176.393	12	6	197	Flagged

Ontario 500 Record

Year	Car	Qual.	S	F	Laps	Speed or Reason Out
1970	Daniels CableVision	177.567	1	23	42	Piston
1971	Utah Stars	174.376	14	4	198	Flagged
1972	Wynn's	185.635	16	17	149	Turbocharger
1973	Commander Homes	188.561	29	28	24	Accident
1974	Unlimited Racing	181.763	6	5	197	Flagged

JOHNNY RUTHERFORD, Ft. Worth, Texas

Indianapolis 500 Record (Passed Driver's Test 1963)

Year	Car	Qual.	S	F	Laps	Speed or Reason Out
1963	U.S. Equipment Co	148.063	26	29	43	Transmission
1964	Bardahl	151.400	15	27	2	Accident
1965	Racing Associates	156.291	11	31	15	Rear end
1967	Weinberger Homes	162.859	19	25	103	Accident
1968	City of Seattle	163.830	21	18	125	Fuel tank
1969	Patrick Petroleum	166.628	17	29	24	Oil leak
1970	Patrick Petroleum	170.213	2	18	135	Brkn. header
1971	Patrick Petroleum	171.151	24	18	128	Flagged
1972	Patrick Petroleum	183.234	8	27	55	Conn. rod
1973	Gulf McLaren	198.413	1	9	124	Flagged
1974	McLaren	190.446	25	1	200	158.589

Pocono 500 Record

Year	Car	Qual.	S	F	Laps	Speed or Reason Out
1971	Patrick Petroleum	165.809	12	7	197	Flagged
1972	Thermo-King	176.872	13	2	200	154.030
1973	Gulf McLaren	188.216	7	5	195	Flagged
1974	McLaren	181.424	5	1	200	156.701

Ontario 500 Record

Year	Car	Qual.	S	F	Laps	Speed or Reason Out
1970	Patrick Petroleum	176.375	3	31	5	Piston
1971	Patrick Petroleum	178.890	5	26	54	Fire
1972	Thermo-King	196.624	24	10	178	Differential
1973	Gulf McLaren	197.109	4	31	13	Accident
1974	McLaren	185.989	2	27	49	Piston

DICK SIMON, Salt Lake City, Utah

Indianapolis 500 Record (Passed Driver's Test 1970)

Year	Car	Qual.	S	F	Laps	Speed or Reason Out
1970	Bryant Heating-Cooling	165.548	31	14	168	Flagged
1971	TraveLodge		33*	14	151	Flagged
	*Qualified by J. Mahler					
1972	TraveLodge	180.424	23	13	186	Flagged
1973	TraveLodge	191.276	27	14	100	Piston
1974	TraveLodge	184.502	10	33	1	Valve

Pocono 500 Record

Year	Car	Qual.	S	F	Laps	Speed or Reason Out
1971	TraveLodge	166.057	11	17	145	Fire-spun out
1972	TraveLodge	174.412	22	16	127	Rear end
1973	TraveLodge	180.054	28	12	163	Turbo fire
1974	TraveLodge	175.584	13	29	18	Manifold

Ontario 500 Record

Year	Car	Qual.	S	F	Laps	Speed or Reason Out
1970	TraveLodge	169.747	27	3	200	159.281
1971	TraveLodge	174.884	28	22	89	Piston
1973	TraveLodge	192.102	14	22	53	Engine
1974	TraveLodge	183.355	12	28	38	Piston

GEORGE SNIDER, Bakersfield, California

Indianapolis 500 Record (Passed Driver's Test 1965)

Year	Car	Qual.	S	F	Laps	Speed or Reason Out
1965	Gerhardt	154.825	16	21	64	Rear end
1966	Sheraton-Thompson	162.521	3	19	22	Accident
1967	Wagner-Lockheed	164.256	10	26	99	Spun out
1968	Vel's Parnelli Jones	162.264	29	31	9	Valve
1969	Sheraton-Thompson	166.914	15	16	152	Flagged
1970	Sheraton-Thomp ITT	167.660	10	20	105	Suspension
1971	G. C. Murphy	171.600	21	33	6	Stalled
1972	ITT-Thompson	181.855	21	11	190	Flagged
1973	Gilmore Racing	190.355	30	12	101	Gearbox
1974	Gilmore Racing	183.993	13	28	7	Valve

Pocono 500 Record

Year	Car	Qual.	S	F	Laps	Speed or Reason Out
1971	G. C. Murphy	166.652	9	33	10	Piston
1972	MVS	176.351	29	21	68	Valve
1973	Gilmore Racing	181.205	19	25	62	Brakes
1974	Gilmore Racing	170.948	31	25	25	Radiator

Ontario 500 Record

Year	Car	Qual.	S	F	Laps	Speed or Reason Out
1971	G. C. Murphy	172.769	20	32	5	Accident
1972	MVS	182.328	22	8	192	Flagged
1973	Gilmore Racing	194.091	18	14	144	Engine
1974	Gilmore Racing	178.749	23	11	192	Flagged

AL UNSER, Albuquerque, New Mexico

Indianapolis 500 Record (Passed Driver's Test 1965)

Year	Car	Qual.	S	F	Laps	Speed or Reason Out
1965	Sheraton-Thompson	154.440	32	9	196	Flagged
1966	STP Oil Treatment	162.272	23	12	161	Accident
1967	Retzloff Chemical	164.594	9	2	198	Flagged
1968	Retzloff Chemical	167.069	6	26	40	Accident
1970	Johnny Lightning 500	170.221	1	1	200	155.749

Year	Car	Qual.	S	F	Laps	Speed or Reason Out
1971	Johnny Lightning 500	174.622	5	1	200	157.735
1972	Viceroy	183.617	19	2	200	160.192
1973	Viceroy	194.879	8	20	75	Piston
1974	Viceroy	183.889	26	18	131	Valve

Pocono 500 Record

Year	Car	Qual.	S	F	Laps	Speed or Reason Out
1971	Johnny Lightning 500	170.365	3	31	32	Oil pump
1972	Viceroy	182.981	4	3	199	Flagged
1973	Viceroy	190.567	2	33	8	Accident
1974	Viceroy	180.905	6	22	64	Conn. rod.

Ontario 500 Record

Year	Car	Qual.	S	F	Laps	Speed or Reason Out
1970	Johnny Lightning 500	175.464	4	9	186	Turbocharger
1971	Johnny Lightning 500	178.713	6	15	160	Gearbox
1972	Viceroy	191.540	4	31	20	Throttle
1973	Viceroy	194.091	9	9	191	Gearbox
1974	Viceroy	183.995	8	2	200	Running

BOBBY UNSER, Albuquerque, New Mexico

Indianapolis 500 Record (Passed Driver's Test 1963)

Year	Car	Qual.	S	F	Laps	Speed or Reason Out
1963	Hotel Tropicana	149.421	16	33	2	Accident
1964	Studebaker STP	154.865	22	32	1	Accident
1965	STP Gas Treatment	157.467	8	19	69	Oil line
1966	Vita Fresh Orange Juice	159.109	28	8	171	Flagged
1967	Rislone	164.752	8	9	193	Flagged
1968	Rislone	169.507	3	1	200	152.882
1969	Bardahl	169.683	3	3	200	154.090
1970	Wagner Lockheed	168.508	7	11	192	Flagged
1971	Olsonite Eagle	175.816	3	12	164	Accident
1972	Olsonite Eagle	195.940	1	30	31	Distributor
1973	Olsonite Eagle	198.183	2	13	100	Conn. rod bolt
1974	Olsonite Eagle	185.176	7	2	200	Running

Pocono 500 Record

Year	Car	Qual.	S	F	Laps	Speed or Reason Out
1971	Olsonite Eagle	171.847	2	9	190	Flagged
1972	Olsonite Eagle	189.473	1	20	77	Gear
1973	Olsonite Eagle	189.613	5	10	167	Clutch
1974	Olsonite Eagle	182.500	1	5	197	Flagged

Ontario 500 Record

Year	Car	Qual.	S	F	Laps	Speed or Reason Out
1970	Wagner Lockheed	173.119	12	22	45	Exhaust valve
1971	Olsonite Eagle	182.066	2	21	117	Accident
1972	Olsonite Eagle	201.374	23	24	72	Engine
1973	Olsonite Eagle	194.932	24	7	195	Flagged
1974	Olsonite Eagle	185.797	3	1	200	157.017

BILL VUKOVICH, Fresno, California

Indianapolis 500 Record (Passed Driver's Test 1968)

Year	Car	Qual.	S	F	Laps	Speed or Reason Out
1968	Wagner Lockheed	163.510	23	7	198	Flagged
1969	Wagner Lockheed	164.843	26	32	1	Brkn. rod
1970	Sugaripe Prune	165.753	30	23	78	Clutch
1971	Sugaripe Prune	171.674	11	5	200	154.563
1972	Sugaripe Prune	184.814	18	28	54	Rear end
1973	Sugaripe Prune	191.103	16	2	133	Flagged
1974	Sugaripe Prune	182.500	16	3	199	Flagged

Pocono 500 Record

Year	Car	Qual.	S	F	Laps	Speed or Reason Out
1971	Sugaripe Prune	165.104	16	5	198	Flagged
1972	Sugaripe Prune	176.912	28	4	198	Flagged
1973	Sugaripe Prune	184.228	13	24	64	Fuel pump
1974	Sugaripe Prune	172.836	19	8	194	Flagged

Ontario 500 Record

Year	Car	Qual.	S	F	Laps	Speed or Reason Out
1971	Sugaripe Prune	171.616	25	10	173	Flagged
1972	Sugaripe Prune	187.344	13	3	199	Flagged
1973	Sugaripe Prune	191.980	16	24	41	Brakes
1974	Sugaripe Prune	182.797	15	21	141	Piston

DAVID (SALT) WALTHER, Dayton, Ohio

Indianapolis 500 Record (Passed Driver's Test 1972)

Year	Car	Qual.	S	F	Laps	Speed or Reason Out
1972	Dayton Steel Wheel	180.542	27	33	0	Magneto
1973	Dayton-Walther	190.739	17	33	0	Accident
1974	Dayton-Walther	183.927	14	17	141	Piston

Pocono 500 Record

Year	Car	Qual.	S	F	Laps	Speed or Reason Out
1972	Dayton Steel Wheel	177.187	12	8	187	Flagged
1974	Dayton-Wlather	170.261	26	20	79	Transmission

Ontario 500 Record

Year	Car	Qual.	S	F	Laps	Speed or Reason Out
1972	Dayton Steel Wheel	185.104	18	6	195	Flagged
1974	Dayton-Walther	179.337	13	22	128	Engine

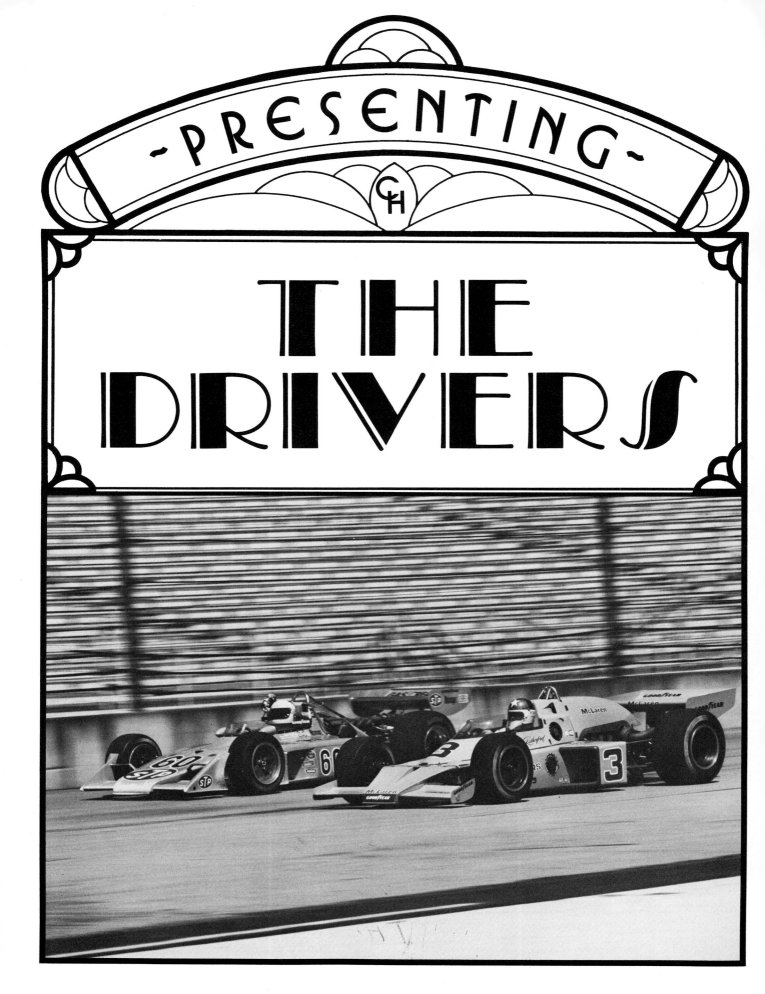

-PRESENTING-

THE DRIVERS

DRIVERS

All Driver Biographies
by Jerry Miller

Photos by Jim Chini and Harry Goode

MARIO ANDRETTI

BIRTHDATE—February 28, 1940; Hometown—Nazareth, Pa.; National Championship division 5th; Dirt Track division 2nd (tie). CAREER HIGHLIGHTS: 1965, '66 and '69 National Champion; 1967 Daytona 500 and Sebring 12 Hours (with Bruce McLaren) winner; First-place finishes: 1965 Hoosier G.P.; 1966 Milwaukee 100, Langhorne 100, Atlanta 300, Hoosier G.P., Milwaukee 200, Hoosier 100, Trenton 200, Phoenix 200; 1967 Trenton 150, IRP 150, Langhorne 150, St. Jovite 100, St. Jovite 100, Milwaukee 200, Hoosier 100, Phoenix 200; 1968 St. Jovite 100, St. Jovite 100, DuQuoin 100, Trenton 200; 1969 Hanford 200, Indianapolis 500, Pikes Peak Hill Climb, Nazareth 100, Trenton 200, Springfield 100, Trenton 300, Kent 100, Riverside 300; 1970 Castle Rock 150; 1973 Trenton 150. Sprint car wins: 9; Stock car win: 1; Midget wins: 1; Dirt Track wins: 2.

Mario Andretti has been at the racing game too long now to have many stars in his eyes.

"Racing to me is definitely a business," says a down-to-earth Andretti. "I don't feel particularly attached to any one area, although I owe a certain loyalty to USAC because this is where I got started.

"By the same token, I feel I'm a businessman and every winter I weigh out the situation and see which way to go."

The way for Mario to go in 1974 turns out to be toward Europe and the Formula I Grand Prix circuit that had sometimes turned him a little starry-eyed in the past.

Andretti, who has won big races in every conceivable type of racing car on every conceivable type of race course, has set aside 1974--and 1975, 1976 and 1977--for his full-scale assault on the Grand Prix tour, starting with the SCCA-USAC Formula 5000 Series this year and culminating, he hopes, with a World Driving Championship in at least one of the succeeding years.

"That has been my top goal since I was a kid and now I'm going to try to realize it," Mario reports, on the Formula I title try. "I've always wanted to drive the Grand Prix circuit full-time and I'm glad my chance finally came with an American team."

That team is the same one that has backed Andretti's Indy car fortunes since 1972, the super-team assembled by former 500 winner Parnelli Jones and his business associate, Vel Miletich. The Vel's-Parnelli Racing operation has provided Mario with a sparkling red-and-white Lola for the F-5000 Series and has its own Formula I car on the drawing boards at its California headquarters.

The venture into Grand Prix racing offers the possibility of several racing milestones for the 34-year-old racing star and his colleagues. Andretti, already the only driver to score victories in the Indianapolis 500, Daytona 500, 24 Hours of Daytona, a Formula I Grand Prix and a Dirt Track Championship race stands ready to become the first to capture both a USAC National Championship and a World Title.

Jones and Miletich, meanwhile, are looking to produce the first American-built Grand Prix Championship car. The two already have distinguished themselves as the owners of cars that have won three USAC national crowns and all three of USAC's Triple Crown 500-mile events.

For Andretti, the new enterprise is the pinacle of a racing career that stretches back to his native Italy, where as a 13-year-old, he raced small Formula cars.

The road led, after World War II left the Andretti family in a displaced persons camp, to America and the world of USAC oval racing. Relocated in Nazareth, Pa., Mario worked his way through the ranks quickly, taking the Sprint car and Midget circuits by storm and landing in the Indy 500 by the time he was 25.

He placed third in the 1965 Indy race and was designated "Rookie of the Year" in a year loaded with outstanding first-year drivers. Driving cars owned by the late Al Dean and tooled by veteran mechanic Clint Brawner, Andretti quickly found his winning ways on the Champ car trail.

He was the USAC National Champion in 1965 and 1966, but his biggest year in Indy car racing was yet to come. That was 1969, when he wheeled Andy Granatelli's entry to a convincing win at Indianapolis and went on to capture his third national crown.

Since then, his Indy car luck has drooped somewhat but he has made up for it with triumphs in a diversity of international racing events. He won the Daytona 500 in 1967, pulled out a last-minute win for Ferrari in the 1900 Daytona 24 Hour Enduro and demonstrated his Formula I potential by winning the pole for the 1968 U.S. Grand Prix in a Lotus and winning the South African Grand Prix and the non-points Questor Grand Prix at Ontario Motor Speedway in 1971.

With all that activity around the world, he still found time to run the Indy car circuit, picking up his 32nd USAC Champ car win at the 1973 Trenton 150. He also won two Dirt Track Championship races that season.

He'll be looking for more of the same in '74, even with one eye toward the glamor and glory of Grand Prix racing. It's still good business, and the 5-5, 140-pound racing heavyweight is a businessman, remember.

"I'm too old to have stars in my eyes," advises Andretti. "I'm pretty practical about the whole thing."

GARY BETTENHAUSEN

BIRTHDATE—November 18, 1941; HOME-TOWN: Monrovia, Ind.; National Champion-ship division 8th; Dirt Track division 17th; Stock car division 77th; Sprint car division 15th; Midget division 19th. CAREER HIGHLIGHTS: 1968 Phoenix 200 winner; 1970 Irish Hills 200 winner; 1972 Trenton 200 winner; 1973 Bryan 200 winner. En-tered Indianapolis 500 from 1968 thru 1974, Ontario 500 from 1970 thru 1974, Pocono 500 from 1971 thru 1974. Sprint Car Champion in 1969 and 1971.

When your name is Bettenhausen, you come to the Indianapolis Speed-way to settle an old score.

You come because it is the wicked and wonderful Speedway that held out its promise to your tough father for 15 years, and then took his life before he could reach it.

When you are Gary Bettenhausen, the strapping, no-nonsense son of Tony Bettenhausen, you come to the big Speedway each year to try to balance the family account. You are 31, have moved away from the family farm in Tinley Park, Ill., to get closer to the Indy track, and are but the first of Tony's three sons to take up the challenge.

You have come close in half as many years as your father spent try-ing. The 1972 race was seemingly yours; you led with less than 20 laps to go when the ignition of your Penske McLaren failed and your teammate won.

You have done your homework on the other tracks, large and small, that teach you the lessons you need to know to be a winner at Indianapolis. You have two USAC Sprint Car Cham-pionships under your belt, as well as Indy car victories from New Jersey to Texas, Michigan to Arizona.

You have come a long way, when your name is Bettenhausen. You've

had to live with the extra scrutiny the son of a famous father receives when he sets out to race.

You have had to overcome history to make your own name on the race tracks of America. "If you want to do something badly enough, it doesn't matter who you are or what your name is," you say now, having estab-lished just how badly you want it.

You have learned to *live* racing to the hilt, just as your father did before you. "I wouldn't quit racing, even if I won Indy five times, the way I feel right now," you say, with a mixture of enthusiasm and determination.

You have the physical tools now to get the job done. Roger Penske is your car owner and his cars are among the best in any type of racing. Your skills have matured in a dozen solid years of racing week in and week out to know what to do with that car.

You have the moral support, too. Your brothers share your dream. Mid-dle brother, Merle, though he lost an arm on the way, still wants what you want. So does youngest brother, Tony Lee, living in Texas and coming up through the NASCAR ranks.

"It's not so much running against my brothers," is how young Tony expresses the trio of hopes. "It's more having the goal of having all three of us in one race at Indianapolis.

"I'd just like to see one of us win it, to have a Bettenhausen in Victory Lane."

So, it is up to you, the eldest son. You have come up the way your father did. You drove everything with wheels on it, from go-karts to Stock cars, Midgets and Sprint cars to the Indianapolis cars.

You are already a well-rounded racing veteran, a big name on the racing trail. You'll race this year in the Indy car races, in the NASCAR Grand Nationals with Penske's red-white-and-blue Matador, and on the Sprint car circuit, when there's time.

You'll win there from time to time. You've already won 29 USAC Sprint car races and 19 Midget races, in addition to your four Indy car triumphs. You have finished fifth at Indianapolis, last year, third in the Indy facsimile at Ontario, Cal., two years before that, and sixth at the other 500 at Pocono, Pa., the same year.

But until you win the big one in Indiana, you haven't done what you set out to do. You have a score to settle, and you have your own special, personal reasons for coming back each

May to the Speedway they call In-dianapolis.

When your name is Bettenhausen, you come to find the end of the rainbow.

EDITOR'S NOTE: Shortly after writer Jerry Miller submitted the fore-going story on Gary Bettenhausen, he was involved in a horrendous crash while "hot lapping" his Championship Dirt car in preparation for a qualifica-tion run at Syracuse, N.Y. on July 4.

Gary sustained a pair of broken collar bones, a shattered right thumb and his left arm was left limp as a result of the multi-flip accident. Ob-servers credited the now mandatory roll-cage assembly utilized on Dirt cars with saving the eldest Bettenhausen's life.

Upon hearing news of his brother's accident, brother Merle, who had lost his right arm in his first Championship start two years prior, announced his retirement from the sport as a driver. Merle had recuperat-ed fully from his fiery and limb-taking crash and was successfully driving again. At the time of Gary's accident, Merle was running second in points in the competitive USAC Midget division and was a threat to win any race on the schedule.

TOM BIGELOW

BIRTHDATE—October 31, 1939; Home-town—Whitewater, Wis.; National Cham-pionship division 25th; Dirt Track division 2nd (tie); Sprint car division 7th; Midget division 21st. CAREER HIGHLIGHTS: 1969 Overall winner Astro Grand Prix; Entered Ontario 500 in 1973 and 1974; Indianapolis 500 in 1974; Pocono 500 in 1973 and 1974. Midget wins: 12; Sprint wins: 8. Dirt Track wins: 1.

You can call Tom Bigelow a "rookie" over at the Indianapolis 500 track if you want, but you couldn't do it anywhere else along the racing trail.

Bigelow, a 34-year-old Whitewater, Wis. product, has been one of USAC racing's most successful and popular "veterans" for quite some time now. He has demonstrated he knows where the winner's circle is, even if 1974 was his first start in the big one called Indy.

In fact, Tom was USAC's most productive winner during the 1972 season. That was the year he recorded 11 wins, seven in the Midgets, three in Sprint cars, and one on the Dirt Track Championship circuit.

Though he first came to USAC racing in 1965, Bigelow has made his presence felt most effectively over the past two or three seasons. He emerged as a big winner on the Midget circuit in 1969, taking the overall championship at the initial Astrodome Midget program.

Since then, he has piled up 12 feature wins in the Midgets. His victory totals in the Sprint cars, where he has gradually worked his way into a full-time role, are catching up rapidly --nine feature victories there, including this year's Indy Sprints card at Raceway Park.

On the USAC Dirt Championship trail, Tom took a win at DuQuoin in 1972 and placed fourth in the point standings. For 1973, he tied Mario Andretti for runnerup honors in the Dirt standings, a third in the Hoosier Hundred giving him the deadlocking points.

Bigelow is no rookie in Indy car racing, either. He has logged 24 Champ car starts since 1968, including the 1973 Pocono 500 and 1973 California 500, where he finished 11th. He placed 10th in the 1974 500-miler at Ontario.

But at Indy, he still wore rookie's stripes before this May's event. Tom qualified Rolla Vollstedt's entry in 1973 but was the victim of an 11th-hour run by Jim McElreath that left him on the sidelines as first alternate. Bigelow was at the wheel of another Vollstedt/Offy this May when he erased the rookie label forever.

Indy fans also learned something of Bigelow's immense popularity at those other stops on the racing circuit. The winning has something to do with it, of course, but so does the unfaltering willingness to stick around after a race, shaking hands, signing autographs, and chatting with his legions of fans.

"I'm a race driver--that's what I do for a living," explains Bigelow,

"and it's those people in the stands who allow me to do that. If you start forgetting about the fans, then you're not going to last very long."

That should tell you that Tom Bigelow was never really a "rookie" to begin with.

LARRY CANNON

BIRTHDATE—April 13, 1937; Hometown —Danville, Ill.; National Championship division 33rd; Sprint car division 13th; Midget division 56th. CAREER HIGHLIGHTS: Entered 1974 Indianapolis 500. Sprint wins: 4. Midget wins: 1.

There is a general tendency to think of Larry Cannon as basically a Dirt Track driver. But he's beginning to get the hang of racing on pavement these days.

"I had to work real hard on getting used to the pavement," advises Larry, "but I think I'm learning."

The records back up Larry there. On the Sprint car trail, where he spends much of his racing time, his statistics on the tougher paved ovals, like Winchester and Salem, have changed from missed features to top 10 finishes over the past few seasons.

And, of course, Larry made the grade this May at the Indianapolis Speedway, which at last report was still a paved track.

Cannon gained his Dirt Track reputation on the small dust bowls around his hometown, Danville, Ill. Both he and his younger brother, Steve, learned the ins and outs of dirt tracking there before making the move to the USAC Sprint and Midget circuits.

Larry, 37, came to USAC late in 1968 and it didn't take him long to flaunt his dirt track talents. He won a Sprint feature at Eldora in 1969 and placed 10th in the season point standings.

He posted Sprint victories at Tri-County (before it was paved) and Reading in 1971, then won at Gardena, Cal. in 1972 on his way to a fifth-place finish in the point standings. He also captured a USAC Midget feature at Springfield in 1969.

In Indy car competition, Larry ran four events in 1973, with an 11th in one of the Michigan International 125s his best finish.

DUANE CARTER JR.

BIRTHDATE—November 6, 1950; Hometown—Huntington Beach, Cal.; Midget division 9th; Dirt Track division 10th; Sprint car division 6th. CAREER HIGHLIGHTS: USAC Midget Champion 1972; Entered 1974 Indianapolis 500 and Pocono 500; 1974 Indianapolis 500 "Rookie of the Year". Midget wins: 12; Sprint car wins: 5.

If you could buy stock in racing drivers, it probably would pay to pick up a few shares in Duane Carter Jr.

"Pancho," at the age of 23, has already established himself as one of the real "growth" stocks on racing's big board.

In less than three full seasons in USAC racing, he has proved to be more bullish on racing than Merrill, Lynch, Pierce, Fenner and Smith are on America.

The curly-haired young Californian comes by it naturally. His father, Duane Sr., put in a lot of miles on the racing trail, winning the AAA Midwest

Sprint car crown in 1950 and running in the Indy 500 11 times.

Pancho has logged a few miles, too. At the age of 5, he was in quarter-midgets and, as a teenager, he was trying his hand at three-quarter Midgets before tackling the full-size Midgets on the West Coast.

Pancho came to USAC racing late in 1971, as soon as he turned 21, and the following season, his first full one, he won the club's national Midget championship. He won eight features during 1972, including a couple of the bigger ones on the calendar, the "Night Before the 500" race at the Indiana State Fairgrounds and the "Hut 100" at Terre Haute.

In 1973, Pancho split his time between the Midgets and the USAC Sprint cars. He didn't win either championship, but his total of nine feature wins--five in Sprints, four in Midgets--made him the winningest driver in USAC that season.

Carter, who graduated from California State College in Long Beach in 1973 with a degree in business administration, then pulled one of the great coups of Indy car history, coming to the 500 Speedway in 1974 with no previous Champ car experience and landing a ride on the Cobre team of Phoenix businessman Bob Fletcher.

Fletcher must know a little bit about the stock market. By hiring the Huntington Beach bachelor, he may have been investing in one of racing's blue chip stocks of the future.

JIMMY CARUTHERS

BIRTHDATE—January 18, 1945; HOMETOWN: Anaheim, Cal.; National Championship division 21st; Midget division 13th. CAREER HIGHLIGHTS: USAC Midget Champion 1970; Entered Indianapolis 500 from 1972 thru 1974, Ontario 500 from 1971 thru 1974, Pocono 500 from 1971 thru 1974. Midget wins: 12; Sprint car wins: 5.

You can guess from his last name that Jimmy Caruthers has been involved with Midget racing at some time in his life.

Most of his life, in fact. Jimmy was racing quarter-midgets almost before he had learned his multiplication tables. That's normal for a Caruthers--a family that thrives on Midget racing.

Doug Caruthers, Jimmy's father, has been a Midget car owner for over 25 years, with drivers from Bill Vukovich (Sr.) to Billy Vukovich (Jr.) wheeling his finely-crafted yellow Midget cars. "Red" Caruthers, Jim's uncle, has also gained a reputation as a Midget car owner, introducing Volkswagen power to the winner's circle in 1973.

Jimmy himself, of course, was the USAC Midget Champion in 1970. His younger brother, Danny, was champion the next year but was tragically killed in a Midget crash at the close of the season.

So, Midget racing has been a way of life for Jimmy for a long time. From the age of seven on, he got the feeling for racing in the Quarters, taking on such tow-head racers as Bruce Walkup and Johnny Parsons. When he reached 16, he moved up to the full-sized Midget action, with a few Stock cars thrown in.

His rapid rise in the Midget ranks was interrupted in 1967 when the U.S. Army called on him for his services. While Jimmy kept up his racing as a serviceman, his discharge saw him more than ready to race to his own drummer, instead of Uncle Sam's.

"I'll take racing to the Army, anytime," chirped the young Anaheim, Cal. racer shortly after his tour of duty. "I really didn't like taking orders from someone else all the time."

He quickly established his own pace on the USAC Midget trail, taking the championship in his second full season in a close battle with veteran campaigner Dave Strickland. He was runnerup to Danny the next season, as the Caruthers brothers totally dominated that brand of racing.

He had also been involved in the bigger USAC cars, debuting at Springfield in '70. His career took a sharp turn upward when Clint Brawner, one

of Indy racing's legendary chief mechanics, took him under his wing on the Champ car scene.

In Brawner's car, Jimmy made the 1972 Indy 500, starting 31st and finishing ninth. He has been a regular starter at Indy--and Pocono and Ontario and Phoenix and so on--ever since, and the fun-loving 29-year-old headed into Indy '74 second to Bobby Unser in the early points race on the strength of fourths at Ontario and Trenton.

His status as Indy car super-star of the near-future hasn't kept Jimmy from keeping up his other pursuits--like riding motorcycles, flying airplanes or helicopters and racing Midgets. He managed to find time to win a pair of Midget features in 1973, pushing his career total to 18.

But then, the name is Caruthers, remember?

WALLY DALLENBACH

BIRTHDATE—December 12, 1936; HOMETOWN: East Brunswick, N.J.; National Championship division 2nd; Midget division 61st. CAREER HIGHLIGHTS: 1973 Milwaukee 200, Ontario 100, Ontario 500 winner; Entered Indianapolis 500 from 1968 thru 1974, Ontario 500 from 1970 thru 1974, Pocono 500 from 1971 thru 1974.

Persistence paid off for Wally Dallenbach.

Dallenbach, the former jalopy driver from East Brunswick, New Jersey, struggled through 89--count 'em, 89--Champ car races without that first victory. A few near-misses and a few not-quites, yes. But trips to the winner's circle, no.

Then all of a sudden (but not really), Wally was a winner. Not once.

Not twice. Three times. . .three times in a row!

For those who believe in the pioneer spirit of dogged determination, it was something to behold. There was Wally, finally with a good car and a little luck, taking a win in the Milwaukee 200, then the 100-mile qualifier at Ontario, and then, best of all, the 1973 California 500 with its top prize of over $100,000.

So, how come? Why do the tables suddenly turn after 89 races and deal out three straight winning hands?

"This win proved what I've felt deep down inside all along," Wally said after the Milwaukee triumph. "I knew I had the capability of finishing first if I could ever get a good ride and have a little luck."

"I'm the same race driver I always was," he added later. "It's George and the team and the equipment that have made the difference."

George, of course, is the one named Bignotti, USAC Championship racing's winningest chief mechanic, and the team was the Patrick Racing operation. Dallenbach joined up with the stable after the 1973 Indy 500--won by Patrick-Bignotti driver Gordon Johncock--and the combination apparently sparked the kind of magic that had always eluded Wally in his eight and one-half years of Indy car campaigning.

The easy-going, soft-spoken Garden Stater started out on the racing road in 1952, driving Modifieds, Stock cars and Drag Racers in the East. By 1964, he was expanding his repertoire to include Midgets and Sprint cars, including some stops in USAC territory.

Then, in 1965, he made his first try at the Indy type cars at Langhorne. He went on trying 88 more times, showing flashes of promise along the way only to be thwarted by mechanical ills and rotten luck.

His luck, ironically, was at its best and worst at his "home" track, Trenton. He invariably would lead at Trenton whenever the big cars raced there, but victory always slipped away. Still, he picked off two seconds and a third between 1968 and 1972.

In the same span, Dallenbach recorded runnerup finishes at Phoenix and Michigan International and a pair of thirds at Langhorne.

In the 500-milers on the Championship calendar, he had not fared so well. Driving for first Tassi Vatis, then Lindsey Hopkins, then Andy Granatelli, then Dan Gurney, Wally could

do no better than 14th in the order in seven shots at Indy, three at Ontario, and two at Pocono before hooking up with the Patrick Racing operation. He didn't do any better at first, placing 29th at Pocono in '73, but his three-straight string turned it all around.

Dallenbach and Johncock dominated the 1973 season in their flame-red Patrick Eagles. Wally added a second at Phoenix and a third back at Trenton to his three wins to finish second in the season's Championship point standings.

It had to be a dream come true for the 37-year-old racer who admittedly had thought about giving up his hopes for the winner's circle. Persistence finally paid off in trips to that circle, big prize money, and even restful nights for Wally Dallenbach.

"You wouldn't believe how much difference it makes in your life, how much better you sleep at night," said Wally, the winner.

A. J. FOYT

BIRTHDATE—January 16, 1935; Hometown—Houston, Tex.; National Championship division 10th; Stock car division 15th; CAREER HIGHLIGHTS: 1960, '61, '63, '64 and '67 National Champion; 1961, '64 and '67 Indianapolis 500 winner; 1960 Eastern Sprint Champion; 1967 LeMans 24 Hours winner (with Dan Gurney); 1968 Stock Car Champion; 1972 Dirt Track Champion; 1973 Pocono 500 winner; All-Time Championship point leader; All-Time USAC Championship standings: 1st. Stock car wins: 28; Midget wins: 20; Sprint car wins: 26; Dirt wins: 2. First race—1953 at Houston, Tex.

Pulling his punches has never been A.J. Foyt's style--on the race track or off.

That is what has made him the best-loved, best-hated (in the sporting sense), most successful, most controversial, most quoted, and least quotable driver in the history of American auto racing. Whatever else he may be, A.J. is never wishy-washy, as a driver or a sports personality.

His racing statistice prove that. Foyt's passion for winning has produced a list of racing achievements unequaled by any driver who has raced in the Indianapolis 500.

The straight-shooter from Houston, Tex. has won 46 Indy car Championship races in his career, more than any other driver. He has also won seven NASCAR Grand National Stock car races, 28 USAC Stock car races, 28 USAC Sprint car features, 20 USAC Midget features and two USAC Dirt Championship races.

He is the only driver to ever win five USAC National Driving Championships. He is the only driver to win USAC titles in four different divisions -- Indy cars, Stocks, Dirt Track and Eastern Sprints.

He is one of only four drivers to win the Indianapolis 500 three times. He is also the first American driver to earn over a million dollars in racing prize money.

That doesn't leave A.J. too many new mountains to climb. But there is one big one he wants to scale in the worst possible way. He wants to become the first driver ever to have his head engraved on Indy's Borg-Warner trophy four times.

"My biggest thrill in racing will be when I win that one for the fourth time," says Foyt, looking toward Indy. "I'll never retire until I win number four."

The importance of that racing goal comes into focus when you ask about another milestone he has a shot at--becoming the first driver to win all three of USAC's Triple Crown 500-milers. "That don't mean anything--I want Indy," he says, with characteristic bluntness.

Foyt, whether he wants it or not, would only have to win the California 500 to collect that secondary accomplishment, having won at Indy and Pocono in past years.

In addition to countless race victories, Foyt has amassed a reputation for saying what's on his mind--when he's in a mood to talk--over the 22 years he's been racing cars. His words often range from harsh to humorous.

For example, he has been outspoken on an incident that took place during the 1973 Indy 500. The Indy crowd, usually in his corner, booed the 39-year-old racing star when he took over a team car driven by George Snider after his own car broke down.

"You know, that's something that really hurts you—when people boo you when they think you've pulled a driver out of a car," A.J. said. "I know that's what the fans thought happened, but it isn't.

"George came in when the race was stopped for Savage's accident and asked me to take the car. I think the accident kinda got to him and he just didn't feel like going.

"After all those wrecks, you know, I really didn't give a damn about getting in that car myself."

On the other hand, he can be downright playful, like when he and Roger McCluskey split a USAC double-header at Michigan last year and someone asked them how it felt to be winning "at their age."

"Hey, what'ya mean, at our age?" Foyt snapped, with mock indignation. "I didn't come here to be insulted."

"Anyway," he added, breaking into a wide smile, "I'm still younger than Roger."

Age has been no barrier to the reaching of new heights for Foyt. This May, he established a new record for most Indy 500 starts, 17, a standard he presumably will keep working on in pursuit of that equally unprecedented fourth victory.

The list of Foyt accomplishments could go on, and probably will. He won the 1967 24 Hours of LeMans with Dan Gurney. He won the pole position at Indy in 1974, his third time in that coveted position.

He also was the pole winner at Ontario for '74 in the Coyote/Foyt he and his father built from the ground up in their Houston shop.

Whatever there has been to do in auto racing, A.J. Foyt has done it. And he has no immediate plans to quit punching more holes in the racing record books.

"As long as my eyes hold out, I'm going to keep right on racing," A.J. reports, still not pulling any punches, "because I really love it."

EDITOR'S NOTE: As we go to press, word has just come from Talladega, Alabama that A.J. Foyt has just put another notch in his long handle of auto racing records: Foyt established a new world's closed course speed record on August 3 of 217.854 mph in his Coyote Indianapolis 500 car.

JERRY GRANT

BIRTHDATE—January 23, 1935; Hometown—Irvine, Cal.; FIA license driver. CAREER HIGHLIGHTS: Entered Indianapolis 500 from 1965 thru 1968 and 1970 thru 1974; Ontario 500 in 1970 and 1972 thru 1974.

Every year at the Indy 500 Victory Banquet, big Jerry Grant concludes his speech by smiling, leaning toward the microphone, and saying, "I guarantee you we will be heard from in the future."

That may leave his fellow competitors a little bewildered--they have been hearing a lot from Jerry on the race track for some time now.

The big, 6-2 and 200 pounds driver from Seattle has already made quite a bit of noise in racing--winning Sports car races, cracking the 200-mph barrier in an Indy car, or almost winning the 1972 Indianapolis 500. Off the track, he is also known for wearing racing's most famous toupee.

The 39-year-old racer got his start driving Midgets and Modified hardtops in the Seattle area. He advanced to Sports cars and, during the 1961 and 1962 seasons, went undefeated in 27 straight races throughout the Pacific Northwest.

He became "Driver of the Year" in the SCCA's Northwest division in 1963.

His career as an Indy 500 driver goes back to 1965, when he qualified for his first start at the Brickyard. He's been a regular starter since then, missing only the '69 and '71 lineups, driving mostly for the man with the Eagles, Dan Gurney.

It was at the wheel of Gurney's "Mystery Eagle" that Grant nearly took the big prize at Indy in 1972. He

was battling Mark Donohue for the lead with just 12 laps to go when he was forced to make an extra pit stop for a tire change.

Jerry returned to the track and was second under the checkered flag behind winner Donohue. But Speedway officials later ruled that the fuel hoses from teammate Bobby Unser's fuel tank had been hooked up to Grant's car during that final pit stop and took away his final 12 laps, dropping his to 12th place in the official standings.

That was the first year Jerry made his banquet remarks about being heard from in the future. It was also the year he became the first driver to officially record a 200-mph lap in a USAC Indy car, putting Gurney's Eagle/Offy on the pole at Ontario with a top lap at 201.414 mph.

Grant never got around to taking the green flag for the Ontario 500-miler, though, as a connecting rod bolt broke on the pace lap.

Jerry continued to make his presence felt at various stops on the Championship circuit in '72 and '73. And, heading for Indianapolis in 1974 as the stand-in for the injured Lee Kunzman on the Cobre Racing stable after finishing third at Ontario two months earlier, there was little doubt that he was already being heard from on the Indy car scene.

But, apparently, Jerry doesn't intend to settle for anything less than being heard accepting the biggest paycheck of them all at one of those Indy 500 Victory Banquets someday soon.

BOB HARKEY

BIRTHDATE—June 23, 1930; Hometown—Indianapolis, Ind. CAREER HIGHLIGHTS: Entered Indianapolis 500 in 1964, '71, '73 and '74; Ontario 500 in 1970 and '74; Pocono 500 1971 thru 1974. Midget wins: 1. First race—1949 (Stock car).

When Bob Harkey isn't out on a race track somewhere, you'll probably have to look to the skies to find him.

Airplanes have been at least a second love for Harkey, if not his first. The veteran racer has done his share of stints as a stunt pilot and has done some parachute jumping when the occasion called for it.

On the racing front, Bob, a native of Charlotte, North Carolina, started out racing Roadsters around nearby Gastonia in 1949. It wasn't long, though, before he took to the Midget circuits, where he made a name for himself in the mid-50s.

Harkey was UMRA champion in 1956 and 1957, as well as NASCAR Midget king in '57. He was NASCAR's Florida Midget champ in 1958. He also picked up a USAC Midget feature victory along the way.

His Indy career has been somewhat rocky, like a sky-diver with a balky rip-cord. He made his first 500 start with Wally Weir's Roadster, starting 27th and driving steadily to finish eighth.

But his chute failed to open at the Brickyard for the next seven years. He qualified cars in both 1967 and 1968, but was bumped from the field at the last minute each time.

That routine was almost repeated in 1971, as Bob sweated out the final minutes of qualifying as the driver on the "bubble," 33rd fastest in the Indy field with Joe Hunt's black No. 99. But he survived and made his second start, dropping out with rear-end problems after 77 laps.

Bob failed to qualify the next year, but was back in the show in 1973 with one of Lindsey Hopkins' entries. The car failed early on, but Hopkins gave Harkey another shot for 1974, expalining, "We didn't do a very good job for Bob last year."

Harkey, who now lives in Indianapolis, has also been a regular competitor on the USAC Dirt Championship circuit, finishing eighth in the 1971 season's standings.

The 43-year-old racer-airman also competed in the Pocono 500, 1971-73, and the California 500, 1970 and 1974.

MIKE HISS

BIRTHDATE—July 7, 1941; HOMETOWN: Tustin, Cal.; National Championship division 14th. CAREER HIGHLIGHTS: 1972 Indianapolis 500 "Rookie of the Year"; 1972 Championship division "Rookie of the Year." Entered Indianapolis 500 from 1972 thru 1974, Ontario 500 in 1972 and 1973, Pocono 500 in 1972 and 1973.

In 1972, Mike Hiss got more "exposure" than any rookie driver in the history of USAC Championship racing. And not all of it was on the race track.

Hiss, a tall, sandy-haired road racer from Tustin, Cal., made plenty of headlines that year with his on-track exploits. But none of them caused quite the stir his appearance as a nude centerfold in a national magazine did.

The centerfold photo, shot in late '72 and published in **Playgirl** magazine in early '73, added a new dimension to Hiss' racing career, one that he admittedly almost backed out of, so to speak.

"I hesitated quite a bit before I did it, and talked it over with everybody who might be involved," Hiss reveals. "It was really funny, a lot of them actually encouraged me to do it--the tire people and some of the sponsors."

And, when it was all said and done, the end apparently justified the means. "Everybody seemed to like it; most of the people I talked to said they did, anyway," Hiss reports.

Mike, born in Norwalk, Conn., first took to the race tracks in sports cars at Eastern road races in 1965. Seven seasons of ever-improving results in SCCA Sports cars and Formula A/5000 and he made the big move to the Indy car scene.

He promptly became "Rookie of the Year" at Indianapolis, driving from 25th starting spot to a seventh-place finish. He kept up the good work at Pocono, placing sixth in the Page Racing Eagle, and at Ontario, where he wheeled Roger Penske's Sunoco McLaren to second place behind winner Roger McCluskey.

Hiss compiled 1,665 points that season, good enough for sixth place on the USAC point standings ladder and "Rookie of the Year" honors on the Championship Trail.

Hiss, whose wife, Arlene, is something of a Sports car racer helself out in California, had a reasonable amount of success in his second season in Indy cars, despite encountering more mechanical setback than usual. He drove the Gerhardt Thermo-King Eagle to third-place finishes in a 100-mile qualifier at Ontario and one of the Michigan International 125s in 1973.

For '74, Mike joined the Penske stable again, replacing the late Peter Revson in one of the Penske McLarens for the Indy 500. The 32-year-old racer appeared to be in a good position to create a few more shock waves in his sport--on the race track, not in a girlie magazine for girls.

"I don't think I'll be doing any more nudes," advises a grinning Mike Hiss, ". . .not for awhile, anyway."

DAVID HOBBS

BIRTHDATE—June 9, 1939; Hometown—Upper Boddington, England; FIA license driver.

In case you hadn't noticed, David Hobbs is British.

In fact, he is **very** British. The bloomin' accent, tells you that. So do the wry wit and tweedy charm, reminiscent of Graham Hill. The only great departure from the Hill tradition is the mustache, which is considerably bushier than Graham's pencil-thin lip garden.

David's racing roots are precisely what you would expect from a lad from Upper Boddington--"That's just north of Lower Boddington, of course," he advises. Driving Sports cars and Formula cars on the great road courses of Europe and America has always been his forte.

The 34-year-old Briton who answers to the name of "Dye-vid Ahbbs" began his racing career in 1959, driving a small Sports car to test his father's invention, the "Hobbs Mechamatic Transmission." He moved through the Sports car and Formula car ranks steadily until he burst onto the international racing scene in 1968.

In the process of rising to the top rungs of the racing ladder, Hobbs drove for some of the most famous racing operations around--Reg Parnell, John Wyer, Penske Racing, Stirling Moss, Carl Haas, Team Surtees, Hogan Racing, Team McLaren.

His Sports car credits include third-place finishes at the 24-hour enduros of LeMans and Daytona, victories in the Monza 1,000km and Six Hours of Nurburgring, and a score of top placings in the Canadian-American Challenge Cup (Can-Am) series. In Formula racing, he has competed in a variety of Formula One and Two events in Europe, but Americans are most familiar with him as the most successful Formula 5000 Continental Series competitor in the history of the Formula.

In five years in the North American Formula Series, first known as Formula A, Hobbs has won the most races, scored the most points, and recorded the most top qualifying laps of any driver. He and Canadian John Cannon were responsible for much of the early success of the Series with their spine-tingling duels for supremacy in 1969 and 1970. Hobbs was the 1971 F-5000 Continental Champion and will again be one of the top contenders in the '74 Series.

But, with all his Road-racing talents and accomplishments, the 6-1 curly-haired Englishman who looks just a little like the great British blues singer Joe Cocker has an appreciation of the kind of racing they do at Indianapolis, where he ran in 1971 for Penske Racing and in 1973 with the Roy Woods Eagle. He made that clear as he headed for the 500 Speedway in 1974 as driver of the second Team McLaren entry.

"I'd dearly love to win Indy," said David. "The money is marvelous and it's **the** race in America. I'm terrifically lucky and awfully glad to be going back there and this time in a new McLaren.

"McLaren's got to be my lucky open-wheeler," added the only foreign driver in the '74 Indy lineup. "The last time I drove a McLaren single-seater, I won. That was in Australia, driving a car the factory lent me for the Tasman Championship."

But, of course--David Hobbs in a Team McLaren car. You can't get any more British than that.

JIM HURTUBISE

BIRTHDATE—December 5, 1932; Hometown—Clermont, Ind.; Stock car division 71st. CAREER HIGHLIGHTS: 1960 Indianapolis 500 "Rookie of the Year"; 1959 Sacramento 100 winner; 1960 Langhorne 100 winner; 1961 Springfield 100 winner; 1962 Springfield 100 winner; Entered Indianapolis 500 from 1960 thru 1966; 1968, 1972 and 1973; Ontario 500 in 1970; Pocono 500 in 1971, '73 and '74. Stock car wins: 3; Sprint car wins: 18. First race—1951 at New York (Stock car).

It must be tough being a legend in your own time--you'd never know what to do for an encore.

But Jim Hurtubise, one of American auto racing's true living legends, never seems to run out of ways to nourish his standing as "people's choice" at the Indianapolis 500 and other big races across the country. It just comes natural to the man who came back from a near-fatal crash in 1964 and later stubbornly defended the virtues of his beloved front-engine roadster.

Hurtubise has been accumulating his legion of fans ever since he came out of North Tonawanda, N.Y., to attack the Sprint car circuits in the late '50s in his own aggressive, gutsy style. He was already gaining a reputation there when he moved up to the big Speedway on West 16th Street and brought the house down in typical Hurtubise fashion.

A rookie qualifying for the 500 usually isn't a big deal, but young Jim shocked the stopwatch watchers in 1960 with an average speed of almost 150 mph. That was a magical barrier in those days and almost three miles an hour faster than Eddie Sachs' pole speed.

The legend of Jim Hurtubise had been born. He sat on the front row at Indy two of the next three years, breaking through the 150 mph barrier with Parnelli Jones in 1963.

Then, in the summer of '64, Jim's Indy car crashed in flames at Milwaukee. Pulled from the wreckage, he was badly burned and barely alive, and doctors gave him no chance of ever driving a race car again.

In fact, the doctors told Jim his flame-ravaged hands would have to be set in a fixed position. Jim calmly told them to set them to fit the contours of a race car's steering wheel.

The doctors were skeptical. Hurtubise insisted. The doctors did as they were told.

Less than a year later, those painfully stiff hands were wrapped around the steering wheel of a mighty Novi and racing in the Indy 500. The doctors were wrong, and racing fans couldn't be happier.

That made Hurtubise a super-hero on the racing scene, but he wasn't done yet. In 1967, he began a one-man crusade to save the honor of the old front-engine roadster in the wake of the new low-slung and fragile rear-engine Indy cars.

While he managed to qualify for only one of the next four Indy races, Hurtubise had demonstrated just how deep his dedication to the endangered species of race car went. "I didn't mind the rear-engines, really, but I decided I wanted to build something better," he would say, in defense of his Mallard roadster.

"If I didn't think it could win, I wouldn't monkey with it."

But finally, in 1972, even Don Quixote had to admit that tilting at windmills wasn't the same as competing in races. So Jim went to a rear-engine car and easily qualified for his ninth Indy start.

He ran out of fuel in that race, took a short-cut through the infield, and was eventually penalized to a 23rd-place finish. He was back in 1973, but was still in the qualifying line when the 6 p.m. gun sounded.

While he was making the switch to the rear-engines, Jim also stepped up the pace of his Indy car and Stock car activities. Moving his wife and family from New York to the Indianapolis area in the fall of '72, racing's living legend pledged to keep the legend going at USAC and NASCAR tracks throughout a full season of racing.

"It's been a nice vacation," said the 41-year-old Hurtubise. "I've spent a lot of time with the wife and kids and done a lot of fishin', but now it's time to go back to work."

GORDON JOHNCOCK

BIRTHDATE—August 5, 1936; Hometown —Phoenix, Ariz.; National Championship division 7th; Stock car division 29th. CAREER HIGHLIGHTS: 1965 Milwaukee 200 winner; 1967 Milwaukee 150, Hanford 200 winner; 1968 Hanford 200, Langhorne 150 winner; 1969 Castle Rock 150, Brainerd 100 winner; 1973 Indianapolis 500, Trenton 200, Phoenix 150 winner. Sprint car wins: 1; Stock car wins: 2. First race—1955 in Hastings, Mich. (Super Modified).

There are two kinds of racing drivers--chargers and strokers. There has never been much doubt about which kind Gordon Johncock is.

"I've never really believed in stroking it," says the 1973 Indianap-olis 500 winner. "Some guys lay back and wait for the hot cars to break down, then they come along and move in. That's not my idea of racing."

Charging has always been Johncock's idea of racing, from the time he began racing Stock cars and Super-modifieds around Hastings, Michigan, back in 1955 to his super-successful 1973 season in USAC Championship cars. He has demonstrated at every turn in the road that he believes it's who's up front that counts.

He proved it in Stock cars and Sprint cars before he burst onto the Indy car scene in 1965. He finished "first in class" that year at Indianapolis, bringing the Weinberger Homes roadster home fifth behind four of the new rear-engine Speedway cars.

Any other year, that would have made him "Rookie of the Year" at the 500. But another promising newcomer by the name of Mario Andretti was in the same race and finished two spots ahead of him.

In 1966, Gordon joined the rear-engine brigade at Indy and moved up to a fourth-place finish.

Away from the Brickyard, the 5-5, curly-haired frontrunner was charging into the winner's circle early and often. His first season, 1965, he won at Milwaukee. Through the succeeding three campaigns, he repeated at Milwaukee, won twice at Hanford, and took a checkered at Langhorne.

Then, in 1969, he attacked Road Racing with equal fervor and success, winning at Castle Rock and Donny-brooke.

All this did not come without some letdowns. Charging has its built-in handicap--the race car isn't always able to keep up the pace. From 1967 through 1972, mechanical failures and accidents put Johncock on the sidelines at Indianapolis.

Then, along came 1973. Though beset by personal and financial problems, Johncock found the most appropriate vehicle for his charging bent, an STP-sponsored Eagle-Offy owned by Pat Patrick and tooled by master mechanic George Bignotti.

That was enough to make Gordon forget just about everything except racing. He closed up the lumber mill he had operated for years in Michigan, moved to Indianapolis, and went racing.

The results were immediate. Johncock brought the flame-red No. 20 car into Victory Lane at the close of the accident-marred, rain-shortened Indy event. He followed up with Champ car wins at Trenton and Phoenix, a seventh-place finish in the point standings, and some impressive showings on the USAC and NASCAR stock car trails with the Chevrolet put together by "Hoss" Ellington.

The end of the season found Johncock listed as the biggest money-maker in racing, accounting for over $300,000 in race purse shares.

Still, the '73 season was as sweet as it could have been. The Indy 500, though the biggest prize any race driver can hope for, had ended 167 miles short under clouds of rain and tragedy.

"I wasn't praying for the rain to end the race," said Johncock after the race. "I wanted to see it go the full 500 miles."

Winning the Indy 332½ wasn't enough to satisfy Gordon Johncock completely. He wanted to come flying toward the flag at full tilt after all 500 miles. When you're a charger, that's the only way you can look at it.

JERRY KARL

BIRTHDATE—April 29, 1941; Hometown —Manchester, Pa.; National Championship division 30th. CAREER HIGHLIGHTS: Entered Ontario 500 from 1972 thru 1974; Indianapolis 500 1973 and 1974; Pocono 500 1972 thru 1974.

Jerry Karl was a part of Indy's "Great Experiment" of 1973.

Jerry, a dark-haired, 33-year-old Pennsylvanian, was the man behind the wheel of a gold-and-black race car that many people saw as the great hope for lowering the costs of competing in the Indy 500 and the rest of the stops along USAC's Championship

Trail. That hope focused on the turbo-charged stock-block Chevrolet engine behind Jerry's head in the Indy car owned by famed Southern mechanic Smokey Yunick.

With a potential commercial price tag of $5,000 for a turbo-Chevy, compared with $30,000 for a traditional racing powerplant, the very future of racing seemed to ride in the cockpit with Jerry Karl, who was also interested in making a future for himself as an Indy 500 driver. The Brickyard rookie had considerable confidence in the whole package.

"We'll either do one of two things--fall flat on our fannies or surprise an awful lot of people," said Jerry, early last May. "I personally think we're going to surprise a lot of people."

And they did, too. When Karl qualified for the '73 500-miler at over 190 mph, the potential of the Chevy mill was clearly demonstrated. Unfortunately, that promise didn't carry over to race day.

The Chevy still had the usual "bugs" in it and Karl spent most of '73 in the pits. Though he was on the track when the race ended, he had managed only 22 laps in the experimental car, 111 laps less than winner Gordon Johncock.

Karl went on to drive Yunick's beauty at Pocono and Ontario, but more insects stung them early in those races. The Chevy question remained unanswered, but at least Jerry Karl had proved himself as a 500-mile driver.

Jerry, who drove ARDC Midgets and URC Sprints for nine seasons and an occasional USAC Sprint program before finishing 10th in his Champ car debut at Dover, Del., in 1969, moved on to the Lindsey Hopkins stable of Indy cars for the '74 season. He qualified for the '74 California 500, dropped out early, and headed for Indy as part of one of the more established and competitive teams in USAC racing.

For Jerry Karl, the experimenting was over.

STEVE KRISILOFF

BIRTHDATE—July 7, 1946; Hometown—Parsippany, N.J.; National Championship division 18th. CAREER HIGHLIGHTS: Entered 1970 Ontario 500; 1971 Indianapolis, Ontario, Pocono; 1972 Indianapolis, Ontario, Pocono; 1973 Indianapolis, Ontario, Pocono; 1974 Ontario, Indianapolis, Pocono.

The story of Steve Krisiloff's rise to fame in Indianapolis-style racing is the kind of tale you'd expect to find only in a Hollywood movie, not in real life.

There was this skinny, shy kid who brought this race car that he had put together himself to Indy for a shot at the biggest race of them all. It was 1970, and the kid's car was old and used an old 255-inch Ford racing engine, hardly in the same class with the new turbocharged racing powerplants.

Everyone in the place figured the car was about 10 miles per hour too slow to make the field.

So, this kid from Parsippany, New Jersey rolled his old car out onto the track and tried to qualify for the big race. He was too slow to make the race, but instead of being 10 miles an hour too slow, he was only three miles an hour below some of the turbocharged cars that qualified for the 500.

That impressed quite a few people on the set. One of the most impressed was the Italian Andy Devine, Andy Granatelli, and before the year was over he had offered the kid from New Jersey a chance to drive one of his shining red STP Racing Team cars.

It had to be something of a dream come true for Krisiloff to have a spanking new car, one of those turbocharged engines, and a whole crew of people to work on the car while he concentrated on driving.

It was a rags-to-riches tale for the young man who spent his teenage years racing go-karts in the East, winning some 100 races in four seasons. After some time at college, Krisiloff had gone racing with URC in the East, finishing second in the 1967 standings and being named "Rookie of the Year" on that circuit.

Steve went to the USAC Sprint car circuit the next year and drove his first Indy car race at Langhorne in 1969. That all led up to his movie-like entry into the Indy spotlight.

Steve, one of the very few drivers of Jewish heritage in big-time racing, put Mr. Granatelli's car into the 1971 Indy field. The engine blew on the 11th lap, however, triggering a three-car pileup that also wiped out his STP teammate, Mario Andretti. He went on to place 10th at Pocono and fifth at Ontario later that year.

For the next two seasons, Krisiloff was the driver of record for Grant King's racing enterprise, making rapid progress back at the original 500 Speedway. He qualified for 10th starting spot in 1972, but dropped out halfway through the race with turbocharger failure.

In 1973, he was seventh fastest in the field and came home sixth in the rain-shortened event.

At season's end, Steve switched to a new car owned by Richard Beith but that association dissolved after the Ontario 500. And, like the Hollywood script, the kid was suddenly racing under those old STP colors as he headed back to the big Indy Speedway as part of Patrick Racing's super-potent three-car team.

ROGER McCLUSKEY

BIRTHDATE—August 24, 1930; Hometown—Tucson, Ariz.; National Championship division 1st; Stock car division 6th. CAREER HIGHLIGHTS: 1973 National Champion; 1972 Ontario 500 winner; 1963 and 1966 Sprint Car Champion; 1969 and 1970 Stock Car Champion; First-place finishes: 1966 Langhorne 150; 1968 Springfield 100; 1973 Michigan 200; Entered Indianapolis 500 from 1961 thru 1974 (except 1964); Ontario 500 from 1970 thru 1974; Pocono 500 from 1971 thru 1974. Midget wins: 4; Sprint wins: 23; Stock car wins: 21. First race—1949 at Tucson, Ariz. (Stock car).

Luck has rarely been a lady to Roger McCluskey.

"Roger's one of the unluckiest drivers in racing," A.J. Foyt once observed. "He should have won a lot of races he didn't."

Mostly, Roger didn't win Indy car races. He won his share of Sprint car and Stock car races, to be sure, raking in two USAC national titles at each of those tables.

But, with 12 seasons of flubs, foul-ups, and fizzles in the Indy cars, anyone betting on McCluskey's chances of winning a big one had the bookies beating a path to his door.

In 1973, though, the fickle femme of fate went a little soft in the heart. Not a lot--just enough to let him beat the house and come away with the USAC National Driving Championship.

"I guess I'm getting old and in the money," said McCluskey, with characteristic good humor, when asked about the apparent turn-around of his racing luck.

"All I know is we had a good year, a damned good year," added the 43-year-old National Champion from Tucson, Arizona.

His hot streak began at the 1972 California 500, where he took Lindsey Hopkins' blue-and-white McLaren into the winner's circle to give the rosy-cheeked Miami businessman the first 500-mile victory of his long stand as a car owner.

That set up the super-successful '73 campaign, as Roger quickly pulled down a third at Indianapolis, a second at Pocono, a fourth at Ontario, and a win at Michigan International in July. That was more than enough for him to clean out the Championship points pot.

It did not come without a touch of the old hard luck, however. At Pocono, the Hopkins McLaren was well into the lead when it came up a gallon short on fuel, and a fellow named Foyt motored past a crestfallen Roger McCluskey on the final lap.

The Indy car crown fit nicely into Roger's trophy case, with the USAC Sprint Car Championship he picked up in 1963 and 1966 and the Stock car titles he took home in 1969 and 1970. His Michigan and California wins also brought his career Indy car victory total to four.

It was, as the man said, a damned good year for the racer who started out racing Stock cars in Arizona 25 years ago and finally came to the USAC Sprint car trail in 1960. In addition to his racing fortune, Roger also won a bride, Jean, at the close of 1973.

For the record, McCluskey attached no special significance to the fact that he had to wait until he was 43 to capture the elusive national Indy car championship.

"I doubt if it means any more now than it would have earlier in my career," Roger said. "Obviously, I wasn't that competitive to have won it then, so I couldn't do it until now."

"The only thing I can say for sure is that doing it at 43 is better than doing it at 44," he added, flashing that familiar wide Roger McCluskey smile.

JIM McELREATH

BIRTHDATE—February 18, 1928; Hometown—Arlington, Tex.; National Championship division 19th. CAREER HIGHLIGHTS: 1970 Ontario 500 winner; 1962 Indianapolis 500 "Rookie of the Year"; 8th in All-Time Championship standings; 1965 Trenton 100, Langhorne 100, Langhorne 125 winner; 1966 Phoenix 150 winner; Entered Indianapolis 500 from 1962 thru 1974 (except 1971); Ontario 500 from 1970 thru 1974; Pocono 500 in 1971, '73 and '74.

Everyone along pit row at Indianapolis just knew something would be missing from the qualifying rituals at Indy this year.

"It won't seem the same without Jim McElreath walking out here about 4 p.m. on the last day of qualifying in his street clothes and looking over the cars in line," was the typical comment from the pits prior to 1974 time trials, "But it's sure good to see Jim hooked up with a good ride at the first of the month," was the typical addition.

It sure was a pleasant change for Jim, but he still didn't shake off that image of an 11th-hour qualifying run to squeeze into the 500 lineup again.

Early on the afternoon of the final day of time trials, there was Jim McElreath, strolling through the pits in his street clothes like he usually had during recent Mays. He wasn't looking over the cars in line for a likely prospect this time, though--two of them already had his name painted on their sides!

To make a long story short, Jim ended up making not just one, but two of his patented near-midnight rides. He qualified the first of the Gerhardt cars at a disappointing 177 mph, then, when the team car came to the front of the line, the first car was withdrawn and the tireless Texan qualified the second machine at an almost identical speed!

"That's really pushing it up there, isn't it?" drawled Jim, when he saw his second four-lap average was only a few hundredths better than his first. But at least he was in the 500 field for the 11th time.

His last-minute qualifying runs--which got him into the 500 in 1970 and 1973 as well, but left him out in 1971 and 1972--had made people temporarily forget Jim's earlier reputation as an up-front driver on the USAC Championship Trail.

The former bricklayer from Arlington, Texas had a different image in the '60s. In his first six starts at Indy, he started in the first seven spots three times and finished in the top six four times. His best was a third in 1966.

McElreath had been no stranger to the winner's circle, either, putting together wins in no less than four USAC racing divisions--one each in Midgets, Sprint cars and Dirt Track Champ cars and five in the Indy cars. His first of three Champ car wins came in 1965, when he won twice at Langhorne and once at Trenton.

The next year, he was first to the flag at Phoenix, on his way to a runnerup finish in the USAC National Championship point standings.

Perhaps his most stirring victory came in 1970, when he won the inaugural California 500 in a last-minute duel with the late Art Pollard.

And he hadn't lost that touch in 1973, as he demonstrated in the Milwaukee 200, leading 16 laps before finishing fourth. Jim, 46, has also been a frequent and strong competitor on the Dirt Track and Sprint car circuits in recent years, too.

There is another McElreath on the racing horizon, as Jim's son, James, is already developing a winning touch of his own on the dirt tracks of Texas.

JOHN MARTIN

BIRTHDATE—March 20, 1939; Hometown—Long Beach, Cal.; National Championship division 17th. CAREER HIGHLIGHTS: Entered Indianapolis 500 from 1972 thru 1974; Ontario 500 from 1972 thru 1974; Pocono 500 from 1972 thru 1974.

Money can't buy happiness. If you can accept that premise, then you can understand why John Martin is a happy man.

"I love what I'm doing and couldn't be happier," says Martin, whose financial shortcomings are near-legend in USAC big car circles. "Right from the start, my goal was to own and drive a Champ car and that's exactly what I'm doing."

But, as John well knows, he's doing it without an unlimited budget and fancy sponsorship deals. Almost every newspaper account of his efforts at Indy racing includes the phrase "low-budget operation" at least once.

Still, the graying former Road Racer from Long Beach, California, seems to get a lot of mileage out of each dollar. He's come a long way from the day in 1961 he decided to tackle Drag Racing on the strips around St. Louis, his home base at the time.

After racking up 52 wins in the Drags, Martin switched to Road Racing. His Corvette made him the A-Production Champion in SCCA's Midwest division in 1964, scoring 13 victories in 14 races.

He was second in the 1968 SCCA American Road Race of Champions and was a team driver for the factory Javelin entries in the 1969 Trans-Am Series. He also drove in NASCAR and USAC Stock car events before tackling the SCCA Formula A Continental Ser-

ies in 1970, where he finished in 11th spot in the season's standings.

Martin then made the move to Long Beach and began planning his low-money, high-happiness try at USAC Championship car racing. He joined that circuit in 1972 and immediately laid the groundwork for his low-budget profile by putting a four-year-old Brabham into the 14th starting spot at the Indianapolis 500.

John qualified for the other two 500s that year, as well as the remaining stops on the Championship Trail. For 1973, he moved up to a year-old McLaren, the one Peter Revson had put on the front row at Indy the year before. Like the earlier Brabham, the McLaren was fondly known as the "Unsponsored Special" owned, mechanicked, and driven by one John Martin.

The red McLaren stunned some of the high-priced outfits by qualifying ninth fastest in the '73 Indy lineup, then finishing eighth in the rain-shortened race. Martin insists that he could have won the 500 if two things hadn't happened--the aforementioned rain that stopped the race short of 500 miles on May 30 and the fiery crash-false start two days earlier that put crimps in both Martin's car and his budget.

"After the crash, there was no way we had a chance of winning and, in fact, it changed our strategy for the whole season," says the 35-year-old racer. "After Indy, we had to run for the dollar, go just fast enough to try and finish in the first five or even the first 10."

MIKE MOSLEY

BIRTHDATE—December 13, 1946; HOME-TOWN—Clermont, Ind.; National Championship division 6th. CAREER HIGHLIGHTS: 1971 Trenton 200 winner; Entered Indianapolis 500 from 1968 thru 1974, Ontario 500 from 1970 thru 1974 (except 1971), Pocono 500 in 1973 and 1974. Sprint car wins: 3.

After hitting the same wall in roughly the same place four times in two years, lesser men might have been persuaded to give up their dreams of racing for the Indianapolis 500's gold. Lesser men than Mike Mosley, that is.

Mosley, the young Californian who has been a big-time racing campaigner most of his adult life, and his "debate" with Indy's fourth-turn wall have become near-legend in the annals of America's most famous auto race. It's not exactly the kind of legend Mike hoped for, but it at least proved just how much determination he was capable of.

Mosley, driving for veteran chief mechanic A.J. Watson, clipped the wall on two successive qualifying tries before the 1971 Indy race. He finally made it around to qualify for the race, but smashed into the concrete again late in the race.

The race crash left Mike seriously injured with burns and broken limbs, but he was back for another try the following May. In the race, shortly after moving his Watson entry into the lead, a wheel flew off and he careened into that same ol' fourth-turn wall again.

Mike suffered burns again, too, but not as severe as the 1971 variety. He was healed in time for the California 500 that fall, but even he had to admit to some doubts about whether 500-milers were his cup of tea.

"I had been thinking about my two bad Indianapolis crashes, but I went ahead and got in the car and ran Ontario," Mike later reported. "I never thought about quitting racing completely, even when I was hurt, but I didn't know if I wanted to run so fast my first time back."

He hasn't stopped running so fast since then. Mosley, only 27, has re-established himself as one of the top contenders for victory laurels at Indy and the other stops on the Champ car trail.

Nothing showed that better than his win in the Phoenix 150 in the spring of '74. That was Mike's second Indy car win, the first coming at Trenton in 1971, on the eve of his string of wall incidents at Indy.

Mosley was born in Oklahoma, but spent most of his early years in LaPuente, California. He was racing early in life, driving go-karts when he was 13 and Midgets when he was 15.

He came to the USAC Sprint car circuit in 1967 and recorded three feature wins there.

He made it into the Indy 500 field for the first time in 1968, running a steady race to finish eighth. Then as now, he drove a Watson-supervised car.

While his later record at Indianapolis was painful, Mosley has been consistently healthy as a finisher in the other 500s. He was fifth at Ontario in 1972 and third the next year. He was fourth at Pocono in 1973—his only start there since his Indy crashes kept him sidelined two years in a row.

The 1973 campaign was one of Mike's most fruitful, which gave him a sixth-place finish in the season point standings. He even got a 10th at Indianapolis, although his car broke down late in the going.

He kicked off what may be an even more productive '74 campaign with his win at Phoenix and a seventh at Ontario.

Mosley, who now calls Clermont, Ind. his home, has obviously pushed aside any gun-shyness from his Indy mishaps and left such things to lesser men.

A lesser man wouldn't have been able to say, as Mike did when they carted him away from his final Indy crash in '72, "I'll be back; racing is still my game."

Someone once asked Rick Muther what he thought of dirt-track racing.

"That's for crazy people," Muther answered, arching his eyebrows then laughing. It was the kind of answer you'd expect from a driver who had spent most of his time racing Sports cars on road courses.

But he left himself an out. "Oh, I might like to go out and try it--if there was nobody else around," Rick added. "It would probably be good for your reactions."

It's a good thing he said that. Otherwise, three years later, at the old fairgrounds track in DuQuoin, Ill., they would have been required to have a psychiatrist on hand at trackside.

There was Rick Muther, driving the dirt like a madman with another score of crazy men and several thousand spectators all around. If that wasn't strange enough, he was doing it in a Dirt Track car with a turbine engine!

Crazy...like a fox. Muther finished eighth there at DuQuoin, becoming about the only driver to earn points in a USAC Championship Dirt race with no previous dirt track experience.

Actually, it was all in keeping with Rick's fading image as a "sports car driver." From the time he came off the Road Racing tour in 1966 to drive Indy cars, he steadily came to be thought of as a USAC Championship Trail driver.

And an Indy 500 driver, of course, After being bumped from the 1969 lineup at the last minute, he made the next two 500's in the Jack Adams cars readied by mechanic Howard Millican--the man who would ultimately have the idea of putting a turbine in a Dirt car that a sane man named Muther would drive at Du-Quoin.

He finished eighth in 1970 and survived a spectacular collision with David Hobbs on the front stretch the next year. He missed the next two Indy races, but logged 500 experience at both Ontario and Pocono.

Back on the Indy car trail in 1974, the bushy-haired Californian had pretty well left his Sports car ties behind. "I started out in them, but I haven't really driven a Sports car for quite awhile," said Rick Muther, Indy and Dirt Track racer.

RICK MUTHER

BIRTHDATE—August 13, 1936; Home-town—Laguna Beach, Cal. CAREER HIGH-LIGHTS: Entered Indianapolis 500 in 1970, '71 and '74; Ontario 500 in 1970, '72 and '74; Pocono 500 in 1972 and 1973.

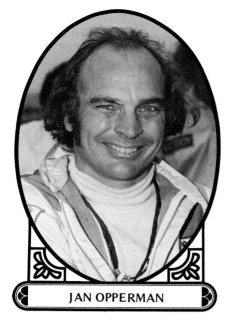

JAN OPPERMAN

Birthdate—Feb. 9, 1939; HOMETOWN: Beaver Crossing, Neb. Career Highlights: National Supermodified Champion, Knoxville, Iowa, 1971; Two time National Super Mod. Champ., Phoenix, Ariz. 1971 & '72. 1973 World Dirt Track Champion. Children, Teacia, Krystal, Jay Lou, Jan.

Racing in the Indianapolis 500 may ruin Jan Opperman's image.

Opperman, considered racing's resident hippie, free spirit, and/or Jesus freak, was a changed man shortly after he arrived at the big track on 16th Street this May. His hair suddenly was as short as Parnelli Jones'; his funky old prospector's hat disappeared, revealing a receding, half-moon hairline, and his iron-cross pendant was tucked nearly inside his fireproof underwear.

When the Speedway opened up May 6, Opperman was wandering around Gasoline Alley in his threadbare bluejeans, beaded necklace, and floppy brown hat. That was strictly in keeping with his image as a vagabond racer who bounced from one backwoods track to another, lived isolated out on the plains of Nebraska, ate organic foods, and practiced a kind of shirt-tail Christianity.

Before the week was over, however, he was seen chumming around with Parnelli Jones, who kept his hair Marine-Corps short for years. Soon, he was sporting a neat haircut, a high forehead, and a shiny new Vel's-Parnelli Racing driving suit.

For those who started to accuse him of selling out, Jan had a quick answer. "Everything costs something, but in this case I think the price was right," he said, rubbing the bare nape of his neck.

"This is really a far-out place," he went on, in his usual idiom. "It kind of scared me at first, but this is what I want to do."

The strange partnership of Opperman and Jones had people shaking their heads in bewilderment for awhile. But Jan's route to Indy, running the so-called "outlaw" tracks and winning as many as 50 features in a single season, struck a personal chord with Parnelli.

"They told me Jan had run 99 races last year and 103 another year," explained the 1963 Indy winner. "That really impressed me—I ran 60 races a year for awhile and I know what that takes."

Opperman, who with his wife and kids constitute most of the population of Beaver Crossing, Neb., had been on the tough road from Sprint car track to Sprint car track until 1974. This season, he came to the USAC Sprint car trail, quickly demonstrating that his racing prowess wasn't restricted to the obscure little dirt tracks of the East and Midwest.

Even with his changing public image at Indy, Opperman held onto his deep spiritual feelings, the ones that had made his approach to racing one of "Praise the Lord and Pass the Competition."

"I've learned to praise the Lord for everything," said the 35-year-old Speedway rookie. "If I went out tomorrow and tore off both my arms in a race car, I'd still get out of the car and praise the Lord."

JOHNNY PARSONS

BIRTHDATE—August 26, 1944; Hometown—Indianapolis, Ind.; National Championship division 22nd; Dirt Track division 4th; Sprint car division 9th; Midget division 29th. CAREER HIGHLIGHTS: Entered 1972, '73 and '74 Ontario 500; 1973 Pocono 500; 1974 Indianapolis 500. Sprint car wins: 1; Midget wins: 4.

For some reason, second-generation racing drivers seem to provide much of the humor and high-jinks on the racing scene. Among the most publicized racing comedy routines are those between Billy Vukovich and Gary Bettenhausen, for example.

It could be that the pressures of having to live up to the images of their famous racing fathers demand a comic relief valve, but it just may be that the second-generation racers feel more "at home" in the racing environment. Whatever, the reasons, Johnny Parsons fits right in.

Known for his flair for humor and horseplay, the ever-smiling, dark-haired Parsons has joined the growing number of sons of racing fathers who have followed their dads into the Indy 500 record books. He and Vukovich now stand as the most likely candidates for the honor of becoming the first son of an Indy 500 winner to visit Victory Lane himself.

Johnny is the 29-year-old son of 1950 Indy winner Johnnie Parsons—their middle names are different, so he's not a Junior. He began racing in California in 1964 and continued racing part-time during a stint as a Los Angeles policeman.

He quit the force in 1967, however, to devote his full energies to the racing beat. He came to the USAC Midgets and Sprints in 1968 and has been a regular competitor in those divisions ever since, rolling up four Midget feature wins and one Sprint victory.

His first full season in USAC big cars was a memorable one, as he won the pole position for the 1970 Hoosier Hundred. He has been an increasingly strong competitor on the Dirt Track Championship circuit, almost winning at Springfield in 1973, taking second at the Hoosier Hundred, and finishing fourth in the '73 point standings.

Parsons' career on the paved track of the Championship Trail went into high gear in the latter part of 1972, when he qualified for the California 500.

In 1973, he ran the Pocono and California 500s and picked up fifth-place finishes in the second Michigan 125 and the Texas 200. He failed to qualify at Indy, but came back this May with a solid run in Tassi Vatis' entry to get his rookie start in the big race his father won 24 years ago.

All jokes aside, young Johnny Parsons who moved from Reseda, Cal. to Indianapolis in 1971, was right at home.

LLOYD RUBY

BIRTHDATE—January 12, 1928; Hometown—Wichita Falls, Tex.; National Championship division 9th. CAREER HIGHLIGHTS: 1961 Milwaukee 200 winner; 1964 Phoenix 200 winner; 1967 Phoenix 150, Langhorne 100 winner; 1966 Milwaukee 150, Milwaukee 200 winner; 1970 Trenton 200 winner. Midget wins: 2. First race—1946 at Wichita Falls, Tex. (Midget).

There are at least three things Lloyd Ruby is an expert at--gin rummy, golf and bad racing luck.

The first two have made Ruby a big winner on the golf course and on improvised card tables back in Gasoline Alley. The third, however, has kept him from winning the one big race he wants to win, the Indy 500.

Lloyd, now 46, has come so close, so often, that even his competitors for the Indy crown would like to see the slow-drawling Texan have some good Indy luck for a change.

"Ol' Rube's gonna win this thing one of these days," said Roger McCluskey, one year at the 500 Victory Banquet, "and, I'll tell you, I'm gonna stay here all night to hear him talk about it."

A Ruby win at Indianapolis would undoubtedly make a lot of people happy--not the least of which, of course, would be Lloyd Ruby. He's been chasing that elusive Indy dream for 15 years now, and he's not about to give it up.

"As long as I feel I can win, I'll keep coming back," says the popular Indy racer out of Wichita Falls, Texas.

It takes some intestinal fortitude for someone to keep coming back to Indianapolis after the incredible doses of hard luck the 500 track has dealt Ruby. Some of the most unlikely things have kept him from that trip to Victory Lane and an all-night speech at the 500 banquet.

In 1966, for instance, Lloyd Ruby was 48 seconds ahead of his nearest challenger with 50 laps to go when he had to be black flagged for an oil leak.

In 1968, he was leading again when a coil went sour and had to be replaced, dropping him to fifth.

In 1968, he and eventual winner Mario Andretti were battling wheel-to-wheel for the victory when Lloyd made a routine pit stop. Ruby started to leave the pits before a fuel hose was disconnected and the move ripped the fuel connector from the side of his car.

In 1970, he came from 25th to first in less than 50 laps only to have a ring-and-pinion gear break.

In 1971, he led Indy again, but his gearbox went up in smoke.

In 1974, he was still in contention when, six laps from the end, he ran out of fuel.

That's the kind of luck Ruby has had at Indy. Elsewhere on the racing trail, he has done considerably better.

Lloyd has had the right kind of luck seven times on the USAC Championship circuit, winning at Milwaukee in 1961, Phoenix in 1964, Phoenix and Langhorne in 1967, Milwaukee twice in 1966, and Trenton in 1970. He has perennially been a contender for the national championship, with a third in 1964, his best points finish.

In his early years in racing, Ruby was known as one of the best young Midget racers to come down the pike in many moons. He won a 10-gallon hat full of races before USAC came into existence, but he also has two USAC Midget victories on the books.

Even his early shots at the Indy 500 featured good luck, if not the winning variety. In his first five starts, he finished in the top eight four times, capped with a third in 1964.

He also placed sixth at the Speedway in 1972. On the other 500-mile tracks, Ruby recorded a fourth at Ontario in 1971 and a third at Pocono in 1973.

So, his luck hasn't completely shut him out of the good things in racing life--just the one he wants so bad he can taste it. But the easy-going, friendly Texas isn't likely to put much stock in the talk about luck having it in for him.

"Luck is a part of racing," observes Rube. "I'm not the only driver who has had bad luck at Indianapolis. I just don't think people should look for excuses like that when things don't go the way they'd like."

JOHNNY RUTHERFORD

BIRTHDATE—March 12, 1938; Hometown—Ft. Worth, Tex.; National Championship division 3rd; Stock car division 32nd; Dirt Track division 16th. CAREER HIGHLIGHTS: 1965 Sprint Car Champion; 1965 Atlanta 250 winner; 1973 Ontario 100, Michigan 125 winner; 1974 Indianapolis 500, Pocono 500 winner; Entered Indianapolis 500 from 1963 thru 1974 (except 1966); Ontario 500 from 1970 thru 1974; Pocono 500 from 1971 thru 1974. Sprint car wins: 8. First race—1959 at Dallas, Tex.

If Indianapolis racing has a Renaissance Man, he is Johnny Rutherford.

Rutherford's personal interests stray radically from the kind of nuts-and-bolts items usually associated with the race driver stereotype. He is into painting--the kind you do with brush and palette, not with a roller--and classical music, among other things.

His painting is prabably John's most developed sideline. His pencil sketches of racing colleagues hang on some of the best walls in the racing world. One of his best-known, a sketch of the late Don Branson, greets you when you enter the offices of the United States Auto Club in Speedway, Indiana.

"I've always enjoyed art, but I don't really know a lot about the Old Masters and such," he relates. "Drawing is just something I've always been good at--I won some art scholarships in school, but I never did take advantage of them."

His musical interests were something else Rutherford never got around to pursuing completely, even though he played a mean trumpet in high school. He did manage to make time, though, to appear as guest conductor with the Indianapolis Symphony Orchestra while he was in town for the 1973 500-miler.

"It was a lot of fun and I really enjoyed it," Johnny says of his night with the baton, "but my musical talents have really been blown up out of proportion."

Other diversions for the Ft. Worth, Texas race driver include motorcycling and flying--a couple of pursuits more in keeping with his profession.

But what Johnny Rutherford is into more than anything is driving race cars--that's what he does most and best.

Johnny started it all in 1959 by racing Stock cars in and around Dallas. The next year, he came north to tackle the UARA Midget circuit as a teammate to Mel Kenyon.

Another year later, he joined IMCA and ran Sprints and Midgets there. He switched to USAC in 1962, driving Sprints and making his big car debut in the Hoosier Hundred.

It had been a rapid climb, from the jalopies to Indy cars in less than four years, but he suddenly hit a few snags--a lot of them, to be exact. Over the next 10 seasons, Rutherford was literally deluged with frustration, most of them inflicted by crash injuries and/or mechanical letdowns.

The only real bright spot in his Indy car career from 1963 to 1973 was the Atlanta 250 in 1965, where Rutherford added the Leader Card Watson/Offy (rear-engine) to his first Champ car victory. By the end of 1972, it was beginning to look like it might be his only visit to the Indy car winner's circle.

Johnny did have some luck in the Sprint cars, winning the USAC national title in 1965. But the following season he broke both arms in a wild flip at Eldora Speedway in Ohio.

At Indy, his fortune was no brighter. He started nine times during his "blue" period and never went further than 135 laps at one time. The one great moment for him at the Brickyard was the first day of qualifying for the 1970 500-miler, when he came within a tick of the stopwatch of knocking Al Unser off the pole with his four-year-old Patrick Racing entry.

By the second half of the '72 season, when he moved over to the Gerhardt Racing stable, things started to get a little better. He took second in the Pocono 500, the only time he had ever gone the full 500 miles to that point, and was third at Milwaukee.

Then, in 1973, he joined forces with England's Team McLaren, and that move got him back on his track

toward the top of the proverbial racing ladder. Johnny was suddenly a winner again, in the papaya-hued McLaren, taking first in a 100-mile qualifier at Ontario and one of the Michigan International twin-125s.

He also picked up a fifth at Pocono. But at Indy, he qualified for the pole with a track record-setting 198.413 mph only to be stricken with persistent oil overflow problems on race day. He spent several minutes in the pits and staggered to a ninth-place finish.

But the winning pattern was already being re-established. "I really can't say enough about this Team McLaren operation," reports Johnny. "I knew right from the beginning that this would be a winning combination."

Fresh from a 1973 season that saw him wind up third in the USAC National Championship standings, Johnny Rutherford came to Indianapolis in 1974 with winning on his mind. And, using his McLaren like a brush, the 36-year-old artist-racer painted himself an almost picture-perfect masterpiece in winning the 1974 Indy 500.

The renaissance of Johnny Rutherford was complete.

DICK SIMON

BIRTHDATE—September 21, 1933; HOMETOWN: Salt Lake City, Utah; National Championship division 20th; Stock car division 85th; Midget division 63rd. CAREER HIGHLIGHTS: Entered Indianapolis 500 from 1970 thru 1974, Ontario 500 from 1970 thru 1974, Pocono 500 from 1971 thru 1974.

They held a five-mile bicycle race at the Indianapolis Motor Speedway a few days before this year's 500. It should have come as no great surprise

to anyone that Dick Simon--together with his teenaged son, Tim--won that race.

Dick Simon has always been the kind of guy who welcomes a new challenge--whether it's a bike race, jumping out of airplanes, flying down a ski slope, racing in the Indy 500, or taking the insurance business by storm. He has tackled them all and usually come away a champion.

Simon, a balding, 40-year-old businessman-sportsman who now hangs his many hats in Salt Lake City, Utah, began taking on the challenges as a teenager in Seattle, Wash., working in the shipyards there to help support his family.

When the financial pressures eased up a little, Dick took his shots at sporting activities, starting with skiing. He won a skiing scholarship to the University of Utah and went on to become Intermountain Ski Jumping Champion twice and took the Landes Ski Jumping trophy three years running.

Parachuting was the next challenge and Simon added a National Parachuting Championship to his collection.

In auto racing, Dick started out in the Supermodifieds in 1962 and, three years later, was champion of the Salt Lake Valley Racing Association. He gradually expanded his racing scope until he hit the USAC Championship Trail in 1970.

He made the Indy 500 on his first try and placed 14th in the 1970 race. He also made the California 500 and finished third in his and Ontario's inaugural.

Simon has been a regular starter at Indy, Ontario and Pocono ever since, missing only the 1972 California 500 lineup. He was bumped at Indy in 1971, but started the race in a team car qualified by John Mahler.

He ran as high as fourth in the 1973 Indy event, but dropped out at 100 laps with a broken piston. He placed 14th again.

While he was doing all these things, Simon was shooting through the pack in the business world, too. His rise from salesman to president of the Majestic Life Insurance Company in Salt Lake City was in keeping with his sporting accomplishments.

For "relaxation," Dick still does some skiing, scuba dives and flies his own plane. He also manages to find time for his wife and their family of seven children--a rather large challenge in itself.

Through it all, Dick Simon has disapproved the old saw about a "jack of all trades" not being able to master anything. He has mastered quite a few despite the skeptics, which included his skiing coach, who insisted Dick give up his other interests to concentrate on skiing, and his first boss at the insurance company, who tried to talk him into giving up racing.

Neither succeeded, but Dick Simon did--proving all things are possible if you stick by your guns. "What I've always tried to do is make a decision and stick with it, whether it's in business or racing or something else," says smiling Dick.

"When you're in a race and you've got to make a split-second decision, there's no time to change your mind, even if you wanted to," he adds. "That's been my philosophy all along, on the race track or off."

BILL SIMPSON

BIRTHDATE—March 14, 1940; Hometown—Hermosa Beach, Cal.; CAREER HIGHLIGHTS: Entered Pocono 500 in 1971, 1972 and 1974; Ontario 500 in 1972 and 1974; Indianapolis 500 in 1974.

Bill Simpson seemed to be a changed man when he came to the Indianapolis Speedway this May.

The change was easy to see. Bill's famed Teddy Roosevelt moustache was gone, and the hair that once fell to his collar was rearranged into a shorter, what you might call egg-beater hairstyle. But the most visible change was the smile, wider and more persistent than ever before.

Simpson had found little to smile about at Indy before. Blown engines, weak equipment, and one wall-banger had managed to dampen his usual good humor during the four previous Mays at the big Speedway. The smile usually disappeared beneath that bushy moustache--which may provide a clue to why it disappeared in '74.

Bill Simpson, who had first tackled Indy with his own cars, finally found a place with a first-line entry where someone else took care of the worries and left the driving to him. California businessman Richard Beith, new to the Indy scene, was the someone else and his American Kids Eagle/ Offy was the equipment that got Simpson his long-sought rookie start in the Indianapolis 500.

Bill, the 34-year-old president of his own racing uniform manufacturing company, is a Los Angeles native who has raced almost every kind of vehicle imaginable since he caught the racing bug in 1956. He started with something called a "straightaway belly tank" on the El Mirage dry lake and moved into NHRA Drag Racing in 1958.

Simpson raced motorboats for a couple of years, then went Road Racing with SCCA from 1962 to 1968. He made his USAC Champ car debut in the Rex Mays 300 at Riverside that year.

In 1969, he spent most of his time on the Indy car trail, then had his fling at the Tasman Series for Formula cars in early 1970, getting a fourth at Christchurch. Later that year, he made the first of his low-mileage runs at Indy.

A sixth-place finish at Milwaukee in '70 helped bring back the smile. But Indy the next year was a frowner, as the engine in Bill's car let go in the final turn of his qualifying run, dropping his speed just enough to get bumped the next weekend.

He made no qualifying attempt in 1972 and crashed during practice the following May.

Simpson, one of racing's more enthusiastic anglers, indicated this May he may surrender some of his fishing time during the summer to run the SCCA-USAC joint-sanctioned Formula 5000 Series.

TOM SNEVA

BIRTHDATE—June 1, 1948; Hometown—Sprague, Wash.; National Championship division 31st; Sprint car division 11th. CAREER HIGHLIGHTS: 1973 Championship "Rookie of the Year." Sprint car wins: 6.

In the spring of 1973, Tom Sneva decided to go racing in a big way.

He packed his racing gear, his wife, and their two young daughters into the family camper, said goodbye to his job as a teacher and administrator in the Sprague, Washington school system, and headed for the race tracks. It was a big step for a man with a family and a secure future as an educator.

"I was racing while I was teaching, and it just got to the point where I couldn't do justice to either one," Sneva explains. "So I decided to go racing, because I enjoy it more right now.

"I'd like to race until I don't enjoy it anymore, then get back into education."

Sneva came to Indianapolis in May of 1973 as an unknown quantity and pretty much stayed that way. The graduate of Eastern Washington State College and the Supermodified tracks of the Northwest passed his rookie's test but failed to qualify for the 500.

But, before the summer of '73 was over, he had made people sit up and take notice. Behind the wheel of Carl Gehlhausen's bullet-shaped rear-engine Sprint car, Sneva proved the soundness of that design and his own talents, winning six features on the USAC Sprint car trail.

The sensational performance on the paved half-miles grabbed the attention of two groups--Champ car owners looking for a young driver and USAC's

Sprint car committee and Board of Directors. On the latter count, the USAC officials banned further rear-engine Sprint car participation for the 1974 season, a move Sneva found disappointing.

"The rear-engines gave the drivers a lot better chance of getting to Indianapolis," he commented at the time. "The upright cars would be fine, if they still ran upright cars at the Speedway."

The other group made up for that, however, as far as getting the 25-year-old ex-teacher to the big Speedway on 16th Street. After his success in Sprints, Sneva found himself in Rolla Vollstedt's Champ car for the final races of the Indy car season, including the California 500, where Sneva made the lineup for the first time.

Moving to Grant King's Kingfish/Offy in '74, the likeable young racer showed rapid improvement. He finished 12th in the March version of the California 500, led at Phoenix before a suspension failure sent him sliding down the backstretch, and qualified second fastest to Mario Andretti at Trenton.

Sneva, who gave up his vagabond existence in '74 in favor of a non-mobile home in Spokane, then headed for Indianapolis as a leading contender for "Rookie of the Year" honors. The school teacher obviously was learning fast.

GEORGE SNIDER

BIRTHDATE—December 8, 1940; Hometown—Bakersfield, Cal.; National Championship division 32nd; Sprint division 21st; Midget division 49th. CAREER HIGHLIGHTS: 1971 Dirt Track Champion. Midget wins: 4; Sprint car wins: 4; Dirt Track wins: 1. First race—1961 at Fresno, Cal.

You won't find "Ziggy Schwartz" listed in your race program. But he's probably out there on the track, just the same.

His given name is George Snider, but to most of the racing fraternity he is "Ziggy." George knows how that nickname got started, even if he's not sure why.

"I don't know what it's supposed to mean, really," Snider relates. "Ronnie Burton (well-known racing artist) was the one who came up with it a few years ago. He just started calling me that, and it kinda stuck."

Whether you call him George Snider or Ziggy Schwartz, the Bakersfield, Cal. native has been a familiar figure in USAC open-cockpit racing for the past decade. A graduate of the California flat tracks, Snider has shown a particular fondness for dirt racing, winning USAC Sprint car and Midget races in that area and becoming the organization's first National Dirt Track Champion in 1971.

He won at DuQuoin and placed second at Springfield and the Hoosier Hundred enroute to the '71 crown. He had also posted runnerup finishes at Springfield (twice) and Sacramento previously, when the dirt-track events were included in the regular National Championship division.

At Indianapolis, Snider has most often been identified as the protege of USAC's winningest driver, A.J. Foyt. In five of his nine Indy appearances before 1974, he was at the wheel of a Foyt car.

That association goes all the way back to 1966 when, as a Speedway sophomore, Snider out-qualified his new boss and started the 500 from the outside spot on the front row.

In 1972, he set a record, of sorts, for USAC 500-mile race competition. It's a record he'd just as soon forget, however, since it amounted to the worst year ever for a driver in the three USAC 500-milers.

Snider was the first entry to drop out at both Indianapolis and Pocono, both due to mechanical failures, and the second driver sidelined at Ontario, this time by an accident. He came back in 1972, however, to record his best season in the Big Three races, finishing 11th at Indy in a Foyt Coyote, his best placing at the Brickyard, and taking 8th at Ontario in a MVS entry.

AL UNSER

BIRTHDATE—May 29, 1939; Hometown—Albuquerque, N.M.; National Championship division 13th; Dirt Track division 1st; Stock car division 45th. CAREER HIGHLIGHTS: 1970 and 1971 Indianapolis 500 winner; 1970 National Champion; 1973 Dirt Track Champion; 1964 and 1965 Pikes Peak Hill Climb winner; 1967 Stock car "Rookie of the Year"; First-place finishes: 1968 Nazareth 100, IRP 100, Langhorne 100, Langhorne 100; 1969 Milwaukee 200, DuQuoin 100, Sacramento 100, Kent 100, Phoenix 200; 1970 Phoenix 150, IRP 150, Springfield 100, Milwaukee 200, DuQuoin 100, Hoosier 100, Sedalia 100, Trenton 300, Sacramento 100; 1971 Rafaela 150, Rafaela 150, Phoenix 150; 1973 Bryan 200. Stock car wins: 4; Dirt Track wins: 4.

Al Unser's approach to driving the Indianapolis 500 track is the essence of simplicity.

"Please don't ask me to explain my driving technique," says Al. "All I know is, I drive as fast as I can on the straightaway and turn left when I hit the corner."

Simple but effective, that's technique. It has worked to perfection for the dark-haired Indy 500 driver, youngest of the fabled Unser brothers from Albuquerque, New Mexico.

Like any other Unser, Al started out on the racing road in the Stock cars and Supermodifieds that perennially flourish around Albuquerque. He raced up the side of Pikes Peak, too, of course--he would hardly qualify as an Unser otherwise.

But it was low-slung, rear-engine USAC Championship cars that little brother proved his mettle. From the time he first came to Indianapolis in 1965, Al Unser has been turning left at the corners with the best of them.

Unser drove A.J. Foyt's second car in his rookie start at Indy and finished a respectable ninth. He followed up with three second-place finishes in the 1966 Champ car season, at Trenton, Phoenix and Indianapolis Raceway Park.

Back at Indy, the young Al Unser was teamed with the great Jim Clark and was running third in his Lotus/ Ford when he smacked the wall exiting the fourth turn. A year later, he proved the promise with a second-place finish behind Foyt in the 1967 Indy go-round.

He finished second four more times that season for his second straight number five ranking in the USAC point standings.

Then, 1968 came along and Al Unser became a winner at someplace other than Pikes Peak. He took five victories on the Championship Trail in George Bignotti's Lola and moved up to third in the point standings.

He crashed at Indy that year, however, as big brother Bobby brought the Unser family its first Indianapolis victory. For 1969, Vel Miletich and Parnelli Jones bought into the Bignotti operation and Al crashed again at Indianapolis, but not on the race track.

Unser broke his leg in a motorcycle accident away from the track and sat out the 500. But when the cast came off, he promptly became the hottest thing on the Championship circuit since "Mom" Unser introduced her famous chili.

Al won five straight in the latter stages of the '69 season and set himself up as the big favorite for Indy glory the following year. He lived up to that role, putting the Vel's Parnelli-Bignotti entry on the pole and winning the 500 going away.

The 1971 Indy event was more closely contested, but Al won anyway, becoming only the fourth driver in history to win the 500 two consecutive years. It had everyone thinking about an unprecedented three straight for Al when 1972 rolled around-- everyone except Al, that is.

Al did his best to keep from thinking of the '72 race as anything more than just another race on the calendar. "I think it's really a great honor to be in a position to win three in a row, but doing it is another thing," he said at the time.

"I really can't look at this race as the chance to win three in a row," he added. "I have to look at it as just another race I have to run and have to try to win."

And try he did. But he was third to the flag in '72, and then inherited second place when Jerry Grant was penalized for a fueling violation.

Al's hot streak cooled off somewhat over the next few seasons, but he still added a win at Texas in 1973 to bring his career total on the USAC Indy car circuit to 27 victories. He also ran a close second to brother Bob at the 1974 California 500.

Al kept up the good work on the Dirt Championship trail, though, winning the 1973 season championship to go along with the Indy car title he had picked up in 1970. He capped off his Dirt crown with another win in the Hoosier Hundred, becoming the first driver to win that event four years in a row.

All in all, not bad for a guy who just "turns left when he gets to the corner"--even if his last name is Unser.

BOBBY UNSER

BIRTHDATE—February 20, 1934; Hometown—Albuquerque, N.M.; National Championship division 12th; Stock car division 43rd. CAREER HIGHLIGHTS: 1956, '58, '59, '60, '61, '62, '63, '66 and '68 Pikes Peak Hill Climb Championship; 1968 National Driving Champion; First-place finishes: 1967 Mosport 100, Mosport 150; 1968 Las Vegas 150, Phoenix 150, Trenton 150, Indianaplis 500; 1969 Langhorne 150; 1970 Langhorne 150; 1971 Milwaukee 200, Trenton 300; 1972 Phoenix· 150, Milwaukee 150, Trenton 300, Phoenix 150; 1973 Milwaukee 150; 1974 Ontario 500. Sprint car wins: 7; Midget wins: 3; Stock car wins: 4. First race—1949 at Roswell, N.M.

For a while, it seemed that Bobby Unser was having the kind of problems associated with a baseball slugger. He was hitting a few home runs, but he was also striking out a lot.

In fact, he either did one or the other, either powdered the ball into the upper deck or walked back to the dugout with his bat resting on his shoulders. Nothing in-between, not even a bloop single.

Translated into racing terms, that means Unser won a lot of pole positions, set a lot of track records, and led a lot of races over the past few seasons, but had a low batting average when it came to finishing and winning –to Bobby, they're basically the same thing--USAC Championship races.

Putting it another way, it became a standing rule that if Bobby hit the ball it left the park. If he finished, he won. He just didn't finish often enough to suit a former Indy 500 winner and USAC National Champion.

As driver of the super fast Eagles produced by Dan Gurney's All-American Racers factory, Bobby U. became known as the fastest of the famous racing Unser brothers (and father, and uncles, etc.) with a flurry of track records beginning in 1971. That was the season when Unser and the immaculate white Eagle set quick time for seven of 11 USAC Indy car events.

The 1972 season saw Bobby set one-lap track records at every stop on the Championship Trail except the second race at Milwaukee. But he only won four of those races--the only four he finished--and placed eighth in the point standings.

He failed to finish any of the three Triple Crown 500-milers, despite being the fastest qualifier for each of them. Still, the lanky, outspoken racer had become the Babe Ruth of speed, making the 200-mph barrier at Indianapolis look like a real possibility for the first time with his 195.9 mph qualifying run.

He was also the first to insist that the 200 mph mark wasn't going to be the last barrier, like Ruth's home-run standard of 714. He may have had a little coaching there from a guy named Aaron.

"There is no limit," said Bobby U. "Speeds will always increase at Indianapolis and other race tracks. It's the American way--you just don't stand still."

Standing still has never been one of Bobby Unser's traits. When you're part of the racing Unsers, you have to keep moving--fast.

Like any good Unser, Bobby started his fast stepping on the side of Pikes Peak. He outdid even his kinfolks by being first to the top at the Peak 11 different times, a Hillclimb record.

He also tried the Modified circuits

around Albuquerque and found them to his liking, winning the New Mexico championship in 1950 and 1951. It was on to the Sprints and Midgets, and Bobby soon was the owner of seven USAC Sprint car feature wins and three Midget victories.

His Indianapolis career began in 1963, but it was three years before he went more than five miles in the race. Crashes knocked him and his Novi out of action in the first two laps for both '63 and '64.

But better times were at hand. He was eighth in '66 and ninth in '67. Then, in 1968, Bobby and the Eagle/Offy owned by the late Bob Wilke outdid the turbines to put themselves in Victory Lane.

The season amounted to everything a racing driver or ballplayer dreams of--home runs, triples, doubles and the World Series. Unser won five Indy car races, finished second in five more, and circled the bases with the USAC national crown on his head.

He also took a third in the Indy 500 the next year.

For the 1971 season, Bobby joined up with the Gurney operation and began building his reputation as the Sultan of Speed.

The biggest barrier-breaker came at Ontario in 1972, when Bobby proved his point about the limitlessness of racing speeds by qualifying at an amazing 201.374 mph for the California 500.

But he didn't win that race, which meant he didn't finish it, either. The 1973 season wasn't much of an improvement, as Unser showed great speed in qualifying but won only one race, the Milwaukee 150, and finished second in another, the Trenton 200. The season was capped with a frightening crash at Phoenix.

The batting slump disappeared dramatically when the '74 campaign for the pennant began, however. In the first four races of the season, Bobby Unser not only won two, but he finished all four. With wins at Ontario and Trenton--bringing his career total to 19--and seconds at Phoenix and Indy, he seemed to have regained his touch for swinging both for distance and average.

Bobby Unser was back in the ballgame.

BILLY VUKOVICH

BIRTHDATE—March 19, 1944; Hometown —Fresno, Cal.; National Championship division 4th; Midget division 58th. CAREER HIGHLIGHTS: 1968 Indianapolis 500 "Rookie of the Year"; Runner-up in 1973 Indianapolis 500; 1973 Michigan 125 winner; Entered Indianapolis 500 from 1968 thru 1974; Ontario 500 from 1971 thru 1974; Pocono 500 from 1971 thru 1974.

There are actually two Billy Vukovichs. Or, rather, there are two distinctly different sides to the one Billy Vukovich.

There is the bright, joyous side, the one that shows in the trackside hi-jinks with other young Indy 500 drivers, in the love for golf, in the backyard games of baseball with his son.

Then there is the darker side, the side that flairs into anger directed toward himself, his car, other drivers, or race officials, the side that sometimes finds him sitting on the inner wall at a track like Indy, his face half in shadows and locked for a moment in a stony, introspective stare at nothing in particular.

There is the Billy Vukovich of unmatched exuberance, who keeps shouting "I'm rich, I'm rich" after finishing second at Indianapolis in 1973. There is the Billy Vukovich of nagging self-doubts, who almost gave up the racing life a few years earlier.

Billy Vukovich is a complex, intriguing individual. As the son of the late Bill Vukovich, an Indy 500 driver of legendary proportions, young Billy knows the feeling of being under a microscope.

"You are put up to constant public criticism," Billy relates. "It's a lot tougher than the average person thinks.

"You come to find out that no matter how good you are somebody is going to say, 'You stink'."

By his own admission, Billy himself has been the one who says it to himself. He was saying it a lot when he considered quitting as a race driver at the close of the 1970 season.

"I wasn't accomplishing anything --nobody even wanted me to drive their car," reports Billy.

But not everyone agreed with that evaluation, least of all California trucking magnate Jerry O'Connell, for whom Billy had driven at Indy after his association with car owner J.C. Agajanian had come to a sudden, but understanding end.

O'Connell convinced Vukovich to stay with it and provided a car for the 1971 season. Not the best car around --as both Jerry and Billy would admit.

"To be honest with you, I've got my eye on something better for the future," said the always-outspoken Vukovich before the '71 campaign.

But O'Connell was looking toward something better, too. And it took the shape of an Eagle from Dan Gurney's factory and one of the best chief mechanics around, Jud Phillips, for the 1972 season.

Billy hasn't had to look any further. With O'Connell, Eagles, and Phillips, he has made his own future as an Indy car driver.

Vukovich, who came up through the Midgets and Sprint cars quickly, has forged a place for himself--as himself, not as anybody's son. He began back with Agajanian, taking "Rookie of the Year" honors in the 1968 Indy 500 with a seventh-place finish.

After those uncertain years, Billy asserted himself with a string of solid seasons in the cars that had long been synonymous with the name of Vukovich. He picked up a lot of seconds, thirds, and fourths in a three-year span that saw him place third ('71), second ('72), and fourth ('73) in the USAC national point standings.

But winning is the name of the game and Billy, naturally, wanted to play. His angry side had to come into the picture in the process, but he did it in the first of the Michigan International twin-125s in the fall of 1973.

Vukovich thought he had won that race, so he was less than calm when race officials told him he had been penalized to third place for passing the pace car on a yellow-light situation.

Billy was both vocal and demonstrative in his displeasure, but in the cool, calm light of the USAC offices a few weeks later, Billy got his first Indy car victory to go along with his 22 USAC Midget wins and two Sprint car triumphs.

It did wonders for that enigmatic face of the 30-year-old racer from Fresno, Cal. It was almost as if someone had said, "Will the real Billy Vukovich please stand up?"

And both of him did.

SALT WALTHER

BIRTHDATE—November 22, 1947; Hometown—West Carrollton, Ohio. CAREER HIGHLIGHTS: Entered 1972 Indianapolis, Pocono and Ontario 500-mile races; 1973 Indianapolis 500-Mile Race; 1947 Ontario, Indianapolis and Pocono 500-mile races.

Headlines--David "Salt" Walther made a lot of those in a year's time.

Given the choice, the dark-haired young racer would probably have declined the privilege of having his name in all the papers the way it was. "Walther Crashes in Flames" wasn't the kind of headline he wanted to make for himself.

But those headlines--the aftermath of the fiery frontstretch pileup that wiped out the original start of the 1973 Indy 500 and left Walther seriously injured--only told the first half of the story. By early 1974, his name was back in the papers, but this time the word "Comeback" appeared in large print beside it.

That quickly became the big story for '74--Salt Walther returning to the racing wars after being shot down in

flames and shrapnel at Indy. As we said, he would have preferred not to have anything to come back from, but it at least took some of the wind out of the "poor little rich kid" image he had worn through most of his racing career.

Salt had been thought of mainly as the son of George Walther, the Dayton, Ohio industrialist who had been entering cars at Indianapolis since 1955. A wide range of drivers, from Jaun Fangio to Bruce Jacobi, had wheeled cars around the Speedway for the president of Dayton-Walther Corp., a maker of cast steel wheels for trucks, trailer supports, and other transportation-oriented items.

But Mr. Walther had an aspiring Indy 500 driver right in his own home. "I can't tell you how I laid awake nights and dreamed of Indy," son Salt related. "There was simply nothing else in life for me."

While he was "bugging" his dad to drive the Indy car, Salt got his feet wet racing the family hydroplane--another long-standing Walther enterprise--and scattered USAC Sprint car races in the late '60s.

By 1971, Salt had convinced his father to give him a shot at the Indy car and he ran four USAC big car programs that year. He came to Indianapolis the following May and, though burdened with a less-than-new car, made the lineup with a surprisingly solid qualifying run.

The young driver with a weight-lifter's physique--because he was one--made it only as far as the second turn on race day, however, as his engine let loose on the first lap. He did better at both Pocono and Ontario, with eighth and sixth place finishes, respectively.

Then came Indy '73. Walther again qualified well, but failed to get through the first half-lap. At the climax of an awkward race start, Salt's blue year-old McLaren pinwheeled down the front straightaway like a fiery meteor.

Walther suffered serious burns and a broken wrist. He lost the tips of the fingers on his left hand to the flames.

But, less than a year later, the 26-year-old racer was the driver of record in the Dayton-Walther Special, qualifying and racing in the '74 California 500. Heading back for that third try at troublesome Indy, Salt Walther had his eyes set on making some new headlines for himself--not as a racing rich kid, not as a wreck survivor, but as Salt Walther, Indy 500 race driver.

TECHNICAL SCENE

A Close-Up Look At Some of The Exotic, Well-Manicured Parts That Make Up Today's Indianapolis 500 Racer

Wally Dallenbach's STP Eagle personifies the "typical" 1974 Indianapolis 500 race car: Frontal area is designed to take full advantage of the air passing over it as evidenced by the "air-splitters" mounted just forward of the front tires.

Yearbook staffer Bob Tronolone took this unusual angle photo of Jerry Grant's mount. For the most part, engine area is virtually ignored as far as bodywork is concerned. The rear wing narrower than the '73 models is the result of a rule change made in an effort to slow the cars down. The idea (which works) is that the wider wing allowed more downforce which in turn allowed the car to "stick" better thru the turns. Drivers report a definite change in handling characteristics.

The car above may be transformed into this condition with about two minutes work with the removal of the all-fiberglass body. This particular Eagle is the one driven by Lloyd Ruby. The tubular assembly up front supports nose and wings which create a teriffic downforce on the vehicle.

There haven't been many McLarens built since the marque first appeared, but those that have appeared have all been successful. The car above is the immaculate machine Gary Bettenhausen drove.

Johnny Rutherford's winning McLaren sported a sleek cover over the engine compartment. Covers over the side radiators are of naugahyde material and are used only when the car is being worked on (so the paint doesn't get scratched!).

To the casual eye, the front end of a McLaren doesn't appear much different than the Eagle on opposite page, but subtle changes may mean the difference between a car that handles well and one that doesn't.

The rear-wing mounting on a McLaren differs greatly from other Speedway cars: Note there is a single pylon mount in the center that is fully adjustable.

Although this rear view makes the rear of the McLaren appear a complex item, photo at left shows how simple it really is.

McLAREN

The complete rear trans-axle assembly of Rutherford's winning McLaren may be removed in a matter of minutes.

Foyt's radically low Coyote presents a rakish look when photographed in a still position. The mysterious cover over the nose was probably psychological warfare, but did serve to hide some never-before seen aerodynamic devices within the nose.

Foyt's long-time assistant, Jack Starnes wheels the wide Coyote up for a tire change. Entire body of the car serves as a wing.

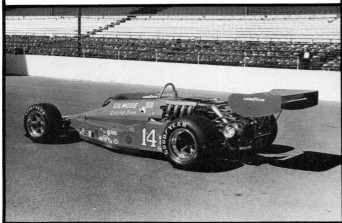

Side Coyote view shows the plexiglass spoiler running alongside left side that Foyt used in an attempt to further cut wind drag.

Dick Simon's Eagle utilized a Foyt engine and a different rear body cover that were dubbed fenders by fellow racers.

Bobby Unser's car showed up at Ontario with the slab-sided wing shown at left but didn't race with it. Fron left, different schools of

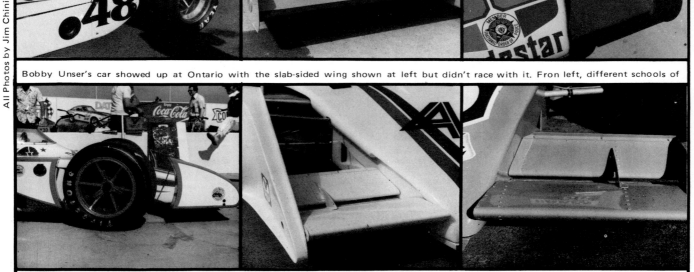

thought are shown in front wing treatment: McLaren, Mosley's Eagle, Mosley's Eagle at Ontario, Simon's Eagle and Jerry Grant's Eagle.

Left, engine builder Carl Cindric puts finishing touches on an Offy. Cindric is currently under tutelage of Herb Porter (center), one of the foremost engine research and development men in the country. Right, Frank DelRoy, tech committee chairman checks out an intake log manifold.

All Photos by Jim Chini

Left, high-quality Premier Supertanium bolts are used throughout most Speedway cars and aircraft safety wire is a precaution against vibration. Right, elbow grease and rubbing compound help make Indy cars the world's shinest.

Foyt (Ford) V-8 requires twice as much turbocharger plumbing as does Rutherford's McLaren, on right. Oil radiator helps keep temperature down and in right photo a back-up ignition is attached in case of failure during race.

Wheel nut safety lock; hydraulic slave cylinder in second photo allows cockpit adjustment of sway bar; the pop-off valve used for qualifying and the tuned exhaust header arrangement on winning McLaren.

THE
CHIEFS

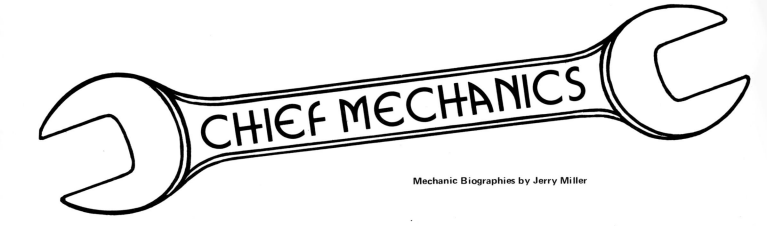

CHIEF MECHANICS

Mechanic Biographies by Jerry Miller

Photos by Jim Chini and Jerry Miller

DON KODA, Car 1

When you win the USAC National Championship in your first full season as an Indy car chief mechanic, you must be doing something right.

Don Koda did, and was. Don, another of the growing number of top-notch Japanese-American mechanics in USAC racing, didn't waste much time in establishing himself as a winner among chief mechanics on the USAC big car trail.

Koda, who spent several years working for veteran 500 mechanic A.J. Watson, became the crew chief for the Lindsey Hopkins McLaren of Roger McCluskey midway through the 1972 season. Almost immediately, he picked off one of the biggest prizes in racing,

the 1973 California 500 at Ontario Speedway.

He followed up by handling the mechanical chores on the car McCluskey drove to the USAC national crown in 1973, winning one race and finishing 12 of 14 events on the circuit. Koda remained on the job as chief mechanic for the radically new Riley/Offy entered for McCluskey in the 1974 Indy 500.

**TYLER ALEXANDER
Cars 3, 73**

Tyler Alexander was only 23-years-old when he joined a small new racing team in England. Now, 10 years later, that team has grown into the racing phenomenon known as Team McLaren and Alexander is recognized as one of the essential elements behind its success.

The Massachusetts-born, sandy-haired mechanic got the racing bug after studying aeronautical engineering. He soon became acquainted with

the Mayer brothers, Teddy and Tim, and worked on their Formula cars from 1961 until Tim's untimely death in 1964.

Tyler and Teddy then joined the new organization being formed by Grand Prix driver Bruce McLaren. Working side by side with McLaren, Alexander learned his racing engineering first-hand as a part of the factory that has turned out winning cars in three main areas--Formula I Grand Prix, USAC Championship cars and Can-Am Group 7 Sports Cars.

Alexander, a bachelor whose enthusiasm for photography is well-known at race tracks around the world, is now director of engineering for McLaren Racing and serves as co-chief mechanic for the Team McLaren cars entered in the 1974 Indianapolis 500 for drivers Johnny Rutherford and David Hobbs.

DENNIS DAVISS, Car 3

Dennis Daviss has been called the

"mystery man" of the Team McLaren crew.

That stemmed mainly from May, 1973, when Johnny Rutherford put a Team McLaren entry on the pole at Indy. When they held the traditional banquet honoring the crew on the pole-winning car, Daviss was auspicious by his absence.

But, in 1974, there was no mystery about the talents of the young Englishman who served as chief mechanic, together with McLaren engineering driector Tyler Alexander, on the No. 3 McLaren again driven by Rutherford. When they honored the winners of the 1974 Indy 500, Daviss was right there at the Victory Banquet to take his place beside Alexander, Rutherford and the rest of the Colnbrook-based McLaren crew.

JUD PHILLIPS, Car 4

Jud Phillips may have the clean-cut appearance and quiet mannerisms of a high school science teacher, but he's a master mechanic. Make no doubt about that.

If you need convincing, just ask the man who provides the Sugaripe Eagle/Offy cars Jud prepares for Billy Vukovich to drive at Indy and the other stops on the Championship Trail. "The guy is really phenomenal," says car owner Jerry O'Connell. "He has been ticklish in everything that he does.

"He just doesn't put a bolt on and let it sit--he analyzes everything he does and makes sure that everything is right. The man is just fantastic in his ability to keep engines running and to keep a chassis together."

That ability, which Jud has nurtured in a racing career that stretches over 21 years, has made the crewcut mechanic a winner in Indianapolis-style racing. Phillips, whose Indy career began as a crewman on the Bob Estes cars of the '50s, has posted 15 victories as a Champ car chief mechanic, including Bobby Unser's 1968 Indy 500 win and Billy Vukovich's first triumph in an O'Connell car at the 1973 Michigan 125.

JOHNNY CAPELS, Car 5

Johnny Capels has never really given up the idea of being a race driver, even with two USAC National Championships under his belt as a chief mechanic.

"I've never officially retired as a driver," says the bushy-haired young man who was in charge of Mario Andretti's 1974 Indy entry. "I'm not really fighting it, though, because it appears I might be able to make a name for myself this way, better than I ever could have as a driver."

Capels, 37, came out of Albuquerque, New Mexico, after racing a couple of guys named Unser on that area's tracks and quickly proved his driving ability by winning a USAC Sprint car feature at Hamburg, New York, in the fall of 1968. But, by 1970, he was firmly entrenched as one of the top wrenches on the Vel's-Parnelli Racing operations, working first on Al Unser's Indy car and then moving over to the team car of Joe Leonard.

Leonard drove a Capels-prepared machine to three Indy car victories and consecutive USAC National Championship titles in 1971 and 1972.

When Leonard was sidelined at Ontario in March, Johnny was designated as chief mechanic for Andretti's Indy 500 effort.

EARLE MACMULLAN, Car 8

Did Earle Macmullan have any idea, 15 years ago when he went to work in a service station, that he would someday be chief mechanic on a top USAC Championship racing car? "Not really," recalls Earle, crew chief for Gary Bettenhausen's Penske Racing McLaren, "but even then, I always enjoyed working on race cars more than anything else."

That enjoyable side of his work eventually led Macmullan to a job in 1969 with Penske Racing, preparing the Camaro that would carry Mark Donohue to the year's Trans-Am Championship. He did the same for Mark's 1971 title-winning Javelin in the same series.

In 1972, Macmullan became chief mechanic for Bettenhausen's Champ car, which promptly won the Trenton 200, led 138 laps at Indianapolis and placed second in the California 500 and Trenton 300. That brought the 40-year-old Bethlehem, Pa., resident a special award as the outstanding first-year chief mechanic on the USAC Championship Trail.

MIKE DEVIN, Car 9

Mike Devin has accomplished a lot in his racing career, but he still points back with pride at a somewhat unofficial record he shared with his boss at the time, Jerry Eisert.

Eisert, of course, was the West Coast Indy car builder who did his best to make a stock-block Chevrolet engine competitive on the USAC trail. "Of the normally-aspirated engines, we lost only one engine in four years of running," notes Devin, reflecting on his tour of duty with Eisert.

He moved on to the Patrick Racing team near the end of the 1969 season, serving as chief mechanic on the Indy car driven by Johnny Rutherford.

GARY BOND, Car 11

Devin, now 34, has been the crew chief for the Eagles driven by veteran campaigner Lloyd Ruby at Indy and elsewhere the past two seasons.

If Duane Carter Jr. was "Rookie of the Year" for the 1974 Indianapolis 500, then so was Gary Bond, his rookie chief mechanic.

Bond, better known until recently as an up-and-coming Midget driver, rose to chief mechanic status in '74 after spending his formative years with such racing luminaries as Clint Brawner, Phil Casey and Jim McGee. Gary was a part of McGee's crew on the 1973 Indy entry driven by Mario Andretti.

Bond drew his first assignment as a crew chief with Richard Beith's American Kids Racer in the '74 California 500 in March. For Indy, Gary was reunited with McGee-who had switched from the Vel's-Parnelli "Super-Team" to the Cobre Firestone operation--as he made his Indy debut as a chief mechanic with Carter and the No. 11 Cobre entry.

A.J. Foyt Sr. has a fairly famous racing son, of course, but he has compiled some pretty impressive racing accomplishments in his own right.

Foyt Sr., for example, shares with George Bignotti the distinction of being the only chief mechanics to have winners in each of the three USAC Triple Crown races. Son A.J. Jr. did the honors at Indianapolis and Pocono, while another Texan, Jim McElreath, put the third jewel in Tony's pocket as winner of the inaugural Ontario 500 in 1970.

Tony Foyt has won a total of 15 USAC Championship races since he took over the mechanical chores for his famous son in 1966. He ranks sixth--with Jud Phillips--on the all-time list of race-winning USAC chief mechanics.

The Foyts, Sr. and Jr., now turn out their super-slick Coyote/Foyt Indy cars in the Houston race shop that formerly housed the family's garage business. Two of the cars were entered for the 1974 Indy 500, with A.J. Jr. and George Snider the assigned drivers.

Chief mechanics don't always have something to smile about, but

that doesn't stop Phil Casey. Some of his colleagues may have more victories, but none of them can match the personable, dark-haired wrench-man in smiles per hour.

Casey, one of those old-school mechanics who believes in enjoying his work, started out as the mechanic on the Midgets and Supermodifieds

A.J. FOYT SR., Car 14, 82

PHIL CASEY, Car 15

George Snider drove when he first came out of California to break into the national racing scene. Phil later moved on to be the crew chief for the Fred and Don Gerhardt entries driven at Indy and elsewhere by Gary Bettenhausen, Jim Malloy, Jim McElreath and Mike Hiss.

Bettenhausen brought Casey his

two USAC Championship wins, at Phoenix in 1968 and Michigan International in 1970. By the 1973 season, Phil had brought his smiles and talents over to the Vel's-Parnelli stable and came to the 1974 Indy go-round as chief mechanic on the No. 15 Eagle piloted by two-time Indy winner Al Unser.

TED SWIONTEK, Car 18

It only takes one quick glance to figure out why they call Ted Swiontek "Tobacco Ted." That bulge in his cheek ain't bubble gum.

Swiontek is known for more than that wad of chewing tobacco around racing circles, though. He first gained recognition as the mechanic on the meticulously-prepared bronze-colored No. 42 Ziegler Sprinter that spent a few seasons on the USAC Sprint car trail with drivers like Herman Wise, Ralph Liguori and Gary Ponzini.

Tobacco Ted made his debut as an Indy car crew chief with the Unsponsored Special of John Martin in 1973. For Indy '74, he was the chief mechanic for Richard Beith's American Kids Eagle/Offy driven by Bill Simpson.

George Bignotti has been to Victory Lane so many times he could probably find the place blindfolded.

The 57-year-old second-generation Italian-American has stepped up beside the silver Borg-Warner trophy at the conclusion of six Indianapolis 500s, more than any other Indy chief mechanic. He has made similar trips to the winner's circle on the USAC

GEORGE BIGNOTTI
Cars 20, 40, 60

Championship Trail 66 times (as of this writing), again more than any other chief mechanic.

It has been a long and glorious road for the acknowledged master of Indy chief mechanics, who began his career in San Francisco by qualifying his own Midget cars and then turning them over to a "hot shoe" for the feature races. He came to Indianapolis racing in 1954 and almost quit four years later because his cars hadn't won a single race.

But he stuck with it and became a big winner, with drivers like Jud Larson, A.J. Foyt, Graham Hill, Al Unser, Joe Leonard, Wally Dallenbach, and 1973 Indy winner Gordon Johncock adding to his ledger of victories. He now has charge of the Patrick Racing Team's trio of Indy Eagle/Offys, driven by Johncock, Dallenbach, and Steve Krisiloff -- prepared in George's immaculate workshop at the Indianapolis headquarters of Louis Meyer Inc.

Bignotti has won so many races he's starting to think about retirement, but he still wants to renew his acquaintance with Victory Lane and its silver trophy just once more. "I'd like to win Indianapolis one more time, then maybe I could turn things over to the younger people," says George.

You have to figure an Indy chief mechanic with 25 Champ car wins on the books would be getting a little middle-aged by now, his hair graying or disappearing and his waist-line developing a "spare tire."

Until you run into Jim McGee,

who still has his youth, his thick black hair, and his waistline. The young Easterner with a gift for things mechanical has shot to the top of his trade in a relatively short number of years.

McGee came to the fore as the right-hand man of long-time Champ car mechanic Clint Brawner in the

JIM McGEE, Car 21

mid-60s. Jim shared 24 USAC victories with Brawner as co-chief mechanic on the cars driven by Mario Andretti, the biggest of the bunch being the win in the 1969 Indianapolis 500.

McGee and Brawner left Andretti and the Andy Granatelli team in 1970 to start their own stable, but Jim returned for the 1971 season. Then, he and Andretti switched over to the Vel's-Parnelli operation in 1972, going on to get another Indy car win at Trenton in 1973.

For 1974, McGee succeeded his former tutor, Brawner, as top wrench on the Cobre Firestone entry driven at Indy by Jimmy Caruthers.

Grant King's racing organization has been described as "the most successful independent racing operation going." It is an apt description.

King, a 40-year-old race car builder born in Canada of Chinese parentage, has gained a reputation as a top racing constructor with an outpouring of winning cars from his Indianapolis shop, from the Sprint cars and Championship Dirt cars that have been big winners on their respective circuits to

RON FALK, Car 55

Ron Falk is another of those amazing young racing mechanics out of California's San Fernando Valley.

The mustachioed mechanic came to Indianapolis racing in the early '60s, after a tour in the U.S. Navy. He was a crew member with the Andy Granatelli stable for several years.

He became crew chief for the Cobre Firestone car driven by Lee Kunzman in the 1973 USAC season. Falk was chief mechanic for that entry at Indy this May but, with Kunzman sidelined with injuries, the car was driven by Jerry Grant.

Among his most talked-about mechanical ventures--if not the most sophisticated--revolves around a '29 Ford pickup he once owned, the engine of which somehow found its way into a Sprint car campaigned by another San Fernando Valleyite, Don Brown.

Hank Higuchi may be Indy's most reluctant chief mechanic.

"I had to take Hank fishing five times to get him to come back and be my chief this year," reported Jim Hurtubise, who finally persuaded Higuchi to serve as crew chief on his 1974 Indy entry.

Hank wasn't always that reluctant. It didn't take nearly so much coaxing for him to come out of Gardena, Cal. in the '50s as mechanic and co-owner of a Sprint car that became a familiar sight on the Sprint circuit. A number of the era's top drivers were behind the wheel at one time or another, including one named Jim Hurtubise.

The quiet-spoken Japanese-American mechanic worked with Herb Porter and the Racing Associates Champ car team before Hurtubise plied him with a few catfish and made him a regular feature of his Indy car operation. Hank was co-chief mechanic with George Morris on Jim's 1973 Indy entry.

HANK HIGUCHI, Car 56

GLENN HALL, Car 59

Glenn Hall tried to take Indy by storm in 1973, but it rained on his parade.

Hall, who had 20 years of experience as a racing mechanic, plunged into the Indy scene in May 1973 as chief mechanic for the Hoffman Racing car driven by rookie Larry Cannon. Hall, who had been the wrenchman for 1968 Drag Racing Champion Norm Ries, was the first to realize he'd tried to accomplish too much too soon.

"Anybody in their right mind wouldn't have come to Indy two weeks before the race and expect to make the show," said the 38-year-old Cincinnati, Ohio mechanic who saw his car make the 500 field the second time around.

For many years, Jim Wright's career was inexorably linked with that of one of racing's great young stars, the late Swede Savage.

Wright began working on the various racing machines driven by Savage back when Swede was under Dan Gurney's wing at the AAR Eagle factory. When Savage moved along to the Patrick Racing operation for the 1972 Indy car campaign, Jim went with him as mechanic and friend.

In 1973, Wright became a member of George Bignotti's crew, working on the Patrick entry driven by Savage until his untimely death at Indianapolis. The burly, sometimes-temperamental mechanic returned to Indy this year as crew chief on the No. 61 Eisenhour-Brayton car driven by Rick Muther.

JIM WRIGHT, Car 61

KARL KAINHOFER, Car 68

HYWEL ABSALOM, Car 73

TOM SMITH, Car 77

Karl Kainhofer isn't the type to shout his own praises. But the man he works for, Roger Penske, will tell you all you want to know about the contributions of the quiet Austrian with the thinning hair and distinctive accent.

"Karl's organizational ability and tireless efforts have set a great example for our people," says the namesake of Penske Racing. "His race cars certainly reflect the fine workmanship it takes to field competitive cars--just look at his track record with us."

Kainhofer, whose mechanical career began with motorcycles in Austria and next led to the Porsche factory in Stuttgart, first met Penske when Roger raced Porsches on the Road Racing trail. Karl helped prepare those cars over two seasons, then joined Penske permanently when the American retired from the cockpit and formed his new racing team in 1966.

Recognition came quickly for Kainhofer. He received the D-A Mechanical Achievement Award in 1971, after driver Mark Donohue smashed the 180 mph barrier at Indy with his Penske McLaren. The same year, Kainhofer and Donohue met in the winner's circle at the Pocono 500 and Michigan 200, then got together again in Victory Lane at Indy the following May.

For 1974, Karl went after his second Indy 500 victory as chief mechanic on the new Penske McLaren driven by Mike Hiss.

Hywel "Hughie" Absalom "just got interested" in racing in 1963. By 1965, he was working on the Formula I Grand Prix cars driven by Jack Brabham and Dan Gurney.

From the Brabham factory, he moved to Lotus in 1967 and worked on that marquee's Indianapolis entries, including the turbine car driven by Art Pollard in 1968. He joined Team McLaren in 1969, working first on their Formula I project and then becoming a regular member of the team's Indianapolis contingent.

For 1974, Absalom, a 30-year-old Welshman, shares responsibility with McLaren engineering manager Tyler Alexander for preparation of the No. 73 McLaren driven at Indianapolis by David Hobbs. While a serious worker at trackside, Hughie is known by his colleagues as "an absolute terror" with his penchant for practical jokes away from the race track.

Tom Smith's approach to preparing racing cars is simple and direct.

"My job is to give the driver, owner and sponsor the fastest, best prepared and safest car I can put together," says Smith, chief mechanic for the Dayton-Walther No. 77 driven by Salt Walther. Smith has been working on George Walther's Indianapolis entries since 1966. Smith, whose command of the language and sense of humor is a cut above the usual mechanic's stereotype, became so tied in with the Walther racing efforts that he moved his racing shop from Indianapolis to Dayton, Ohio, site of Walther's headquarters, and now Tom also calls it home.

Don Kenyon has been working on racing cars so long now that most people don't realize he used to do a little race driving, too.

Don and brother Mel both were familiar figures at tracks in Illinois and Iowa when they started out in the late '50s. Both drove Midgets in UARA back then, but when Mel Kenyon took

DON KENYON, Car 79

GRANT KING, Car 24

Cars built, designed and/or prepared by King have won USAC Championship races at Milwaukee, Wis., Dover, Del., the Pikes Peak Hillclimb and innumerable Dirt Champ and Sprint car features.

Ted Hall is probably used to being called a "boy wonder" by this time.

Hall burst onto the racing scene at a rather tender age, coming along as car owner and chief mechanic for fellow Missourian Greg Weld while still a teenager. The exploits of the two Kansas City area teenagers on the Supermodified circuits eventually led them both to the garage of veteran race car builder Grant King.

Weld drove for King on the Championship Trail from 1969 to 1972 and Hall rapidly matured his own mechanical talents. The trio had been nothing short of sensational on the Dirt Champ circuit, putting King's Plymouth-powered machine on the pole for four of the big car events in 1969.

By 1974, former boy wonder Ted Hall was designated as co-chief mechanic with King on the No. 24 Kingfish/Offy to be driven by Indy rookie Tom Sneva.

DICK OEFFINGER, Car 27

his famous "Chinese McLaren" and "Kingfish" Indianapolis-style machines. And, as the word "independent" indicates, it has all been done without the luxury of being independently wealthy or having gigantic sponsorship contracts.

King, who came to Indy in 1974 as owner, builder and co-chief mechanic on the No. 24 Kingfish driven by rookie Tom Sneva, served his racing apprenticeship working for the Indy car operations of people like Rolla Vollstedt, Jim Robbins Racing and STP Racing over the past 10 years. He formed his own racing team in mid-1970 and he and his attractive blonde wife, Doris, have become among the most familiar and popular figures in USAC racing.

October 13, 1968 is a date Dick Oeffinger isn't likely to forget.

That was the day his name went into the record books as a race-winning chief mechanic on the USAC Championship Trail. The car, the Weinberger Homes Eagle/Offy, wasn't the newest car on the scene and its driver, Sports Car racer Ronnie Bucknum, had never won a USAC race--in fact, he's never driven on any oval track except Indy before that day--but they were the big news of USAC's 250-miler at the brand-new Michigan International Speedway.

Oeffinger has been a regular in USAC Championship racing ever since. For the 1974 version of the Indy 500, he returned as chief mechanic on the new Rolla Vollstedt entry, driven by Indy rookie Tom Bigelow.

early Supermodifieds, has gone on to gain a stature approaching Gordon's on the USAC Championship racing scene. As an Indy car chief mechanic, Duane has recorded seven Championship wins, those victories coming from 1965-69 with Johncock.

After Gordon dropped his own racing operations to drive for Team McLaren in 1972, Glasgow signed on with the Lindsey Hopkins stable, serving as crew chief on the car driven by Lee Kunzman in the 1973 Indianapolis 500. For 1974, Duane was the chief mechanic on the Hopkins Eagle/Offy piloted at Indy by Jerry Karl.

TED HALL, Co-Chief Mechanic
Car 24

When Gordon Johncock burst onto the national racing scene in the early '60s, so did Duane Glasgow.

The yellow-haired mechanic, who had been the mechanic on Johncock's

DUANE GLASGOW, Car 42

KEITH RANDOL, Car 44

Lynn Reid has been bitten by two of the world's most persistent "bugs" in his life--the racing bug and the photography bug.

Reid, who holds a bachelor's degree in photography from the Rochester Institute of Technology, keeps saying he plans to retire from racing to run the camera store he owns in Logansport, Ind. So far, he hasn't quite made it.

The young, mustachioed mechanic served his racing apprenticeship as an assistant to Jack Beckley on the Lindsey Hopkins racing team. He joined the Gerhardt Racing operation in 1972 and succeeded Phil Casey as chief mechanic on the car driven by Mike Hiss in 1973.

For '74, Lynn came to Indianapolis--not Logansport, mine you--as crew chief for the No. 45 Gerhardt entry driven by veteran Jim Mc-Elreath.

Though Wayne Leary has been involved with almost every imaginable type of racing machinery, he has now become mainly identified as the man who puts Dan Gurney's fabulous racing Eagles into shape.

Leary, the dark-haired mechanical

The Eagles built by Gurney, driven by Unser, and prepared by Leary have been the fastest things on wheels on the Indy car circuit since 1971. The low-slung white cars have set track records at every track on the USAC trail at least once and still hold the ultimate lap record of 201.965 mph at Ontario Motor Speedway.

Fresh from a victory in the 1974 California 500, Leary returned to Indy this May as crew chief for the No. 48 Eagle entry.

**JIMMY DILAMARTER
Car 51**

Keith Randol learned his craft from a master.

Randol got his early mechanical training in the racing garage of Jud Phillips, one of the most respected and successful Indy car mechanics around. Working with Phillips, who prepared the famed Bob Estes cars and Bruce Homeyer's Konstant Hot Roadsters, Keith learned the ins and outs of being a first-line chief mechanic.

And now he are one. Randol was designated as the crew chief for the No. 44 Eagle/Foyt owned and driven by Dick Simon in the 1974 Indy 500.

WAYNE LEARY, Car 48

whiz who has been involved with Gurney's racing efforts since the early '60s, has recorded a total of 16 USAC Championship Trail victories. Gurney posted seven of those when he was still behind the wheel; the other nine have come after Gurney retired and Bobby Unser stepped into the cockpit.

Almost everyone agrees that Jimmy Dilamarter is a young man with a bright future in auto racing.

Dilamarter, another of the "young lions" among Indy 500 mechanics, has, in a few short years, become a key figure in the racing fortunes of the Vel's-Parnelli racing team. He was a crew member on the Vel's-Parnelli cars driven to victory by Al Unser in 1970 and 1971, working at the side of the dean of Indy crew chiefs, George Bignotti.

Over the past few seasons, Jimmy has served in various capacities on the crews preparing Vel's-Parnelli cars for Unser and teammate Mario Andretti. He was with the Unser entry in 1973 and, for Indy '74, was chief mechanic on the Vel's-Parnelli car driven by rookie Jan Opperman.

LYNN REID, Car 45

his shot at USAC racing in the early '60s brother Don decided to devote himself to the mechanical end of things.

Kenyon has been preparing the Midgets and Indy cars Mel drives ever since, sometimes working on a stable of two Midgets and two Champ cars at the same time in the Kenyon brothers' shop at Lebanon, Ind.

While Mel Kenyon's entry was still in line when qualifications for the '74 Indy 500 came to a close, the second Lindsey Hopkins-owned car under Don's care was in the starting lineup.

There was a new face among Gasoline Alley's chief mechanics. It belonged to a 30-year-old Californian named Mike Mullins, crew chief for the red No. 89 McLaren/Offy driven by John Martin.

Mike, with a mechanical background in Midgets, Sprints and Drag Racing cars on the West Coast, had never even been to the Indy track before his arrival this May. He joined the Automotive Technology crew over the past winter and worked his first Indy car race at the California 500 in March.

The Cypress, Cal., resident admitted he was doing a lot of learning in his first try as an Indy chief mechanic. "I've just been fortunate that John

(Martin) has a lot of patience and has been willing to show me how things are done here," Mullins said.

Bill Finley may be the last of a particular breed of racing mechanic-- the kind that really enjoys getting their hands dirty and their brows sweaty.

Finley, a 47-year-old long-term mechanic with a skimpy mustache and a craftsman's love for building race cars with his bare hands, has been at it for a long time. He drove Sprint cars when he was 20 and eventually drifted into the mechanical side of his chosen sport.

For the past several years, he has been building, designing and pampering the Indianapolis 500 cars owned by Greek shipping mogul Tassi Vatis. For 1974, Finley was in charge of the No. 94 Vatis car he designed himself and Johnny Parsons put it in the race.

While his cars admittedly have not been the most expensive pieces of machinery at the Speedway, no one questions the fact that each part of those racing cars has been put together with the love, care and sweat of a dedicated racing mechanic. Anyone who has been around Gasoline Alley at all knows the picture of Bill Finley-- bent down over his race car, periodi-

cally wiping his grimy hands on his smeared mechanic's trousers and wiping the glistening sweat from his mechanic's brow.

A.J. Watson admittedly has had some problems adjusting to the switch from front-engine roadsters to rear-engined cars at the Indianapolis 500.

"Yes, I have had a couple of problems with them," A.J. has said, of the newer rear-engine Indy cars. Of course, they're not really that much of a problem--if you can build things, you can build them front-engine or rear-engine."

There has never been much doubt about Watson's ability to build things, especially those famous Indy roadsters of the '50s and early '60s. From 1955 to 1965, roadsters built and/or prepared by Watson, or copied from his blueprints, rolled into Victory Lane at Indy eight times.

Working with Eagles from Dan Gurney's shops and relying on the driving talents of young Mike Mosley, Watson has returned to the winning ways of his roadster years. Two victories, including the Phoenix 150 this March, have pushed Watson's career total to 27 in USAC Championship competition.

MIKE MULLINS, Car 89

BILL FINLEY, Car 94

A.J. WATSON, Car 98

THE FACTS

TIMES AND AVERAGES

STATISTICS OF THE 1911 500-MILE RACE

Honorary Referee—R. P. Hooper *Starter*—Fred J. Wagner *Pacemaker*—Carl G. Fisher

Open to Cars with a Piston Displacement of 600 Cubic Inches or Under

Pos.	No.	Car and Driver	Cyldrs.	Bore	Stroke	Piston Displace.	Time	M. P. H.
1	32	Marmon, Harroun	6	4½	5	447.1	6:42:08	74.59
2	33	Lozier, Mulford	4	5⅜	6	544.6	6:43:51	74.29
3	28	Fiat, Bruce-Brown	4	5	7½	589.0	6:52:29	72.73
4	11	Mercedes, Wishart	4	5.1	7.1	580.2	6:52:57	72.65
5	31	Marmon, Dawson	4	4.5	7	445.3	6:54:34	72.34
6	2	Simplex, Ralph De Palma	4	5¾	5¾	597.2	7:02:02	71.13
7	20	National, Merz	4	5	5 9/16	436.8	7:06:20	70.37
8	12	Amplex, Turner	4	5 5/16	5	443.3	7:15:56	68.82
9	15	Knox, Belcher	6	5	4¾	559.1	7:17:09	68.63
10	25	Jackson, Cobe	4	5	5½	431.9	7:21:50	67.90

Finished—Stutz, Anderson; Mercer, Hughes.

Running at the finish—Firestone, Frayer; National, Wilcox; Mercer, Bigelow; Inter-State, H. Endicott; Velie, Hall; Benz, Knipper, Benz, Burman; Simplex, Beardsley; Fiat, Hearne-Parker; Pope-Hartford, Fox; Cutting, Delaney; Jackson, Tower; McFarlan, Marquette; Cole, W. Endicott.

Also started—National, Aitken, 125 laps; Case, Jones, 122; Case, Strang, 109; Westcott, Knight, 90; Case, Jagersberger, 87; Apperson, Lytle, 82; Alco, Grant, 51; Buick, C. Basle, 46; Pope-Hartford, Disbrow, 45; Buick, A. Chevrolet, 30; Fiat, Bragg, 24; Jackson, Ellis, 22; Lozier, Tetzlaff. 20; Amplex, Greiner, 12.

STATISTICS OF THE 1912 500-MILE RACE

Honorary Referee—R. P. Hooper *Starter*—Fred J. Wagner *Pacemaker*—Carl G. Fisher

Open to Cars with a Piston Displacement of 600 Cubic Inches or Under

Pos.	No.	Car and Driver	Cyldrs.	Bore	Stroke	Piston Displace.	Time	M. P. H.
1	8	National, Dawson	4	5	6¼	490.8	6:21:06	78.72
2	3	Fiat, Tetzlaff	4	5	7½	589.0	6:31:29	76.6
3	21	Mercer, Hughes	4	4⅜	5	300.7	6:33:09	76.31
4	20	Stutz, Merz	4	4¾	5½	389.9	6:34:40	76.01
5	18	Schacht, W. Endicott	4	4¾	5½	389.9	6:46:28	73.81
6	2	Stutz, Zengel	4	4¾	5½	389.9	6:50:28	73.09
7	14	White, Jenkins	6	4¼	5¾	489.4	6:52:38	72.70
8	22	Lozier, Horan	4	5⅜	6	544.6	6:59:38	71.49
9	9	National, Wilcox	4	5	7½	589.0	7:11:30	69.52
10	19	Knox, Mulford	6	4.8	5½	597.16	8:53:00	56.29

Also started—Mercedes, R. DePalma, 198 laps; Cutting, Burman, 156; Mercedes, Wishart, 82; Simplex, Dingley, 116; Lozier, Matson, 107; Stutz, Anderson, 79; Marquette-Buick, Liesaw, 72; Case, Disbrow, 67; McFarlan, Marquette, 63; Case, Hearne, 54; Firestone, Rickenbacker, 44; National, Bruce-Brown, 24; Lexington, Knight, 7; Opel, Ormsby, 5.

STATISTICS OF THE 1913 500-MILE RACE

Honorary Referee—Laurens Enos *Starter*—Charles P. Root *Pacemaker*—Carl G. Fisher

Open to Cars with a Piston Displacement of 450 Cubic Inches or Under

Pos.	No.	Car and Driver	Cyldrs.	Bore	Stroke	Piston Displace.	Time	M.P.H.
1	16	Peugeot, Goux	4	4.246	7.875	448.13	6:35:05.00	75.933
2	22	Mercer, Wishart	4	4.370	5.000	299.00	6:48:13.40	73.49
3	2	Stutz, Merz	4	4.813	5.500	399.97	6:48:49.25	73.38
4	9	Sunbeam, Guyot	6	3.540	6.290	367.52	7:02:58.95	70.92
5	23	Mercedes-Knight, Pilette	4	3.937	5.118	251.33	7:20:13.00	68.15
6	12	Gray Fox, Wilcox	4	4.750	5.500	389.90	7:23:26.55	67.65
7	29	Mercedes, Mulford	4	4.489	7.087	448.66	7:28:05.50	66.95
8	31	Case, Disbrow	4	5.100	5.500	449.00	7:29:09.00	66.80
9	35	Mason, Haupt	4	4.316	6.000	350.50	7:52:35.10	63.48
10	25	Tulsa, Clark	4	4.752	5.500	340.10	7:56:14.25	62.99

Running at the finish—Keeton, Burman.

Also started—Stutz, Anderson, 187 laps; Mason, Evans, 158; Anel, Liesaw, 148; Mercer, Bragg, 128; Henderson, Knipper, 125; Isotta, Tetzlaff, 118; Case, Nikrent, 67; Mason, Tower, 51; Isotta, Trucco, 39; Nyberg, H. Endicott, 23; Peugeot, Zuccarelli, 18; Mercer, R. DePalma, 15; Isotta, Grant, 14; Schacht, Jenkins, 13; Stutz, Herr, 7; Case, W. Endicott, 1.

STATISTICS OF THE 1914 500-MILE RACE

Honorary Referee—John A. Wilson *Starter*—Thomas J. Hay *Pacemaker*—Carl G. Fisher

Open to Cars with a Piston Displacement of 450 Cubic Inches or Under

Pos.	No.	Car and Driver	Cyldrs.	Bore	Stroke	Piston Displace.	Time	M. P. H.
1	16	Delage, Thomas	4	4.13	7.08	380.2	6:03:45	82.47
2	14	Peugeot, Duray	4	3.07	6.18	183.0	6:10:24	80.99
3	10	Delage, Guyot	4	4.13	7.08	380.2	6:14:01	80.21
4	6	Peugeot, Goux	4	3.94	7.08	345.0	6:17:24	79.49
5	3	Stutz, Oldfield	4	4.80	6.00	434.3	6:23:51	78.15
6	9	Excelsior, Christiaens	6	3.80	6.20	446.6	6:27:24	77.44
7	27	Sunbeam, Grant	6	3.14	5.90	273.0	6:36:22	75.69
8	5	Beaver Bullet, Keene	4	5.10	5.50	449.4	6:40:57	74.82
9	25	Maxwell, Carlson	4	4.20	8.00	445.3	7:02:42	70.97
10	42	Duesenberg, Rickenbacker	4	4.40	6.00	360.5	7:03:34	70.83

Finished—Mercedes, Mulford; Duesenberg, Haupt; Keeton, Knipper.

Also started—Peugeot, Boillot, 148 laps; Bugatti, Friedrich, 134; Burman, Disbrow, 128; Mercer, Wishart, 122; Stutz, Cooper, 118; Mercer, Bragg, 117; King, Klein, 87; Braender, Chandler, 69; Gray Fox, Wilcox, 67; Mason, Mason, 66; Burman, Burman, 47; Marmon, Dawson, 44; Stutz, Anderson, 42; Isotta, Gilhooley, 41; Maxwell, Tetzlaff, 38; Sunbeam, Chassagne, 20; Ray, Brock, 5.

STATISTICS OF THE 1915 500-MILE RACE

Referee—A. R. Pardington *Starter*—Thomas J. Hay *Pacemaker*—Carl G. Fisher

Open to Cars with a Piston Displacement of 300 Cubic Inches or Under

Pos.	No.	Car and Driver	Cyldrs.	Bore	Stroke	Piston Displace.	Time	M.P.H.
1	2	Mercedes, R. DePalma	4	3.620	6.500	274.0	5:33:55.51	89.84
2	3	Peugeot, Resta	4	3.620	6.670	276.0	5:37:24.94	88.91
3	5	Stutz, Anderson	4	3.800	6.480	295.3	5:42:27.58	87.60
4	4	Stutz, E. Cooper	4	3.800	6.480	295.3	5:46:19.36	86.62
5	15	Duesenberg, O'Donnell	4	3.980	6.000	299.0	6:08:13.27	81.47
6	8	Peugeot, Burman	4	3.650	7.100	296.0	6:13:19.61	80.36
7	1	Stutz, Wilcox	4	3.816	6.484	298.5	6:14:19.73	80.14
8	10	Duesenberg, Alley	4	3.980	6.000	299.0	6:15:08.01	79.97
9	19	Maxwell, Carlson-Hughes	4	3.750	6.750	298.0	6:19:55.90	78.96
10	7	Sunbeam, Van Raalte	4	3.700	6.300	274.0	6:35:23.43	75.87

Finished—Emden, Haupt.

Also started—Sunbeam, Grant, 184 laps; Maxwell, Orr, 168; Sunbeam, Porporato, 164; Sebring, J. Cooper, 154; Duesenberg, Mulford, 124; Peugeot, Babcock, 117; Kleinart, Klein, 111; Maxwell, Rickenbacker, 103; Cornelian, Chevrolet, 76; Delage, J. DePalma, 41; Mais, Mais, 23; Bugatti, Hill, 20; Purcell, Cox, 12.

TIMES AND AVERAGES

STATISTICS OF THE 1916 300-MILE RACE

Referee—Howard Marmon   *Starter*—George M. Dickson   *Pace Car*—Premier "6"

Open to Cars with a Piston Displacement of 300 Cubic Inches or Under

Pos.	No.	Car and Driver	Cyldrs.	Bore	Stroke	Piston Displace.	Time	M.P.H.
1	17	Peugeot, Resta	4	3.62	6.65	274	3:34:17	84.00
2	1	Duesenberg, D'Alene	4	3.75	6.75	299	3:36:15	83.24
3	10	Peugeot, Mulford	4	3.60	6.70	274	3:37:56	82.59
4	14	Sunbeam, Christiaens	6	3.18	5.90	299	3:46:36	79.44
5	15	Delage, Oldfield	4	3.72	6.30	275	3:47:19	79.18
6	4	Maxwell, Henderson	4	3.75	6.75	298	3:49:56	78.28
7	29	Premier, Wilcox	4	3.60	6.70	274	3:54:31	76.75
8	26	Crawford, Johnson	4	3.75	6.75	298	4:01:54	74.41
9	24	Crawford, Chandler	4	3.75	6.75	298	4:02:43	74.16
10	9	Osteweg, Haibe	4	4.34	5.00	296	4:03:10	74.02

Finished—Ogren, Alley.

Also started—Frontenac, L. Chevrolet, 82 laps; Premier, Anderson, 75; Crawford, Lewis, 71; Peugeot, Aitken, 69; Delage, DeVigne, 61; Premier, Rooney, 48; Frontenac, A. Chevrolet, 35; Peugeot, Merz, 25; Maxwell, Rickenbacker, 9; Peusun, Franchi, 9.

STATISTICS OF THE 1919 500-MILE RACE

Referee—E. V. Rickenbacker   *Starter*—E. C. Patterson   *Pace Car*—Packard V-12

Open to Cars with a Piston Displacement of 300 Cubic Inches or Under

Pos.	No.	Car and Driver	Cyldrs.	Bore	Stroke	Piston Displace.	Time	M.P.H.
1	3	Peugeot, Wilcox	4	3.60	6.70	274.6	5:40:42.87	88.05
2	14	Durant, Hearne	4	3.81	6.50	298.6	5:44:29.04	87.09
3	6	Peugeot, Goux	4	3.60	6.70	274.6	5:49:06.18	85.93
4	32	Ballot, Guyot	8	2.92	5.52	296.0	5:55:16.27	84.44
5	26	Bender, Alley	4	3.625	7.00	289.0	6:05:03.92	82.18
6	4	Packard, R. DePalma	12	2.657	4.50	299.2	6:10:10.64	81.04
7	7	Frontenac, L. Chevrolet	4	3.875	6.375	299.5	6:10:10.92	81.04
8	27	Hudson, I. Vail	6	3.500	5.00	288.6	6:12:42.00	80.49
9	21	Stickel, Hickey	4	3.500	5.00	288.6	6:13:57.24	80.22
10	41	Frontenac, G. Chevrolet	4	3.875	6.375	299.5	6:17:21.79	79.50

Finished—Ballot, Thomas; Stutz, Cooper; Shannon, Shannon; Hudson, Haibe.

Also started—Baby Peugeot, Boillot, 195 laps; Peugeot, Howard, 130; Duesenberg, D'Alene, 120; Roamer, Le Cocq, 96; Peugeot, Klein, 70; Detroit, Kirkpatrick, 69; Duesenberg, O'Donnell, 60; Ballot, Bablot, 63; Duesenberg, Milton, 50; Roamer, Hitke, 56; Chevrolet, Durant, 54; Ballot, Wagner, 44; Thurman, Thurman, 44; Toft, Toft, 44; Frontenac, Boyer, 30; Frontenac, Mulford, 37; McCoy, McCoy, 36; Richards, Brown, 14; Oldfield, Sarles, 8.

STATISTICS OF THE 1920 500-MILE RACE

Referee—Hon. Clifford Ireland   *Starter*—E. C. Patterson   *Pace Car*—Marmon "34"

Open to Cars with a Piston Displacement of 183 Cubic Inches or Under

Pos.	No.	Car and Driver	Cyldrs.	Bore	Stroke	Piston Displace.	Time	M.P.H.
1	4	Monroe, Gaston Chevrolet	4	3.125	5.9375	182.5	5:38:32.00	88.62
2	25	Ballot, Rene Thomas	8	2.56	4.41	181.0	5:44:51.60	86.99
3	10	Duesenberg, Tommy Milton	8	2.5	4.625	181.5	5:45:02.48	86.95
4	12	Duesenberg, Jimmy Murphy	8	2.5	4.625	181.5	5:52:31.35	85.10
5	2	Ballot, Ralph DePalma	8	2.56	4.41	181.0	6:05:19.15	82.12
6	31	Duesenberg, Eddie Hearne	8	2.5	4.625	181.5	6:10:21.55	81.00
7	26	Ballot, Jean Chassagne	8	2.56	4.41	181.0	6:15:16.65	79.94
8	28	Monroe, Joe Thomas	4	3.125	5.9375	182.5	6:21:41.55	78.60
9	33	Mulford, Ralph Mulford	8	2.5	4.625	181.5	7:17:14.25	68.61
10	15	Revere, Henderson-Alley	8	2.5	4.625	181.5	7:23:53.95	67.58

Also started—Richards Special, John Boling, 199 laps; Frontenac, Joe Boyer, 192; Peugeot, Ray Howard, 150; Duesenberg, Eddie O'Donnell, 149; Peugeot, Jules Goux, 148; Meteor, Willie Haupt, 146; Frontenac, Bennie Hill, 115; Monroe, Louis Chevrolet, 94; Peugeot, Howard Wilcox, 65; Monroe, Roscoe Sarles, 58; Frontenac, Art Klein, 40; Gregoire, Jean Porporato, 23; Peugeot, Andre Boillot, 16.

STATISTICS OF THE 1921 500-MILE RACE

Honorary Referee—David Beecroft   *Starter*—Thomas J. Hay   *Pace Car*—HCS "6"

Open to Cars with a Piston Displacement of 183 Cubic Inches or Under

Pos.	No.	Car and Driver	Cyldrs.	Bore	Stroke	Piston Displace.	Time	M.P.H.
1	2	Frontenac, Tommy Milton	8	2.625	4.093	182.5	5:34:44.65	89.62
2	6	Duesenberg, Roscoe Sarles	8	2.5	4.625	183.835	5:38:34.03	88.61
3	23	Frontenac, Percy Ford	4	3.125	5.937	182.12	5:52:50.30	85.02
4	5	Duesenberg, Eddie Miller	8	2.5	4.625	183.835	5:54:24.98	84.65
5	16	Sunbeam, Ora Haibe	8	2.56	4.415	181.36	5:55:58.20	84.28
6	9	Duesenberg, Albert Guyot	8	2.5	4.625	182.672	6:01:17.70	83.03
7	3	Leach Special, Ira Vail	8	2.687	4.00	181.48	6:14:17.47	80.15
8	21	Duesenberg, Bennie Hill	8	2.5	4.625	183.334	6:19:06.74	79.13
9	8	Frontenac, Ralph Mulford*	8	2.625	4.093	182.552	6:20:08.64	69.84

*Flagged 177th lap; awarded 9th place; only car running.

Also started—Sunbeam, Rene Thomas, 144 laps; Frontenac, Tom Alley, 133; Ballot, Ralph DePalma, 112; Revere, Eddie Hearne, 111; Duesenberg, Jimmy Murphy, 107; Junior Special, R. J. Brett, 91; Frontenac, C. W. Van Ranst, 87; Duesenberg, Joe Boyer, 74; Peugeot, Jean Chassagne, 65; Frontenac, Jules Ellingboe, 49; Talbot-Darracq, Andre Boillot, 41; Junior Special, Louis Fontaine, 33; Duesenberg, Joe Thomas, 24; Peugeot, Howard Wilcox, 22; Frontenac, entered but did not qualify; Durant-Duesenberg (withdrawn), Tommy Milton.

STATISTICS OF THE 1922 500-MILE RACE

Referee—Richard Kennerdell   *Starter*—E. V. Rickenbacker   *Pace Car*—National 8

Open to Cars with a Piston Displacement of 183 Cubic Inches or Under

Pos.	No.	Car and Driver	Cyldrs.	Bore	Stroke	Piston Displace.	Time	M.P.H.
1	35	Murphy Special, Jas. A. Murphy	8	2.685	4.0	181.44	5:17:30.79	94.48
2	12	Duesenberg, Harry Hartz	8	2.508	4.5	181.9	5:20:44.39	93.53
3	15	Ballot, Eddie Hearne	8	2.56	4.218	180.1	5:22:26.06	93.04
4	17	Duesenberg, Ralph DePalma	8	2.531	4.5	181.15	5:31:04.65	90.61
5	31	Duesenberg, Ora F. Haibe	8	2.49	4.5781	177.14	5:31:13.45	90.57
6	24	Duesenberg, G. W. Wonderlich	8	2.503	4.5	181.58	5:37:52.84	88.79
7	21	Duesenberg, I. P. Fetterman	8	2.49	4.625	180.2	5:40:55.54	88.00
8	1	Disteel-Duesenberg, Ira Vail	8	2.501	4.656	183.33	5:48:19.16	86.13
9	26	Monroe, Tom Alley	4	3.125	5.9375	181.54	5:55:53.46	84.30
10	10	Duesenberg, Joe Thomas	8	2.507	4.5	181.28	6:03:24.23	82.55

Finished—Frontenac, E. G. Baker; Durant Special, R. Clifford Durant; Bentley, W. Douglas Hawkes.

Also started—Monroe, Wilbur D'Alene, 160 laps (flagged) Leach Special, Frank Elliott, 195; Monroe, Lora L. Corum, 169; Fronty-Ford, C. Glenn Howard, 165; Frontenac, Ralph Mulford, 161; Fronty-Ford, John Curtner, 160; Frontenac, Peter DePaolo, 110; Frontenac, Art Klein, 105; Frontenac, Leon Duray, 94; Frontenac, Roscoe Sarles, 88; Leach Special, Tommy Milton, 44; Ballot, Jules Goux, 25; Duesenberg, Jules Ellingboe, 25; Peugeot, Howard Wilcox, 7.

TIMES AND AVERAGES

STATISTICS OF THE 1923 500-MILE RACE

Honorary Referee—John Oliver La Gorce   *Starter*—E. V. Rickenbacker   *Pace Car*—Duesenberg 8

Open to Cars with an Engine Piston Displacement of 122 Cubic Inches or Under

Single-Seat Bodies

Pos.	No.	Car and Driver	Cyldrs.	Bore	Stroke	Piston Displace.	Time	M.P.H.
1	1	H. C. S. Special, Tommy Milton	8	2.344	3.500	120.75	5:29:50.17	90.95
2	7	Durant Special, Harry Hartz	8	2.344	3.500	120.75	5:33:05.90	90.06
3	5	Durant Special, James Murphy	8	2.344	3.500	120.75	5:40:36.54	88.08
4	6	Durant Special, Eddie Hearne	8	2.344	3.500	120.75	5:46:14.23	86.6?
5	23	Barber-Warnock Sp'l, L. L. Corum	4	3.115	4.000	122.00	6:03:16.81	82.58
6	31	Durant Special, Frank R. Elliott	8	2.531	3.000	120.80	6:04:52.87	82.22
7	8	Durant Special, R. C. Durant	8	2.344	3.500	120.75	6:05:06.30	82.17
8	15	Mercedes Special, Max Sailer	4	2.765	5.020	119.40	6:11:49.60	80.68
9	19	Bugatti Special, Prince de Cystria	8	2.362	3.468	121.75	6:26:24.78	77.64
10	34	Duesenberg Special, Phil Shafer	8	2.374	3.422	121.40	6:40:04.98	74.98

Finished—Mercedes Special, Christian Werner.

Also started—Bugatti, Pierre de Viscaya, 166 laps; Durant Special, Leon Duray, 136; Packard, Dario Resta, 88; Packard, Ralph DePalma, 69; Durant Special, Harlan Fengler, 69; H. C. S. Special, Howard Wilcox, 60; Packard, Joe Boyer, 59; Miller Special, J. Bennett Hill, 41; Bugatti, Count L. Zborowski, 41; Durant Special, Earl P. Cooper, 22; Bugatti, Raoul Riganti, 19; Mercedes Special, C. Lautenschlager, 14; Bugatti Special, Martin de Alsaga, 6.

STATISTICS OF THE 1924 500-MILE RACE

Honorary Referee—Henry Ford   *Starter*—W. S. Gilbreath   *Pace Car*—Cole V-8

Open to Cars with an Engine Piston Displacement of 122 Cubic Inches or Under

Single-Seat Bodies

Pos.	No.	Car and Driver	Cyldrs.	Bore	Stroke	Piston Displace.	Time	M.P.H.
1	15	Duesenberg Special, L. L. Corum and Joe Boyer	8	2.380	3.422	121.9	5:05:23.51	98.23
2	8	Studebaker Special, Earl Cooper	8	2.343	3.50	120.75	5:06:47.18	97.79
3	2	Miller Special, James Murphy	8	2.343	3.50	120.75	5:08:25.39	97.27
4	4	Durant Special, Harry Hartz	8	2.343	3.50	120.75	5:10:44.39	96.54
5	3	Miller Special, Bennett Hill	8	2.343	3.50	120.75	5:11:00.07	96.46
6	12	Duesenberg Special, Peter De Paolo	8	2.380	3.422	121.9	5:18:08.55	94.30
7	14	Durant Special, Fred Comer	8	2.343	3.50	120.75	5:21:06.91	93.42
8	6	Ira Vail Special, Ira Vail	8	2.343	3.50	120.75	5:24:30.07	92.45
9	32	Mourre Special, Antoine Mourre	8	2.343	3.50	120.75	5:26:55.62	91.76
10	19	Miller Special, Robert McDonogh	8	2.343	3.50	120.75	5:31:26.73	90.51

Finished—Miller Special, Jules Ellingboe; Durant Special, G. W. Wonderlich.

Also started—Miller Special, Tommy Milton, 110 laps; Durant Special, R. C. Durant, 199 laps; Duesenberg Special, Joe Boyer, 177 laps; Duesenberg Special, Antserberg, 2 laps; Durant Special, E. Hearne, 151 laps; Barber-Warnock Special, Wm. Hunt, 191 laps (flagged); Barber-Warnock Special, F. L. Harder, 176 laps (flagged); Barber-Warnock Special, A. E. Moss, 177 laps (flagged); Schmidt Special, Ora Haibe, 182 laps (flagged); Miller Special, Frank Elliott, 149.

STATISTICS OF THE 1925 500-MILE RACE

Honorary Referee—Charles Schwab   *Starter*—Seth Klein   *Pace Car*—Rickenbacker "8"

Open to Cars with a Piston Displacement of 122 Cubic Inches or Under

Single-Seat Bodies

Pos.	No.	Car and Driver	Cyldrs.	Bore	Stroke	Piston Displace.	Time	M.P.H.
1	12	Duesenberg Special, Peter De Paolo	8	2.380	3.421	121.780	4:56:39.46	101.13
2	1	Junior Eight Special, * D. N. Lewis	8	2.343	3.500	120.750	4:57:33.15	100.82
3	9	Duesenberg Special, Phil E. Shafer	8	2.373	3.406	120.580	4:59:26.79	100.18
4	16	Miller Special, Harry A. Hartz	8	2.343	3.500	120.750	5:03:21.59	98.89
5	4	Miller Special, Tommy Milton	8	2.342	3.500	120.700	5:08:25.72	97.27
6	28	Miller Special, Leon Duray	8	2.343	3.500	120.750	5:09:34.01	96.91
7	8	Miller Special, Ralph De Palma	8	2.343	3.500	120.750	5:09:46.06	96.85
8	38	Duesenberg Special, Peter Kreis	8	2.373	3.406	120.580	5:11:26.86	96.32
9	15	Miller Special, Dr. W. E. Shattuc	8	2.373	3.406	120.580	5:11:51.10	96.24
10	22	Fiat Special, Pietro Bordino	8	2.375	3.437	121.000	5:13:20.48	95.74

*Front Drive model.

Finished—Miller Special, Fred Comer; Miller Special, Frank R. Elliott.

Also started—Miller Special, Earl Devore, 198 laps; Miller Special, Robert McDonogh, 188; Duesenberg Special, W. D. Morton, 165; Miller Special, Ralph Hepburn, 144; Junior Eight Special, Earl P. Cooper, 127; Miller Special, Bennett Hill, 69; Jones-Whitaker Special, L. H. Jones, 69; R. J. Special, Ira Vail, 63; Skelly Special, M. C. Jones, 33; Miller Special, Jules Ellingboe, 25.

STATISTICS OF THE 1926 500-MILE RACE

Honorary Referee—Arthur Brisbane   *Starter*—Seth Klein   *Pace Car*—Chrysler

Open to Cars of a Piston Displacement of 91½ Cubic Inches or Under

(Race Called at 400 Miles Account Rain)

Single-Seat Bodies

Pos.	No.	Car and Driver	Cyldrs.	Bore	Stroke	Piston Displ.	Miles Driven When Flagged	Time	Average
1	15	Miller Special, F. Lockhart	8	2.1875	3.00	90.2	400	4:10:14.95	95.904
2	3	Miller Special, Harry Hartz	8	2.1875	3.00	90.2	395	4:10:50.49	94.482
3	36	Boyle Spec., Cliff Woodbury	8	2.344	2.625	90.2	395	4:11:46.55	94.131
4	8	Miller Special, Fred Comer	8	2.1875	3.00	90.2	387½	4:11:49.99	92.323
5	12	Duesenberg Special, P. DePaolo	8	2.286	2.750	90.3	382½	4:10:41.90	91.544
6	6	Miller Special, Frank Elliott	8	2.344	2.625	90.6	380	4:10:46.64	90.917
7	14	Miller Special, Norman Batten	8	2.344	2.625	90.6	377½	4:10:53.91	90.276
8	19	Miller Special, Ralph Hepburn	8	2.344	2.625	90.6	377½	4:11:59.68	89.883
9	18	Elcar Special, John Duff	8	2.344	2.625	90.6	367½	4:11:51.10	87.551
10	4	Miller Special, Phil Shafer	8	2.1875	3.00	90.2	365	4:11:26.66	87.097

Also started—Miller Special, Tony Gulotta, 142 laps; Miller Special, Bennie Hill, 136; Abell Special, Thane Houser, 102; Eldridge Special, W. D. Hawkes, 92; Miller Special, Dave Lewis, 92; Miller Special, Earl Cooper, 74; Locomobile Special, Cliff Durant, 61; Duesenberg Special, Ben Jones, 54; Eldridge Special, E. A. D. Eldridge, 46; Schmidt Special, Lora Corum, 45; Schmidt Special, Steve Nemesh, 42; Miller Special, Jules Ellingboe, 39; Locomobile Special, Leon Duray, 33; Nickel Plate Special, Fred Lecklider, 25; Hamlin Special, Jack McCarver, 24; Miller Special, "Bon" MacDougall, 19; Miller Special, Dr. Wm. E. Shattuc, 16; Guyot Special, Albert Guyot, 9.

STATISTICS OF THE 1927 500-MILE RACE

Honorary Referee—Charles F. Kettering   *Starter*—Geo. Townsend   *Pace Car*—LaSalle

Open to Cars of a Piston Displacement of 91½ Cubic Inches or Under

Single-Seat Bodies

Pos.	No.	Car and Driver	Cyldrs.	Bore	Stroke	Piston Displace.	Time	M.P.H.
1	32	Duesenberg, George Souders	8	2.250	2.34375	90.0	5:07:33.08	97.545
2	10	Miller, Earl Devore	8	2.1875	3.000	90.2	5:19:35.95	93.868
3	27	Miller, Tony Gulotta	8	2.1875	3.000	90.2	5:22:05.88	93.139
4	29	Jynx Special, Wilbur Shaw	8	2.34375	2.625	90.6	5:22:12.05	93.110
5	21	Duesenberg, Dave Evans	8	2.28125	2.750	90.5	5:30:27.71	90.782
6	12	Cooper Special, Bob McDonogh	8	2.1875	3.000	90.2	5:31:49.34	90.410
7	16	Miller Special, Eddie Hearne	8	2.1875	3.000	90.2	5:33:05.74	90.064
8	6	Detroit Special, Tommy Milton	8	2.1875	3.000	90.2	5:52:36.21	85.081
9	25	Miller Special, Cliff Bergere	8	2.1875	3.000	90.6	6:15:20.07	79.929
10	5	Junior Eight Special, Frank Elliott	8	2.34375	2.625	90.6	6:23:25.69	78.244

Also started—Miller Special, George Fernic, 199 laps; Nickel Plate Special, Jim Hill, 197; Perfect Circle Duesenberg, Ben Shoaff, 198; Thompson Valve Duesenberg, Wade Morton, 152; Miller Special, Al Melcher, 144; Miller Special, Louis Schneider, 137; Cooper Special, Peter Kreis, 123; Perfect Circle Miller, Frank Lockhart, 120; Boyle Valve Special, Cliff Woodbury, 108; Miller Special, Dutch Bauman, 90; Miller Special, Al Cotey, 87; Miller Special, William E. Shattuc, 83; Miller Special, H. Kohlert, 49; Boyle Valve Special, Ralph Hepburn, 32; Miller F. W. D. Special, Harry Hartz, 38; Perfect Circle Miller, Peter De Paolo, 31; Miller F. W. D. Special, Leon Duray, 26; Cooper Special, Bennett Hill, 26; Cooper Special, Jules Ellingboe, 25; Miller Special, Norman Batten, 24; Duesenberg Special, Babe Stapp, 24; Boyle Valve Special, Jack Petticord, 22; Miller F. W. D. Special, Dave Lewis, 21.

TIMES AND AVERAGES

STATISTICS OF THE 1928 500-MILE RACE

***Honorary Referee*—Larry P. Fisher** ***Starter*—Lt. Chester Maitland** ***Pace Car*—Marmon**

Open to Cars of a Piston Displacement of 91½ Cubic Inches or Under

Single-Seat Bodies

Pos.	No.	Car and Driver	Cyldrs.	Bore	Stroke	Piston Displace.	Time	M.P.H.
1	14	Miller Special, Louis Meyer	8	2.1875	3.000	90.2	5:01:33.75	99.482
2	28	Miller Special, Lou Moore	8	2.1875	3.000	90.2	5:02:17.64	99.241
3	3	S. A. I. Special, George Souders	8	2.1875	3.000	90.2	5:06:01.04	98.034
4	15	Simplex P. R. Special, Ray Keech	8	2.1875	3.000	90.2	5:21:28.45	93.320
5	22	Miller Special, Norman Batten	8	2.1875	3.000	90.2	5:21:47.51	93.228
6	7	Miller Special, Babe Stapp	8	2.1875	3.000	90.2	5:23:50.40	92.638
7	43	Boyle Valve Special, Billy Arnold	8	2.1875	3.000	90.2	5:29:16.09	91.111
8	27	S. A. I. Special, Fred Frame	8	2.2812	2.750	90.5	5:33:02.38	90.079
9	25	Boyle Valve Special, Fred Comer	8	2.1875	3.000	90.2	5:37:29.89	88.889
10	8	Stutz Special, Anthony Gulotta	8	2.1875	3.000	90.2	5:37:30.11	88.888

Finished—Armacost Special, Louis Schneider; Boyle Valve Special, Dave Evans.

Also started—Elgin Piston Pin Special, Henry Kohlert, flagged at 450 miles; Miller Special, Deacon Litz, flagged at 402.5 miles; Duesenberg Special, Jimmy Gleason, out at 195 laps; Detroit Special, Cliff Durant, 175; Marmon Special, Johnny Seymour, 151; Chromolite Special, Earl Devore, 163; Miller Special, Leon Duray, 133; Aranem Special, Sammy Ross, 132; Duesenberg Special, Ira Hall, 115; Marmon Special, Peter Kreis, 73; Boyle Valve Special, Cliff Woodbury, 55; Miller Special, Ralph Hepburn, 48; Flying Cloud Special, Wilbur Shaw, 42; Duesenberg Special, Benny Shoaff, 35; Green Special, C. W. Belt, 32; Miller Special, Cliff Bergere, 7; Marmon Special, Russell Snowberger, 4.

STATISTICS OF THE 1929 500-MILE RACE

***Honorary Referee*—H. S. Firestone** ***Starter*—L. P. Fisher** ***Pace Car*—Studebaker**

Open to Cars of a Piston Displacement of 91½ Cubic Inches or Under

Single-Seat Bodies

Pos.	No.	Car and Driver	Cyldrs.	Bore	Stroke	Piston Displace.	Time	M.P.H.
1	2	Simplex Piston Ring Special, Ray Keech	8	2.1875	3.000	90.2	5:07:25.42	97.585
2	1	Miller Special, Louis Meyer	8	2.1875	3.000	90.2	5:13:49.21	95.596
3	53	Duesenberg Special, Jimmy Gleason	8	2.2860	2.750	90.1	5:20:10.46	93.699
4	43	Marchese Special, Carl Marchese	8	2.3440	2.500	91.5	5:20:42.95	93.541
5	42	Duesenberg Special, Fred Winnai	8	2.1950	3.000	91.0	5:37:52.05	88.792
6	48	Chromolite Special, W. H. Gardner	8	2.1875	3.000	90.2	5:39:24.27	88.390
7	6	Delage Special, Louis Chiron	8	2.1969	2.992	89.9	5:41:57.85	87.728
8	9	Boyle Valve Special, Billy Arnold	8	2.1875	3.000	90.2	5:57:31.77	83.909
9	25	Armacost-Miller Special, Cliff Bergere	8	2.1875	3.000	90.2	6:11:44.00	80.703
10	34	Cooper Special, Fred Frame	8	2.1875	3.000	90.2	Flagged 193 laps	

Also started—Burbach Special, Frank Brisko, flagged at 450 miles; Miller Special, Phil Shafer, flagged at 375 miles; Miller-Majestic Special, Lou Moore, out at 198 laps; Miller Special, Frank Farmer, 140; Miller Special, Wesley Crawford, 127; Detroit Special, Pete Kreis, 91; Packard Cable Special, Anthony Gulotta, 91; Miller Special, Bob McDonogh, 74; Pittsburgh-Miller Special, Bill Lindau; 70; Armacost-Miller Special, Herman Schurch, 70; Cooper Special, Johnny Seymour, 65; Packard Cable Special, Leon Duray, 65; Miller Special, Rickliffe Decker, 61; Rusco-Durac Special, Deacon Litz, 56; Richard Brothers Special, Albert Karnatz, 50; Buckeye Duesenberg Special, Ernest Triplett, 48; Cooper Special, Russell Snowberger, 45; Spindler-Miller Special, Babe Stapp, 40; Thompson Products Special, Jules Moriceau, 30; Boyle Valve Special, Peter DePaolo, 25; Packard Cable Special, Ralph Hepburn, 14; Duesenberg Special, Bill Spence, 14; Boyle Valve Special, Cliff Woodbury, 3.

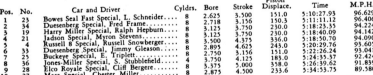

STATISTICS OF THE 1930 500-MILE RACE

***Honorary Referee*—Vincent Bendix** ***Starter*—Grantland Rice** ***Pace Car*—Cord**

Open to Cars with a Piston Displacement of 366 Cubic Inches or Under

Pos.	No.	Car and Driver	Cyldrs.	Bore	Stroke	Piston Displace.	Time	M.P.H.
1	4	Miller Hartz Special, Billy Arnold	8	2.625	3.500	151.5	4:58:39.72	100.448
2	16	Miller-Schofield Special, Wm. Cantlon	4	3.750	4.125	183.0	5:05:57.18	98.054
3	23	Bowes Seal Fast Special, L. Schneider	8	2.344	3.500	121.0	5:10:04.21	96.752
4	1	Sampson Special, Louis Meyer	16	2.3125	5.000	201.0	5:14:57.07	95.253
5	6	Duesenberg Special, Wm. Cummings	8	2.875	4.625	243.5	5:20:35.11	93.579
6	24	Jones & Maley Special, Dave Evans	8	2.500	3.750	138.0	5:24:04.50	92.571
7	15	Coleman Special, Phil Shafer	4	3.750	4.125	183.0	5:29:57.37	90.921
8	22	Russell 8 Special, Russell Snowberger	8	3.500	4.375	336.0	5:36:26.96	89.166
9	25	Allen-Miller Special, Leslie Allen	4	3.750	4.125	183.0	5:49:51.51	85.749
10	27	Stutz Special, L. L. Corum	8	3.375	4.500	322.0	5:51:32.09	85.340

Also started—V-eight Special, Claude Burton, flagged at 196 laps; Maserati Special, L. P. Cucinotta, flagged at 185; Fronty Special, Chester Miller, flagged at 161; Butcher Bros. Special, Harry Butcher, flagged at 127; Mavv Special, Mel Kenealy, out at 114; Miller Special, Zeke Meyer, 115; Guiberson Special, Ernie Triplett, 125; Romthe Special, J. C. McDonald, 112; Slade Special, Roland Free, 69; Mavv Special, Tony Gulotta, 79; Betholine Special, Frank Farmer, 69; Empire State Special, Wilbur Shaw, 54; Gauss Special, Joe Huff, 48; Alberti Special, Joe Caccia, 43; Nardi Special, Bill Denver, 41; Nardi Special, Cy Marshall, 29; Du Pont Special, Charles Moran, Jr., 22; Waverly Oil Special, Jimmy Gleason, 22; Coleman Special, Lou Moore, 23; Duesenberg Special, Deacon Litz, 22; Duesenberg Special, Babe Stapp, 18; Gauss Special, Johnny Seymour, 21; Duesenberg Special, Peter DePaolo, 20; Trexler Special, Marion Trexler, 20; Miller Special, Speed Gardner, 14; Maserati Special, B. Borzachini, 7; Hoosier Special, Rick Decker, 8; Buckeye Special, Chet Gardner, 1.

STATISTICS OF THE 1931 500-MILE RACE

***Honorary Referee*—W. S. Knudsen** ***Starter*—Barney Oldfield** ***Pace Car*—Cadillac**

Open to Cars with a Piston Displacement of 366 Cubic Inches or Under

Pos.	No.	Car and Driver	Cyldrs.	Bore	Stroke	Piston Displace.	Time	M.P.H.
1	23	Bowes Seal Fast Special, L. Schneider	8	2.625	3.500	151.0	5:10:27.93	96.629
2	34	Duesenberg Special, Fred Frame	8	2.718	3.156	150.3	5:11:11.12	96.406
3	19	Harry Miller Special, Ralph Hepburn	8	3.125	3.750	230.0	5:18:23.35	94.224
4	21	Jadson Special, Myron Stevens	8	3.125	3.750	230.0	5:18:40.09	94.142
5	4	Russell 8 Special, Russell Snowberger	8	3.500	4.375	336.0	5:18:50.70	94.090
6	33	Duesenberg Special, Jimmy Gleason	8	2.895	4.625	243.0	5:20:29.76	93.605
7	25	Buckeye Special, E. Triplett	8	2.750	3.156	151.0	5:22:26.24	93.041
8	36	Jones-Miller Special, S. Stubblefield	4	3.750	4.125	183.0	5:24:35.37	92.424
9	28	Elco Royale Special, Cliff Bergere	8	3.375	5.000	358.0	5:26:39.62	91.839
10	27	Marr Special, Chester Miller	8	2.875	4.500	233.6	5:34:53.75	89.580

Finished—G. H. N. Special, George Howie; Shafer 8 Special, Phil Shafer; Cummins Diesel Special, Dave Evans; Alberti Special, Al Aspen; Miller Special, Sam Ross.

Also started—Goldberg Special, Joe Huff, 180 laps; Maley Special, Deacon Litz, 177; Hunt Special, Tony Gulotta, 167; Miller-Hartz Special, Billy Arnold, 162; Bill Richards Special, Luther Johnson, 156; Hoosier Pete Special, Billy Winn, 138; Brisko-Atkinson Special, Frank Brisko, 138; Fronty Special, Gene Haustein, 117; Russo Special, Joe Russo, 109; Nutmeg State Special, "Speed" Gardner, 107; Boyle Valve Special, Lou Moore, 103; Harry Miller Special, "Shorty" Cantlon, 88; Empire State Special, Bill Cummings, 70; Bowes Seal Fast Special, Freddie Winnai, 60; Duesenberg Special, Phil Pardee, 60; Empire State Special, Paul Bost, 35; Milt Jones Special, Frank Farmer, 32; Wingerter Special, Geo. Wingerter 29; Sampson Special, Louie Meyer, 28; Rigling-Henning Special "Babe" Stapp, 9; Morton & Brett Special, John Boling, 7; Leon Duray Special, Leon Duray, 6; Butcher Bros. Special, Harry Butcher, 6; Hoosier Pete Special, Herman Schurch, 5; Tucker-Tappet Ford Special, Francis Quinn, 3.

STATISTICS OF THE 1932 500-MILE RACE

***Honorary Referee*—Edsel Ford** ***Starter*—Gar Wood** ***Pace Car*—Lincoln**

Open to Cars with a Piston Displacement of 366 Cubic Inches or Under

Pos.	No.	Car and Driver	Cyldrs.	Bore	Stroke	Piston Displace.	Time	M.P.H.
1	34	Miller Hartz Special, Fred Frame	8	2.875	3.500	182.0	4:48:03.79	104.144
2	6	Lion Head Special, Howdy Wilcox	4	4.062	4.250	220.0	4:48:47.45	103.881
3	22	Studebaker Special, Cliff Bergere	8	3.500	4.375	336.7	4:52:13.24	102.662
4	61	Meyer Special, Bob Carey	8	3.250	3.750	249.0	4:55:57.90	101.363
5	4	Hupp Com. Special, Russell Snowberger	8	3.500	4.687	361.0	4:57:38.72	100.791
6	37	Studebaker Special, Zeke Meyer	8	3.500	4.375	336.7	5:04:38.52	98.476
7	35	Duesenberg Special, Ira Hall	8	2.895	4.625	243.0	5:05:28.72	98.207
8	65	Foreman Axle S. Spl., Fred Winnai	8	2.750	3.187	151.0	5:07:53.49	97.437
9	2	Duesenberg Special, Billy Winn	8	2.750	3.156	151.0	5:07:56.43	97.421
10	55	Highway Parts Special, Joe Huff	16	2.187	3.000	183.0	5:42:31.25	87.586

Also started—Phil Shafer, Shafer 8 Special, flagged at 197 laps; Kelly Petillo, Jones Miller Special, flagged at 189 laps; Tony Gulotta, Studebaker Special, flagged at 184 laps; H. W. Stubblefield, Gilmore Lion Special, flagged at 178 laps; Peter Kreis, Studebaker Special, out at 178 laps; Luther Johnson, Studebaker Special, 164 laps; Wilbur Shaw, Veedol Special, 157 laps; Deacon Litz, Bowes Seal Fast Special, 152 laps; Bill Cummings, Bowes Seal Fast Special, 151 laps; Malcolm Fox, Richards Special, 132 laps; Chester Miller, Hudson Special, 125 laps; Ernie Triplett, Floating Power Special, 125 laps; Louis Schneider, Bowes Seal Fast Special, 125 laps; Joe Russo, Art Rose Special, 107 laps; Lou Moore, Boyle Valve Prod. Special, 79 laps; Juan Gaudino, Golden Seal Special, 71 laps; Al Miller, Hudson Special, 66 laps; Geo. MacKenzie, Brady Special, 65 laps; Frank Brisko, Brisko-Atkinson Special, 81 laps; Ray Campbell, Folly Farm Special, 60 laps; Billy Arnold, Miller-Hartz Special, 59 laps; Bryan Saulpaugh, Harry Miller Special, 55 laps; Louis Meyer, Sampson Special, 50 laps; Al Aspen, Brady-Nardi Special, 31 laps; John Kreiger, Consumers Petroleum Special, 30 laps; Wesley Crawford, Boyle Valve Prod. Special, 28 laps; Paul Bost, Empire State Special, 18 laps; Bob McDonogh, Miller F. W. D. Special, 17 laps; Gus Schrader, Harry Miller Special, 7 laps; Al Gordon, Lion Tamer Special, 3 laps.

TIMES AND AVERAGES

STATISTICS OF THE 1933 500-MILE RACE

Honorary Referee—Larry P. Fisher   *Starter*—Gar Wood   *Pace Car*—Chrysler

Open to Cars with a Piston Displacement of 366 Cubic Inches or Under

Pos.	No.	Car and Driver	Cyldrs.	Bore	Stroke	Piston Displace.	Time	M.P.H.
1	36	Tydol Special, Louis Meyer............	8	2.3125	3.750	258	4:48:00.75	104.162
2	17	Mallory Special, Wilbur Shaw.........	4	4.0625	4.250	220	4:54:42.64	101.795
3	37	Foreman Axle Special, Lou Moore....	4	4.125	4.500	255	4:55:16.79	101.599
4	21	Sampson-Radio Special, Chet Gardner..	16	2.3125	3.000	201	4:56:29.71	101.182
5	8	Shafer "8" Special, H. W. Stubblefield..	8	3.125	4.625	284	4:57:43.82	100.762
6	38	Art Rose Special, Dave Evans........	8	3.1875	4.250	260	4:58:43.82	100.425
7	34	Studebaker Special, Tony Gulotta.....	8	3.500	4.375	336	5:02:48.75	99.071
8	4	Russell "8" Special, Russell Snowberger.	8	3.500	4.375	336	5:02:59.84	99.011
9	9	Studebaker Special, Zeke Meyer........	8	3.500	4.375	336	5:05:44.49	98.122
10	46	Studebaker Special, Luther Johnson....	8	3.500	4.375	336	5:08:22.22	97.286

Finished—Studebaker Special, Cliff Bergere; Studebaker Special, L. L. Corum; Jack C. Carr Special, Willard Prentiss; Golden Seal Special, Raul Riganti.

Also started—Martz Special, Eugene Haustein, 197 laps; Bowes Seal Fast Special, Deacon Litz, 197 laps; Wonder Bread Special, Joe Russo, 192 laps; Brady Special, Doc McKenzie, 192 laps; Sacks Bros. Special, Kelly Petillo, 168 laps; Marr Special, Chet Miller, 163 laps; Marr Special, Al Miller, 161 laps; Goldberg Special, Bennett Hill, 158 laps; Boyle Products Special, Babe Stapp, 156 laps; Boyle Valve Special, Wesley Crawford, 147 laps; Boyle Products Special, Wm. Cummings, 136 laps; Miller Special, Lester Spangler, 132 laps; Kemp Special, Fred Winnai, 125 laps; Universal Service Special, Malcolm Fox, 121 laps; Miller-Hartz Special, Fred Frame, 85 laps; Kemp Mannix Special, Mark Billman, 79 laps; Lencki & Madis Special, John Sawyer, 77 laps; Floating Power Special, Ernie Triplett, 61 laps; Frame-Miller Special, Pete Kreis, 63 laps; Sullivan & O'Brien Special, Wm. Cantlon, 50 laps; Gilmore Special, Mauri Rose, 48 laps; F. W. D. Special, Frank Brisko, 47 laps; Denny Duesenberg Special, Ira Hall, 37 laps; Highway Truck Parts Special, Ralph Hepburn, 33 laps; G. & D. Special, Ray Campbell, 24 laps; Frame-Miller Duesenberg, Paul Bost, 13 laps; Miller Special, Rick Decker, 13 laps; Edelweiss Special, Louis Schneider, 1 lap.

STATISTICS OF THE 1934 500-MILE RACE

Honorary Referee—Roy D. Chapin   *Starter*—Roscoe Turner   *Pace Car*—LaSalle

Open to Cars with a Piston Displacement of 366 Cubic Inches or Under

Fuel Limit—45 Gallons   Oil Limit—6½ Gallons

Pos.	No.	Car and Driver	Cyldrs.	Bore	Stroke	Piston Displace.	Time	M.P.H
1	7	Boyle Products Special, Wm. Cummings..	4	4.1250	4.1250	220	4:46:05.20	104.863
2	9	Duray Special, Mauri Rose...........	4	4.0625	4.250	220	4:46:32.43	104.697
3	2	Foreman Axle Special, Lou Moore......	4	4.250	4.500	255	4:52:19.63	102.625
4	12	Stokely Food Special, Deacon Litz...	4	4.0625	4.250	220	4:57:46.27	100.749
5	16	Duesenberg Special, Joe Russo........	8	3.500	3.625	275	5:00:19.21	99.893
6	36	Shafer Eight Special, Al Miller......	8	3.125	4.625	286	5:05:18.08	98.264
7	22	Floating Power Special, Cliff Bergere..	4	4.0625	4.250	220	5:06:41.54	97.818
8	10	Russell Eight, Russell Snowberger.....	4	3.500	4.375	336	5:08:20.05	97.297
9	32	F. W. D. Special, Frank Brisko......	4	4.250	4.500	255	5:09:57.63	96.787
10	24	Lucenti Special, Herb Ardinger........	8	3.250	4.000	265	5:12:42.47	95.936

Finished—Red Lion Special, Kelly Petillo; Cummins-Diesel Special, H. W. Stubblefield.

Also started—Detroit Gasket Special, Chas. Crawford, 110 laps; Miller Special, Ralph Hepburn, 164; Boyle Products Special, George Barringer, 161; Shafer Eight Special, Phil Shafer, 130; Schroder Special, Tony Gulotta, 94; Ring Free Special, Louis Meyer, 92; Cummins-Diesel Special, Dave Evans, 81; Sullivan and O'Brien Special, Wm. Cantlon, 76; Sampson Radio Special, Chester Gardner, 72; Abels-Fink Special, Al Gordon, 66; Miller-Duesenberg Special, Rex Mays, 53; Superior Trailer Special, Dusty Fahrnow, 28; Burd Piston Ring Special, Johnny Sawyer, 27; Streamline-Miller Special, Johnny Seymour, 22; Carter Carburetor Special, Rick Decker, 17; Lion Head Special, Wilbur Shaw, 15; Cresco Special, Doc MacKenzie, 15; Martz Special, Gene Haustein, 13; DeBaets Special, Harry McQuinn, 13; Scott Special, George Bailey, 12; Bohnalite Special, Chester Miller, 11.

STATISTICS OF THE 1935 500-MILE RACE

Honorary Referee—Amelia Earhart   *Starter*—Seth Klein   *Pace Car*—Ford V-8

Open to Cars with a Piston Displacement of 366 Cubic Inches or Under

Fuel Limit—42½ Gallons   Oil Limit—6½ Gallons

Pos.	No.	Car and Driver	Cyldrs.	Bore	Stroke	Piston Displace.	Time	M.P.H.
1	5	Gilmore Speedway Special, Kelly Petillo..	4	4.250	4.625	262	4:42:22.71	106.240
2	14	Pirrung Special, Wilbur Shaw.......	4	4.0625	4.250	220	4:43:02.73	105.990
3	1	Boyle Products Special, Bill Cummings..	4	4.125	4.125	221	4:46:22.48	104.758
4	22	Abels & Fink Special, Floyd Roberts.....	4	4.250	4.500	255	4:50:37.05	103.228
5	21	Veedol Special, Ralph Hepburn.......	8	3.3125	3.750	258	4:50:45.73	103.177
6	9	Sullivan & O'Brien Spl., Shorty Cantlon..	4	4.0625	4.250	220	4:56:37.07	101.140
7	18	Sampson Radio Special, Chester Gardner	4	4.0625	4.250	220	4:56:39.02	101.129
8	16	Shaler Rislone Special, Deacon Litz......	4	4.0625	4.250	220	4:57:18.22	100.907
9	8	Pirrung Special, Doc Mackenzie........	4	4.0625	4.250	220	4:58:13.01	100.598
10	34	Milac Front Drive Special, Chet Miller..	8	2.625	3.500	151	4:58:35.16	100.474

Finished—Miller-Hartz Special, Fred Frame; Ring Free Special, Louis Meyer.

Also started—Victor Gasket Special, Cliff Bergere, 196 laps; Mikan & Carson Special, Harris Insinger, 185 laps; Boyle Products Special, Al Miller, 178 laps; Ford V-8 Special, Ted Horn, 145 laps; Gilmore Special, Rex Mays, 123 laps; Foreman Axle Special, Lou Moore, 116 laps; Marks Miller Special, George Connor, 112 laps; F. W. D. Special, Mauri Rose, 103 laps; Bowes Seal Fast Special, Anthony Gulotta, 102 laps; Blue Prelude Special, Jimmy Snyder, 97 laps; Art Rose Special, Frank Brisko, 79 laps; Ford V-8 Special, Johnny Seymour, 71 laps; Marks Miller Special, Babe Stapp, 70 laps; Ford V-8 Special, George Bailey, 65 laps; Boyle Products Special, Russell Snowberger, 59 laps; Burd Piston Ring Special, Louis Tomei, 47 laps; Ford V-8 Special, Bob Soll, 47 laps; Cocktail Hour Cigarette Special, Al Gordon, 17 laps; Duesenberg Special, Freddie Winnai, 16 laps; Bowes Seal Fast Special, Clay Weatherly, 9 laps; DeBaets Special, Harry McQuinn, 4 laps.

STATISTICS OF THE 1936 500-MILE RACE

Honorary Referee—Ralph DePalma   *Starter*—Seth Klein   *Pace Car*—Packard

Open to Cars with a Piston Displacement of 366 Cubic Inches or Under

Fuel Limit—37½ Gallons   Oil Limit—6½ Gallons

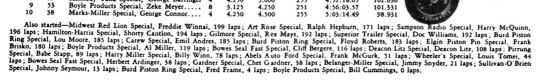

Pos.	No.	Car and Driver	Cyldrs.	Bore	Stroke	Piston Displace.	Time	M.P.H.
1	8	Ring Free Special, Louis Meyer.........	4	4.250	4.500	255	4:35:03.39	109.069
2	22	Hartz Special, Ted Horn..............	8	2.875	3.500	182	4:37:20.54	108.170
3	10	Gilmore Speedway Spl., Doc MacKenzie	4	4.250	4.625	262	4:39:10.36	107.460
4	36	F. W. D. Special, Mauri Rose........	4	4.250	4.500	255	4:39:39.85	107.272
5	18	Boyle Products Special, Chet Miller......	8	2.625+	3.500	152	4:40:35.17	106.919
6	41	Fink Auto Special, Ray Pixley........	4	3.6875	4.750	203	4:45:01.58	105.253
7	3	Gilmore Special, Wilbur Shaw........	4	4.250	4.500	255	4:47:49.00	104.233
8	17	Kennedy Tank Special, George Barringer	4	4.250	5.000	255	4:52:18.65	102.630
9	53	Boyle Products Special, Zeke Meyer.....	8	3.125	4.500	251	4:56:03.57	101.331
10	38	Marks-Miller Special, George Connor....	4	4.250	4.500	255	5:03:14.49	98.931

Also started—Midwest Red Lion Special, Freddie Winnai, 199 laps; Art Rose Special, Ralph Hepburn, 171 laps; Sampson Radio Special, Harry McQuinn, 196 laps; Hamilton-Harris Special, Shorty Cantlon, 194 laps; Gilmore Special, Rex Mays, 192 laps; Superior Trailer Special, Doc Williams, 192 laps, Burd Piston Ring Special, Lou Moore, 185 laps; Carew Special, Emil Andres, 185 laps; Burd Piston Ring Special, Floyd Roberts, 183 laps; Elgin Piston Pin Special, Frank Brisko, 180 laps; Boyle Products Special, Al Miller, 119 laps; Bowes Seal Fast Special, Cliff Bergere, 116 laps; Deacon Litz Special, Deacon Litz, 108 laps; Pirrung Special, Babe Stapp, 89 laps; Harry Miller Special, Billy Winn, 78 laps; Abels Auto Ford Special, Frank McGurk, 51 laps; Wheeler's Special, Louis Tomei, 44 laps; Bowes Seal Fast Special, Herbert Ardinger, 38 laps; Gardner Special, Chet Gardner, 38 laps; Belanger-Miller Special, Jimmy Snyder, 21 laps; Sullivan-O'Brien Special, Johnny Seymour, 13 laps; Burd Piston Ring Special, Fred Frame, 4 laps; Boyle Products Special, Bill Cummings, 0 laps.

TIMES AND AVERAGES

STATISTICS OF THE 1937 500-MILE RACE

Honorary Referee—W. S. Knudsen   *Starter*—Seth Klein   *Pace Car*—LaSalle

Open to Cars with a Piston Displacement of 366 Cubic Inches or Under

Fuel restricted to "Commercial Gasoline." Quantity not limited. Oil Limit—6½ Gallons

Pos.	No.	Car and Driver	Cyldrs.	Bore	Stroke	Piston Displace.	Time	M.P.H.
1	6	Shaw Gilmore Special, Wilbur Shaw....	4	4.250	4.500	255	4:24:07.80	113.580
2	8	Hamilton-Harris Sp'l, Ralph Hepburn..	4	4.250	4.500	255	4:24:09.96	113.565
3	3	Miller Hartz Special, Ted Horn........	8	2.875	3.500	182	4:24:28.87	113.434
4	2	Boyle Special, Louis Meyer...........	8	3.375	3.750	268	4:30:55.70	110.730
5	45	Mid-West Red Lion Sp'l, Cliff Bergere...	4	4.250	4.500	255	4:35:23.60	108.935
6	16	Boyle Special, Bill Cummings.........	4	4.250	4.500	255	4:40:03.03	107.124
7	28	Miller Special, Billy DeVore..........	4	4.250	4.500	255	4:40:23.17	106.995
8	38	Burd Piston Ring Sp'l, Athy. Gulotta..	4	4.250	4.500	255	4:45:40.42	105.015
9	17	Marks Miller Special, George Connor..	4	4.250	4.500	255	4:48:56.00	103.830
10	53	S. S. Engineering Co. Sp'l, L. Tomei...	8	3.500	4.375	336.7	4:54:37.33	101.825

Also started—Burd Piston Ring Special, Chet Gardner, 199 laps; Topping Special, Ronney Householder, 194 laps, Thorne Special, Floyd Roberts, 190 laps; Motorola Special, Deacon Litz, 191 laps; Thorne Special, Floyd Davis, 190 laps; Bowes Seal Fast Special, Shorty Cantlon, 182 laps; Thorne Special, Al Miller, 170 laps; Burd Piston Ring Special, Mauri Rose, 127 laps; Lucky Teetor Special, Kenneth Fowler, 116 laps; Petillo Special, Kelly Petillo, 109 laps; Duray-Sims Special, George Bailey, 107 laps; Chicago Raw Hide Oil Seal Special, Herbert Ardinger, 106 laps; Elgin Piston Pin Special, Frank Brisko, 105 laps; Duray Special, Frank Wearne, 99 laps; F. W. D. Special, Tony Willman, 95 laps; Miller Special, Billy M. Winn, 85 laps; Snowberger Special, Russell Snowberger, 66 laps; Fink Auto Special, Bob Swanson, 52 laps; Sullivan O'Brien Special, Harry McQuinn, 47 laps; Boyle Special, Chet Miller, 36 laps; Topping Special, Babe Stapp, 36 laps; Sparks Special, Jimmy Snyder, 27 laps; Bowes Seal Fast Special, Rex Mays, 24 laps.

STATISTICS OF THE 1938 500-MILE RACE

Honorary Referee—Harvey S. Firestone, Jr.   *Starter*—Seth Klein   *Pace Car*—Hudson

Non-Stock Supercharged Motors 183.060 Cubic Inches (3,000 cc.) Piston Displacement or Less
and Non-Stock Non-Supercharged Motors 274.59 Cubic Inches (4,500 cc.)
Piston Displacement or Less—One or Two Seated Bodies

Pos.	No.	Car and Driver	Cyldrs.	Bore	Stroke	Piston Displace.	Time	M.P.H.
1	23	Burd Piston Ring Spl., Floyd Roberts.....	4	4.937	4.625	270	4:15:58.40	117.200
2	1	Shaw Special, Wilbur Shaw............	4	4.000	4.250	256	4:19:33.67	115.580
3	3	I. B. E. W. Special, Chet Miller.......	4	4.250	4.500	255	4:20:59.51	114.946
4	2	Miller-Hartz Special, Ted Horn........	8	2.875	3.500	182	4:27:22.39	112.203
5	38	Burd Piston Ring Spl., Chet Gardner.....	4	4.260	4.500	257	4:31:57.48	110.311
6	54	Offenhauser Special, Herb Ardinger......	4	4.250	4.500	255	4:31:45.15	109.843[1]
7	45	Marchese Special, Harry McQuinn......	8	2.875	3.500	151	4:31:51.80	108.694[2]
8	58	P. R. & W. Special, Billy DeVore......	4	4.250	4.500	255	4:31:49.00	102.080[3]
9	22	Thorne Engineering Spl., Joe Thorne....	4	4.260	4.500	256	4:32:02.05	102.009[4]
10	29	Indiana Fur Special, Frank Wearne.....	4	4.260	4.750	270.8	4:32:44.82	99.543[5]

Flagged before completing full distance, due to rain, as follows: [1] 497½ mile; [2] 492½ miles; [3] 462½ miles; [4] 462½ miles; [5] 452½ miles.

Also started—Kohlert Special, Duke Nalon, 178 laps; Barbasol Special, George Bailey, 166 laps; I. B. E. W. Special, Mauri Rose, 165 laps; Thorne-Sparks Special, Ronney Householder, 154 laps; Sparks-Thorne Special, Jimmy Snyder, 150 laps; Bowes Seal Fast, Louis Meyer, 149 laps; Hamilton-Harris Special, Tony Gulotta, 130 laps; Domonts Pepsi-Cola Special, Al Miller, 125 laps; Marks-Miller Special, George Connor, 119 laps; Kraft's Real Rye, Cliff Bergere, 111 laps; Kimmel Special, Henry Banks, 109 laps; Petillo Special, Kelly Petillo, 100 laps; P. O. B. Perfect Seal Special, Louis Tomei, 88 laps; I. B. E. W. Special, Bill Cummings, 72 laps; D-X Special, Russ Snowberger, 56 laps; McCoy Auto Service Special, Babe Stapp, 54 laps; Belanger Special, Tony Willman, 47 laps; Alfa Romeo Special, Rex Mays, 45 laps; Elgin Piston Pin Special, Emil Andres, 45 laps; Ira Hall, Greenfield Super Service Special, 44 laps; Shur-Stop Mechan. Brake Equalizer Special, Frank Brisko, 39 laps; Troy Tydol Special, Al Putnam, 15 laps; Kamm's Special, Shorty Cantlon, 13 laps.

STATISTICS OF THE 1939 500-MILE RACE

Honorary Referee—Roscoe Turner   *Starter*—Seth Klein   *Pace Car*—Buick

Non-Stock Supercharged Motors 183.060 Cubic Inches (3,000 cc.) Piston Displacement or Less
and Non-Stock Non-Supercharged Motors 274.59 Cubic Inches (4,500 cc.)
Piston Displacement or Less—One or Two Seated Bodies

Pos.	No.	Car and Driver	Cyldrs.	Bore	Stroke	Piston Displace.	Time	M.P.H.
1	2	Boyle Special, Wilbur Shaw............	8	2.720	4.000	183	4:20:47.39	115.035
2	10	Thorne Engineer. Spl., Jimmy Snyder...	6	3.203	3.750	182	4:22:35.61	114.245
3	54	Offenhauser Special, Cliff Bergere......	4	4.3125	4.625	270	4:23:51.40	113.698
4	4	Boyle Special, Ted Horn..............	8	3.375	3.750	268	4:28:08.82	111.879
5	31	Alfa-Romeo, "Babe" Stapp............	8	3.000	3.200	181	4:29:42.68	111.230
6	41	Bill White Special, Geo. Barringer......	4	4.135	4.250	228	4:30:12.60	111.025
7	8	Thorne Engineer. Spl., Joe Thorne......	6	3.535	4.625	271.8	4:31:42.04	110.416
8	16	Wheelers Special, Mauri Rose	4	4.260	4.500	256.4	4:33:51.80	109.544
9	14	Burd Piston Ring Spl., Frank Wearne...	4	4.500	4.250	270	4:38:16.65	107.806
10	26	Leon Duray Barb. Spl., Billy DeVore...	4	3.8125	4.000	182	4:47:43.37	104.207

Finished—Burd Piston Ring Special, Tony Gulotta.

Also started—Bowes Seal Fast Special, Louis Meyer, 197 laps; Marks Special, George Connor, 191 laps; Burd Piston Ring Special, Tony Willman, 188 laps; Alfa-Romeo, Louis Tomei, 186 laps; Thorne Engineering Special, Rex Mays, 145 laps; Miller-Hartz Special, Herb Ardinger, 141 laps; Kay Jeweler's Special, Kelly Petillo, 141 laps; Joe Thorne, Inc. Special, Mel Hansen, 113 laps; Elgin Piston Pin Special, Harry McQuinn, 110 laps; Boyle Special, Chet Miller, 107 laps; Hamilton-Harris Special, Ralph Hepburn, 107 laps; Burd Piston Ring Special, Floyd Roberts, 94 laps; Greenfield Sup. Ser. Special, Ira Hall, 89 laps; D-X Special, Russell Snowberger, 50 laps; Miller Special, George Bailey, 47 laps; W. B. W. Special, Floyd Davis, 43 laps; Kennedy Tank Special, Al Miller, 41 laps; National Seal Special, Frank Brisko, 38 laps; Chicago Flash Special, Emil Andres, 22 laps; S. M. I. Special, Bob Swanson, 19 laps; Automotive Service Special, Shorty Cantlon, 15 laps; Maserati Special, Deacon Litz, 7 laps.

STATISTICS OF THE 1940 500-MILE RACE

Honorary Referee—Paul G. Hoffman   *Starter*—Seth Klein   *Pace Car*—Studebaker

Non-Stock Supercharged Motors 183.060 Cubic Inches (3,000 cc.) Piston Displacement or Less
and Non-Stock Non-Supercharged Motors 274.59 Cubic Inches (4,500 cc.)
Piston Displacement or Less—One or Two Seated Bodies

Pos.	No.	Car and Driver	Cyldrs.	Bore	Stroke	Piston Displace.	Time	M.P.H.
1	1	Boyle Special, Wilbur Shaw...........	8	2.718	4.000	179.2	4:22:31.17	114.277
2	33	Bowes Seal Fast Special, Rex Mays....	8	2.96875	3.250	179.6	4:23:45.31	113.742
3	7	Elgin Piston Pin Special, Mauri Rose....	4	4.3125	4.625	270	4:24:08.96	113.572
4	3	Boyle Special, Ted Horn..............	8	3.375	3.750	268	*199 laps	flagged
5	8	Thorne Donnelly Special, Joe Thorne....	6	3.531	4.625	271	*197 "	"
6	32	Sampson Special, Bob Swanson.......	16	2.000	3.000	183	*196 "	"
7	9	Boyle Special, Frank Wearne..........	4	4.625	4.500	257.2	*195 "	"
8	31	Hartz Special, Mel Hansen............	4	2.875	5.500	182.1	*194 "	"
9	16	Elgin Piston Pin Special, Frank Brisko...	6	3.625	4.375	271	*193 "	"
10	49	Lucy O'Reilly Schell Spl., Rene LeBegue..	8	2.145	3.280	183	*192 "	"

*Flagged after first car finished 200 laps on account of rain.

Also started—Harry McQuinn, Hollywood's Payday Spl., 192 laps; Emil Andres, Belanger-Foltz Special, 192 laps; Sam Hanks, Duray Special, 192 laps; George Barringer, Hollywood's Payday Spl., 191 laps; Joie Chitwood, Kennedy Tank Special, 190 laps; Louis Tomei, Falstaff Special, 190 laps; Chet Miller, Alfa-Romeo, 189 laps; Billy DeVore, Bill Holabird Special, 181 laps; Al Putnam, Refinoil Special, 179 laps; Floyd Davis, Lencki Special, 157 laps; Kelly Petillo, Indiana Fur Special, 128 laps; Duke Nalon, Marks Special, 120 laps; George Robson, Keller Special, 67 laps; Babe Stapp, Surber Special, 64 laps; Doc Williams, Quillen Brothers, 61 laps; George Connor, Lencki Special, 52 laps; Cliff Bergere, Noc-Out Hose Clamp Spl., 51 laps; Paul Russo, Elgin Piston Pin Special, 48 laps; Ralph Hepburn, Bowes Seal Fast Special, 47 laps; Al Miller, Alfa-Romeo, 41 laps; Russell Snowberger, Snowberger Special, 38 laps; Tommy Hinnershitz, Marks Special, 32 laps; Raul Riganti, Maserati Special, 24 laps.

TIMES AND AVERAGES

STATISTICS OF THE 1941 500-MILE RACE

Honorary Referee—Guy Vaughn   *Starter*—Seth Klein   *Pace Car*—Chrysler

Non-Stock Supercharged Motors 183.060 Cubic Inches (3,000 cc.) Piston Displacement or Less
and Non-Stock Non-Supercharged Motors 274.59 Cubic Inches (4,500 cc.)
Piston Displacement or Less—One or Two Seated Bodies

Pos.	No.	Driver and Car	Cyldrs.	Bore	Stroke	Piston Displace.	Time	M.P.H.
1	16	Floyd Davis and Mauri Rose, Noc-Out Hose Clamp Special	4	4.3125	4.625	270	4:20:36.24	115.117
2	1	Rex Mays, Bowes Seal Fast Special	8	2.968	3.250	179.8	4:22:06.19	114.459
3	4	Ted Horn, T.E.C. Special	6	3.204	3.750	181.4	4:23:28.39	113.864
4	54	Ralph Hepburn, Bowes Seal Fast Special	8	3.125	2.9375	180.1	4:24:00.79	113.631
5	34	Cliff Bergere, Noc-Out Hose Clamp Spl	4	4.3125	4.625	270	4:24:15.10	113.528
6	41	Chet Miller, Boyle Special	8	3.375	3.750	268	4:28:02.75	111.921
7	15	Harry McQuinn, Ziffrin Special	8	3.010	3.200	181	4:28:20.96	111.795
8	7	Frank Wearne, Bill Holabird Special	4	4.250	4.500	255	4:30:42.92	110.818
9	45	Paul Russo, Leader Card Special	8	2.480	3.500	137	4:44:00.88	105.628
10	29	Tommy Hinnershitz, Mark Special	4	4.3125	4.625	270	4:45:18.05	105.152

Finished—Louis Tomei, H-3 Special; Al Putnam, Schoof Special.

Also started—Overton Phillips, Phillips Special, 187 laps; Joie Chitwood, Blue Crown Spark Plug, 177 laps; Duke Nalon, Elgin Piston Pin Special, 173 laps; George Connor, Boyle Special, 167 laps; Everett Saylor, Bowes Special; 155 laps; Wilbur Shaw, Boyle Special, 151 laps; Billy DeVore, Hollywood Pay Day C. Bar S, 121 laps; Tony Willman, Lyons Special, 117 laps; Russell Snowberger, Jim Hussey's Sptm., 107 laps; Deacon Litz, Sampson 16 Special, 89 laps; Frank Brisko, Zollner Piston Special, 70 laps; Merrill "Doc" Williams, Indiana Fur Special, 68 laps; George Robson, Gilmore Red Lion Special, 66 laps; Mauri Rose, Elgin Piston Pin Special, 60 laps; Kelly Petillo, American Airline Sand. Sp., 48 laps; Al Miller, Miller Special, 22 laps; Mel Hansen, Fageol Special, 11 laps; Emil Andres, Kennedy Tank Special, 5 laps; Joe Thorne, Thorne Engineering Special, 5 laps.

STATISTICS OF THE 1946 500-MILE RACE

Honorary Referee—Jack Dempsey   *Starter*—Seth Klein   *Pace Car*—Lincoln-Continental

Non-Stock Supercharged Motors 183.060 Cubic Inches (3,000 cc.) Piston Displacement or Less
and Non-Stock Non-Supercharged Motors 274.59 Cubic Inches (4,500 cc.)
Piston Displacement or Less—One or Two Seated Bodies

Pos.	Car No.	Driver	Car	Cyldrs.	Bore	Stroke	Piston Displace.	Time	MPH
1	16	Geo. Robson,	Thorne Eng. Sp	6	3.205	3.750	183.	4:21:26.70	114.820
2	61	Jimmy Jackson,	Jackson Special	4	4.275	4.500	255.	4:22:00.74	114.498
3	29	Ted Horn,	Boyle Maserati Sp	8	2.718	4.000	179.2	4:33:19.60	109.819
4	18	Emil Andres,	Elgin Piston Pin Sp	4	2.702	4.000	183.	4:35:28.65	108.902
5	24	Joie Chitwood,	Noc-Out Hose Clamp Sp.	4	4.4125	4.625	270.	4:36:45.30	108.399
6	33	Louis Durant,	Alfa-Romeo Special	8	2.7165	3.937	182.	4:45:30.88	105.073
7	52	Gigi Villoresi,	Maserati Sp	8	3.070	3.070	181.78	4:57:40.23	100.783
8	7	Frank Wearne,	Wolfe-Tulsa Sp	4	4.375	4.500	271.	4:58:05.00 flg. 197 lps.	
9	39	Bill Sheffler,	Jack Maurer Sp	4	4.250	4.500	255.	(flagged 139 laps)	
10	17	Billy DeVore,	Schoof Sp	4	4.250	4.250	255.	(out at 167 laps)	

Also started—Mel Hansen, Page Offenhauser Special, 143 laps; Russ Snowberger, Jim Hussey Special, 134 laps; Harry McQuinn, Mobile Gas Special, 124 laps; Ralph Hepburn, Novi Governor Special, 121 laps; Al Putnam, L.G.S. Spring Clutch Special, 120 laps; Cliff Bergere, Noc-Out Hose Clamp Special, 82 laps; Duke Dinsmore, Johnston Special, 82 laps; Chet Miller, Miller Special, 64 laps; Jimmy Wilburn, Mobile Oil Special, 52 laps; Tony Bettenhausen, Bristow-McManus Special, 47 laps; Danny Kladis, Grancor V-8 Special, 46 laps; Duke Nalon, Maserati Special, 45 laps; Mauri Rose, Blue Crown Spark Plug Special, 40 laps; George Connor, Walsh Offenhauser Special, 38 laps; Hal Robson, Phillips Miller Special, 37 laps; Louis Tomei, Boxar Tool Special, 34 laps; Henry Banks, Auto Shippers Special, 32 laps; Shorty Cantlon, H-3 Special, 28 laps; George Barringer, Tucker Torpedo Special, 27 laps; Rex Mays, Bowes Seal Fast Special, 26 laps; Sam Hanks, Spike Jones Special, 18 laps; Hal Cole, Alfa-Romeo Special, 16 laps; Paul Russo, Fageol Twin-Coach Special, 16 laps.

STATISTICS OF THE 1947 500-MILE RACE

Honorary Referee—Governor Ralph Gates   *Starter*—Seth Klein   *Pace Car*—Nash Ambassador

Non-Stock Supercharged Motors 183.060 Cubic Inches (3,000 cc.) Piston Displacement or Less and
Non-Stock Non-Supercharged Motors 274.59 Cubic Inches (4,500 cc.)
Piston Displacement or Less—One or Two Seated Bodies

Pos.	Car No.	Driver	Car	Cyldrs.	Bore	Stroke	Piston Displace.	Time	MPH
1	27	Mauri Rose,	Blue Crown Spark Plug Sp.	4	4.312	4.625	270.	4:17:52:17	116.338
2	16	Bill Holland,	Blue Crown Spark Plug Sp.	4	4.312	4.625	270.	4:18:24:29	116.097
3	1	Ted Horn,	Bennett Bros. Sp	8	68.9MM	101.6MM	179.2	4:20:52:55	114.997
4	54	Herb Ardinger,	Novi Gov. Mobile Sp	8	3.125	2.937	181.	4:24:32:52	113.404
5	7	Jimmy Jackson,	Jim Hussey Sp	4	4.275	4.500	258.3	4:25:52:65	112.834
6	9	Rex Mays,	Bowes Seal Fast Sp	8	2.9687	3.250	179.6	4:30:08:05	111.056
7	33	Walt Brown,	Permafuse Sp	8	69MM	100 MM	183.0	4:54:51:47	101.744
8	34	Cy Marshall,	Tattersfield Sp	8	3.010	3.200	182.16	4:56:22:07	Flg. 197 Laps
9	41	Fred Agabashian,	Ross Page Sp	4	3.812	4.000	183.	Flagged	191 Laps
10	10	Duke Dinsmore,	Wolfe Sp	4	4.312	4.625	270.	Flagged	167 Laps

Also Started—Les Anderson, Kennedy Tank Special, 131 laps (Flagged); Pete Romcevich, Camco Motors Special, 168 laps; Emil Andres, Tucker Bros. Special, 150 laps; Frank Wearne, Superior Ind. Special, 128 laps; Ken Fowler, Alfa Romeo Special, 121 laps; Duke Nalon, Don Lee Special, 119 laps; Roland Free, Bristow McManus Special, 87 laps; Tony Bettenhausen, Belanger Special, 79 laps; Russ Snowberger, Federal Engineering Special, 74 laps; Hal Robson, Palmer Special, 67 laps; Cliff Bergere, Novi Governor Mobile Special, 62 laps; Joie Chitwood, Peters Special, 51 laps; Shorty Cantlon, Auto Shippers Special, 40 laps; Henry Banks, Federal Engineering Co., 36 laps; Al Miller, Preston Tucker Special, 33 laps; George Connor, Walsh Special, 32 laps; Mel Hansen, Thorne Engineering Special, 32 laps; Paul Russo, Wolfe Special, 24 laps; Chas. Van Acker, Preston Tucker Partner Special, 24 laps; Milt Fankhouser, Milt Frankhouser Special, 16 laps.

STATISTICS OF THE 1948 500-MILE RACE

Honorary Referee—Mayor Al Feeney   *Starter*—Seth Klein   *Pace Car*—Chevrolet

Non-Stock Supercharged Motors, 183,060 Cubic Inches (3,000 cc.) Piston Displacement or Less, and Non-Stock Non-Supercharged Motors, 274.59 Cubic Inches (4,500 cc.) Piston Displacement or Less—One or Two-Seated Bodies

Pos.	Car No.	Driver	Car	Cyldrs.	Bore	Stroke	Piston Displ.	Time	M.P.H.
1	3	Mauri Rose,	Blue Crown Spark Plug Special	4	4.312	4.625	270	4:10:23.33	119.814
2	16	Bill Holland,	Blue Crown Spark Plug Special	4	4.312	4.625	270	4:11:47.40	119.147
3	54	Duke Nalon,	Novi Grooved Piston Special	8	3.125	2.937	181	4:14:09.78	118.034
4	1	Ted Horn,	Bennett Bros. Special	8	2.718	4.000	179.2	4:14:34.47	117.844
5	35	Mac Hellings,	Don Lee Special	4	4.132	4.625	270	4:24:38.52	113.361
6	63	Hal Cole,	City of Tacoma Special	4	4.125	4.625	247	4:28:50.86	111.587
7	91	Lee Wallard,	Iddings Special	4	4.062	4.500	233	4:34:47	109.177
8	33	John Mauro,	Phil Kraft Special	8	69MM	100MM	183	Flagged	198 Laps
9	7	Tommy Hinnershitz,	Kurtis Kraft Special	4	4.312	4.625	270	Flagged	198 Laps
10	61	Jimmy Jackson,	Howard Keck Special	4	4.312	4.625	270	Left Spindle Broken	193 Laps

Also started—Charles Van Acker, South Bend Special, flagged 192 laps; Billy DeVore, Pat Clancy Special, flagged 190 laps; Johnny Mantz, Kurtis Kraft Special, flagged 185 laps; Tony Bettenhausen, Belanger Special, 167 laps; Hal Robson, Palmer Special, 164 laps; Bill Cantrell, Fageol Twin Special, 161 laps; Joie Chitwood, Nyquist Special, 138 laps; Bill Sheffler, Sheffler Offy Special, 132 laps; Rex Mays, Bowes Seal Fast Special, 129 laps; Chet Miller, Don Lee Special, 108 laps; Jack McGrath, Sheffler Offy Special, 70 laps; Duane Carter, Belanger Motors Special, 59 laps; Fred Agabashian, Page Offenhauser, 58 laps; Les Anderson, Kennedy Tank Special, 58 laps; Mel Hansen, Shafer Gear Works Special, 42 laps; Sam Hanks, Flavelle Duffy Special, 34 laps; Spider Webb, Bromme Special, 27 laps; George Connor, Bennett Bros. Special, 24 laps; Doc Williams, Clark Auto Co. Special, 19 laps; Mike Salay, Terman Supply Special, 13 laps; Emil Andres, Tuffy's Auto Special, 11 laps; Paul Russo, Federal Eng. Detroit Special, 7 laps; Harry McQuinn, Frank Lynch Special, 1 lap.

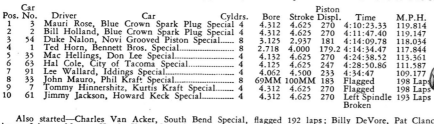

TIMES AND AVERAGES

STATISTICS OF THE 1949 500-MILE RACE

Honorary Referee—J. Emmett McManamon   *Starter*—Seth Klein   *Pace Car*—Oldsmobile

Non-Stock Supercharged Motors, 183.060 Cubic Inches (3,000 cc.) Piston Displacement or Less; Non-Stock Non-Supercharged Motors, 274.59 Cubic Inches (4,500 cc.) Piston Displacement or Less; and Diesel Engines, 402.68 Cubic Inches (6,600 cc.) Piston Displacement or Less (One or Two-Seated Bodies, No Weight Limits.)

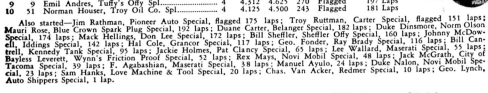

Pos.	Car No.	Driver	Car	Cyldrs.	Bore	Stroke	Piston Displ.	Time	M.P.H.
1	7	Bill Holland, Blue Crown Spark Plug Spl.		4	4.312	4.625	270	4:07:15.97	121.327
2	12	Johnny Parsons, Kurtis-Kraft Spl.		4	4.312	4.625	270	4:10:26.97	119.785
3	22	George Connor, Blue Crown Spark Plug Spl.		4	4.312	4.625	270	4:10:50.78	119.595
4	2	Myron Fohr, Marchese Spl.		4	4.312	4.625	270	4:12:32.65	118.791
5	77	Joie Chitwood, Wolfe Spl.		4	4.312	4.625	270	4:12:36.97	118.757
6	61	Jimmy Jackson, Howard Keck Spl.		4	4.312	4.625	270	4:14:31.00	117.870
7	98	Johnny Mantz, Agajanian Spl.		4	4.312	4.625	270	4:16:06.01	117.601
8	19	Paul Russo, Tuffy's Offy Spl.		4	4.312	4.625	270	4:28:11.28	111.862
9	9	Emil Andres, Tuffy's Offy Spl.		4	4.312	4.625	270	Flagged	197 Laps
10	51	Norman Houser, Troy Oil Co. Spl.		4	4.125	4.500	243	Flagged	181 Laps

Also started—Jim Rathman, Pioneer Auto Special, flagged 175 laps; Troy Ruttman, Carter Special, flagged 151 laps; Mauri Rose, Blue Crown Spark Plug Special, 192 laps; Duane Carter, Belanger Special, 182 laps; Duke Dinsmore, Norm Olson Special, 174 laps; Mack Hellings, Don Lee Special, 172 laps; Bill Sheffler, Sheffler Offy Special, 160 laps; Johnny McDowell, Iddings Special, 142 laps; Hal Cole, Grancor Special, 117 laps; Geo. Fonder, Ray Brady Special, 116 laps; Bill Cantrell, Kennedy Tank Special, 95 laps; Jackie Holmes, Pat Clancy Special, 65 laps; Lee Wallard, Maserati Special, 55 laps; Bayless Leverett, Wynn's Friction Proof Special, 52 laps; Rex Mays, Novi Mobil Special, 48 laps; Jack McGrath, City of Tacoma Special, 39 laps; F. Agabashian, Maserati Special, 38 laps; Manuel Ayulo, 24 laps; Duke Nalon, Novi Mobil Special, 23 laps; Sam Hanks, Love Machine & Tool Special, 20 laps; Chas. Van Acker, Redmer Special, 10 laps; Geo. Lynch, Auto Shippers Special, 1 lap.

STATISTICS OF THE 1950 500-MILE RACE (Called at 345 Miles Because of Rain)

Honorary Referee—Clarence Beesemyer   *Starter*—Seth Klein   *Pace Car*—Mercury

Non-Stock Supercharged Motors, 183.060 Cubic Inches (3,000 cc.) Piston Displacement or Less; Non-Stock Non-Supercharged Motors, 274.59 Cubic Inches (4,500 cc.) Piston Displacement or Less; and Diesel Engines, 402.68 Cubic Inches (6,600 cc.) Piston Displacement or Less (One or Two-Seated Bodies, No Weight Limits.)

Pos.	Car No.	Driver	Car	Cyldrs.	Bore	Stroke	Piston Displ.	*Time	M.P.H.
1	1	Johnny Parsons, Wynn's Friction Proofing Spl.		4	4.3125	4.625	270	2:46:55.97	124.002
2	3	Bill Holland, Blue Crown Spark Plug Spl.		4	4.3125	4.625	270	2:47:33.97	122.638
3	31	Mauri Rose, Offenhauser Spl.		4	4.3125	4.625	270	2:48:44.96	121.778
4	54	Cecil Green, John Zink Spl.		4	4.3125	4.625	270	2:48:45.97	121.766
5	17	Joie Chitwood, Wolfe Spl.		4	4.3125	4.625	270	2:47:32.99	121.755
6	8	Lee Wallard, Blue Crown Spark Plug Spl.		4	4.3125	4.625	270	2:48:34.97	121.009
7	98	Walt Faulkner, Grant Piston Ring Spl.		4	4.3125	4.625	270	2:47:13.55	121.094
8	5	George Conner, Blue Crown Spark Plug Spl.		4	4.3125	4.625	270	2:47:14.25	121.086
9	7	Paul Russo, Russo-Nickels Spl.		4	4.3125	4.625	270	2:48:48.32	119.961
10	59	Pat Flaherty, Granatelli-Sabourin Spl.		4	4.3125	4.625	270	2:48:49.02	119.952

Also started—Myron Fohr, Bardahl Special, 133 laps; Duane Carter, Belanger Special, 133 laps; Mack Hellings, Tuffy's Offy, 132 laps; Jack McGrath, Hinkle Special, 131 laps; Troy Ruttman, Bowes Seal Fast Special, 130 laps; Gene Hartley, Troy Oil Special, 128 laps; Jimmie Davies, Pat Clancy Special, 128 laps; Johnny McDowell, Wales Special, 128 laps; Walt Brown, Tuffy's Offy, 127 laps; Spider Webb, Fadely-Anderson Special, 126 laps; Jerry Hoyt, Morris Special, 125 laps; Walt Ader, Sampson Special, 123 laps; Jackie Holmes, Norm Olsen Special, 123 laps; Jim Rathmann, Pioneer Auto Special, 122 laps; Henry Banks, I.R.C. Special, 112 laps; Bill Schindler, Auto Shippers Special, 111 laps; Bayliss Levrett, Palmer Special, 108 laps; Fred Agabashian, Wynn's Friction Proofing Special, 64 laps; Jimmy Jackson, Cummins Diesel Special, 52 laps; Sam Hanks, Merz Engineering Special, 42 laps; Tony Bettenhausen, Blue Crown Spark Plug Special, 30 laps; Dick Rathmann, City of Glendale Special, 25 laps; Duke Dinsmore, Brown Motors Special, 10 laps.

* Laps completed: Parsons, 138; Holland, Rose, Green, 137; Chitwood, Wallard, 136; Faulkner, Conner, Russo and Flaherty, 135.

STATISTICS OF THE 1951 500-MILE RACE

Honorary Referee—Clarence Beesemyer   *Starter*—Seth Klein   *Pace Car*—Chrysler

Non-Stock Supercharged Motors, 183.060 Cubic Inches (3,000 cc.) Piston Displacement or Less; Non-Stock Non-Supercharged Motors, 274.59 Cubic Inches (4,500 cc.) Piston Displacement or Less; and Diesel Engines, 402.68 Cubic Inches (6,600 cc.) Piston Displacement or Less (One or Two-Seated Bodies, No Weight Limits.)

Pos.	Car No.	Driver	Car	Cyldrs.	Bore	Stroke	Piston Displ.	Time	M.P.H.
1	99	Lee Wallard, Belanger Spl.		4	4.250	4.250	241	3:57:38.05	126.244
2	83	Mike Nazaruk, Jim Robbins Spl.		4	4.3125	4.625	270	3:59:25.31	125.302
3	9	Jack McGrath & Manuel Ayulo, Hinkle Spl.		4	4.3125	4.625	270	4:00:29.42	124.745
4	57	Andy Linden, Leitenberger Spl.		4	4.3125	4.625	270	4:02:18.06	123.812
5	52	Bobby Ball, Blakely Spl.		4	4.3125	4.625	270	4:02:30.27	123.709
6	1	Henry Banks, Blue Crown Spark Plug Spl.		4	4.3125	4.625	270	4:03:18.02	123.304
7	68	Carl Forberg, Auto Shippers Spl.		4	4.3125	4.625	270	Flagged	193 Laps
8	27	Duane Carter, Mobilgas Spl.		4	4.322	4.625	272	Flagged	180 Laps
9	5	Tony Bettenhausen, Mobilgas Spl.		4	4.3125	4.625	270	Out	178 Laps
10	18	Duke Nalon, Novi Purelube Spl.		8	3.187	2.840	181	Out	151 Laps

Also started—Gene Force, Brown Motor Company Spl., 142 laps; Sam Hanks, Peter Schmidt Spl., 135 laps; Bill Schindler, Chapman Spl., 129 laps; Mauri Rose, Pennzoil Spl., 126 laps; Walt Faulkner, Agajanian Grant Piston Ring Spl., 123 laps; Jimmy Davies, Parks Offenhauser Spl., 110 laps; Fred Agabashian, Granatelli Bardahl Spl., 109 laps; Carl Scarborough, McNamara Spl., 100 laps; Bill Mackey, Karl Hall Spl., 97 laps; Chuck Stevenson, Bardahl Spl., 93 laps; Johnny Parsons, Wynn's Friction Proofing Spl., 87 laps; Cecil Green, John Zink Company Spl., 80 laps; Troy Ruttman, Agajanian Featherweight Spl., 78 laps; Duke Dinsmore, Brown Motor Company Spl., 73 laps; Chet Miller, Novi Purelube Spl., 56 laps; Walt Brown, Federal Engineering Spl., 55 laps; Rodger Ward, Deck Manufacturing Company Spl., 34 laps; Cliff Griffith, Morris Spl., 30 laps; Bill Vukovich, Central Excavating Spl., 29 laps; George Connor, Blue Crown Spark Plug Spl., 29 laps; Mack Hellings, Tuffanelli & Derrico Spl., 18 laps; Johnny McDowell, W & J Spl., 15 laps; Joe James, Lincoln-Mercury Spl., 8 laps.

STATISTICS OF THE 1952 500-MILE RACE

Honorary Referee—Raymond C. Firestone   *Starter*—Seth Klein   *Pace Car*—Studebaker

Non-Stock Supercharged Motors, 183.060 Cubic Inches (3,000 cc.) Piston Displacement or Less; Non-Stock Non-Supercharged Motors, 274.59 Cubic Inches (4,500 cc.) Piston Displacement or Less; and Diesel Engines, 402.68 Cubic Inches (6,600 cc.) or Less (One or Two-Seated Bodies, No Weight Limits.)

Pos.	Car No.	Driver	Car	Cyldrs.	Bore	Stroke	Piston Displ.	Time	M.P.H.
1	98	Troy Ruttman, Agajanian Spl.		4	4.322	4.500	264	3:52:41.88	128.922
2	59	Jim Rathman, Grancor Wynn's Spl.		4	4.312	4.625	270	3:56:44.24	126.723
3	18	Sam Hanks, Bardahl Spl.		4	4.312	4.625	270	3:58:53.48	125.580
4	1	Duane Carter, Belanger Motors Spl.		4	4.323	4.500	264	3:59:30.21	125.259
5	33	Art Cross, Bowes Seal Fast Spl.		4	4.312	4.625	270	4:01:22.08	124.292
6	77	Jimmy Bryan, Peter Schmidt Spl.		4	4.312	4.625	270	4:02:06.23	123.914
7	37	Jimmy Reece, John Zink Spl.		4	4.312	4.625	270	4:03:17.15	123.312
8	54	George Connor, Fed. Eng. Det. Spl.		4	4.312	4.625	270	4:04:42.50	122.595
9	22	Cliff Griffith, Tom Saratoff Spl.		4	4.372	4.500	270	4:05:05.65	122.402
10	5	Johnnie Parsons, Jim Robbins Spl.		4	4.352	4.500	270	4:06:19.71	121.789

Also started—Jack McGrath, Hinkle Special, 200 laps; Jim Rigsby, Bob Estes Special, 200 laps; Joe James, Bardahl Special, 200 laps; Bill Schindler, Chapman Special, 200 laps; George Fonder, Leitenberger Special, 197 laps; Eddie Johnson, Central Excavating Special, 193 laps; Bill Vukovich, Fuel Injection Engineering Special, 191 laps; Chuck Stevenson, Springfield Welding's Smith Special, 187 laps; Henry Banks, Blue Crown Spark Plug Special, 184 laps; Manuel Ayulo, Coast Grain Company Special, 184 laps; Johnny McDowell Special, 182 laps; Spider Webb, Granatelli Enterprises Special, 162 laps; Rodger Ward, Federal Engineering Detroit Special, 130 laps; Tony Bettenhausen, Blue Crown Spark Plug Special, 93 laps; Duke Nalon, Novi Pure Oil Special, 84 laps; Bob Sweikert, McNamara Special, 77 laps; Fred Agabashian, Cummins Diesel Special, 71 laps; Gene Hartley, Mel-Rae Special, 65 laps; Bob Scott, Morris Special, 49 laps; Chet Miller, Novi Pure Oil Special, 41 laps; Alberto Ascari, Ferrari Special, 40 laps; Bobby Ball, Ansted Rotary Special, 34 laps; Andy Linden, Miracle Power Special, 20 laps.

TIMES AND AVERAGES

STATISTICS OF THE 1953 500-MILE RACE

Honorary Referee—Henry Ford II   *Starter—Seth Klein*   *Pace Car—Ford Sunliner*

Non-Stock supercharged engines, 183.060 Cubic Inches (3,000 cc.) Piston Displacement or Less and Non-Stock Non-Supercharged Engines, 274.59 Cubic Inches (4,500 cc.) Diesel Engines, 402.68 Cubic Inches (6,600 cc.) or Less. Turbine Motors, no size limitation. (No weight limits.)

Pos.	Car No.	Driver	Car	Cyldrs.	Bore	Stroke	Piston Displ.	Time	M.P.H.
1	14	Bill Vukovich, Fuel Injection Spl.		4	4.375	4.500	270	3:53:01.69	128.740
2	16	Art Cross, Spfg. Welding's Clay Smith Spl.		4	4.312	4.500	263	3:56:32.56	126.827
3	3	Sam Hanks & Duane Carter, Bardahl Spl.		4	3.375	3.500	270	3:57:13.24	126.465
4	59	Fred Agabashian & Paul Russo, Grancor-Elgin Piston Pin Special		4	4.375	4.500	270	3:57:40.91	126.219
5	5	Jack McGrath, Hinkle Special		4	4.312	4.625	270	4:00:51.33	124.556
6	48	Jimmy Daywalt, Sumar Special		4	4.312	4.625	270	4:01:11.88	124.379
7	2	Jim Rathmann & Eddie Johnson, Travelon Trailer Special		4	4.375	4.500	270	4:01:47.65	124.072
8	12	Ernie McCoy, Chapman Special		4	4.312	4.625	270	4:03:06.23	123.404
9	98	Tony Bettenhausen & Gene Hartley Agajanian Special		4	4.312	4.500	263	4:00:05.49	122.453
10	53	Jimmy Davies, Pat Clancy Special		4	4.375	4.500	274	4:02:51.81	119.203

Also started—Duke Nalon, Novi Governor Special, 191 laps; Carl Scarborough and Bob Scott, McNamara Special, 190 laps; Manuel Ayulo, Peter Schmidt Special, 184 laps; Jim Bryan, Blakely Oil Special, 183 laps; Bill Holland and Jim Rathmann, Crawford Special, 177 laps; Rodger Ward, M. A. Walker Special, 177 laps; Walt Faulkner and Johnny Mantz, Automobile Shippers Special, 176 laps; Marshall Teague, Hart Fullerton Special, 169 laps; Spider Webb and Jackie Holmes, Lubri-Loy Special, 166 laps; Bob Sweikert, Dean Van Lines Special, 151 laps; Mike Nazaruk, Kalamazoo Special, 146 laps; Pat Flaherty, Peter Schmidt Special, 115 laps; Jerry Hoyt and Andy Linden, John Zink Special, 107 laps; Duane Carter, Miracle Power Special, 94 laps; Paul·Russo, Federal Engineering Detroit Special, 89 laps; Johnnie Parsons, Belond Equa-Flow Exhaust Special, 86 laps; Don Freeland, Bob Estes Special, 76 laps; Gene Hartley, Federal Engineering Detroit Special, 53 laps; Chuck Stevenson, Agajanian Special, 42 laps; Cal Niday, Miracle Power Special, 30 laps; Bob Scott, Belond Equa-Flow Exhaust Special, 14 laps; Johnny Thomson, Dr. Sabourin Special, 6 laps; Andy Linden, Cop-Sil-Loy Brake Special, 3 laps.

NOTE: Relief drivers listed only when they finished a car started by someone else.

STATISTICS OF THE 1954 500-MILE RACE

Honorary Referee—Ralph DePalma   *Starter—W. H. Vandewater*   *Pace Car—Dodge*

Non-Stock supercharged engines, 183,060 Cubic Inches (3,000 cc.) Piston Displacement or Less and Non-Stock Non-Supercharged Engines, 274.79 Cubic Inches (4,500 cc.) Diesel Engines, 402.68 Cubic Inches (6,600 cc.) or Less. Turbine Motors, no size limitation. (No weight limits.)

Pos.	Car No.	Driver	Car	Cyldrs.	Bore	Stroke	Piston Displ.	Time	M.P.H.
1	14	Bill Vukovich, Fuel Injection Spl.		4	4.375	4.500	271	3:49:17.27	130.840
2	9	Jimmy Bryan, Dean Van Lines Spl.		4	4.312	4.500	263	3:50:27.26	130.178
3	2	Jack McGrath, Hinkle Spl.		4	4.312	4.625	270	3:50:36.97	130.086
4	34	Troy Ruttman, Automobile Shippers Spl.		4	4.375	4.500	271	3:52:09.90	129.218
5	73	Mike Nazaruk, McNamara Spl.		4	4.375	4.500	271	3:52:41.85	128.923
6	77	Fred Agabashian, Merz Engr. Spl.		4	4.385	4.500	272	3:53:04.83	128.711
7	7	Don Freeland, Bob Estes Spl.		4	4.375	4.500	271	3:53:30.65	128.474
8	5	Paul Russo and Jerry Hoyt, Ansted Rotary Engr. Spl.		4	4.375	4.500	271	3:54:18.39	128.037
9	28	Larry Crockett, Fed. Engr. Det. Spl.		4	4.312	4.625	270	3:56:24.56	126.899
10	24	Cal Niday, Jim Robbins Spl.		4	4.375	4.500	271	3:56:24.93	126.895

Also started—Art Cross and Jimmie Davies, Bardahl Special, 200 laps; Chuck Stevenson and Walt Faulkner, Agajanian Special, 199 laps; Manuel Ayulo, Schmidt Special, 197 laps; Bob Sweikert, Lutes Truck Parts Special, 197 laps; Duane Carter and Jimmy Jackson, Automobile Shippers Special, 196 laps; Ernie McCoy, Crawford Special, 194 laps; Jimmy Reece, Malloy Special, 194 laps; Ed Elisian and Bob Scott, Chapman Special, 193 laps; Frank Armi, Martin Bros. Special, 193 laps; Sam Hanks and Jim Rathmann, Bardahl Special, 191 laps; Pat O'Connor, Hopkins Special, 181 laps; Rodger Ward, Dr. Sabourin Special, 172 laps; Gene Hartley and Marshall Teague, John Zink Special, 168 laps; Johnny Thomson and Bill Homeier, Chapman Special, 165 laps; Andy Linden and Bob Scott, Brown Motor Co. Special, 138 laps; Jerry Hoyt, Belanger Special, 130 laps; Jimmy Daywalt, Sumar Special, 111 laps; Jim Rathmann and Pat Flaherty, Bardahl Special, 110 laps; Tony Bettenhausen, Mel Wiggers Special, 105 laps; Spider Webb and Danny Kladis, Advance Muffler Special, 104 laps; Len Duncan and George Fonder, Ray Brady Special, 101 laps; Johnnie Parsons, Belond Equa-Flow Exhaust Special, 79 laps; Bill Homeier, Jones and Maley Special, 74 laps.

NOTE: Relief drivers listed only when they finished a car started by someone else.

STATISTICS OF THE 1955 500-MILE RACE

Honorary Referee—R. A. Stranahan, Jr.   *Starter—W. H. Vandewater*   *Pace Car—Chevrolet*

Non-Stock supercharged engines, 183.060 cubic inches (3,000 cc.) Piston Displacement or Less; Non-Stock non-supercharged engines, 274.59 cubic inches (4,500 cc.) or Less; Diesel Engines, 335.57 cubic inches (5,000 cc.) or Less; Turbine Motors, no size limitation. (No weight limits.)

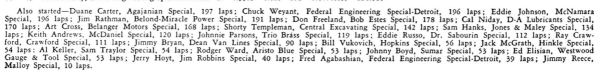

Pos.	Car No.	Driver	Car	Cyl.	Bore	Stroke	Piston Displ.	Time	M.P.H.
1	6	Bob Sweikert, John Zink Spl.		4	4.3125	4.625	270	3:53:59.13	128.209
2	10	Tony Bettenhausen, Chapman Spl.		4	4.375	4.500	270	3:56:43.11	126.733
3	15	Jimmy Davies, Bardahl Spl.		4	4.375	4.500	270	3:57:31.89	126.299
4	44	Johnny Thomson, Schmidt Spl.		4	4.3125	4.625	270	3:57:38.44	126.241
5	77	Walt Faulkner, Merz Engineering Spl.		4	4.375	4.500	270	3:59:16.66	125.377
6	19	Andy Linden, Massaglia Spl.		4	4.375	4.500	270	3:59:57.47	125.022
7	71	Al Herman, Martin Bros. Spl.		4	4.3125	4.625	270	4:00:23.81	124.794
8	29	Pat O'Connor, Ansted-Rotary Spl.		4	4.3125	4.625	270	4:00:41.09	124.644
9	48	Jimmy Daywalt, Sumar Spl.		4	4.375	4.500	270	4:01:09.39	124.401
10	89	Pat Flaherty, Dunn Engineering Spl.		4	4.3325	4.625	272	4:01:46.05	124.086

Also started—Duane Carter, Agajanian Special, 197 laps; Chuck Weyant, Federal Engineering Special-Detroit, 196 laps; Eddie Johnson, McNamara Special, 196 laps; Jim Rathman, Belond-Miracle Power Special, 191 laps; Don Freeland, Bob Estes Special, 178 laps; Cal Niday, D-A Lubricants Special, 170 laps; Art Cross, Belanger Motors Special, 168 laps; Shorty Templeman, Central Excavating Special, 142 laps; Sam Hanks, Jones & Maley Special, 134 laps; Keith Andrews, McDaniel Special, 120 laps; Johnnie Parsons, Trio Brass Special, 119 laps; Eddie Russo, Dr. Sabourin Special, 112 laps; Ray Crawford, Crawford Special, 111 laps; Jimmy Bryan, Dean Van Lines Special, 90 laps; Bill Vukovich, Hopkins Special, 56 laps; Jack McGrath, Hinkle Special, 54 laps; Al Keller, Sam Traylor Special, 54 laps; Rodger Ward, Aristo Blue Special, 53 laps; Johnny Boyd, Sumar Special, 53 laps; Ed Elisian, Westwood Gauge & Tool Special, 53 laps; Jerry Hoyt, Jim Robbins Special, 40 laps; Fred Agabashian, Federal Engineering Special-Detroit, 39 laps; Jimmy Reece, Malloy Special, 10 laps.

STATISTICS OF THE 1956 500-MILE RACE

Honorary Referee—Herman Teetor   *Starter—W. H. Vandewater*   *Pace Car—De Soto*

Non-Stock Supercharged Engines 183.060 Cubic Inches (3,000 cc.) Piston Displacement or Less; Non-Stock Non-Supercharged Engines 274.59 Cubic Inches (4,500 cc.) or Less; Diesel Engines 335.57 Cubic Inches (5,500 cc.) or Less; Turbine Motors, no size limitation. (No weight limits.)

Pos.	Car No.	Driver	Car	Cyl.	Bore	Stroke	Piston Displ.	Time	M.P.H.
1	8	Pat Flaherty, John Zink Spl.		4	4.3125	4.625	270	3:53:28.84	128.490
2	4	Sam Hanks, Jones & Maley Spl.		4	4.3125	4.625	270	3:53:49.30	128.303
3	16	Don Freeland, Bob Estes Spl.		4	4.3125	4.625	270	3:54:59.07	127.668
4	98	Johnnie Parsons, Agajanian Spl.		4	4.250	4.125	270	3:56:54.48	126.631
5	73	Dick Rathmann, McNamara Spl.		4	4.3125	4.625	270	3:57:50.65	126.133
6	1	Bob Sweikert, D-A Lubricant Spl.		4	4.500	4.375	270	3:59:03.83	125.489
7	14	Bob Veith, Fed. Engr. Spl., Detroit		4	4.3125	4.625	270	3:59:54.50	125.048
8	19	Rodger Ward, Filter Queen Spl.		4	4.3125	4.625	270	4:00:01.15	124.990
9	26	Jimmy Reece, Massaglia Hotels Spl.		4	4.3125	4.625	270	4:00:07.11	124.938
10	27	Cliff Griffith, Jim Robbins Spl.		4	4.3125	4.625	270	4:01:45.48	123.471

Also started—Gene Hartley, Central Excavating Special, 196 laps; Fred Agabashian, Federal Engineering Special, Detroit, 196 laps; Bob Christie, Helse Special, 196 laps; Al Keller, Sam Traylor Special, 195 laps; Eddie Johnson, Central Excavating Special, 195 laps; Billy Garrett, Greenman-Casale Special, 194 laps; Duke Dinsmore, Shannon's Special, 191 laps; Pat O'Connor, Ansted-Rotary Special, 187 laps; Jimmy Bryan, Dean Van Lines Special, 185 laps; Jim Rathmann, Hopkins Special, 175 laps; Johnnie Tolan, Trio Brass Foundry Special, 173 laps; Tony Bettenhausen, Belanger Motors Special, 160 laps; Ed Elisian, Hoyt Machine Special, 160 laps; Jimmy Daywalt, Sumar Special, 134 laps; Jack Turner, Travelon Trailer Special, 131 laps; Andy Linden, Chapman Special, 98 laps; Keith Andrews, Dunn Engineering Special, 94 laps; Al·Herman, Bardahl Special, 74 laps; Ray Crawford, Crawford Special, 49 laps; Johnny Boyd, Bowes Seal Fast Special, 35 laps; Troy Ruttman, John Zink Special, 22 laps; Johnny Thomson, Schmidt Special, 22 laps; Paul Russo, Novi Vespa Special, 21 laps.

TIMES AND AVERAGES

STATISTICS OF THE 1957 500-MILE RACE

Honorary Referee—Louis Schwitzer, Sr.   *Starter*—W. H. Vandewater   *Pace Car*—Mercury

Non-Stock Supercharged Engines 170.856 Cubic Inches (2,800 cc.) Piston Displacement or Less; Non-Stock Non-Supercharged Engines 256.284 Cubic Inches (4,200 cc.); Diesel Engines 335.57 Cubic Inches (5,500 cc.) or Less; Turbine Motors, no size limitation. (No weights limits.)

Pos.	Car No.	Driver Car	Cyl.	Bore	Stroke	Piston Displ.	Time	M.P.H.
1	9	Sam Hanks, Belond Exhaust Spl..........	4	4.156	4.625	250.	3:41:14.25	135.601
2	26	Jim Rathmann, Chiropractic Spl..........	4	4.3125	4.375	255.	3:41:35.75	135.382
3	1	Jimmy Bryan, Dean Van Lines Spl.........	4	4.21875	4.500	251.6	3:43:28.25	134.246
4	54	Paul Russo, Novi Auto. Air Cond. Spl.	8	3.200	2.625	168.6*	3:44:11.10	133.818
5	73	Andy Linden, McNamara Veedol Spl.......	4	4.250	4.500	255.3	3:44:28.55	133.645
6	6	Johnny Boyd, Bowes Seal Fast Spl.......	4	4.21875	4.500	251.6	3:45:49.55	132.846
7	48	Marshall Teague, Sumar Spl.............	4	4.250	4.500	255.3	3:45:59.85	132.745
8	12	Pat O'Connor, Sumar Spl...............	4	4.250	4.500	255.3	3:46:47.35	132.281
9	7	Bob Veith, Bob Estes Spl..............	4	4.250	4.500	255.3	3:47:31.35	131.855
10	22	Gene Hartley, Massaglia Hotels Spl.....	4	4.21875	4.500	251.6	3:48:24.40	131.345

Also started—Jack Turner, Bardahl Special, 200 laps; Johnny Thomson, D-A Lubricant Special, 199 laps; Bob Christie, Jones & Maley Special, 197 laps; Chuck Weyant, Central Excavating Special, 196 laps; Tony Bettenhausen, Novi Auto. Air Cond. Special, 195 laps; †Johnnie Parsons, Sumar Special, 195 laps; Don Freeland, Ansted-Rotary Special,* 192 laps; Jimmy Reece, Hoyt Machine Special, 182 laps; Don Edmunds, McKay Special, 170 laps; Johnnie Tolan, Greenman-Casale Special, 138 laps; Al Herman, Dunn Engineering Special, 111 laps; Freddie Agabashian, Bowes Seal Fast Special, 107 laps; Eddie Sachs, Schmidt Special, 105 laps; Mike Magill, Dayton Steel Foundry Special 101 laps; Eddie Johnson, Chapman Special, 93 laps; Bill Cheesbourg, Seal Line Special, 81 laps; Al Keller, Bardahl Special, 75 laps; Jimmy Daywalt, Helse Special, 53 laps; Ed Elisian, McNamara Special, 51 laps; Rodger Ward, Wolcott Fuel Injection Special, 27 laps; Troy Ruttman, John Zink Special, 13 laps; Eddie Russo, Sclavi & Amos Special, 0 laps; Elmer George, Travelon Trailer Special, 0 laps.

† Drove car qualified by D. Rathmann.

* Supercharged.

STATISTICS OF THE 1958 500-MILE RACE

Honorary Referee—R. A. Stranahan, Jr.   *Starter*—W. H. Vandewater   *Pace Car*—Pontiac

Non-Stock Supercharged Engines 170.856 Cubic Inches (2,800 cc.) Piston Displacement or Less; Non-Stock Non-Supercharged Engines 256.284 Cubic Inches (4,200 cc.); Diesel Engines 335.57 Cubic Inches (5,500 cc.) or Less; Turbine Motors, no size limitation. (No weights limits.)

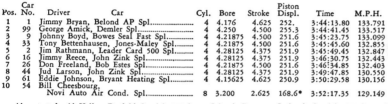

Pos.	Car No.	Driver Car	Cyl.	Bore	Stroke	Piston Displ.	Time	M.P.H.
1	1	Jimmy Bryan, Belond AP Spl..........	4	4.176	4.625	252.	3:44:13.80	133.791
2	99	George Amick, Demler Spl..........	4	4.250	4.500	255.3	3:44:41.45	133.517
3	9	Johnny Boyd, Bowes Seal Fast Spl......	4	4.21875	4.500	251.6	3:45:23.75	133.099
4	33	Tony Bettenhausen, Jones-Maley Spl.......	4	4.21875	4.500	251.6	3:45:45.60	132.855
5	2	Jim Rathmann, Leader 500 Spl........	4	4.28125	4.375	251.9	3:45:49.45	132.847
6	16	Jimmy Reece, John Zink Spl..........	4	4.28125	4.375	251.9	3:46:30.75	132.443
7	26	Don Freeland, Bob Estes Spl.........	4	4.21875	4.500	251.6	3:46:34.85	132.403
8	44	Jud Larson, John Zink Spl...........	4	4.28125	4.375	251.9	3:49:47.85	130.550
9	61	Eddie Johnson, Bryant Heating Spl......	4	4.15625	4.625	250.9	3:50:29.58	130.156
10	54	Bill Cheesbourg, Novi Auto Air Cond. Spl.	8	3.200	2.625	168.6*	3:52:17.35	129.149

Also started—Al Keller, Bardahl Special, 200 laps; Johnnie Parsons, Gerhardt Special, 200 laps; Johnnie Tolan, Greenman Casale Special, 200 laps; Bob Christie, Federal Engineering Special, 189 laps; Dempsey Wilson, Sorenson Special, 151 laps; A. J. Foyt, Dean Van Lines Special, 148 laps; Mike Magill, Dayton Steel Foundry Special, 136 laps; Paul Russo, Novi Auto Air Conditioning Special, 122 laps; Shorty Templeman, McNamara Special, 106 laps; Rodger Ward, Wolcott Fuel Injection Special, 93 laps; Billy Garrett, Chapman Special, 80 laps; Eddie Sachs, Schmidt Special, 68 laps; Johnny Thomson, D-A Lubricant Special, 52 laps; Chuck Weyant, Dunn Engineering Special, 38 laps; Jack Turner, Massaglia Hotels Special, 21 laps; Bob Veith, Bowes Seal Fast Special, 1 lap; Dick Rathmann, McNamara Special, 0 laps; Ed Elisian, John Zink Special, 0 laps; Pat O'Connor, Sumar Special, 0 laps; Paul Goldsmith, City of Daytona Beach Special, 0 laps; Jerry Unser, McKay Special, 0 laps; Len Sutton, Jim Robbins Special, 0 laps; Art Bisch, Helse Special, 0 laps.

* Supercharged.

STATISTICS OF THE 1959 500-MILE RACE

Honorary Referee—Vernon A. Bellman   *Starter*—W. H. Vandewater   *Pace Car*—Buick

Non-Stock Supercharged Engines 170.856 Cubic Inches (2,800 cc.) Piston Displacement or Less; Non-Stock Non-Supercharged Engines 256.284 Cubic Inches (4,200 cc.); Diesel Engines 335.57 Cubic Inches (5,500 cc.) or Less; Turbine Motors, no size limitation. (No weights limits.)

Pos.	Car No.	Driver Car	Cyl.	Bore	Stroke	Piston Displ.	Time	M.P.H.
1	5	Rodger Ward, Leader Card 500 Rdstr......	4	4.28125	4.375	251.9	3:40:49.20	135.857
2	16	Jim Rathmann, Simoniz Special........	4	4.28125	4.375	251.9	3:41:12.47	135.619
3	2	Johnny Thomson, Racing Associates Spl..	4	4.28125	4.375	251.9	3:41:39.85	135.340
4	1	Tony Bettenhausen, Hoover Motor Exp. Spl.	4	4.28125	4.375	251.9	3:42:36.25	134.768
5	99	Paul Goldsmith, Demler Special......	4	4.250	4.500	255.3	3:42:55.60	134.573
6	33	Johnny Boyd, Bowes Seal Fast Spl......	4	4.28125	4.375	251.9	3:44:06.23	133.867
7	37	Duane Carter, Smokey's Reverse Torq. Spl.	4	4.28125	4.375	251.9	3:44:59.15	133.342
8	19	Eddie Johnson, Bryant Htg. & Cool. Spl.	4	4.15625	4.625	250.9	3:44:59.69	133.336
9	45	Paul Russo, Bardahl Special........	4	4.21875	4.500	251.6	3:45:00.24	133.331
10	10	A. J. Foyt, Dean Van Lines Spl........	4	4.21875	4.500	251.6	3:45:03.65	133.297

Also started—Gene Hartley, Drewry's Special, 200 laps; Bob Veith, John Zink Heater Special, 200 laps; Al Herman, Dunn Engineering Special, 200 laps; Jimmy Daywalt, Federal Engineering Special, 200 laps; Chuck Arnold, Hall-Mar Special, 200 laps; Jim McWithey, Ray Brady Special, 200 laps; Eddie Sachs, Schmidt Special, 182 laps; Al Keller, Helse Special, 163 laps; Pat Flaherty, John Zink Heater Special, 162 laps; Dick Rathmann, McNamara Chiropractic Special, 150 laps; Bill Cheesbourg, Greenman-Casale Special, 147 laps; Don Freeland, Jim Robbins Special, 136 laps; Ray Crawford, Meguiar's Mirror Glaze Special, 115 laps; Don Branson, Bob Estes Special, 112 laps; Bob Christie, Federal Engineering Special, 109 laps; Bobby Grim, Sumar Special, 85 laps; Jack Turner, Travelon Trailer Special, 47 laps; Chuck Weyant, McKay Special, 45 laps; Jud Larson, Bowes Seal Fast Special, 45 laps; Mike Magill, Dayton Steel Foundry Special, 45 laps; Red Amick, Wheeler-Foutch Special, 45 laps; Len Sutton, Wolcott Special, 34 laps; Jimmy Bryan, Belond AP Muffler Special, 1 lap.

STATISTICS OF THE 1960 500-MILE RACE

Honorary Referee—Vernon A. Bellman   *Starter*—W. H. Vandewater   *Pace Car*—Oldsmobile

Non-Stock Supercharged Engines 170.856 Cubic Inches (2,800 cc.) Piston Displacement or Less; Non-Stock Non-Supercharged Engines 256.284 Cubic Inches (4,200 cc.); Diesel Engines 335.61 Cubic Inches (5,500 cc.) or Less; Turbine Motors, no size limitation. (No weights limits.)

Pos.	Car No.	Driver Car	Cyl.	Bore	Stroke	Piston Displ.	Time	M.P.H.
1	4	Jim Rathmann, Ken-Paul Spl........	4	4.28125	4.375	251.9	3:36:11.36	138.767
2	1	Rodger Ward, Leader Card 500 Rdstr.......	4	4.28125	4.375	251.9	3:36:24.03	138.631
3	99	Paul Goldsmith, Demler Spl........	4	4.250	4.500	255.3	3:39:18.58	136.792
4	7	Don Branson, Bob Estes Spl.........	4	4.28125	4.375	251.9	3:39:19.28	136.785
5	3	Johnny Thomson, Adams Quarter Horse Spl..	4	4.28125	4.375	251.9	3:39:22.65	136.750
6	22	Eddie Johnson, Jim Robbins Spl.......	4	4.28125	4.375	251.9	3:40:21.88	136.137
7	98	Lloyd Ruby, Agajanian Spl.........	4	4.21875	4.500	251.6	3:40:36.88	135.983
8	44	Bob Veith, Schmidt Spl...........	4	4.28125	4.375	251.9	3:41:28.78	135.452
9	18	Bud Tingelstad, Jim Robbins Spl......	4	4.28125	4.375	251.9	3:44:21.17	133.717
10	38	Bob Christie, Federal Engineering Spl........	4	4.1862	4.625	254.6	3:44:51.54	133.416

Also started—Red Amick, King O'Lawn Special, 200 laps; Duane Carter, Thompson Industries Special, 200 laps; Bill Homeier, Ridgewood Builders Incorporated Special, 200 laps; Gene Hartley, Sumar Special, 200 laps; Chuck Stevenson, Leader Card 500 Roadster, 196 laps; Bobby Grim, Bill Forbes Special, 194 laps; Shorty Templeman, Federal Engineering Special, 191 laps; Jim Hurtubise, Travelon Trailer Special, 185 laps; Jimmy Bryan, Metal-Cal Special, 152 laps; Troy Ruttman, John Zink Heater Special, 134 laps; Eddie Sachs, Dean Van Lines Special, 132 laps; Don Freeland, Ross Babcock Traveler Special, 129 laps; Tony Bettenhausen, Dowgard Special, 125 laps; Wayne Weiler, Ansted-Rotary Special, 103 laps; A. J. Foyt, Bowes Seal Fast Special, 90 laps; Eddie Russo, Go-Kart Special, 84 laps; Johnny Boyd, Bowes Seal Fast Special, 77 laps; Gene Force, McKay Special, 74 laps; Jim McWithey, Hoover Motor Express Special, 60 laps; Len Sutton, S-R Racing Enterprises Special, 47 laps; Dick Rathmann, Jim Robbins Special, 42 laps; Al Herman, Joe Hunt Magneto Special, 34 laps; Dempsey Wilson, Bryant Heating & Cooling Special, 11 laps.

TIMES AND AVERAGES
STATISTICS OF THE 1961 500-MILE RACE

Honorary Referee—Raymond Firestone   *Starter—W. H. Vandewater*   *Pace Car—Ford Thunderbird*

Non-Stock Supercharged Engines 170.856 Cubic Inches (2,800 cc.) Piston Displacement or Less; Non-Stock Non-Supercharged Engines 256.284 Cubic Inches (4,200 cc.) or Less; Diesel Engines 335.61 Cubic Inches (5,500 cc.) or Less; Turbine Motors, no size limitation. (No weight limits.)

Pos.	Car No.	Driver Car	Cyl.	Bore	Stroke	Piston Displ.	Time	M.P.H.
1	1	A. J. Foyt, Bowes Seal Fast Spl.	4	4.28125	4.375	251.9	3:35:37.49	139.130
2	12	Eddie Sachs, Dean Van Lines Spl.	4	4.28125	4.375	251.9	3:35:45.77	139.041
3	2	Rodger Ward, Del Webb's Sun City Spl.	4	4.28125	4.375	251.9	3:36:32.68	138.539
4	7	Shorty Templeman, B. Forbes Rac. Tm. Spl.	4	4.28125	4.375	251.9	3:39:10.84	136.873
5	19	Al Keller, Konstant Hot Spl.	4	4.29100	4.375	253.0	3:40:31.94	136.034
6	18	Chuck Stevenson, Metal-Cal Spl.	4	4.28125	4.375	251.9	3:41:00.45	135.742
7	31	Bobby Marshman, Hoover Motor Exp. Spl.	4	4.28125	4.375	251.9	3:41:20.77	135.534
8	5	Lloyd Ruby, Autolite Spl.	4	4.30100	4.375	254.0	3:42:27.14	134.860
9	17	Jack Brabham, Cooper-Climax Spl.	4	3.78000	3.740	167.6	3:43:41.22	134.116
10	34	Norm Hall, Federal Engineering Spl.	4	4.18620	4.625	254.6	3:43:42.39	134.104

Also started—Gene Hartley, John Chalik Spl., 198 laps; Parnelli Jones, Agajanian Willard Battery Spl., 192 laps; Dick Rathmann, Jim Robbins Spl., 164 laps; Paul Goldsmith, Racing Associates Spl., 160 laps; Wayne Weiler, Hopkins Spl., 147 laps; Dempsey Wilson, Lysle Greenman Spl., 145 laps; Bob Christie, North Electric Spl., 132 laps; Eddie Johnson, Jim Robbins Spl., 127 laps; Len Sutton, Bryant Heating and Cooling Spl., 110 laps; Troy Ruttman, John Zink Trackburner Spl., 105 laps; Johnny Boyd, Leader Card 500 Roadster, 105 laps; Jim Hurtubise, Demler Spl., 102 laps; Ebb Rose, Meyer Speedway Spl., 93 laps; Cliff Griffith, McCulloch Spl., 55 laps; Jack Turner, Bardahl Spl., 52 laps; A. J. Shepherd, Travelon Trailer Spl., 51 laps; Roger McCluskey, Racing Associates Spl., 51 laps; Bill Cheesbourg, Dean Van Lines Spl., 50 laps; Don Davis, Dart-Kart Spl. by Rupp, 49 laps; Jim Rathmann, Simoniz Spl., 48 laps; Jimmy Daywalt, Schulz Fueling Equipment Spl., 27 laps; Bobby Grim, Thompson Industries Spl., 26 laps; Don Branson, Hoover Motor Express Spl., 2 laps.

STATISTICS OF THE 1962 500-MILE RACE

Honorary Referee—R. A. Stranahan   *Starter—Pat Vidan*   *Pace Car—Studebaker Lark*

Non-Stock Supercharged Engines 170.856 Cubic Inches (2,800 cc.) Piston Displacement or Less; Non-Stock Non-Supercharged Engines 256.284 Cubic Inches (4,200 cc.) or Less; Diesel Engines 335.61 Cubic Inches (5,500 cc.) or Less; Turbine Motors, no size limitation. (No weight limits.)

Pos.	Car No.	Driver Car	Cyl.	Bore	Stroke	Piston Displ.	Time	M.P.H.
1	3	Rodger Ward, Leader Card 500 Rdstr.	4	4.28125	4.375	251.9	3:33:50.33	140.293
2	5	Len Sutton, Leader Card 500 Rdstr.	4	4.28125	4.375	251.9	3:34:01.85	140.167
3	2	Eddie Sachs, Dean Autolite Spl.	4	4.28135	4.375	252	3:34:10.26	140.075
4	27	Don Davis, J. H. Rose Truck Line Spl.	4	4.28125	4.375	251.9	3:34:38.46	139.768
5	54	Bobby Marshman, Bryant Htg. & Cool. Spl.	4	4.28125	4.375	251.9	3:36:09.27	138.790
6	15	Jim McElreath, Schulz Fuel. Equip. Spl.	4	4.28125	4.375	251.9	3:36:22.02	138.653
7	98	Parnelli Jones, Agajanian's Wlrd. Btry. Spl.	4	4.28125	4.375	251.9	3:36:33.18	138.534
8	12	Lloyd Ruby, Thompson Industries Spl.	4	4.29125	4.375	253.4	3:37:06.33	138.182
9	44	Jim Rathmann, Simoniz Vista Special	4	4.28125	4.375	251.9	3:39:07.05	136.913
10	38	Johnny Boyd, Metal-Cal Special	4	4.28125	4.375	251.9	3:39:37.19	136.600

Also started—Shorty Templeman, Bill Forbes Racing Team Spl., 200 laps; Don Branson, Mid-Continent Securities Spl., 200 laps; Jim Hurtubise, Jim Robbins Spl., 200 laps; Ed Rose, J. H. Rose Truck Line Spl., 200 laps; Bud Tingelstad, Konstant Hot Spl., 200 laps; Roger McCluskey, Bell Lines Trucking Spl., 169 laps; Elmer George, Sarkes Tarzian Spl., 147 laps; Troy Ruttman, Jim Robbins Spl., 141 laps; Bobby Grim, Morcroft Spl., 97 laps; Dan Gurney, Thompson Harvey Aluminum Spl., 93 laps; Chuck Hulse, Federal Engineering Spl., 92 laps; Jimmy Daywalt, Albany New York Spl., 75 laps; A. J. Foyt, Bowes Seal Fast Spl., 70 laps; Dick Rathmann, Chapman Spl., 52 laps; Eddie Johnson, Polyaire Foam Spl., 39 laps; Paul Goldsmith, American Rubber & Plastics Spl., 27 laps; Gene Hartley, Drewrys Spl., 24 laps; Paul Russo, Denver-Chicago Trucking Co. Spl., 21 laps; Jack Turner, Bardahl Spl., 18 laps; Bob Christie, North Electric Spl., 18 laps; Allen Crowe, S-R Racing Enterprise Spl., 18 laps; Chuck Rodee, Travelon Trailer Spl., 18 laps; Bob Veith, Meguiars Mirror Glaze Spl., 13 laps.

STATISTICS OF THE 1963 500-MILE RACE

Honorary Referee—Baxter F. Ball   *Starter—Pat Vidan*   *Pace Car—Chrysler 300 J*

Non-Stock Supercharged Engines 170.856 Cubic Inches (2,800 cc.) Piston Displacement or Less; Non-Stock Non-Supercharged Engines 256.284 Cubic Inches (4,200 cc.) or Less; Diesel Engines 335.61 Cubic Inches (5,500 cc.) or Less; Turbine Motors, no size limitation. (No weight limits.)

Pos.	Car No.	Driver Car	Cyl.	Bore	Stroke	Piston Displ.	Time	M.P.H.
1	98	Parnelli Jones, Agajanian Willard Spl.	4	4.28125	4.375	251.9	3:29:35.40	143.137
2	92	Jim Clark, Lotus Powered By Ford	8	3.760	2.870	255.6*	3:30:09.24	142.752
3	2	A. J. Foyt, Sheraton-Thompson Spl.	4	4.28125	4.375	251.9	3:30:57.34	142.210
4	1	Rodger Ward, Kaiser Aluminum Spl.	4	4.28125	4.375	251.9	3:32:37.80	141.090
5	4	Don Branson, Leader Card 500 Roadster	4	4.28125	4.375	251.9	3:32:58.11	140.866
6	8	Jim McElreath, Forbes Racing Team Spl.	4	4.28125	4.375	251.9	3:32:58.43	140.862
7	93	Dan Gurney, Lotus Powered By Ford	8	3.760	2.870	255.6*	3:34:10.61	140.071
8	10	Chuck Hulse, Dean Van Lines Spl.	4	4.28125	4.375	251.9	3:34:11.26	140.064
9	84	Al Miller, Thompson Harvey Alum. Spl.	8	3.750	2.880	255 *	3:35:00.98	139.524
10	22	Dick Rathmann, Chapman Spl.	4	4.28125	4.375	251.9	3:36:04.09	138.845

Also started—Dempsey Wilson, Vita Fresh Orange Juice Special, 200 laps; Troy Ruttman, J. R. Autocrat Seat Belt Special, 200 laps; Bob Christie, Travelon Trailer Special, 200 laps; Ebb Rose, Sheraton-Thompson Special, 200 laps; Roger McCluskey, Konstant Hot Special, 198 laps; Bobby Marshman, Econo-Car Rental Special, 196 laps; Eddie Sachs, Bryant Heating & Cooling Special, 181 laps; Paul Goldsmith, Demler Special, 149 laps; Lloyd Ruby, John Zink Trackburner Special, 126 laps; Eddie Johnson, Drewrys Special, 112 laps; Chuck Stevenson, Bardahl Special, 110 laps; Jim Hurtubise, Hotel Tropicana Special, #102 laps; Duane Carter, Mickey Thompson Harvey Aluminum Special,* 100 laps; Jim Rathmann, Coral Harbour Special, 99 laps; Bobby Grim, Morcroft Special, 79 laps; Bob Veith, Sheraton-Thompson Special, 74 laps; Allen Crowe, Gabriel Shocker Special, 47 laps; Bud Tingelstad, Hoover Inc. Special, 46 laps; Johnny Rutherford, U.S. Equipment Special, 43 laps; Elmer George, Sarkes Tarzian Special, 21 laps; Art Malone, S.T.P. Special, # 18 laps; Johnny Boyd, Bowes "Seal Fast" Special, 12 laps; Bobby Unser, Hotel Tropicana Special, # 2 laps.

* — rear engine   # — supercharged

STATISTICS OF THE 1964 500-MILE RACE

Honorary Referee—Raymond Firestone   *Starter—Pat Vidan*   *Pace Car—Ford Mustang*

Non-Stock Supercharged Engines 170.856 Cubic Inches (2,800 cc.) Piston Displacement or Less; Non-Stock Non-Supercharged Engines 256.284 Cubic Inches (4,200 cc.) or Less; Diesel Engines 335.61 Cubic Inches (5,500 cc.) or Less; Turbine Motors, no size limitation. (No weight limits.)

Pos.	Car No.	Driver Car	Cyl.	Bore	Stroke	Piston Displ.	Time	M.P.H.
1	1	A. J. Foyt, Sheraton-Thompson Spl.	4	4.28125	4.375	251.9	3:23:35.83	147.350
2	2	Rodger Ward, Kaiser Aluminum Special	8	3.760	2.874	255.2*	3:25:00.18	146.339
3	18	Lloyd Ruby, Bill Forbes Racing Team Sp.	4	4.28125	4.375	251.9	3:27:52.31	144.320
4	99	Johnny White, Demler Special	4	4.28125	4.375	251.9	3:29:29.30	143.206
5	88	Johnny Boyd, Vita Fresh Orange Juice Sp.	4	4.28125	4.375	251.9	3:30:45.31	142.345
6	15	Bud Tingelstad, Federal Engineering Special	4	4.28125	4.375	251.9	Flagged	198 laps
7	23	Dick Rathmann, Chapman Special	4	4.28125	4.375	251.9	Flagged	197 laps
8	4	Bob Harkey, Wally Weir Mobilgas Spl.	4	4.28125	4.375	251.9	Flagged	197 laps
9	68	Bob Wente, Morcroft-Taylor Special	4	4.28125	4.375	251.9	Flagged	197 laps
10	16	Bobby Grim, Konstant Hot Special	4	4.28125	4.375	251.9	Flagged	197 laps

Also started—Art Malone, Studebaker STP Special #, 194 laps; Don Branson, Wynn's Friction Proofing Special*, 187 laps; Walt Hansgen, MG-Liquid Suspension Special*, 176 laps; Jim Hurtubise, Tombstone Life Special, 141 laps; Len Sutton, Bryant Heating & Cooling Special*, 140 laps; Bill Cheesbourg, Arizona Apache Airlines Special, 131 laps; Dan Gurney, Lotus-Ford*, 110 laps; Troy Ruttman, Dayton Steel Wheel Special, 99 laps; Bob Veith, MG-Liquid Suspension Special*, 88 laps; Jack Brabham, John Zink-Urschel Trackburner*, 77 laps; Jim McElreath, Studebaker STP Special#, 77 laps; Bob Mathouser, Dayton Disc Brake Special, 77 laps; Parnelli Jones, Agajanian Bowes Seal Fast Special, 47 laps; Jim Clark, Lotus-Ford*, 47 laps; Bobby Marshman, Pure Oil Firebird Special*, 39 laps; Eddie Johnson, Mickey Thompson Sears Allstate Special*, 6 laps; Johnny Rutherford, Bardahl Special, 2 laps; Chuck Stevenson, Diet Rite Cola Leader Card Roadster, 2 laps; Dave MacDonald, Mickey Thompson Sears Allstate Special*, 1 lap; Eddie Sachs, American Red Ball Special*, 1 lap; Ronnie Duman, Clean Wear Service Company Special, 1 lap; Bobby Unser, Studebaker STP Special#, 1 lap; Norm Hall, Hurst Special, 1 lap.

*—rear engine   #—supercharged

TIMES AND AVERAGES

STATISTICS OF THE 1965 500-MILE RACE

Honorary Referee—Raymond C. Firestone   Starter—Pat Vidan   Pace Car—Plymouth Sports Fury

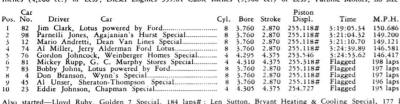

Non-Stock Supercharged Engines 170.856 Cubic Inches (2,800 cc.) Piston Displacement or Less; Non-Stock Non-Supercharged Engines 256.284 Cubic Inches (4,200 cc.) or Less; Diesel Engines 335.61 Cubic Inches (5,500 cc.) or Less; Turbine Motors, no size limitation. (No weight limits.)

Pos.	Car No.	Driver	Car	Cyl.	Bore	Stroke	Piston Displ.	Time	M.P.H.
1	82	Jim Clark,	Lotus powered by Ford	8	3.760	2.870	255.118#	3:19:05.34	150.686
2	98	Parnelli Jones,	Agajanian's Hurst Special	8	3.760	2.870	255.118#	3:21:04.32	149.200
3	12	Mario Andretti,	Dean Van Lines Special	8	3.760	2.870	255.118#	3:21:10.70	149.121
4	74	Al Miller,	Jerry Alderman Ford Lotus	8	3.760	2.870	255.118#	3:24:39.89	146.581
5	76	Gordon Johncock,	Weinberger Homes Special	4	4.295	4.375	253.546	3:24:53.62	146.417
6	81	Mickey Rupp,	G. C. Murphy Stores Special	4	4.310	4.375	255.318#	Flagged	198 laps
7	83	Bobby Johns,	Lotus powered by Ford	8	3.760	2.870	255.118#	Flagged	197 laps
8	4	Don Branson,	Wynn's Special	8	3.760	2.870	255.118#	Flagged	197 laps
9	45	Al Unser,	Sheraton-Thompson Special	8	3.760	2.870	255.118#	Flagged	196 laps
10	23	Eddie Johnson,	Chapman Special	4	4.305	4.375	254.727	Flagged	195 laps

Also started—Lloyd Ruby, Golden 7 Special, 184 laps#; Len Sutton, Bryant Heating & Cooling Special, 177 laps#; Johnny Boyd, George Bryant & Staff Special, 140 laps#; Walt Hansgen, MG Liquid Suspension Special, 117 laps#; A. J. Foyt, Jr., Sheraton-Thompson Special, 115 laps#; Bud Tinglestad, American Red Ball Special, 115 laps; Billy Foster, Jim Robbins-Autotron Electronics Special, 85 laps#; Arnie Knepper, Konstant Hot Special, 80 laps; Bobby Unser, STP Gasoline Treatment Special, 69 laps°*; Jim McElreath, Zink-Urschel Trackburner, 66 laps#; George Snider, Gerhardt Offy Special, 64 laps#; Ronnie Duman, Travelon Trailer-H & H Bookbinding Special, 62 laps#; Masten Gregory, George Bryant & Staff Special, 59 laps#; Bob Veith, MG Liquid Suspension Special, 58 laps#; Chuck Stevenson, Vita Fresh Orange Juice Special, 50 laps; Dan Gurney, Yamaha Special, 42 laps#; Jerry Grant, Bardahl MG Special, 30 laps#; Chuck Rodee, Weir's Mobiloil Special, 28 laps#; Joe Leonard, All American Racers Special, 27 laps#; Roger McCluskey, All American Racers Special, 18 laps#; Johnny Rutherford, Racing Associates Special, 15 laps#; Bill Cheesbourg, WIFE Good Guy Special, 14 laps#; Jim Hurtubise, STP-Tombstone Life Special, 1 lap*.

#—rear engine   *—supercharged   °—four wheel drive

STATISTICS OF THE 1966 500-MILE RACE

Honorary Referee—Raymond C. Firestone   Starter—Pat Vidan   Pace Car—Mercury Comet Cyclone GT

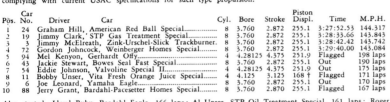

Supercharged four-cycle overhead camshaft engines, 170.856 cubic inches (2,800 cc) or less; non-supercharged four-cycle overhead camshaft engines, 256.284 cubic inches (4,200 cc) or less; American stock production block design, single non-overhead camshaft, removable head, supercharged engines, 203.4 cubic inches (3,333 cc) or less; American stock production block design, single non-overhead camshaft, removable head, non-supercharged engines, 305.1 cubic inches (5,000 cc) or less; two-cycle engines, supercharged or not, 170.856 cubic inches (2,800 cc) or less; diesel engines, supercharged or not, two or four cycle, 335.61 cubic inches (5,500 cc) or less; rotating combustion engines, not supercharged, 256.284 cubic inches (4,200 cc) or less, based on maximum volume minus minimum volume of one working chamber; and turbine engines, energy or fuel cells, hydraulic accumulators and steam engines complying with current USAC specifications for such type propulsion.

Pos.	Car No.	Driver	Car	Cyl.	Bore	Stroke	Piston Displ.	Time	M.P.H.
1	24	Graham Hill,	American Red Ball Special	8	3.760	2.872	255.1	3:27:52.53	144.317
2	19	Jimmy Clark,	STP Gas Treatment Special	8	3.760	2.872	255.1	3:28:33.66	143.843
3	3	Jimmy McElreath,	Zink-Urschel-Slick Trackburner.	8	3.760	2.872	255.1	3:28:42.42	143.742
4	72	Gordon Johncock,	Weinberger Homes Special	8	3.760	2.872	255.1	3:29:40.00	143.084
5	94	Mel Kenyon,	Gerhardt Offy	4	4.28125	4.375	251.9	Flagged	198 laps
6	43	Jackie Stewart,	Bowes Seal Fast Special	8	3.760	2.872	255.1	Out	190 laps
7	54	Eddie Johnson,	Valvoline Special II	4	4.28125	4.375	251.9	Out	175 laps
8	11	Bobby Unser,	Vita Fresh Orange Juice Special	4	4.125	3.125	168 †	Flagged	171 laps
9	6	Joe Leonard,	Yamaha Eagle	8	3.760	2.872	255.1	Out	170 laps
10	88	Jerry Grant,	Bardahl-Pacesetter Homes Special	8	3.760	2.870	255.1	Flagged	167 laps

Also started—Lloyd Ruby, Bardahl Eagle, 166 laps; Al Unser, STP Oil Treatment Special, 161 laps; Roger McCluskey, G. C. Murphy Special, 129 laps; Parnelli Jones, Agajanian's Rev 500 Special, 87 laps*; Rodger Ward, Bryant Heating & Cooling Special, 74 laps*; Carl Williams, Dayton Steel Wheel Special, 38 laps; Jim Hurtubise, Gerhardt Offy, 29 laps†; Mario Andretti, Dean Van Lines Special, 27 laps; George Snider, Sheraton-Thompson Special, 22 laps; Chuck Hulse, Wynn's Special, 22 laps; Bud Tingelstad, Federal Engineering Special, 16 laps*; Johnny Boyd, Prestone Special, 5 laps; Don Branson, Leader Card Racer #4; Billy Foster, Jim Robbins Special; Gary Congdon, Valvoline Special; A. J. Foyt, Jr., Sheraton-Thompson Special; Dan Gurney, All American Racers Eagle; Cale Yarborough, Jim Robbins Special; Arnie Knepper, Sam Liosi Special; Al Miller, Jerry Alderman Ford Lotus; Bobby Grim, Racing Associates Special†; Larry Dickson, Michner Petroleum Special; Ronnie Duman, Harrison Special.

*—supercharged   †—turbocharged

STATISTICS OF THE 1967 500-MILE RACE

Honorary Referee—Raymond C. Firestone   Starter—Pat Vidan   Pace Car—Chevrolet Camaro

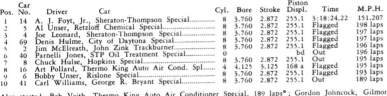

Supercharged four-cycle overhead camshaft engines, 170.856 cubic inches (2,800 cc) or less; non-supercharged four-cycle overhead camshaft engines, 256.284 cubic inches (4,200 cc) or less; American stock production block design, single non-overhead camshaft, removable head, supercharged engines, 203.4 inches (3,333 cc) or less; American stock production block design, single non-overhead camshaft, removable head, non-supercharged engines, 302.1 cubic inches (5,000 cc) or less; two-cycle engines, supercharged or not, 170.856 cubic inches (2,800 cc) or less; diesel engines, supercharged, two or four cycle, 203.4 cubic inches (3,333 cc) or less; diesel engines, nonsupercharged, two or four cycle, 305.1 cubic inches (5,000 cc) or less; gas turbine engines incorporating axial flow design compressors, total inlet annulus area of 23 square inches or less, measured at the entrance to the first moving stage of the compressor section; gas turbine engines incorporating centrifugal design compressors, total inlet annulus area of 28.5 square inches or less; rotating combustion engines, not supercharged, 256.284 cubic inches (4,200 cc) or less, based on maximum volume minus minimum volume of one working chamber; energy or fuel cells, hydraulic accumulators and steam engines complying with USAC specifications for such type propulsion.

Pos.	Car No.	Driver	Car	Cyl.	Bore	Stroke	Piston Displ.	Time	M.P.H.
1	14	A. J. Foyt, Jr.,	Sheraton-Thompson Special	8	3.760	2.872	255.1	3:18:24.22	151.207
2	5	Al Unser,	Retzloff Chemical Special	8	3.760	2.872	255.1	Flagged	198 laps
3	4	Joe Leonard,	Sheraton-Thompson Special	8	3.760	2.872	255.1	Flagged	197 laps
4	69	Denis Hulme,	City of Daytona Special	8	3.760	2.872	255.1	Flagged	197 laps
5	2	Jim McElreath,	John Zink Trackburner	8	3.760	2.872	255.1	Flagged	196 laps
6	40	Parnelli Jones,	STP Oil Treatment Special	0			bd	Out	196 laps
7	8	Chuck Hulse,	Hopkins Special	8	3.760	2.872	255.1	Out	195 laps
8	16	Art Pollard,	Thermo King Auto Air Cond. Spl	4	4.125	3.125	168 a	Flagged	195 laps
9	6	Bobby Unser,	Rislone Special	8	3.760	2.872	255.1	Flagged	193 laps
10	41	Carl Williams,	George R. Bryant Special	8	3.760	2.872	255.1	Out	189 laps

Also started—Bob Veith, Thermo King Auto Air Conditioner Special, 189 laps°; Gordon Johncock, Gilmore Broadcasting Special, 188 laps; Bobby Grim, Racing Associates Special, 187 laps°; Bud Tingelstad, Federal Engineering Special, 182 laps; Larry Dickson, Vita Fresh Orange Juice Special, 180 laps; Mel Kenyon, Thermo King Auto Air Conditioner Special, 177 laps°; Cale Yarborough, Bryant Heating & Cooling Special, 176 laps; Jackie Stewart, Bowes Seal Fast Special, 168 laps; Roger McCluskey, G. C. Murphy Special, 165 laps; Jerry Grant, All American Racers Eagle, 162 laps; Dan Gurney, Wagner Lockheed Brake Fluid Eagle, 160 laps; Arnie Knepper, M.V.S. Special, 158 laps; Ronnie Duman, Agajanian's Rev 500 Special, 154 laps*; Jochen Rindt, Wagner Lockheed Brake Fluid Eagle, 108 laps; Johnny Rutherford, Weinberger Homes Special, 103 laps; George Snider, Wagner Lockheed Brake Fluid Special, 99 laps; Lee Roy Yarbrough, Jim Robbins Seat Belt Company Special, 87 laps; Al Miller, Cleaver-Brooks Special, 74 laps; Wally Dallenbach, Valvoline Special, 73 laps°; Mario Andretti, Dean Van Lines Special, 58 laps; Jim Clark, STP Oil Treatment Special, 35 laps; Graham Hill, STP Oil Treatment Special, 23 laps; Lloyd Ruby, Red Ball Special, 3 laps°.

*—supercharged   °—turbocharged   b—turbine powered   c—front wheel drive
d—four wheel drive

STATISTICS OF THE 1968 500-MILE RACE

Honorary Referee—Raymond C. Firestone   Starter—Pat Vidan   Pace Car—Ford Torino

Supercharged four-cycle overhead camshaft engines, 170.856 cubic inches (2,800 cc) or less; non-supercharged four-cycle overhead camshaft engines, 256.284 cubic inches (4,200 cc) or less; American stock production block design, single non-overhead camshaft, removable head, supercharged engines, 203.4 cubic inches (3,333 cc) or less; American stock production block design, single non-overhead camshaft, removable head, non-supercharged engines, 305.1 cubic inches (5,000 cc) or less; two-cycle engines, other than diesel engines, supercharged or not, 170.856 cubic inches (2,800 cc) or less; diesel engines, supercharged, two or four cycle, 203.4 cubic inches (3,333 cc) or less; diesel engines, nonsupercharged, two or four cycle, 305.1 cubic inches (5,000 cc) or less; gas turbine engines, total inlet annulus area of 15.999 square inches or less, measured at the entrance to the first moving stage of the compressor section; rotating combustion engines, not supercharged, 256.284 cubic inches (4,200 cc) or less, based on maximum volume minus minimum volume of one working chamber.

Pos.	Car No.	Driver	Car	Cyl.	Bore	Stroke	Piston Displ.	Time	M.P.H.
1	3	Bobby Unser,	Rislone Special	4	4.125	3.125	168 a	3:16:13.76	152.882
2	48	Dan Gurney,	Olsonite Eagle	8	4.007	3.000	305	3:17:07.57	152.187
3	15	Mel Kenyon,	City of Lebanon Indiana	4	4.125	3.125	168 a	3:21:02.43	149.224
4	42	Denis Hulme,	Olsonite Eagle	8	3.760	2.872	255.1	3:21:08.71	149.146
5	25	Lloyd Ruby,	Gene White Company	4	4.125	3.125	168 a	3:21:58.83	148.529
6	59	Ronnie Duman,	Cleaver-Brooks Special	4	4.125	3.125	168 a	3:21:23.09	148.224
7	98	Bill Vukovich,	Wagner-Lockheed Brake Fluid Spl...	4	4.125	3.125	168 a	3:22:00.12	147.028
8	90	Mike Mosley,	Zecol-Lubaid Special	8	3.760	2.872	255.1	3:21:18.84	146.786
9	94	Sam Sessions,	Valvoline Special	4	4.125	3.125	168 a	3:21:47.34	146.440
10	6	Bobby Grim,	Gene White Company	4	4.125	3.125	168 a	3:21:48.25	145.686

Also started—Bob Veith, Thermo King Auto Air Conditioner Special, 196 laps(a); Joe Leonard, STP Oil Treatment Special, 191 laps(bd); Art Pollard, STP Oil Treatment Special, 188 laps(bd); Jim McElreath, Greer Special, 179 laps; Carl Williams, Sheraton-Thompson Special, 163 laps; Bud Tingelstad, Federal Engineering Special, 158 laps(a); Wally Dallenbach, Valvoline Special, 146 laps(a); Johnny Rutherford, City of Seattle, 125 laps; Graham Hill, STP Oil Treatment Special, 110 laps(bd); A. J. Foyt, Jr., Sheraton-Thompson Special, 86 laps: Ronnie Bucknum, Weinberger Homes Special, 76 laps; Jim Malloy, Jim Robbins Seat Belt Company Special, 64 laps(a); Jerry Grant, Bardahl Eagle, 50 laps(a); Gary Bettenhausen, Thermo King Auto Air Conditioner Special, 43 laps(a); Arnie Knepper, Bryant Heating & Cooling Special, 42 laps(a); Al Unser, Retzloff Chemical Special, 40 laps(ad); Gordon Johncock, Gilmore Broadcasting Special, 37 laps(a); Larry Dickson, Overseas National Airways Special, 24 laps; Roger McCluskey, G. C. Murphy Special, 16 laps(a); Jim Hurtubise, Pepsi-Frito Lay Special, 9 laps(a); George Snider, Vel's Parnelli Jones Special, 9 laps; Jochen Rindt, Repco Brabham, 5 laps; Mario Andretti, Overseas National Airways Special, 2 laps(a).

(a)—turbocharged (b)—turbine powered (d)—four wheel drive

TIMES AND AVERAGES

STATISTICS OF THE 1969 500-MILE RACE

Honorary Referee—Raymond C. Firestone ***Starter—Pat Vidan*** ***Pace Car—Chevrolet Camaro***

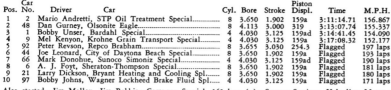

Supercharged four-cycle overhead camshaft engines, 161.703 cubic inches (2,650cc) ; non-supercharged four-cycle overhead camshaft engines, 256.284 cubic inches (4,200cc) ; American stock production block design, single non-overhead camshaft, removable head, supercharged engines, 203.4 cubic inches (3,333cc) ; American stock production block design, single non-overhead camshaft, removable head, non-supercharged engines, 320.355 cubic inches (5,250cc) ; Special rocker arm, single non-overhead camshaft, removable head, non-supercharged engines, 305.1 cubic inches (5,000cc) ; two-cycle engines, other than diesel engines, supercharged or not, 170.856 cubic inches (2,800cc) ; diesel engines, supercharged, two or four cycle, 203.4 cubic inches (3,333cc) ; diesel engines, non-supercharged, two or four cycle, 305.1 cubic inches (5,000cc) ; gas turbine engines, total inlet annulus area of 11.999 square inches measured at the entrance to the first moving stage of the compressor section ; rotating combustion engines, not supercharged, 256.284 cubic inches (4,200cc) or less, based on maximum volume minus minimum volume of one working chamber.

Pos.	Car No.	Driver	Car	Cyl.	Bore	Stroke	Piston Displ.	Time	M.P.H.
1	2	Mario Andretti,	STP Oil Treatment Special	8	3.650	1.902	159a	3:11:14.71	156.867
2	48	Dan Gurney,	Olsonite Eagle	8	4.113	3.000	319	3:13:07.74	155.337
3	1	Bobby Unser,	Bardahl Special	4	4.030	3.125	159ad	3:14:41.45	154.090
4	9	Mel Kenyon,	Krohne Grain Transport Special	4	4.030	3.125	159a	3:17:08.32	152.177
5	92	Peter Revson,	Repco Brabham	8	3.655	3.030	254.3	Flagged	197 laps
6	44	Joe Leonard,	City of Daytona Beach Special	8	3.650	1.902	159a	Flagged	193 laps
7	66	Mark Donohue,	Sunoco Simoniz Special	4	4.030	3.125	159ad	Flagged	190 laps
8	6	A. J. Foyt,	Sheraton-Thompson Special	8	3.650	1.902	159a	Flagged	181 laps
9	21	Larry Dickson,	Bryant Heating and Cooling Spl.	8	3.650	1.902	159a	Flagged	180 laps
10	97	Bobby Johns,	Wagner Lockheed Brake Fluid Spl.	4	4.030	3.125	159a	Flagged	171 laps

Also started—Jim Malloy, Jim Robbins Company Special, 165 laps (a) ; Sammy Sessions, Valvoline Motor Oil Special, 163 laps (a) ; Mike Mosley, Zecol-Lubaid Special, 162 laps (a) ; Roger McCluskey, G. C. Murphy Special, 157 laps (a) ; Bud Tingelstad, Vel's Parnelli Jones Ford Special, 155 laps (ad) ; George Snider, Sheraton-Thompson Special, 152 laps (a) ; Sonny Ates, Krohne Grain Transport Special, 146 laps (a) ; Denis Hulme, Olsonite Eagle, 145 laps (a) ; Gordon Johncock, Gilmore Broadcasting Special, 137 laps (a) ; Lloyd Ruby, Wynn's Spitfire, 105 laps (a) ; Wally Dallenbach, Sprite Special, 82 laps (a) ; Arnie Knepper, M.V.S. Special, 82 laps (a) ; Lee Roy Yarbrough, Jim Robbins Company Special, 65 laps (a) ; Jack Brabham, Repco Brabham, 58 laps ; Carl Williams, STP Gasoline Treatment Special, 50 laps (a) ; Gary Bettenhausen, Thermo King Auto Air Conditioner Special, 35 laps (a) ; George Follmer, Retzloff Special, 26 laps (a) ; Jim McElreath, Jack Adams Special, 24 laps (a) ; Johnny Rutherford, Patrick Petroleum Eagle, 24 laps (a) ; Ronnie Bucknum, Weinberger Homes Special, 16 laps (a) ; Art Pollard, STP Oil Treatment Special, 7 laps (ad) ; Bill Vukovich, Wagner Lockheed Brake Fluid Special, 1 lap (a) ; Bruce Walkup, Thermo King Auto Air Conditioner Special, 0 laps (a).

a—Turbo Charged d—Four Wheel Drive

STATISTICS OF THE 1970 500-MILE RACE

Honorary Referee—Raymond C. Firestone ***Starter—Pat Vidan*** ***Pace Car—Oldsmobile 4-4-2***

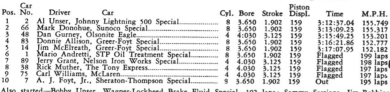

Supercharged four-cycle overhead camshaft engines, 161.703 cubic inches (2,650cc) ; non-supercharged four-cycle overhead camshaft engines, 256.284 cubic inches (4,200cc) ; American stock production block design, single non-overhead camshaft, removable head, supercharged engines, 203.4 cubic inches (3,333cc) ; American stock production block design, single non-overhead camshaft, removable head, non-supercharged engines, 320.355 cubic inches (5,250cc) ; Special rocker arm single non-overhead camshaft, removable head, non-supercharged engines, 305.1 cubic inches (5,000cc) ; two-cycle engines, other than diesel engines, supercharged or not, 170.856 cubic inches (2,800cc) ;diesel engines, supercharged, two or four cycle, 203.4 cubic inches (3,333cc) ; diesel engines, non-supercharged, two or four cycle, 305.1 cubic inches (5,000cc) ; gas turbine engines, total inlet annulus area of 11.999 square inches measured at the entrance to the first moving stage of the compressor section ; rotating combustion engines, not supercharged, 256.284 cubic inches (4,200cc) or less, based on maximum volume minus minimum volume of one working chamber.

Pos.	Car No.	Driver	Car	Cyl.	Bore	Stroke	Piston Displ.	Time	M.P.H.
1	2	Al Unser,	Johnny Lightning 500 Special	8	3.650	1.902	159	3:12:37.04	155.749
2	66	Mark Donohue,	Sunoco Special	8	3.650	1.902	159	3:13:09.23	155.317
3	48	Dan Gurney,	Olsonite Eagle	4	4:030	3.125	159	3:15:49.25	153.201
4	83	Donnie Allison,	Greer-Foyt Special	8	3.650	1.902	159	3:16:21.86	152.777
5	14	Jim McElreath,	Greer-Foyt Special	8	3.650	1.902	159	3:17:07.95	152.182
6	1	Mario Andretti,	STP Oil Treatment Special	8	3.650	1.902	159	Flagged	199 laps
7	89	Jerry Grant,	Nelson Iron Works Special	4	4.030	3.125	159	Flagged	198 laps
8	38	Rick Muther,	The Tony Express	4	4.030	3.125	159	Flagged	197 laps
9	75	Carl Williams,	McLaren	4	4.030	3.125	159	Flagged	197 laps
10	7	A. J. Foyt, Jr.,	Sheraton-Thompson Special	8	3.650	1.902	159	Out	195 laps

Also started—Bobby Unser, Wagner-Lockheed Brake Fluid Special, 192 laps; Sammy Sessions, Jim Robbins Co. Special, 190 laps; Jack Brabham, Gilmore Broadcasting Brabham, 175 laps; Dick Simon, Bryant Heating and Cooling Special, 168 laps; Ronnie Bucknum, M.V.S. Special, 162 laps; Mel Kenyon-Roger McCluskey, Sprite Special, 160 laps; Wally Dallenbach, Sprite Special, 143 laps; Johnny Rutherford, Patrick Petroleum Special, 135 laps; Lee Roy Yarbrough, Jim Robbins Company Special, 107 laps; George Snider, Sheraton-Thompson Special, 105 laps; Mike Mosley, G. C. Murphy Special, 96 laps; Peter Revson, McLaren, 87 laps; Billy Vukovich, Sugaripe Prune Special, 78 laps; Joe Leonard, Johnny Lightning 500 Special, 73 laps; Roger McCluskey, Quickick Special, 62 laps; Gary Bettenhausen, Thermo King Auto Air Conditioner Special, 55 laps; Lloyd Ruby, Daniels Cablevision Special, 54 laps; Gordon Johncock, Gilmore Broadcasting Special, 45 laps; Bruce Walkup, Wynn's Kwik-Kool Special, 44 laps; Art Pollard, Art Pollard Car Wash Systems Special, 28 laps; George Follmer, STP Oil Treatment Special, 18 laps; Greg Weld, Art Pollard Car Wash Systems Special, 12 laps; Jim Malloy, Stearns Manufacturing Transi-Tread Special, 0 laps.

STATISTICS OF THE 1971 500-MILE RACE

Honorary Referee—Raymond C. Firestone ***Starter—Pat Vidan*** ***Pace Car—Dodge Challenger***

Supercharged four-cycle overhead camshaft engines, 161.703 cubic inches (2,650cc) ; non-supercharged four-cycle overhead camshaft engines, 256.284 cubic inches (4,200cc) ; American stock production block design, single non-overhead camshaft, removable head, supercharged engines, 203.4 cubic inches (3,333cc) ; American stock production block design, single non-overhead camshaft, removable head, non-supercharged engines, 320.355 cubic inches (5,250cc) ; Special rocker arm single non-overhead camshaft, removable head, non-supercharged engines, 305.1 cubic inches (5,000cc) ; two-cycle engines, other than diesel engines, supercharged or not, 170.856 cubic inches (2,800cc) ; diesel engines, supercharged, two or four cycle, 203.4 cubic inches (3,333cc) ; diesel engines, non-supercharged, two or four cycle, 305.1 cubic inches (5,000cc) ; gas turbine engines, total inlet annulus area of 11.999 square inches measured at the entrance to the first moving stage of the compressor section; rotating combustion engines, not supercharged, 256.284 cubic inches (4,200cc) or less, based on maximum volume minus minimum volume of one working chamber.

Pos.	Car No.	Driver	Car	Cyl.	Bore	Stroke	Piston Displ.	Time	M.P.H.
1	1	Al Unser,	Johnny Lightning Special	8	3.760	1.800	158	3:10:11.56	157.735
2	86	Peter Revson,	McLaren	4	4.030	3.125	159	3:10:34.44	157.415
3	9	A. J. Foyt, Jr.,	ITT-Thompson Special	8	3.650	1.902	159	3:12:13.37	156.069
4	42	Jim Malloy,	Olsonite Eagle	4	4.281	2.750	158	3:14:04.65	154.577
5	32	Billy Vukovich,	Sugaripe Prune Special	4	4.281	2.750	158	3:14:05.77	154.563
6	84	Donnie Allison,	Purolator Special	8	3.650	1.902	159	Flagged	199 laps
7	58	Bud Tingelstad,	Sugaripe Prune Special	4	4.030	3.125	159	Flagged	198 laps
8	43	Denny Zimmerman,	Fiore Racing Ent. Special	4	4.030	3.125	159	Flagged	189 laps
9	6	Roger McCluskey,	Sprite Special	8	3.650	1.902	159	Flagged	188 laps
10	16	Gary Bettenhausen,	Thermo King Special	4	4.030	3.125	159	Flagged	178 laps

Also started—Lloyd Ruby, Utah Stars Special, 174 laps; Bobby Unser, Olsonite Eagle, 164 laps; Mike Mosley, G. C. Murphy Special, 159 laps; Dick Simon, Travelodge Sleeper, 151 laps; George Follmer, Spirit of Indianapolis, 147 laps; Cale Yarborough, Gene White Firestone, 140 laps; Denis Hulme, McLaren, 137 laps; Johnny Rutherford, Patrick Petroleum Special, 128 laps; Joe Leonard, Samsonite Special, 123 laps; David Hobbs, Penske H.P.P. Special, 107 laps; Rick Muther, Arkansas Aviation, 85 laps; Bob Harkey, Joe Hunt Magneto Special, 77 laps; Bentley Warren, Classic Wax Special, 76 laps; Wally Dallenbach, Sprite Special, 69 laps; Mark Donohue, Sunoco Special McLaren, 66 laps; Art Pollard, Gilmore Racing Team, 45 laps; Sammy Sessions, Wynn's Kwik-Kool Special, 43 laps; Larry Dickson, Spirit of Indianapolis, 33 laps; Gordon Johncock, Norris Industries Special, 11 laps; Mario Andretti, STP Oil Treatment Special, 11 laps; Steve Krisiloff, STP Gasoline Treatment Special, 10 laps; Mel Kenyon, Sprite Special, 10 laps; George Snider, G. C. Murphy Special, 6 laps.

All Cars Turbo Charged.

STATISTICS OF THE 1972 500-MILE RACE

Honorary Referee—Lucien Smith ***Starter—Pat Vidan*** ***Pace Car—Hurst/Olds***

Supercharged four-cycle overhead camshaft engines, 161.703 cubic inches (2,650 cc) ; non-supercharged four-cycle overhead camshaft engines, 274.590 cubic inches (4,500 cc) ; stock production block design, single non-overhead camshaft, removable head, supercharged engines, 209.3 cubic inches (3,430 cc) ; stock production block design, single non-overhead camshaft, removable head, non-supercharged engines, 355.136 cubic inches (5,820 cc) ; special rocker arm, single non-overhead camshaft, removable head, supercharged engines, 180 cubic inches (2,950 cc) ; special rocker arm, single non-overhead camshaft, removable head, non-supercharged engines, 320.355 cubic inches (5,250 cc) ; two-cycle engines, other than diesel engines, supercharged or not, 170.856 cubic inches (2,800 cc) ; diesel engines, supercharged, two or four cycle, 203.4 cubic inches (3,333 cc) ; diesel engines, non-supercharged, two or four cycle, 305.1 cubic inches (5,000 cc) ; gas turbine engines, total inlet annulus area of 11.999 square inches measured at the entrance to the first moving stage of the compressor section; rotating combustion engines, not supercharged, 256.284 cubic inches (4,200 cc), based on maximum volume minus minimum volume of one working chamber times two, times number of rotors.

Pos.	Car No.	Driver	Car	Cyl.	Bore	Stroke	Piston Displ.	Time	M.P.H.
1	66	Mark Donohue,	Sunoco McLaren	4	4.281	2.750	159	3:04:05.54	162.962
2	4	Al Unser,	Viceroy Special	4	4.281	2.750	159	3:07:16.49	160.192
3	1	Joe Leonard,	Samsonite Special	4	4.281	2.750	159	3:08:17.51	159.327
4	52	Sam Sessions,	Gene White Firestone Special	8	3.760	1.800	159	3:09:22.88	158.411
5	34	Sam Posey,	Norris Eagle	4	4.281	2.750	159	Flagged	198 laps
6	5	Lloyd Ruby,	Wynn's Special	8	3.760	1.800	159	Flagged	196 laps
7	60	Mike Hiss,	STP-Pylon Wind. Wiper Blade Spl.	4	4.281	2.750	159	Flagged	196 laps
8	9	Mario Andretti,	Viceroy Special	4	4.281	2.750	159	Out of fuel	194 laps
9	11	Jimmy Caruthers,	Steed U.S. Armed Forces Spl.	8	3.760	1.800	159	Flagged	194 laps
10	21	Cale Yarborough,	Bill Daniels GOP Special	8	3.760	1.800	159	Flagged	193 laps

Also started—George Snider, I.T.T.-Thompson Special, 190 laps; Jerry Grant, Mystery Eagle, 188 laps; Dick Simon, Travelodge Sleeper, 186 laps; Gary Bettenhausen, Sunoco McLaren, 182 laps; Wally Dallenbach, STP Oil Treatment Special, 182 laps; John Martin, Unsponsored Special, 161 laps; Lee Kunzman, Caves Buick Co. Special, 131 laps; Mel Kenyon, Gilmore Racing Team Special, 126 laps; Denny Zimmerman, Bryant Heating and Cooling Special, 116 laps; Gordon Johncock, Gulf McLaren, 113 laps; Steve Krisiloff, Ayr-Way-Lloyd's Special, 102 laps; John Mahler, Harbor Fuel Oil Special, 99 laps; Jim Hurtubise, Miller High Life Special, 94 laps; Roger McCluskey, American Marine Underwriters Special, 92 laps; A. J. Foyt, Jr., I.T.T.-Thompson Special, 60 laps; Mike Mosley, Vivitar Special, 56 laps; Johnny Rutherford, Patrick Petroleum Special, 55 laps; Billy Vukovich, Sugaripe Prune Special, 54 laps; Carl Williams, City of Terre Haute, 52 laps; Bobby Unser, Olsonite Eagle, 31 laps; Peter Revson, Gulf McLaren, 23 laps; Swede Savage, Michner Industries Special, 5 laps; Salt Walther, Dayton Steel Wheel Special, 0 laps.
All Cars Turbo Charged.

TIMES AND AVERAGES

STATISTICS OF THE 1973 500-MILE RACE (Called at 332½ Miles Because of Rain)

Honorary Referee—Charles W. Duncan   Starter—Pat Vidan   Pace Car—Cadillac

Eligibility: supercharged four-cycle overhead camshaft engines will be limited to a maximum piston displacement of 161.703 cubic inches (2,650cc); non-supercharged four-cycle overhead camshaft engines will be limited to a maximum piston displacement of 274.590 cubic inches (4,500cc); stock production block design, single non-overhead camshaft, removable head, supercharged engines will be limited to a maximum piston displacement of 209.3 cubic inches (3,430cc); stock production block design, single non-overhead camshaft, removable head, non-supercharged engines will be limited to a maximum piston displacement of 355.136 cubic inches (5,820cc); special rocker arm, single non-overhead camshaft, removable head, supercharged engines will be limited to a maximum piston displacement of 180 cubic inches (2,950cc); special rocker arm, single non-overhead camshaft, removable head, non-supercharged engines will be limited to a maximum piston displacement of 320.355 cubic inches (5,250cc); two-cycle engines, other than diesel engines, supercharged or not, will be limited to a maximum displacement of 170.856 cubic inches (2,800cc); diesel engines, supercharged, two or four cycle, will be limited to a maximum displacement of 203.4 cubic inches (3,333cc); diesel engines, non-supercharged, two or four cycle, will be limited to a maximum displacement of 305.1 cubic inches (5,000cc); gas turbine engines will be limited to a maximum total inlet annulus area of 11.999 square inches measured at the entrance to the first moving stage of the compressor section; and all cars powered by gas turbine engines must have facilities as stipulated by USAC to prevent escapement of debris resulting from turbine wheel failure; rotating combustion engines, not supercharged, will be limited to a maximum of 256.284 cubic inches (4,200cc), based on maximum volume minus minimum volume of one working chamber times two, time number of rotors.

Pos.	Car No.	Driver	Car	Cyl.	Bore	Stroke	Piston Displ.	Time	M.P.H.
1	20	Gordon Johncock,	STP Double Oil Filters	4	4.375	2.600	157	2:05:26.59	159.036
2	2	Billy Vukovich,	Sugaripe Prune Special	4	4.281	2.750	159	2:06:51.50	157.262
3	3	Roger McCluskey,	Lindsey Hopkins Buick Co. Spl.	4	4.281	2.750	159	Flagged	131 laps
4	19	Mel Kenyon,	Atlanta Falcons Special	8	3.760	1.800	159	Flagged	131 laps
5	5	Gary Bettenhausen,	Sunoco-DX McLaren	4	4.281	2.750	159	Flagged	130 laps
6	24	Steve Krisiloff,	Elliot's Norton Special	4	4.281	2.750	159	Flagged	129 laps
7	16	Lee Kunzman,	Ayr-way/Lloyd's Special	4	4.281	2.750	159	Flagged	127 laps
8	89	John Martin,	Unsponsored Special	4	4.281	2.750	159	Flagged	124 laps
9	7	Johnny Rutherford,	Gulf McLaren	4	4.281	2.750	159	Flagged	124 laps
10	98	Mike Mosley,	Lodestar Special	4	4.281	2.750	159	Out	120 laps

Also started—David Hobbs, Carling Black Label Special, 107 laps; George Snider, Gilmore Racing Team, 101 laps; Bobby Unser, Olsonite Eagle, 100 laps; Dick Simon, Travelodge Eagle, 100 laps; Mark Donohue, Sunoco-DX Eagle, 92 laps; Graham McRae, STP Gas Treatment, 91 laps; Mike Hiss, Thermo King Special, 91 laps; Joe Leonard, Samsonite Special, 91 laps; Jerry Grant, Olsonite Eagle, 77 laps; Al Unser, Viceroy Special, 75 laps; Jimmy Caruthers, Cobre Special, 73 laps; Swede Savage, STP Oil Treatment, 57 laps; Jim McElreath, Norris Eagle, 54 laps; Wally Dallenbach, Olsonite Eagle, 48 laps; A. J. Foyt, Jr., Gilmore Racing Team, 37 laps; Jerry Karl, Oriente Express, 22 laps; Lloyd Ruby, Commander Motor Homes Special, 21 laps; Sam Sessions, M.V.S. Special, 17 laps; Bob Harkey, Bryant Heating and Cooling Special, 12 laps; Mario Andretti, Viceroy Special, 4 laps; Peter Revson, Gulf McLaren, 3 laps; Bobby Allison, Sunoco-DX McLaren, 1 lap; Salt Walther, Dayton-Walther Special, 0 laps. All cars turbo charged.

"NEVER MIND...HE JUST TRIED IT."

"I THINK WE'VE SOLVED MOST OF THE CHASSIS WEIGHT PROBLEM BY ELIMINATING IT !!"

"...AND THEN I THOUGHT — WHY NOT PUT THEM TO WORK?!"

"LET ME KNOW WHEN IT'S READY FOR THE AFTERNOON RUN"

THAT'LL BE THE DAY!

"THEY SAY IT WILL GET 47 MPG...
BUT IT TAKES 200 GALLONS TO START IT"

All CARTOONS BY TOM BUTTERS

"NAH, THERE WASN'T NOTHING WRONG WITH
MY CAR. THOSE OTHER GUYS JUST DROVE FASTER"

Knox